TREATMENT OF DEPRESSION AND RELATED MOODS

TREATMENT OF DEPRESSION AND RELATED MOODS

A Manual for Psychotherapists

Daniel W. Badal, M.D.

Jason Aronson Inc.
Northvale, New Jersey
London

Library of Congress Cataloging-in-Publication Data

Badal, Daniel W.
    Treatment of depression and related moods.

    Includes bibliographies and index.
    1. Depression, Mental.   2. Affective disorders.
I. Title.   [DNLM: 1. Affective Disorders—diagnosis.
2. Affective Disorders—therapy.   3. Depression—
diagnosis.   4. Depression therapy.   WM 207 B132t]
RC537.B3   1988   616.85′27   87–33665
ISBN 0–87668–981–0

Manufactured in the United States of America. Jason Aronson Inc. offers books and cassettes. For information and catalog write to Jason Aronson Inc., 230 Livingston Street, Northvale, NJ 07647.

CONTENTS

Preface   ix

Acknowledgments   xiii

Introduction   xv

PART I: GENERAL PRINCIPLES

Chapter 1.   Definitions   3

Mood and Affect • Mood (Affective) Disorders • Depression
• Biological Psychiatry and the Affective Disorders

Chapter 2.   Causes   13

The Multifactorial Basis • Genetics: How Important?

Chapter 3.   Epidemiology   23

Frequency in the Population • Sex and Race Differences
• Suicide and Murder • Depression and the Personality

Chapter 4.   History of Current Concepts   33

Emil Kraepelin • Psychobiology • Interpersonal Psychiatry
• Freud—History of Psychoanalytic Studies • Self Psychology
• Psychoanalytic Contributions to the Study of Transferences
• Widening Scope of Analysis • Derivative Systems:
Interpersonal Psychiatry and Behavioral Therapy

PART II: DIAGNOSIS

Chapter 5.   Preparation for Making Diagnoses   49

The Therapist • Ethics • Interviewing the Patient

Chapter 6.   Diagnosis and Evaluation   63

Accountability • Planning Treatment • Limitations of Diagnosis •
Clinical History • Mental Status • Integration of History and
Mental Status • Disguises of Depression (The Struggle against
Pain)

Chapter 7.   Formal Diagnostic Classifications   77

DSM-III-R • Diagnosis in Practice • Diagnostic Categories and
Clinical Descriptions • Clinical Syndromes: Types of Affective
Disorders • Subtypes of Major Mood Disorders • Frequency of
Diagnostic Types • Organic Mood (Affective) Disorders •
Diagnosis of Personality Disorders and Trends • Personality
Disorders: *DSM-III-R,* AXIS II, Diagnosis of Personality Disorders,
and Maladaptive Personality Trends • Aggression • Problems and
Suggestions for Solution in Diagnosis of Personality Disorders •
Appendix: *ICD-9-CM* and *DSM-III-R* Compared

Chapter 8.   Psychodynamics and Psychopathology   125

Early Development • The Person in Crisis • Self Psychology

Chapter 9.   Differential Diagnosis   135

Medical Illness and Effects of Medication • Depression Misdiagnosed as Medical Illness • Other Psychiatric Illnesses • Organic
Affective Syndromes

Chapter 10.   Borderlands of Affective Disorders   147

Normal Depression and Depressive Affects • Fatigue • Rejection
• Loss, Grief, and Mourning • Separation and Nostalgia • Return
of the Repressed in Melancholia • Boredom and Apathy •
Affects Resulting from Loss of Defenses • Loneliness • Biological
Functions of Affects • Signs of Withdrawal, Alienation, or Retreat
• Loss of Self-Esteem and the Self-Image • Depressive
Equivalents: The Inability to Perceive Affects

Chapter 11.   Suicide and the Mood Disorders   169

Epidemiology • Age-Related Considerations • Risk Factors •
Psychology and Motivation • Personality and Psychodynamics •
Suicide and Treatment • Medical-Legal Considerations

PART III: TREATMENT AND MANAGEMENT

Chapter 12.   Strategy   195

Geographical Setting for Therapy • Process of Treatment • Stages of Treatment • Emergency Situations • Role of Families in Treatment and Patient's Responsibility • Advice to Families • Living with a Manic Patient • Living with a Depressed Person • Advice to Patients

Chapter 13. Biological Therapy   217

Definition • Clinical Basis for Biological Therapy • Psychosomatic Processes – The Somatic Basis • Medicine and Responsibility • The Patient and Psychopharmacology • Purposes and Functions of Medication • Psychopharmacology • Drugs Currently Used in Affective Disorders • Tricyclics and Other Antidepressants • Psychic Energizers and Stimulants • Tranquilizers • Lithium • Carbamazepine (Tegretol) for Bipolar Illness and as an Antidepressant • Chronic Disability • Timing of Medication According to Stage of Development of Depression • Clusters of Symptoms and Drug Treatment • Drugs and Prevention • Noncompliance • Other Biological Treatments • Electroconvulsant Therapy (ECT) • Use in Depression

Chapter 14. Psychotherapy   271

Effectiveness of Psychotherapy in Affective Disorders • Early Stages of Therapy • Short-term Psychotherapy without Medication • Long-term Developments and Working Through

Chapter 15. Combined Treatment:
Drugs and Psychotherapy   297

Eclectic Therapy • Advice to Therapists (Social Workers, Psychologists, Clergymen, Nurse Clinicians, Counselors, and Psychiatrists) • Advice to Psychiatrists and Physicians • Some Interactions of Drugs and Psychotherapy

Chapter 16. Course, Outcome, and Prognosis   315

Factors Influencing Outcome • Acute Depression in Ambulatory Patients • Hospitalized Patients

PART IV: AFFECTIVE DISORDERS AND THE LIFE CYCLE

Chapter 17. Childhood   323

Variations in Clinical Signs and Symptoms with Age • Developmental Stages: The Life Cycle • Affective Disorders in Preadolescent Children

Chapter 18. Adolescence   345

Psychopathology and Clinical Diagnosis • Treatment and
Prevention • Adolescent Suicide

Chapter 19. Early Adult Life   381

Sexual Problems • Career • Moods and the Menstrual Cycle •
Pregnancy and Parenthood

Chapter 20. Late Life   397

Importance of Affective Disorders in the Elderly • Integrated
Therapy • Biological Treatment in the Elderly • Psychotherapy

References   411

Additional Readings   425

Index   437

PREFACE

It has become common practice for nonmedical professionals to be involved in the treatment of depressed people—an enormous responsibility. These therapists are in a position to influence lives in highly significant ways, and they must be prepared to do this with educated judgment and skill.

Clinical psychiatry as a discipline has been doing these very things for a long time. As a field of collective endeavors, psychiatry has certain insights to offer psychotherapists. The purpose of this book is to present these essential insights in a condensed but sufficiently comprehensive way in order to give nonpsychiatrists an intensive course in the clinical psychiatry of mood (affective) disorders.

I became aware of the need for such a book over the last several years while conducting seminars for psychotherapists of various disciplines on the subject of psychoanalytic contributions to the understanding of depressions. A book of this nature was needed as a supplement and preparation for the course. None of the textbooks seemed to represent fully the view of psychiatry I wanted to represent. I then wrote a manual for the course, containing what I think psychotherapists should know about the clinical psychiatry of mood disorders. The groups to whom I gave it found it very useful. These groups were made up of physicians, psychiatrists, social workers, nurses, psychologists, and psychoanalysts.

In this book I discuss specific illnesses, that is, mood disorders, as well as related dysphoric moods and affects. There is material on combinations of treatments, areas in which biological psychiatry, psychopharmacology, and psychotherapy overlap.

USING THE MANUAL

To provide a basic orientation, the first four chapters contain a summary of definitions, causes, epidemiology, and history. Although directed primarily to the nonpsychiatrist, it can also orient the seasoned professional to the theory basic to the practical methods described in later chapters.

The chapters on meeting the patient and on the preparation of the therapist for making a diagnosis introduce the concept of the therapist's empathy as a diagnostic tool and should be read before the chapter on making the formal diagnosis.

For formal diagnosis – in the United States, at present – it seems advisable to adhere to the official diagnostic of the American Psychiatric Association as set forth and fully described in the *Diagnostic and Statistical Manual of Mental Disorders* (Third Edition) of the American Psychiatric Association, published in Washington, D.C., 1980, and the Third Edition – Revised, 1987, hereafter called *DSM-III* and *DSM-III-R. The International Classification of Diseases* (Ninth Revision) and the *Clinical Modification* thereof, *ICD-9* and *ICD-9-CM*, are in some ways more satisfactory because they take into account more clinical variables and have a richer range of clinical pictures. For those who prefer the international classification, there is a listing of the various affective disorders and a comparison with *DSM-III-R* in the Appendix to Chapter 7. (To do justice to the classifications and to use them properly, it is necessary to read the original manuals.)

The chapter on borderlands of affective disorders is of particular importance to the psychotherapist. A good many patients with these disturbances get to nonpsychiatrists, rather than to psychiatrists, who tend to see more fully established, complete syndromes.

Suicide deserves and gets a separate chapter. Special age-related aspects of suicide are taken up in the section on the life cycle.

The chapters on treatment should be supplemented by study of the separate techniques referred to: acute care, group therapy, couples therapy, cognitive and interpersonal therapies, psychoanalysis and psychoanalytic psychotherapy. The method described for medications, although the author's own approach, agrees essentially with that described by most practicing psychiatrists.

Complete tables of antidepressant and anxiolytic drugs are given with their generic and trade names, doses, side effects, and dangers. Tables are given for differential diagnosis and for a comparison of the chief diagnostic schedules, *The Diagnostic and Statistical Manual of Mental Disorders (DSM-III-R)* and the *International Classification of Diseases (ICD-9-CM)*. Other features include a table on results and methods of treatment, a flow chart for a typical treatment, and a table listing the types of personality problems seen in patients with affective disorders.

The chapters on age-related disorders supplement the general text and should be read after the general text.

With the information provided in this book, psychotherapists should be able to acquire a general grasp of their own place and function in relation to the large field of mood or affective disorders and to the various related depressive states, such as sadness and grief, which are unavoidable aspects of the human experience.

ACKNOWLEDGMENTS

During the writing and production of this book I have received a great deal of encouragement and support from a number of persons who have, in so many ways, made the work possible.

I wish to thank in particular my colleagues and friends at the Cleveland Psychoanalytic Institute for their encouragement and interest throughout this project. Also, the Department of Psychiatry of Case Western Reserve University, the University Hospitals of Cleveland, and St. Luke's Hospital have provided a sound and stimulating clinical and academic setting for my work.

I was helped a great deal by Mrs. Erna Furman and Mrs. Jean Kushleika, child therapists and psychoanalysts, who read some portions of the manuscript and made valuable comments.

The editorial work of many professionals contributed significantly to the final product, starting with Sue Sahli, Ph.D., who helped put the first draft together. The editorial staff at Jason Aronson, starting with Joan Langs, did a great service by insisting on clear language, without unnecessary baggage, and they put a great deal of work toward that end.

Especially I thank my wife, Eleanor B. Badal, M.S.W., a clinical social worker, for her critical reading of portions of the manuscript, her assistance in the bibliography on grief, her insight into the understanding of the mourning process, and her unending patience.

INTRODUCTION

Clinical psychiatry is accumulating new knowledge at an accelerating pace. The progress in the understanding and treatment of the affective disorders is particularly impressive. Since the introduction of antidepressant drugs nearly three decades ago, much of the work of psychiatrists on the depressions and manias has been directed toward increasing specificity of diagnosis for specific treatment. Tests are becoming more specific for isolating particular chemical variations. The field of psychopharmacology has blossomed.

At the same time, psychotherapy and its basic psychological theory have been enriched by an impressive accumulation of observations on a number of substantive issues, for example, how depressive affects and depressive thinking can originate in childhood, the relationship of grief to depression and depressive affects, the importance of loss as a trauma, the origin of pathological guilt and suicidal ideas, and the influence of interpersonal relationships in precipitating depressions.

For a long time, the use of antidepressant drugs tended to polarize psychiatrists into those who "believed in" medication and those who did not, or, to reverse it, those who believed in psychotherapy and those against it. Fortunately, the middle ground — combined treatments or electicism, for decades the standard procedure — is coming more and more to be recognized by the polarized groups.

Combined treatment of medication and psychotherapy has been the standard psychiatric method but was not identified as a separate entity, as it now is with the advent of psychotropic drugs, such as antidepressants, neuroleptics, and lithium. These drugs make accessible to psychotherapy many individuals who, two decades ago, had to live with disabling symptoms and personal problems. The psychotherapist needs to have some knowledge of medication, including diagnosis, side effects, dosage, when to stop the drug, effects of medication on psychotherapy, who should prescribe the drugs, and how to handle emergencies.

Many physicians are not especially trained in psychotherapy, and it is incumbent upon them to know when to advise psychotherapy and available psychotherapeutic techniques, regardless of whether or not the physicians employ those techniques themselves. The physician has to have an appreciation of the importance of precipitating psychosocial factors, the impact on families, the interpersonal relations, and the intrapsychic (personality) trends that breed depressions, and whether or not these should be treated. Clinical psychiatry addresses these issues.

The subject is divided in this book into two separate but related parts: (1) mood (affective) disorders, that is, the definitive clear-cut diagnosable illnesses, seen from the medical perspective; and (2) depressive affects, equivalents, existential depressions, and related symptoms, that is, the partial expression of depressive moods, such as pessimism, sadness, grief, disillusionment, despair, and hopelessness. These subjects are related because often, especially early in the course of the disorders, the depressive symptom complex has not developed fully; at early stages of the depressive illness, the clinical picture may be indistinguishable from a normal response to trauma or loss. Moreover, depressive *affects* may precede, merge with, and follow depressive *illness*, and often must be treated to prevent further breakdown and to improve the quality of life. This is the arena in which psychotherapists fight their battles. Many patients "in remission" or in partial remission belong here also.

Although some depressive moods are not illnesses, the mood (affective) disorders themselves are illnesses; they are psychosomatic in the sense that there is a physical change in the nervous system that is influenced by psychological factors. This physical change involves neurotransmitters and hormones; the chemicals used to treat these disorders are those that influence the neuro-transmitters norepinephrine, dopamine, and serotonin. In order to treat patients, it is necessary to know both psychological and somatic components of the psychosomatic disorder.

The future may teach us to exercise a direct influence, by means of particular chemical substances, upon the amounts of energy and their distribution to the mental apparatus. It may be that there are undreamt-of possibilities of therapy.
— Sigmund Freud, "An Outline of Psychoanalysis"

It is clear from all I have been saying that I advocate a change in role and value orientation for the psychiatrist who engages in mental health work. He must still be a fully established clinical diagnostician, but he must also have knowledge of the possible precursors of disease (as exemplified by grief reactions). Together with social scientists, he will have to address himself to social systems, whether family, kinship circle, small group, work team, institution, or whole community. Problems of transition and crises of adaptation are challenges for the right kind of mental health services, and they are also opportunities for investigation.
— Erich Lindemann, "Mental Health Aspects
of Rapid Social Change"
In *Beyond Grief: Studies in Crisis Intervention*

Depression can be understood as concurrently a disorder of biogenic amine metabolism, a syndrome arising out of the intrapsychic consequences of object loss, a disturbance of family relationships, and a learned response pattern with adaptive utility
— Gene Usdin, *Depression: Clinical, Biological, and
Psychological Perspectives*

PART I

GENERAL PRINCIPLES

1

DEFINITIONS

MOOD AND AFFECT

Use of the words "affect" and "affective" requires explanation. Very likely the technical use in psychiatry comes from the German word *affekt*, translated as "emotion" or as "passion or affection," used to distinguish this group of disturbances from those with the more characteristic thinking disorder seen in the schizophrenias.

The terms *emotion, affect, mood,* and *feelings* are often used interchangeably, but some distinctions are developing. The official diagnostic manual used from 1980 to 1987 in the United States, *Diagnostic and Statistical Manual of Mental Disorders*, 3rd edition (The American Psychiatric Association, Task Force on Nomenclature and Statistics 1980), hereafter referred to and cited as *DSM-III*, states that it employs the term *affective disorders* for the group, and, although the correct term should be *mood disorders*, "common usage and historical continuity favor retention of the term 'Affective Disorders'" (p. 205). "Mood" is defined therein as "a prolonged emotion that colors the whole psychic life; it generally involves either depression or elation" (p. 205). In *DSM-III-R* (1987), mood disorders is given preference.

The term *affect* refers to immediate and short-term responses to stimuli, both external and intrapsychic. The more sustained, prolonged, and fixed mood states are referred to as *mood disorders*. *Affects* are the feelings that play into the more prolonged mood states. Because both affective states and specific prolonged entities known as mood disorders are discussed here, the terms are used in places interchangeably.

The psychodynamic definition of affect is in agreement with this distinction. Affect, as defined in the psychoanalytic glossary of The American Psychoanalytic Association (Moore and Fine 1967) is said to be "Subjectively experienced feeling states, usually perceived as pleasurable or unpleasurable in relation to the gratification or frustration of instinctual drives, to *realistic* achievements, and to the fulfillment of ideals" (p. 13). There are also physiological components, somatic manifestations, and unconscious elements.

Biological Function and the Psychology of Affects

Affects perform the same function for the whole person as physical sensations do for parts of the body, that is, they signal psychic pain or pleasure, often when instinctual drives are involved, and contribute to homeostasis (the maintenance of health). They can be sudden, transitory, or sustained.

Mood disorders involve two principal affects: anxiety and depression. Anxiety affect is linked to danger and apprehension, whereas depressive affect is associated with something that has already happened, such as a loss, trauma, or catastrophe. There is a range of intensity, from normal to pathological, that depends on the severity or persistence of the reaction.

Three central components of affects are (1) feeling (pain or pleasure of some degree), (2) ideational (i.e., cognition), and (3) somatic. In depressive affect there are ideas of loss, hopelessness, helplessness, shame, guilt, and so on. The ideas may be thoughts, memories, wishes, fantasies, or dreams, and may not be clearly conscious or easy to express. Patients often do not complain of being sad; it can be inferred from their story or demeanor.

Because of the painful nature of the depressive affect, various defenses may be built up against it. These include denial, repression, displacement, projection, psychosomatic symptoms, the use of drugs or alcohol, and acting out. In adolescents, delinquency, physical complaints, acting out, and outbursts of anger or withdrawal may mask or ward off the depressive affect. In children, school failure, hyperactivity, withdrawal, delinquency, and physical complaints may be equivalents of, or symptoms of, depressive affect.

Other affects seen in various types and degrees of depression are sadness, grief, gloom, pessimism, apathy, sorrow, emptiness, boredom, nostalgia, alienation, and despair, all of which are accompanied by some degree of psychic pain and suffering. Not unusual also, especially in the early stages, are various degrees and varieties of anxiety, ranging from emotional tension and restlessness to overwhelming panic and agitation. Anxiety may so confuse the clinical picture that the depressive features, even serious ones, are hidden and masked.

The affects seen in mania and hypomania, as well as in the active phase of the cycles of the cyclothymic personality, are opposite to those in depression, ranging from good spirits and joyousness, an energetic – indeed irrational – optimism, and happiness ("I never felt better in my life"), to elation, euphoria, excitement, and frenzy. Sometimes there is an overwhelming pressure to be active; then the person becomes irritable, or angry, and very aggressive when crossed or opposed. An underlying depression may also be detected; it is not unusual to see a mixed picture of depression and mania. For the most part, in mania and hypomania the affects are pleasurable, in contrast to those in depression.

Clinical Manifestations
of Affects and Moods

Affects are expressed in different ways in different people; they can be repressed or inhibited, or expressed. Some affects are *flattened*, as in schizophrenia, where there is no emotional expression. Some depressed persons may appear expressionless and flat.

Individuals who develop depressions tend to deal with affects in characteristic ways. One type is the person whose affects are inhibited, that is, not expressed openly and easily, except possibly through irritability or impatience. The cyclothymic's affects tend to cycle through high (euphoric) and low (depressed) periods. Hysterics tend to express (and feel) affect in an exaggerated manner; they overreact. The obsessive, restricted personalities seem almost without affect and tend to intellectualize without expressing much feeling, although it is there but inhibited. The schizoid person seems to lack affect.

Labile affect, which is too easily laughing, crying, or becoming angry, is seen in people with organic brain disease such as cerebral arteriosclerosis, toxic states, or brain tumor. Often this difference from depression or mania helps make a clear-cut diagnosis of a somatic disease even when the patient has an affective disorder also.

MOOD (AFFECTIVE) DISORDERS

Mood disorders are illnesses in which an abnormal mood is the central symptom. That mood may either be elevated, as in mania and hypomania, or it may be lowered, as in the various depressive disorders. In the elevated states, there is a speeding up of thought processes, along with the elevated, euphoric, overly optimistic mood. In the depressive disorders, pessimistic thinking is usually present with the depressed mood, and sometimes slowing down of thought processes, the pathognomonic sign of major depression.

Depressive disorders are states of depression that go beyond those passing moments of sadness or grief common and normal in the human experience. They are illnesses. Diagnostically important is a persistent low mood which does not vanish with a good night's sleep, or in a day or two when things should look better. This disorder must be looked at from the medical point of view, that is, with a view to objective diagnosis and treatment. This medical model provides a measure of the several types of depression that require different treatment. Like other illnesses, they go through characteristic stages of onset and decline or resolution. Understanding these variations and knowing at what point a problem becomes an illness can require the utmost skill and attention.

DEPRESSION

Depression can be a normal feeling but is also the symptom of an illness. Healthy people can have the "blues" (a feeling of sadness or depression) as a reaction to a situation of loss, disappointment, or grief. The mood or affect is familiar and normal. When the intensity of the feeling is out of proportion to the situation, it becomes a symptom. When the depression has a relentless grip, a persistence that cannot be shaken off, even after many days, it becomes a syndrome or an illness in which a pervasive lowering of spirits and pessimism takes over the thinking and outlook, with ideas of guilt and lowered self-esteem.

In a fully developed major depression, the subject finds it difficult to concentrate; work slows down and thoughts tend to be pessimistic day after day, week after week. There may be feelings of helplessness and hopelessness. There are physical symptoms of weakness, unaccountable fatigue, loss of appetite, insomnia, digestive symptoms, and even cessation of menses. Besides these bodily complaints, there is loss of interest and pleasure (anhedonia) and a tendency to withdraw from life. There may be guilt feelings and thoughts of suicide. People afflicted by depression know that something is wrong, but often do not understand *what* it is even though they may be severely incapacitated and unable to function. They may blame themselves, find fault with their own behavior, or not complain but suffer in silence. This cluster of specific symptoms, such as guilt, self-criticism, and self-abasement, works to disguise the illness and prevent the sufferer from seeking help.

The depressive constellation of symptoms can occur separately, in which case it becomes one of the several varieties of mood disorders: major depressive disorder, bipolar (if manic attacks are interspersed), or depressive neurosis (dysthymia). The syndrome may be an effect of medication (e.g., steroids), part of another psychiatric illness (e.g., schizophrenia), or secondary to a medical illness, including organic cerebral disease (e.g., cerebral arteriosclerosis). For any of these causes, it may be simply a classical affective illness precipitated by the stimulus, or a depressive affect which is relieved when the underlying condition is treated.

Depressions that are clear-cut illnesses have certain essential features:

- There is a special quality of the painful mood, with accompanying ideation/physical symptoms and persistence.

- The clinical picture and course follow specific patterns with marked uniformity.

- The somatic changes, although reversible, have the specificity and relentlessness of illness: a slowing of bodily processes, including thinking and talking, salivation, bowel activity, menses, and a change in the diurnal rhythm, with resultant early waking and feelings of exhaustion in the morning.

The classical depression gives the impression that the sources of energy have been depleted and all functions are at a lowered rate of speed and intensity. Indeed, some patients describe the feeling as diseaselike or as a toxic state, outside their control, much as one feels when a fever or malady takes over.

In the opposite direction, that is, when a person has a manic attack, it is as if that person were given a toxic substance that speeds up everything so that all processes, including thinking, ambition, drive, sex, and digestion, go faster, and the person seems tireless. The impersonal nature of the process, like an intoxication, is evident once it is set off. It is persistent and unrelenting until it runs its course or is treated.

Some depressive disorders and elations are so deceptively mild that they seem like normal mood swings rather than illnesses. However, because this particular milder group has a pattern and symptomatology exactly like the more serious and severe depressions, except for intensity, it belongs in the same class as the more severe major depressions.

Depressed persons may have some resistance to hearing that they are suffering from an illness. They may not want to hear that they are considered sick, especially when they feel otherwise, such as that they are no good, or useless, or that they brought it on themselves.

Depressions are so common that almost everyone has seen them at some time in family, friends, associates, or even themselves. Depression causes serious problems, sometimes even tragedy, since any depressed person is a potential suicide. At the very least, discomfort and misery occur, progressing to loss of work and resources, and damage to important relationships.

Careers are affected, as are marriages. Furthermore, emotional disturbance in parents affect children too, and depressions do this in very special ways, mainly because the depressed parent lacks the energy and concentration to attend to the child's needs.

Moreover, sometimes certain depressed people develop manic or hypomanic states; they become speeded up—the opposite of depression. This is the bipolar disorder (manic-depressive disease, as it has been known in the past), which can cause serious difficulties for patients and their families because of irrational behavior—overenthusiastic business deals, fantasies of power and great wealth, and possibly delusions.

Finally, the established mood disorders differ from neuroses in that there is a partial or complete breakdown of defenses, sometimes to the extent that the patient is completely overwhelmed by the painful affect and requires relief and protection.

BIOLOGICAL PSYCHIATRY AND THE AFFECTIVE DISORDERS

Biological psychiatry is the approach to psychiatric illnesses through physical, chemical, and other somatic mechanisms.

Psychiatry has participated in the ongoing revolution in biomedical science, which, as it involves psychiatry, is "neuroscience," "neurobiology," "neurochemistry," "psychochemistry," and "psychopharmacology." There has been a spectacular growth in theory, research, and practical consequences, especially through the discovery of new and useful drugs (Meltzer 1987). The psychotherapist often has to deal with patients who take medicines and needs to know the rationale for their use.

Mood disorders are accompanied by changes in the body. The bipolar disorders and major depression are accompanied by changes in the physiology of chemical substances in the cells of the brain and also possibly by hormonal changes in endocrine metabolism through the hypophysis. Some of these changes or the potential for them appear to run in families and have genetic roots, especially in bipolar illness. Environmental stress can influence these changes in the predisposed person.

Biological psychiatry is an integral component of general psychiatry, along with the other special fields of study. A recent textbook from the American College of Psychiatrists states the case for integration of disciplines thus: "Depression can be understood as *concurrently* a disorder of biogenic amine metabolism, a syndrome arising out of the intrapsychic consequences of object loss, a disturbance of family relationships, and a learned response pattern with adaptive utility (Usdin 1977, p. xiii).

The manner in which this seemingly contradictory state of affairs comes about is not yet fully explained, but biological mechanisms are gradually being uncovered. To date, the most important basic fact is that the synapses of the brain are governed in their actions by chemical transmitters. By altering the action of these transmitters, either chemically or by stress, changes can be brought about in the symptoms of both schizophrenia and manic-depressive disease.

The transmitter systems include dopamine, noradrenalin, serotonin, and acetylcholine, as well as polypeptides and amino acids, which not only transmit but modulate the action of other transmitters. Some of these actions are stress related, thus bringing the environment and the experience of the individual to play on the final action of the nervous system. The genetic endowment of the individual apparently supplies the basic mechanisms, which can then be influenced by a variety of chemical substances, as well as by stress.

Historical Development of Biological Psychiatry

The idea that psychiatric disturbances such as depression have biological (i.e., somatic) roots is not new in modern medicine. Consider the following quotation: "Melancholia, whose definition fluctuates even in descriptive psychiatry, takes on various clinical forms the grouping together of which into a single unity does not seem to be established with certainty; and some of these forms suggest somatic rather than psychogenic affections" (Freud 1917, p. 243).

The following events are the most significant in the history of biological psychiatry:

1933 Pentamethylene tetrazol (Cardiazol, Metrazol) found to relieve depression by inducing seizures. This dramatic discovery initiated modern biological psychiatry.

1938 Electroconvulsant therapy (ECT) introduced.

1949 Inception of the use of lithium salts for mania.

1951 Monoamine oxidase inhibitors (MAOs) found to relieve depression.

1952 Rauwolfia serpentina found to calm mania.

1952 Chlorpromazine found effective in psychoses.

1958 Imipramine (Tofranil) synthesized. The first of many tricyclic antidepressants, which have revolutionized the treatment of depressive illnesses.

1960 Synthesis of the first of many benzodiazepines, chlordiazepoxide (Librium), a potent anxiolytic. These have largely replaced the older sedatives and hypnotics.

1960 The explosion of psychopharmacology as a science. The further development of animal testing, mass trials, and controlled studies to ensure the safety and efficacy of the new drugs. The discovery and synthesis of numerous new anxiolytic and antipsychotic (neuroleptic) and antidepressant drugs.

1980 to the present (1) The discovery that some of the new antidepressants do not work like the tricyclics, casting doubt on the catecholamine hypothesis. (2) Acknowledgement that the new drugs are not cure-alls, resulting in a resurgence of clinical interest, emphasis on diagnosis, and interest in the integration of biological, psychological, and environmental/social factors and influences. (3) Combinations of psychotherapy and drugs found to work better than either alone in most studies. In a few studies psychotherapy was better.

The future New techniques offering promise of diagnostic and therapeutic applications. Computerized axial tomography (CAT scan) may show tumor, atrophy, or other changes that facilitate diagnosis. New radiological techniques, nuclear magnetic resonance

(NMR), and magnetic resonance imaging (MRI), positron emission tomography (PET), should soon make contributions to understanding the cerebral physiological changes of illness. By using labeled molecules with these newer techniques, it has been possible to visualize chemical changes in the brain that have heretofore not been detected. Further developments of therapy with light and the manipulation of sleep.

2

CAUSES

THE MULTIFACTORIAL BASIS

In the several distinct varieties of mood disorders, there are a number of both predisposing and precipitating causes, with different degrees of influence in each disorder.

Predisposing causes

1. Genetic influences are proved and significant in bipolar and recurrent unipolar disorders, major depression, and cyclothymic disorder. They are absent in dysthymia (depression neurosis).
2. Developmental (i.e., environmental) influences of early infantile experiences and childhood trauma probably can influence the occurrence and cause of major disorders. They are essential to the development of depressive neurosis (dysthymia) and characteriological depressions. Their influence in bipolar illness is under study currently and appears to vary with the individual case.

Precipitating causes

1. Psychosocial stressors, including interpersonal relationships, usually are found to influence profoundly the onset and resolution of all major and minor (neurotic) disorders.
2. Physical influences, a variety of drugs, a number of illnesses, unusual fatigue, major geographical moves, and other major changes, especially losses, can have a profound effect in precipitating illness.

From the standpoint of the life history of the individual, a simple equation represents the development of the illness:

$$\text{PREDISPOSED PERSON} + \text{PRECIPITATING CAUSE} = \text{AFFECTIVE DISORDER}$$

The predisposing causes are both genetic and developmental. The latter influences traits of personality that may be treatable.

The precipitating cause may have a special significance to the patient involving the individual's needs, wishes, intrapsychic object relations, ideals, and fantasies. For example, if a woman has an abortion, and her husband experiences the abortion as either murder or a loss of male authority and male dominance, the husband may be troubled enough by it to feel the loss deeply. If he has unipolar or bipolar illness, he may become depressed and require more therapy or medicine. On the other hand, if he sees the incident as relieving himself and his wife of an overwhelming burden, he may have a good conscience about the abortion and no regrets. There is a special personal meaning in connection with the events of every life; in the case of depression-prone persons, they require careful evaluation, particularly as the significance may be unconscious and require searching for, because the patients are often unable to identify it themselves.

GENETICS: HOW IMPORTANT?

Those who treat persons with affective disorders sometimes have to answer questions about heredity, sometimes to counteract misinformation. One needs to know what influence family history has on diagnosis, choice of treatment, and the attitude and well-being of the patient and his or her family.

It is surprising how few people bring up the question of inheritance. Perhaps the depressed person and his or her family are suffering enough without addressing additional painful possibilities. Questions sometimes come up indirectly, however. For example, the siblings of a patient with bipolar disorder had planned not to have children because of the risk of inheritance.

This report by a patient opened the door to discussing her own questions about heredity. Recently a depressed woman whose second son had just had a manic attack was feeling guilty because she had heard that "it comes from the mother's side." The therapist informed her that this has not been validated scientifically.

Another question that comes up is, "Should we get married?" or "Should we have children?" The answer depends on several things, first of which is the diagnosis. Because the affective disorders are a group of entities that differ in their biological base as well as in the clinical picture, treatment, and outcome, they should be discussed separately. Bipolar and unipolar disorders come first because they are the only affective disorders in which a clear-cut genetic factor has actually been proved.

Bipolar and Unipolar Disorder

For a long time clinicians have observed that affective disorders occur in families, which raises the question as to what that means genetically; that is, can specific genetic inheritance be identified? Is it nature or nurture? It is now known that there is a major genetic factor in bipolar illness, a less important factor in unipolar illness, and probably none or a very minor factor in the most common illness, depressive neurosis.

Clinical Observations

Some practitioners relate stories of families with cases of illness occurring in three generations, whereas others counter with stories of families with no evidence of inheritance. The impression is that inheritance and family history are important, but that other factors, such as personality, individual vulnerability, object relations, and social stressors, also can play a crucial role in treatment, outcome, and prognosis.

Consider the contrast in the histories of two sets of identical twins. The first set is two women in their sixties. One, a single schoolteacher, had a severe depression of several years' duration treated successfully with electroconvulsant therapy, a result that generally indicates a diagnosis of major depressive disorder. The other twin is married to a competent, protective husband, and has never worked. In striking contrast, she has never been clinically depressed.

The second set of identical twins, men in their thirties, have both been treated for recurrent depression. One of the twins, who was drafted and who served in Vietnam, has had almost continuous disabling depressions over the 14 years since discharge from service. He has also had one brief three-month period of hypomania. Throughout he has had great resistance to medical treatment, which has deprived him of appropriate chemotherapy. The other twin, not drafted into the armed services, has had similar depressions and hypomania, not disabling, for which he has received medication. He has been able to function and hold a job throughout this time. Apparently these identical twins have the same illness but are affected by it differently.

Controlled Studies and Surveys

A number of both surveys and twin studies reveal that in bipolar disorder about 67 percent of the identical twins of patients also have bipolar disorder, as contrasted with fraternal twins, in whom only about 20 percent of the twins of affected persons have the illness, a figure comparable to that seen in all siblings. Yet one-fourth of the identical twins of the patient do not have the illness. For the unipolar illness of recurrent depressions without mania, the figures are less impressive: 40 percent of identical and 11 percent of fraternal twins have the same illness. The figures for identical twins are similar whether reared apart or together (Gershon 1983).

In first-degree relatives, that is, immediate family, there is a higher incidence of affective disorder than in the general population, that is, about 18 percent compared with 0.9 percent in the population of controls, using the criterion of strictly confirmed diagnosis (Gershon 1983).

The conclusion is that there is a strong genetic component in bipolar and unipolar illness, but not an exclusive one, meaning that other factors are involved. Even with bipolar illness, which shows the most evidence for a major genetic factor, it has not been possible to show a single-locus genetic source. A multifactorial basis is postulated, including the proposition that influences other than genetic are influential in causing illness.

In a recent workshop on genetics, one of the conclusions drawn by a group of geneticists was that genetic studies should not be made in isolation; the role of nongenetic factors such as environment, continuity between child and adult disorders, and other factors should be studied also (Blehar et al. 1988).

Summary of Studies

Concerning family studies of both bipolar and unipolar illness, Gershon (1983) reports that even sound studies show marked inconsistencies. He reports that the risk of bipolar illness in first-degree relatives of bipolar patients in thirteen studies from 1966 to 1982 varied from 2.5 to 17.7 percent (mean 5.8 percent), compared with normal controls of 0.2, 0.5, and 1.8 percent. The risk of unipolar illness in families of bipolar patients varied from 0.5 to 22.4 percent, with a mean of 10.6 percent, compared with normal controls with 0.7, 5.6, and 5.8 percent, a much smaller proportion.

Starting with unipolar patients as index cases in eight studies, the risk of first-degree relatives having bipolar illness varied from 5.9 to 17.5 percent, with a mean of 8.3–14.2 percent, compared with normals of 0.7, 5.6, and 5.8 percent, a much smaller figure. There is no doubt that unipolar and bipolar illness demonstrate a considerably higher risk for first-degree relatives than for well controls.

Cognitive or cultural factors lead to differences in rates (Gershon 1983), with urban setting, younger generation, and American nationality associated with higher rates. The rate of affective illness is consistently several times higher in relatives of patients than in controls, which is evidence of a strong familial influence. The first-degree relative of a bipolar patient has from a one-in-seven to a one-in-twelve chance of having unipolar illness and about one chance in sixteen of having bipolar illness. These figures may be useful in discussing genetics with the families because the odds are not overwhelming.

Other Affective Disorders

The preceding data are for clear-cut bipolar and unipolar illness. Data for the other forms, which are much more numerous in the practice of the psychotherapist, are scarce. There are some figures for schizoaffective disorder, which is a fairly uncommon illness and probably related to bipolar illness. For single-episode depression without mania, for depressive neurosis (dysthymia), and for secondary depressions, clinical experience suggests a very weak to absent genetic component.

In comparing the incidence of cyclothymic personality and schizoaffective disorder in relatives of bipolar patients with the incidence of these disorders in families of normal probands, evidence is found that these disorders are part of a bipolar spectrum, which is a clinically useful piece of information for planning therapy. For example, if you see a patient's first-degree relative with a clinically confusing picture, you are likely to be correct if you lean toward a diagnosis of an affective disorder.

Children of Parents with Bipolar and Unipolar Disorder

The chance of a child with one parent with clear-cut bipolar or unipolar illness becoming affectively ill has been reported at 27 percent (i.e., about one in four). With two parents so affected the risk is 50–70 percent (Gershon 1983).

It is quite clear that in counseling a patient with definite bipolar or unipolar illness concerning the risk of illness in future offspring, these figures should be kept in mind, remembering that a great deal of the data was collected from studies on severely ill and hospitalized patients, and the extrapolation of the data to the average depressed patient is open to some question.

There is also evidence that, with milder forms in the parents, the offspring are less likely to be affected, possibly because of a smaller degree of expression (penetrance) of the genetic factor. There are other rather remarkable exceptions. For example, there was one family with ten siblings, of whom eight had bipolar and two had unipolar illnesses. These ten siblings collectively had fourteen children, all of them now past the age of risk, (i.e., 40 years of age), and only one of the fourteen has had any affective illness (unipolar depression), suggesting that something diluted the genetic factor in the next generation.

Infants of Parents with Bipolar Illness: Nature Plus Nurture

There are ongoing efforts to study the relationship of a genetic predisposition to the quality of the nurturing environment by the direct examination of infants and parents with illness in their family setting. Bipolar illness has been studied the most intensively, with comparison to normal controls (Cytryn et al. 1984). These studies, although with small numbers (thirty-four index families of patients and thirty-four control families) and followed for 4 years in one group and from age of 12 months to 24 months in the other, showed significantly more pathology in the infants of manic-depressive mothers than in controls. The principal findings in the infants were an increase of an "insecure, ambivalent attachment" from 12 to 18 months, and less capacity for "self-regulation of their emotional equilibrium." Only one infant showed a depressed mood. In older children, aged 2–3 and 5–8 years, about one-third showed attachment difficulties and "marked variability of mood and behavior" (Cytryn et al. 1984, p. 221). A summary of the principal literature to 1978 is given in Reid and Morrison (1983).

Cytryn and colleagues (1984) discuss the relationship of nature (genetics) and nurture, pointing out that most studies show a frequency of serious pathology in families with an affectively ill parent. The parents exhibit "disorganization, tension, and unhappiness, coupled with a relative lack of effectiveness [in parenting, no doubt] and more negative affect toward their children . . . ." (p. 221). They add, "The frequency of disturbances in children reared in such an environment would be difficult to explain on a genetic basis alone" (p. 221).

The important question of whether early symptoms are related to later depressions also comes up, that is, "continuity verses discontinuity." The problem has been addressed by others (Decina et al. 1983) who found higher rates of childhood psychopathology in the older children (age 7 to 14) bipolar probands than in controls. The degree of pathology was such that 50 percent of the children might require therapy.

At present one cannot separate out genetic, environmental, and developmental factors. Nevertheless, the rearing of children at risk is a fruitful field for therapeutic intervention and prevention. Techniques must be employed to help depressed mothers with infants and their children, some of whom may be genetically at risk or certainly vulnerable because of the special relationship of the depressed mother with her baby. The psychotherapist of the adult may very well be treating the child by counselling the mother, or referring to a child therapist.

Clinical Applications

Knowing the potential influence of a genetic component can be useful with patients who are difficult diagnostic problems. An example is a 35-year-old woman with a sibling who has clear-cut bipolar disease, and other affected first-degree relatives. Her therapist had taken a leave of absence. The patient plunged into a severe panicky depression in which she sought emergency consultation. After a chance to tell her story to a new psychiatrist she felt much better, but the next day awoke early, feeling "speeded up." During the day she experienced an unpleasant excited feeling which lasted into the next day, preventing her from sleeping. She explained it as due to so much relief and excitement at finding someone who would listen to her.

This woman was a genetically susceptible person with a brief psychogenic depression, induced by separation, followed by a brief hypomanic spell, brought on by the excitement of finding a new listener. If she did not have a family history of bipolar disorder, we would be puzzled by the reaction and would probably consider it a hysterical overreaction, but we would wonder about the excessive elation. Because it is known that, in the families of bipolar patients, relatives such as our patient often experience rapid cycles of emotion we can lean toward her having cyclothymia.

The family history may be especially helpful in adolescents and young adults in whom the initial attack often presents a disguised or atypical picture. These young people may be seen by a school counselor who is not trained to recognize major disorders. The diagnosis may be missed, with unfortunate results, possibly even suicide, or at best an unnecessary failure in school. A college student whose work had been outstanding was not able to finish her assignments and take examinations. She was scolded by her teachers, went to the counselor, a young psychiatrist who had little background in major disorders. When he learned that she had just lost her boyfriend, he advised her to learn to be tough and to adjust. She dropped out of school; when seen a week later by another psychiatrist it was evident that she had a major depression with endogenous signs, particularly mental slowing and inability to concentrate. Her mother and sister had had similar depressions. At college her depression had been masked by her personal problem, which she had presented to the psychiatrist as her reason for seeing him; this is an error all too easily made in the early stages of a major depression; it arises out of the obvious trauma of a loss such as a disappointing love affair. This mistake can be avoided by taking a careful family history for affective disorders.

Bipolar illness and recurrent unipolar illness run in families and have a definite genetic factor in their etiology. The illnesses overlap in some families, showing that these two forms have a genetic relationship to each other. When there is a definite bipolar or unipolar disorder in one or both parents, the children are at high risk, and every effort should be made to protect and nurture them, with this vulnerability in mind, through parent guidance, family therapy, or the use of child therapists. The presence of a strong family history of either bipolar or unipolar disease can influence the therapist toward a diagnosis of similar endogenous disease in questionable cases, such as first attacks in young adults or adolescents who tend to present atypical clinical pictures.

Search is underway for genetic markers and other evidence of the mode of inheritance, so far revealing only that it does not seem to be a single-locus transmission and that factors other than straight inheritance also influence the outcome (i.e., the occurrence of illness). In other mood disorders, depressive neurosis, and characterological depressions, there appears to be little or no inheritance. In treatment, other factors, such as personal history, life style, stress factors, and personal relationships must be weighed, along with family history and genetics.

3

EPIDEMIOLOGY

Psychiatric illness and psychotherapies are intimately interwoven with their sociocultural settings. The illnesses are the results or expressions of disharmonies within a person and between him and his society.

— Jerome Frank, *Persuasion and Healing:*
A Comparative Study of Psychotherapy

FREQUENCY IN THE POPULATION

The latest figures from a study released in 1984 by the National Institute of Mental Health (Robins et al. 1984) show that affective disorders were the third most widespread of psychiatric disorders, after anxiety and alcohol and drug abuse. The figures are shown in Table 3–1. The survey was made in Baltimore, St. Louis, and New Haven; nearly 10,000 people were questioned. The method of identification was by the clinical criteria described in the *Diagnostic and Statistical Manual of Mental Disorders (DSM-III)*, so that what are described are actual clinical disorders, and not merely moods or attitudes, as in the *Midtown Manhattan Study* (Srole et al. 1978).

Surveys have defects, one being that sometimes questions do not suffice to make a valid diagnosis, but the criteria of *DSM-III* are fairly definitive, so that all the figures are probably somewhere near the actual occurrence, except anxiety disorder in Baltimore, which seems to be exaggerated.

Although depressions are found in people of all nations and

Table 3-1
Lifetime Prevalence Rates of Psychiatric Disorders in Three Sites

Disorder	Percent of total population		
	New Haven	Baltimore	St. Louis
Any disorder	28.8	38.0	31.0
Substance use (alcohol, drugs)	15.0	17.0	18.1
Anxiety disorders, including phobia, panic, obsessive-compulsive, and somatization	10.4	25.1	11.1
Affective disorders	9.5	6.1	8.0
Manic episode	1.1	0.6	1.1
Major depression	6.7	3.7	5.5
Dysthymia (depressive neurosis)	3.2	2.1	3.8

Source: Robins, L. N., Helzer, J. E., Weissman, M. M., Orvaschel, H., Gruenberg, E., Burke, J. D., Jr., and Regier, D. A. (1984). Lifetime prevalence of specific psychiatric disorders in three sites. Archives of General Psychiatry 41:952. Copyright © 1984 by the American Medical Association. Adapted by permission.

nationality groups, in the cities and in the country, there are some interesting differences in frequency. The classical *Midtown Manhattan Study,* although a few years old, gave some valuable data, obtained from a population survey (Srole et al. 1978) in New York City. It showed that 23.6 percent of the surveyed group had depressive symptoms; that is, about one-fourth of the population studied had a tendency toward depression, defined as a pessimistic viewpoint toward life situations, health problems, and interpersonal relationships. Other studies show similar figures. (Martinson et al. 1957)

The number of people who need help from a physician is high enough so that most physicians have had considerable experience with depressed patients. Indeed, general practitioners often treat patients with milder forms of depression without referring them to psychiatry. The number of people who go on to become patients of psychiatrists is great enough to constitute the largest single group in the general psychiatrist's practice. About 40 percent of women and 17.2 percent of men discharged from general hospital psychiatric inpatient units had a primary diagnosis of depressive disorder. These percentages also show a preponderance of women over men.

Another significant comparison is contained in a study (Martin et al. 1957) of a group near London, England, where 10 percent of the men and 24 percent of the women complained of depression. In general, in any locale, approximately two to three times as many women as men have depressions. However, in the United States, more men—almost three times as many—commit suicide. The rate of suicide increases with age in both men and women. At age 55 the rate for women falls off, but the rate for men continues to rise (Silverman 1968, p. 57).

In summary, it is evident that where depression is defined more strictly by clinical symptoms, the occurrence rate is 6–10 percent, and where the diagnosis is made on the basis of a depressive (i.e., pessimistic) attitude, the frequency can be as high as 23.6 percent, and includes many people who are untreated.

The quotation at the head of this chapter simply reminds us that the struggle of individuals, within themselves and in their society, is still understood to be at the heart of everyday work with troubled people.

SEX AND RACE DIFFERENCES

We do not know why more women than men have depressions. Perhaps there are hereditary and other biological factors that cause women to break down more readily than men. There are psychological factors too; little girls have been taught to be nice (i.e., passive). Some women cannot let out their normal aggression, which accumulates until it is unbearable. Some women carry an abnormally heavy load of aggression and hostility which they have suppressed all their lives. There are circumstances in our society that are unbearable for such women; for example, consider the narrowness of some women's lives. Consider also the restrictions of an intolerable marriage from which society, circumstances, and the woman's passivity allow no escape. Eventually disappointment, hopelessness, and despair may overcome her.

Why do more men (almost three times as many) commit

suicide than women, especially in the older age group? (Silverman 1968, p. 57). Loneliness may be a factor, or lack of self-esteem. There are men whose self-esteem has been destroyed by the losses of age, by the stresses of society, or possibly in childhood, by an environment that failed to provide them with a strong self-image. One sees mothers whose circumstances or whose unconscious hostility to the male prevents them from giving the child a strong self-image and may endow him with life-long guilt. There are fathers who have implanted impossible goals and excessive guilt. There are men, like the women described above, who were taught to suppress their aggression and to be "good." Out of guilt, they turn their anger against themselves. When society has no function for them by which to enable them to feel useful, what is left? The idea that "I'm no good" or "The world would be better off without me," may then overwhelm the desire for life.

SUICIDE AND MURDER

"Blacks kill each other. Whites kill themselves," one black Cleveland City councilman said recently. Nevertheless, in recent years, more and more blacks are found who are subject to depressions, and more black patients are seen with the same affective symptoms as the whites. We suspect that better distribution of medical care may be one of the reasons for the change. It seems likely that these differences are not racial, but are cultural and environmental. Data for educated blacks differs very little from those for educated whites.

Nevertheless, psychotherapists working with blacks living in a white society are going to have to deal with some of the specific psychological problems of the minority group—low self-esteem, rebellion, and reality problems—which can be overriding.

Hendin (1969) states that among young urban black men, between 20 and 35 years of age, suicide is twice as frequent as among white men of the same age group. Black homicide reaches its peak in the same age group. In a study using psychoanalytic technique, he was able to demonstrate that the pressures and conflicts of urban Negro life and the frustrations and anger of the black ghetto can lead to suicide as well as homicide. The part played by definitive affective disorders per se is not described in this article.

If you get yourself killed in a gunfight, is that not a form of suicide? Such deaths certainly resemble suicide in that victims bring it on themselves. Persons who subject themselves to the risk of a gunfight must have a low estimation of the importance of their own lives. Friedman and colleagues (1987) surveyed, using an anonymous questionnaire, students at an academically selective New York City public high school. Of the 380 students who responded, 201 (62 percent) had thought about killing themselves, and 9 percent had made a suicide attempt. Fifty-eight had worked out a plan for killing themselves, but only in 15 did the suicidal thoughts persist for more than a week. Among the 143 who had not had a plan, seventeen had persistent suicidal thoughts. Of the thirty-three who had actually attempted suicide, most were girls. Half of these had made more than one attempt, usually by unreliable methods, such as drug overdoses or wrist-slashing. One-quarter expected to die, one-quarter were unsure, and one-half did not. The rate of attempted suicide reported here is higher than in the adult population.

Actually, the suicide rate among young black males (10 to 40 years) is higher than in young white males and parallels the homicide rate. In the older groups, 40 or more years of age, the rate for white males is much higher (Hendin 1969).

Suicide and the Young

Another group with a high suicide rate is the young (see also Chapter 17). A number of people (e.g., Rome 1974) have pointed out that a serious suicide risk group in the United States is found among young persons, especially males, of college age. Among college students, suicide is now the second largest cause of death, with a national rate 50 percent higher than for other Americans of comparable age. The rate for young men is said to have increased by 50 percent between 1970 and 1980 (New York Times 1985).

Why is this so? Why should young adults, with their lives before them, fortunate enough to be privileged to obtain higher education, take their own lives? There are a number of reasons, but perhaps the most important is that this is the age at which young adults go out on their own to face life and to try themselves out. Those with a low self-esteem and high ambitions may too easily get a sense of failure and defeat. If there are feelings of guilt and worthlessness, they may choose suicide as a solution, especially if they feel very much alone and have no one to turn to for help. Rome (1974) discusses alienation from an impersonal society and its effect on young college students. He or she may actively protest and rebel, with a disregard for his or her own life, or he or she may become disenchanted and withdraw into a depression.

DEPRESSION AND THE PERSONALITY

Depression can occur in very effective, accomplished people. It can be found at all social levels, and, indeed, there are many examples of famous and capable people who have suffered from depression. Senator Eagleton withdrew as running mate to candidate George McGovern in the 1972 presidential campaign because of the public reaction to his past history of mental breakdown treated (successfully) with electroshock therapy. Although he was well when the story was announced, suddenly depression "went public." The public was awakened to the possibility that mental illness is treatable and curable.

A generation earlier, following World War II, the American Secretary of Defense James Forrestal, suffering from a mental breakdown of depressive type, was confined to the Naval Hospital in Bethesda, Maryland. One night at 3:00 A.M. he went into a small kitchen, found a window he could open and threw himself to the ground seventeen stories below, ending his life, destroying the talent and superb mind that had brought him to a position of eminence. Speculation was widespread as to the reason for this self-destruction. Was it some government secret or was it some personal problem? The answer was simpler than these guesses; it was evidently a depression of a type occurring in middle life in certain conscientious, hard-working people, that is, a specific illness, known as psychotic depression or involutional melancholia.

In our own generation, the actress Marilyn Monroe, America's sex symbol, supremely successful in her career (but not in her private life), at the top of her profession, was found dead from an overdose of drugs. She had been under treatment for chronic depression. Another generation was awakened publicly to the existence of mental illness and the seeming inconsistency of where it strikes. Her depression was apparently dysthymia (depressive neurosis) and differs from that of Senator Eagleton or Secretary Forrestal; it is chronic, comes from lifelong insecurity, anxiety, and the absence of love and care in childhood.

Lessons of History

Fortunately there are, in fact, far more examples with less tragic outcomes. History tells us of famous people who have been victims of depression. Among those who had serious depressive spells include Abraham Lincoln, Winston Churchill, the musician Robert Schumann, and William James, professor of philosophy at Harvard. These people suffered with their problems, but continued to be productive. We know from their biographies how much they suffered.

There are practical lessons of history for the psychotherapist. One is that depression and its related problems—mania, disability, suffering, and suicide—are no respectors of persons. In addition to those mentioned above, there have been many others: Queen Elizabeth I of England, Gioacchino Rossini (the composer of *The Barber of Seville* and other enduring musical masterpieces), and King Ludwig II of Bavaria all suffered from clinically disabling depression.

A second point is that childhood losses seem, in most of these famous persons, to predispose to adult depression, just as they do today. Rossini's mother and father left him at age 6 with his grandmother as they went off on concert tours. Lincoln's mother died when he was 9 years old. In his adult years, his first disabling depression came after the death of his fiancée, Anne Rutledge. Queen Elizabeth I was separated from her mother, Anne Boleyn, in infancy, and was brought up by others. When she was 3 years old, her mother was beheaded by order of her father, King Henry VIII—truly an inauspicious climate for a young child.

Today, one tries ideally to see children through such traumas with support and understanding. In the book, *A Child's Parent Dies* (Furman 1974), the author describes methods of lessening the damage done at such times by assisting in the process of mourning.

There are also some lessons in history on suicide prevention. For example, in his book on Marilyn Monroe's last days, written years after her death, Summers (1985) illustrates the fact that Miss Monroe gave hidden signals for a long time and, at the end, directly warned at least one person, who for reasons of his own, did not intervene and to his regret learned that she died that night of an overdose of medication.

In the case of Forrestal, the physicians failed to recognize two truths; one, that a very dangerous time is when the patient is beginning to get some energy back and become more active, but is still influenced by the same thinking; and two, that a person can be suicidal even if he or she does not talk about it.

Parenthetically, the old belief that if a person threatens suicide he or she is not going to do it is wrong also. In the story of King Ludwig II of Bavaria (Alexander 1954), he had threatened suicide many times and eventually succeeded. The mistake there was on the part of the psychiatrist who did not rule the King's therapy with an iron hand, but allowed the King to influence him to walk alone and unprotected with him along a lake. The King, after a horrendous struggle, drowned them both.

The Seriousness of Depression

People may be suffering with depressive illness without others being aware of it until something brings it forcibly to attention, such as the tragedy of suicide. As a woman stated after her husband's suicide, "I knew something was wrong, but he never complained. He just kept worrying about business and brooding about failure. I didn't know how serious it was." Sometimes people do not want to see it. The closer we are to the victim, the harder it gets, because we do not want to believe that there is such a thing as a mental state beyond our voluntary control.

Often the tendency of the onlooker is, through denial, to minimize or disparage the symptom in an effort to encourage the sufferer, and to try to keep the person from "giving in" to his or her symptoms. This is based on the fantasy that there is really nothing wrong with the individual and that his or her symptoms will go away if he or she straightens up and shows a little more determination. Alas, such advice usually makes the patient worse. As a symptom of the illness, the sufferer already feels much too guilty and useless, sometimes to the point of suicide; this threat to life is the greatest danger in depression. The patient has already called him or herself "lazy," "useless," or "no good" because of a lack of drive; one has to be careful not to increase guilty feelings in the patient. Depression occurs in very conscientious persons who do not need anyone to tell them their duty. Even the physician can fall into the error of trying to shame the seeming laggard into action, thinking it may act as a stimulus to increase his or her drive, whereas the opposite may happen; that is, the individual may become more ashamed and more withdrawn and slowed down.

Depression and Disability

Depressed people can lose a great deal of time from their lives. A depression can last months, or even years. Add to this the fact that depressions tend to recur, and some depressed persons can be susceptible to another attack in the future if untreated. Careers are cut short tragically, effectiveness is slowed down in all areas of life, if treatment is not pursued. A brilliant scientist or businessperson may not be able to function half of the time; a parent may be separated from the family for weeks or months, resulting in serious damage to the marriage and to their children's lives. Many depressions are brief, fortunately, and modern treatment can also shorten them significantly, but there are also many untreated people who go on in misery for years, who could have been helped.

Then there are also substantial numbers of people with partial depressions, the dysphoric moods of pessimism, boredom, sadness, grief, and despair which do not prevent functioning but which affect the quality of life, as suggested by the Manhattan study quoted earlier (Srole et al. 1978).

4

HISTORY OF
CURRENT CONCEPTS

Melancholia is thoroughly embedded in our civilization, as history tells us (Jackson 1986). It is revealing to know that these depressive illnesses are not unique to our day, and that something as human as a tendency to melancholia must be a very powerful, fundamental force to show such persistence. Perhaps it makes melancholia respectable. For practical purposes, modern insights can be said to have started with Freud's (1917) essay "Mourning and Melancholia" and with Kraepelin's (1921) descriptions of manic-depressive illness.

In the introduction to his very thorough historical study, Jackson (1986) says that some melancholic and depressive states have always, over the centuries, been recognized (by good clinical observers) as disease, and some as not disease, either normal human experience or an experience that goes beyond the normal.

EMIL KRAEPELIN

The concepts behind the classification of affective disorders in use currently can be said to have started with Emil Kraepelin. In 1896, he presented a classification of mental illness (Kraepelin 1921) in which he separated mental illness into two main groups on the basis of prognosis: (1) with benign outcome, manic-depressive and (2) with poor outcome, dementia praecox (called schizophrenia, after Bleuler). This classification had the advantage of making each entity more specific, with a definite beginning, a typical course, and a typical outcome, like any illness. The concept, by following a medical or disease-oriented model, made it feasible to look for definite causes as well as definite symptoms and changes, both physical and psychological. There is a comforting soundness in having this kind of medical model, with its demand for cause, specific course, and implied potential for treatment; it is appealing and, because of extensive study over the years, is becoming more and more applicable to certain specific groups of affective illnesses, as more is learned about their genetics and their chemistry and physiology. The official classifications, *ICD-9-CM* and *DSM-III-R*, used in the United States today for psychiatric conditions, is a modified adaptation of the descriptive approach of Kraepelin. A difference is that now all the entities are called "disorders," rather than "reactions," with their implied etiological meaning, as in *DSM-II* (1968), the earlier manual which followed the ideas of Adolph Meyer.

In his book *Manic Depressive Insanity and Paranoia,* Kraepelin (1921) had this to say about what we call mood (affective) disorders:

> Manic-depressive insanity, as it is to be described in this section, includes on the one hand the whole domain of so-called *periodic and circular insanity,* on the other hand *simple mania,* the greater part of the morbid states termed *melancholia* and also a not inconsiderable number of cases of *amentia.* Lastly, we include here certain slight and slightest colourings of *mood,* some of them periodic, some of them continuously morbid, which on the one hand are to be regarded as the rudiment of more severe disorders, on the other hand pass over without sharp boundary into the domain of *personal predisposition.* In the course of the years I have become more and more convinced that all the above-mentioned states only represent manifestations of a *single morbid process.* [p. 1]

What Kraepelin meant by a morbid process reflected the medical climate of his day. He thought there should be microscopic changes in the brain that could be detected by pathological examination. Although this has turned out to be an error, he is not to be discredited, because something similar is now being demonstrated in the way of chemical changes in certain of the disorders listed under this rubric. As Lewin (1950) said in his monograph, *The Psychoanalysis of Elation*, "Nevertheless, it must be something more than respect for authority that has kept us Kraepelinians, tacitly, when we speak in psychiatric terms. We probably cannot account for the attraction of the Kraepelian terminology" (p. 42). The attraction is, I think, that this group, now called affective or mood disorders, does have a common denominator, which is a generally nondeteriorating course, and a central core of depressive (or manic) symptoms.

Note here that Kraepelin says, "We include here certain slight and slightest colourings of *mood*, some of them periodic, some of them continuously morbid, which on the one hand are to be regarded as the rudiment of more severe disorders, on the other hand pass over without boundary into the domain of *personal predisposition*." He means that the ambulatory cases that present-day psychotherapists see in their work every day are to be included under the same rubric, that is, illnesses, as the more gross and severe forms of bipolar illness. This is truly a modern attitude because it implies a common denominator of all affective disorders, a concept found, with some differences, in *DSM-III*.

The differences in *DSM-III* are that the whole general class he called manic-depressive is now called mood disorders, and it is divided into major mood disorders, which include bipolar and major depression, and minor forms called cyclothymic disorder and dysthymia (neurotic depression).

When we use a descriptive method we cannot go very far from Kraepelin, even though it still leaves us somewhat unsatisfied. We feel that something is missing. Fortunately, there soon appeared someone on the scene to supply some of the missing ingredients, which had to do with not just the disease, but an awareness of the person with the disease.

PSYCHOBIOLOGY

The new actor on the stage was Adolph Meyer. He overlapped in time with Kraepelin, and in the United States there was a great deal of interest in his work (Meyer 1948a). He followed a different path altogether, with the central concept that the illnesses are "reactions" rather than fixed entities. The diverse groups of illnesses were then called reaction types; for example, schizophrenia became schizophrenic reaction, and depression became depressive reaction. This concept, based on what Meyer called "psychobiology," has had a powerful influence on American psychiatry because it opened up doors to understanding and helping the patients through insight into the various developmental, individual, and environmental factors that lead to breakdown. It also explained the diversity of the individual's symptoms. Perhaps because of his Swiss humanist background, Meyer was able to see and teach how the personal life experiences of hospitalized patients affected their illnesses. What an important insight this was to be! And how extraordinary that the state hospitals at the turn of the century provided the setting for Meyer to see how the life histories of the individuals played into their illnesses at the onset, affecting their quality and duration. It has turned out to be of lasting value that he was able to say,

> Today we study mental activity and behavior—the topic of psychology—as the function and activity of the unified organism, just as we view physiology as the science studying the behavior and function of the various organs and parts. The study of the *total behavior of the individual and its integration as it hangs together as part of a life history of a personality in distinction from the life history of a single organ*—that is our great interest in psychology and psychopathology. [Meyer 1948c, p. 492]

With characteristic interest in causes of the breakdown in functioning, Meyer wrote,

> We look for concrete mismanagement of home situations, for discrepancies of ambition and performance, existing difficulties and failures, problems of adaptation and problems of desensitization; and doing so, we shall be helpful to our patient instead of sacrificing him at the

altar of vocabularies dealing with terminal states and
with fixed fatalistic "constitutions" and too dogmatically
fixed "disease entities." [Meyer 1948b, p. 572]

We suspect that here he was referring to the tendency in American psychiatry to follow Kraepelin's descriptive approach slav-
ishly without also examining the personal history and psychological influences which Meyer emphasized.

Meyer called his approach "psychobiology" (Meyer 1957),
meaning the total integration of body and mind to form an
inseparable entity. Nowadays there is a tendency (which Meyer
deplored) to consider, after the manner of Kraepelin, that the
biological features make up a fixed constitutional and genetic
alteration in physiology and that psychological changes are secondary. To call that concept psychobiology is in direct contradic-
tion of Meyer's views. Meyer clearly used the concept of psychobiology to mean *all* the processes by which the individual adapted
to the challenges of the environment, including interpersonal
relations, not merely the limited biochemical areas.

To encourage and expedite the longitudinal approach to the
study of psychiatric problems, Meyer designed a life chart, which
allowed one to show schematically the lines of development
through life, through illness and health, of all levels of the personality, physical and mental, as a unit. Through this concept, illness
then became an understandable developmental event in a human
life. All too often, in our pragmatic viewpoint, where we seek
quick solutions, we are prone, especially because of the use of
effective medications, to take a short-sighted, cross-sectional
view, instead of the more comprehensive longitudinal view of
Meyer, which, fortunately, influenced several generations of outstanding pupils.

INTERPERSONAL PSYCHIATRY

An important outgrowth of the Meyerian school was an increased
interest in the concept of interpersonal relations, that is, the
relationships of individuals with those who have an influence on

their lives—family, friends, neighbors, and social and work groups—and the manner in which these persons influence the lives and symptoms of individuals. An extension of this area of interest into societal factors promoted the growth of the American group of social psychiatrists, who emphasize the influence of society on psychiatric disorders and the concept that improvements in society would help prevent psychiatric disorders.

It is evidence of the continuing influence of Meyerian psychiatry that the *DSM-III-R* emphasizes the importance of an evaluation of psychosocial factors along with the diagnostic appraisal; in fact, it gives a special diagnostic "axis" to psychosocial factors. Specifically in the case of mood disorders, the interaction between the patient and spouse, family, friends, or employer and the atmosphere created by this interaction may force the patient in the direction of illness and may help or hinder recovery. For these reasons, nowadays, one is increasingly likely to get families involved in the treatment and recovery processes. Yet to go even more deeply into causes it should be noted here that interpersonal factors cannot produce any reaction without the cooperation of the intrapersonal (i.e., intrapsychic) factors, such as those described by psychoanalysts and developed in considerable detail over the last several decades. These intraspsychic factors are described in the following section.

FREUD—HISTORY OF PSYCHOANALYTIC STUDIES

At the same time descriptive psychiatry has been making some necessary standardizations, psychological science—behavioral, societal, and psychoanalytic—has also been growing, accumulating a wealth of observations on psychodynamics, personality development, and the place of early and later childhood influences in the background of those who become ill with affective disorders. These observations are being integrated with the entire field of psychiatry. The jumping-off point of this work is Freud's (1917) paper "Mourning and Melancholia," in which he acknowledged that some melancholias (depressions) are somatic in origin, but that others seem to be psychogenic and show deficits in self-esteem, problems of pathological identification, inability to cope with aggression, and regressive phenomena, as components and processes involved in experience of depression.

A series of accumulated contributions since that time by Jacobson (1953, 1971), Bibring (1953), Rado, Deutsch (1933, 1937), Anna Freud (1937), Mahler (1979a, 1979b), and many others has led to the recognition that depressive tendencies may arise out of early experiences, particularly the mother–child relationships, suggesting that prevention is possible. These observations may well implement an oncoming emphasis on prevention which can burgeon in the next generation.

Social psychiatry which studies the effects of society, interpersonal psychology and family therapy all have to be mentioned here because these approaches, growing in interest in recent decades, can contribute to the understanding, treatment, and prevention of affective disorders.

Generally, psychiatry, excluding psychoanalysis, tends to work with the here and now, that is, immediate precipitating stresses and current social and interpersonal problems. It leaves treatment of the character symptoms and traits and more long-range difficulties in object relations to the field of psychoanalysis, although recently there is growing acknowledgment of the existence of long-term interpersonal and intrapsychic problems in the affective disorders. These problems create chronicity and recurrences with untold amounts of suffering. It is to be hoped that this new awareness will counteract the emphasis, a very limiting one, on the immediate precipitants and obvious "events," and focus more on the importance of the chronic, ongoing reality and intrapsychic situations that cause most breakdowns.

The antipsychological attitude of some psychiatric researchers of the 1960s and 1970s sometimes reached polemic proportions, but by the late 1970s and early 1980s things began to change, and there emerged a renewed awareness of psychogenetic possibilities in the affective disorders and the potential, indeed, the necessity of psychological intervention. A review by Malan (1973) confirming the effectiveness of psychotherapy in psychiatric disorders is a case in point. The contemporary reemphasis on grief and mourning and the resurgent interest in Lindemann's (1944) work on grief is another. The increased sophistication clinically of social workers and nurses and their acceptance to do psychotherapy, group work, and family therapy in clinics and private offices of their own or of psychiatrists is now universal. This is certainly an era of the integration of psychodynamic psychology in the treatment of affective disorders. Chapter 16 discusses developmental issues in more detail.

With renewed interest in psychological treatments, there has been an increased interest in psychoanalysis, both as a psychology for understanding the development of affective disorders and in the treatment. Psychotherapists are interested in psychoanalytic concepts and want training in the field. In the development of the psychoanalytic theories of depression there have been five overlapping historical eras (see Table 4–1). Each subsequent era has added to the observation of the previous, with consequent extension of the theory into new areas of study of mental functioning.

A number of studies have been done over the last decade on the manner in which aggression is handled, from childhood on. The concept of "splitting" helps to explain the ambivalence toward love objects, as follows: Developing children acquire a rejecting posture toward the "bad" parts of themselves, the unlovable parts. They internalize these parts as separated from themselves by splitting, rather than by simple repression. When they are forced to look at these bad parts, their anger and hostility are turned on them, and they wish to destroy this part of themselves, resulting in suicidal desires. Unresolved hostility toward others is thus internalized, but usually its presence is betrayed by irritability, impatience, sullenness, and inability to deal with interpersonal conflict in a straightforward way. These insights have spread to general psychiatric education and are used by psychotherapists of all schools of thought.

Psychoanalytic contributions to other approaches have been considerable. There is a concept of the behavioral school called "learned helplessness," which is acknowledged to come from an interpretation, in behavioral terms, of the work of Bibring (1953). Beck (1973), with a psychoanalytic background, has done much to develop the use of cognitions in understanding the psychology of depressions. This is a very useful device no matter what background the therapist has, provided he or she remembers to look for the origin of the ideas.

Study of cognitions has not only theoretical value but also has great practical value for identifying the depressive complex whenever it occurs, regardless of the setting, whether in depressive illness, in the presence of a physical illness, or after a personal catastrophe. Cognitions, ideas, and fantasies provide material with which the psychotherapist can work.

SELF PSYCHOLOGY

Valuable insights have recently grown out of a self psychology that identifies a mental mechanism used unconsciously by those depressives who have some of the characteristics of borderline personalities, especially the tendency to project, identify, and involve others at the same time. One such characteristic is projective identification (Ogden 1983). An example is guilty patients who project their guilt on the therapist and think that the therapist considers them bad rather than owning their own guilt. "You think I'm bad, and if you don't think so, you ought to," typifies this defense, which can induce the therapist to behave as though it were true. What occurs is a splitting of the self into separate selves, each capable of a life of its own and resistances of its own during therapy. For example, there is in some depressives a masochistic trend consisting not of an isolated symptom, but of a whole masochistic self which can function, defend, repress, and assert itself. This is a "vertical" split, in contrast to the "horizontal" split which is repression.

Interpersonal therapy and psychoanalysis have in common that they both deal with object relations, which historically has always been studied intensively by psychoanalysts, from Freud to the present day. "Object relations" refers to the intrapsychic images and their interrelationships, as contrasted to interpersonal relations, which deals with external relationships between people.

An enormous interest in the field of self psychology has grown, especially exemplified by the work of Kohut (1977) and that of Kernberg (1975, 1976), both of whom have described the special therapeutic attitudes required of the therapist working with personalities with atypical trends such as borderline and

Table 4–1
History of Psychoanalytic Concepts of Affective Disorders

Historical eras	Proponent	Concepts
1911–1924		Fixation points; ambivalence; love relations; regression (classic concepts)
	Abraham (1911)	Infantile predisposition to oral sadism and regression to early stages. Guilt over aggression. Unconscious hostility
	S. Freud (1917)	Comparison of melancholia and mourning. Ambivalence toward love object. Introjection of projected anger. Narcissistic injury in early life. Loss of love
1924–1953		Defenses and needs, ego mechanisms
	Lewin (1932)	Optimism in mania
	Angel [Katan] (1934)	Optimism in mania
	A. Freud (1936)	Defense mechanisms—denial
	Fenichel (1945)	Need for "supplies." Dependency. Loss of self-esteem
	Spitz (1946)	Anaclitic depression in infants
	Bibring (1953)	Need to be good, strong, successful. Need to be lovable. Disappointment and helplessness in achieving goals
1953–1966		Object relations, ego functions, early development, mourning
	Jacobson (1953)	Primal depression. Object relations theory. The self. Dependency. The theme of loss

Table continued on next page

Table 4–1 continued

Historical eras	Proponent	Concepts
	Mahler (1961, 1966)	Sadness and grief in childhood. Depressive affect—a basic mood. Separation–individuation
	Bowlby (1961a)	Childhood mourning. Separation and loss in childhood
1965–1985		Studies of affect and cognition. Basic affective theory
	Joffe and Sandler (1965, 1968)	Basic psychobiological affective response in children. Reaction to helplessness. Response to mental pain
	Beck (1967)	The cognitive triad: negative interpretation of experience (pessimism), devaluation of one's self, and negative view of future
	Dorpat (1977)	Denial and loss of reality testing
	Brenner (1982)	Depressive affect, a primary affective response. Denial and loss of reality testing
1950 to present		Widening scope of psychoanalysis
	Stone (1954)	Emphasis on object relations theory, projections and identifications and applications in therapy. Narcissistic personality development. Treatment of more severe forms by analytic methods. Studies of the uses of empathy
	Kohut (1971, 1977)	
	Kernberg (1975, 1976)	
	Frosch (1983)	

depressive. Short-term psychotherapy requires the therapist to look for the interpersonal relationship with the key person and note that the patient has transferred some of his or her parental images on that person. This also occurs in long-term therapy involving personality characteristics. The therapist, especially in analytic psychotherapy, has to work through the early roots of the relationship from which it is transferred, including family relationships. For example, as Cohen (1954) demonstrated, the family member who breaks down in a family that is genetically vulnerable to manic-depressive illness is often the one who feels that it is his or her role to rescue and represent the family. This attitude can result in unrealistic demands with unattainable goals which cannot be achieved and may require considerable psychotherapeutic work.

PSYCHOANALYTIC CONTRIBUTIONS TO THE STUDY OF TRANSFERENCES

Jacobson (1971) followed patients with affective disorders over the long term, giving her an opportunity to study the kinds of transferences these patients develop and to describe how these transferences affect the therapy. She observed that the transferences are characterized by great dependency, are often childlike, and that the severe depressive, even between attacks, often requires special handling. Particularly, the therapist should not terminate abruptly, but have long tapering-off trial periods, reducing the number of visits slowly to permit adjustment on the part of the patient to going it alone, if possible. Empathy guides these decisions.

WIDENING SCOPE OF ANALYSIS

Stone (1954) has discussed some issues in the application of psychoanalytic methods to the treatment of more severe illnesses. Although he was referring to borderline personalities, his ideas can apply to affective disorders in which early infantile attachments occur and in which marked regressions may take place.

Analysts no longer consider severely depressed people in remission outside the range of analysis, but believe that analysis is, par excellence, the appropriate therapy for the kind of personality problem likely to be found in persons with major affective disorders, usually when the major disabling symptoms are controlled with medication. The disorders seen are usually obsessive-compulsive, masochistic, or dependent. Kohut and his followers, particularly, perhaps as an extension of Jacobson's concepts, stress the importance of special considerations of empathy and nurturance with these special persons. The psychotherapist who works with people who are vulnerable to depressive and manic attacks sees that they have a limited tolerance to separation and loss and that one must be alert to impending decompensations, which take the form of the patient's characteristic breakdown.

DERIVATIVE SYSTEMS: INTERPERSONAL PSYCHIATRY AND BEHAVIORAL THERAPY

Although an offshoot of Meyerian psychiatry, the interpersonal approach owes a lot to the studies of object relations done by analysts. The behavioral method, founded on learning theory, has emphasized that neurotic mechanisms are learned rather than inherited, a concept shared with psychoanalysis. For example, the idea of "learned helplessness" (Seligman 1975) as a basis for depression is admittedly derived from the work of Bibring, mentioned earlier in this chapter.

For a summary of the history of psychotherapy, which gives some insight into the place of Sullivan, Fromm, Horney, and Kelmann on culture and interpersonal relationships, see Ehrenwald (1976), who also describes existential psychiatry and discusses Jung and Adler.

PART II

DIAGNOSIS

5

PREPARATION FOR MAKING DIAGNOSES

THE THERAPIST

We psychiatrists pay a high and unacknowledged price these days for our great advances: More and more we ignore the clinical skills that detect, at all levels of awareness, what another person feels. The shift is clearly marked in our practice, research, teaching, literature, and ideal for professional identity. Brain replaces mind, miraculously erasing the great philosophical problem. [Emphasis added]

—R. Stoller, "Psychiatry's Mind–Brain Dialectic,
or the *Mona Lisa* Has No Eyebrows"

The therapist needs sensitivity and awareness to recognize suffering and empathize with the sufferer, yet still be objective even when emotionally affected: to be detached, but not too detached; to be kind, but not maudlin. Integrity and honesty are also basic qualities in this kind of work.

Each therapist has a particular professional training in the traditional techniques of his or her speciality and its insights, but also, unfortunately, its limitations. Whatever their speciality, therapists cannot help but be influenced in their judgment by the ideas with which they are most familiar. Each speciality has its strengths and its weaknesses and tends to overlook the knowledge available in the other specialities while acquiring great depth in its own. With advanced knowledge of psychopharmacology, some persons may tend to prescribe medicines too readily. Others, with advanced knowledge of psychological techniques, may neglect medication even in the presence of the somatic symptoms that indicate the illness of depression; psychomotor retardation, changes in diurnal rhythm, anorexia, weight loss, cessation of menses, and loss of sexual drive. This resistance to medicate is common. Indeed, one sometimes sees in families, patients, and even in some therapists an unawareness of those symptoms which distinguish depressive illness from normal everyday depression. There can be a profound resistance, even in patients themselves to seeing it as an illness and a stubborn insistence that it is merely wrongheaded errors on their own part, to be corrected by sheer willpower.

Some antimedicationists, which include both patients and therapists, take the position that all medicines are a dangerous indulgence, immoral, likely to lead to addiction, and to be avoided at all costs. This group includes some therapists who are not thoroughly familiar with biological psychiatry, although in treating troubled people they will eventually, of necessity, encounter some clients who need medication.

The psychology behind this attitude varies. In some patients it is a kind of paranoid feeling that the medication is a persecutory device. On others it is a fear of being taken over. In families, it may be an admission of their own guilt to accept medication for the patient. Although there are not a large number of therapists, patients, and families who object this vigorously to medication, one should be prepared for it.

To balance off this group who neglect psychopharmacology, there are those who often err in the opposite direction. They are skillful in pursuing the medical treatments, but cannot detect the problems that need psychotherapy.It seems that some attention is usually, but secondarily, given by these biological psychiatrists to immediate psychosocial problems, but they are less likely to see long-term maladjustments, such as, personality problems which require long-term therapy. More emphasis on prevention may help correct this in the future, but at present it seems to be a neglected area in the practice of otherwise very good biological psychiatry.

The therapist also needs a basic, thorough knowledge of the field—its science, its basic fundamentals of research, of classification, of what to look for, and of how to recognize and appraise symptoms. It takes learning through supervision, training, text-book work, and field work to be really educated professionally with respect to the subject. Another need is an awareness of the society, the milieu, and a knowledge of what happens to people in life.

One should write careful notes, go back over them, write papers, give case reports, and never stop learning. With some patients one has to put off note writing until afterward because it is distracting to them. A personal psychoanalysis can go a long way to speeding up the learning process, even for those therapists who are reasonably healthy.

Feelings of the Therapist

The importance of the therapist's personality is helpful in diagnosis in a very special way, namely, through the use of awareness of his or her own emotional reaction to the patient as a measuring stick to assess what is going on in the patient. The patient is not alone in having feelings—therapists have feelings too, and as scholars of feelings, have to be aware of their own. The following are some significant examples of the range of feelings a therapist might have.

Empathy

Awareness of another person's feelings—empathy—is not always present in dealings with patients. Stoller (1984) recently said, "I have an awful suspicion: Many psychiatrists cannot decipher the subtle, pervasive, nonverbal communications that are the way humans express their interior." He adds that many do not feel it important, and that "they don't know what they are missing" (p. 554).

Sensitivity to what the patient is feeling has diagnostic value. It helps the patient, who of course can respond, open up, and reveal more. It expedites compliance with therapy. In short, it makes it possible to be an effective psychotherapist.

Technical uses of trained empathy in psychotherapy go beyond the common usage of the term. Empathy can become a tool for gathering data on the inner life of the patient, a tool which can be trained and focused on particular unconscious elements in the patient's thinking and feeling, and ultimately can become a curative device (Berger 1987).

Kindness

The ability to be kind to your patients enables you to care enough about them to fill the role to which your contract with the patient has assigned you, that is, the role of therapist, physician, and helper. Kindness is an essential preliminary quality that implies the capacity to act, to take responsibility, to perform the function of applying your science, your art, and your skill, in the patient's behalf.

Compassion

The uses of compassion are various. Principally, as with empathy, compassion, the "feeling with" the other person, is a tool for perceiving the suffering and pain the patient is going through. What is required is the ability to identify with the patient, yet without becoming maudlin. This means you can empathize but not lose your objectivity. For example, you may feel angry over the circumstances that led to the patient's predicament, you may feel like crying with him or her, scolding the society, the parents, spouse, employer, or child who is causing such trouble, but you still recognize how it came about, the patient's role in it, and the need for treatment. Most important, compassion implies action to relieve the suffering, whereas empathy is passive.

Through the eyes of compassion you are able to observe when the patient is "at the end of his rope," when he or she is at risk of suicide, to be aware of when he or she needs support or rescue and to take the necessary action. Parenthetically, in this day of malpractice suits, the compassionate, careful therapist does not get sued or taken to court. The seemingly indifferent therapist does.

In a way this is just, for when patients trust themselves to your care they are in a sense making a contract with you and putting you in the role of a caretaker, like a parent. By taking them as patients, you are accepting the contract. They rightly expect that you will fill this role seriously, although not necessarily perfectly, unless they are so regressed as to be infantile in their dependency, in which case the rules change. For patients who are not that seriously regressed, it is satisfactory if you are a "good enough" parent who can make some reasonable mistakes without creating serious resentment, because your heart is in the right place, as are your efforts. You are kind and compassionate. You can then give them bad news and have them accept it because they see your compassion. If you do not have compassion and make mistakes, you may have created an enemy. This basis for malpractice suits is not necessarily a legal basis, but certainly will create a patient who wants to retaliate.

Attraction

It helps to like the patient. The patient will be aware of this and will respond to it, usually positively; but there is a dangerous side to this too. It is important that liking the patient does not get out of hand, especially if the patient is so hungry for love that he or she is capable of forgetting the professional nature of the relationship. If the therapist has the same need to be loved by everyone, it is even more dangerous.

Dislike

While compassion is the helpful emotion you experience when you are empathic enough to know what the patient is feeling, it is possible to feel the opposite also, namely, aversion, or even disgust, if some of the patient's symptoms go against your rules, prejudices, or sensitivities. Adolescents who are rebellious and provocative for the purpose of covering up anxiety or depression can easily make you feel like fighting back. Don't do it! Recognize their underlying guilt and don't be led astray. Don't get drawn into a battle. Often "bad" people are anxious. Pay more attention to their anxiety than to their "badness."

Negative emotions, such as aversion, can interfere with treatment. Probably, you should not try to treat someone you dislike too much or are too afraid of. It is hard enough to take care of depressed and manic patients and accept the normal anxieties of this work if you like them and are drawn to them. The patient will eventually pick up your feelings. It can interfere with the work.

Impatience

You have to be especially alert to your impatience because depressed persons move slowly, and their symptoms give up their hold with painful reluctance. You hear the same thing over and over again and wonder if things are ever going to change.

Also, what is more likely to happen, the very personality characteristics, such as passivity and masochism, which got them into their problem can interfere with their getting better, particularly passivity, dependence, submissiveness, and masochistic trends. It can try your tolerance to see a patient who repeatedly gives in to a dominating spouse and then continues to complain about the results of his or her own submissiveness. Equally difficult are those who dominate and control with their symptoms and find them too useful to give up. One cannot treat too many patients with this kind of depression; it can become enormously fatiguing.

Honesty

Why do we have to discuss honesty? Isn't it obvious? It must be, and it surely is, apparent to all professionals that they must be honorable in their dealings. Surely, everyone knows that if the spouse of a patient under psychotherapy calls you, on one's own, you have to tell the spouse that you must tell the patient about the call because it will interfere with the therapy. Of course, as an aside, you say to yourself that you know very well that the spouse will tell the patient if you don't, and thus insert a wedge, unconsciously or on purpose, between you and the patient. Complete openness is easy in such instances, but it is not always so simple. What if you have a very fragile patient who would become not only exceedingly resentful if he knew, but might actually become violent? There you have to weigh the factors involved and make the best decision possible. Most of the time honesty is your best defense against being manipulated and misused.

Another difficult situation is in labels. What if a patient asks if he or she is a schizophrenic or if a parent asks what a schizophrenic child's diagnosis is? In this case honesty about the various meanings of the term is important. It is not necessary to hit someone with this diagnosis without compassion and a knowledge that preliminary diagnoses are not always correct. Thoughtfulness, full explanation, and "being with" the patient and family go a long way to making honesty workable.

Countertransference

This term describes a complex phenomenon that occurs in the therapist when the patient, in the course of the therapy, awakens and mobilizes in the therapist an old object relationship. The therapist then feels toward, or reacts toward, the patient as though the patient were the old image from the therapist's past. The process may be conscious or unconscious, or a combination, and can cause serious complications in therapy.

Problems that can result from countertransference are several, but have the common denominator that the therapist's reaction is appropriate neither to the situation nor to the client who has aroused this ghost in the therapist's closet. Therapists can become too resistant, attracted, resentful, etc., and must examine their own feelings and the origins, when they feel their emotions being stirred up. Especially they must watch for acting out on their own part, which may be unconscious (seductiveness, domination, controlling behavior, preaching, nagging, etc.), breaking and changing appointments, being late consistently, dozing off, interrupting the patient too much, and other actions can all point to an interfering countertransference.

Countertransferences can develop rapidly, as soon as the patient's reactions begin, in the course of the therapy, to impinge on the therapist and arouse a need to react. Generally, in the initial stages of a therapy, our responses, as therapists, to the patient are benign, momentary, and transitory, based on our impressions and guided by an objective diagnostic appraisal. Later, as therapy goes on and working with the patient progresses, our interactions begin to affect our own unconscious, and our own old relationships are revived, so that we have to contend with our own memories and unconscious responses. This may be particularly difficult with patients who project, because they tend to put their "bad feelings," such as guilt, on us. This subject is discussed further in the section on psychotherapy in Chapter 14.

Insight

A final consideration is the organized insight into the patient's inner life, and it is essential to both diagnosis and treatment. It gives a framework to what is otherwise chaos. This means a knowledge of drives, defenses, resistances, and symptoms as well as their interactions. Reading, studying, experience, and supervision can contribute to these insights, but, in addition, a personal psychoanalysis is invaluable. If you refer patients who need psychotherapy of any kind to therapists who have had personal psychoanalysis, you know that they will look at the patients' problems in depth. If they are kind as well, you know they will give the help needed, whatever it may be, when intrapersonal and interpersonal conflicts are at the heart of the matter.

Add to this some insight into family dynamics. Psychoanalytically trained therapists can help in understanding the impact of illness on children, particularly, but also on other members of the family.

There are many excellent therapists who neither have had

nor need personal psychoanalysis. However, to carry the work of therapy beyond the immediate present conflicts, it is essential. There are patients with affective disorders who need long-term dynamic therapy or psychoanalysis, and we need a body of trained people to ensure treatment for them.

ETHICS

No penetrating discussion of clinical psychiatry can be complete without at least a mention of the importance of ethics. Psychiatry, as a branch of medicine, shares with medicine some essential inherited moral and ethical principles. This tradition does give us a useful code by which we can be piloted, fortunately for us, through some rather dangerous waters with our patients. Your personal moral values have to be measured by this code.

Start with *primum non nocere*. Yes, indeed, Latin! It means, "first and foremost, don't do the patient any harm!" Add to this the rest of the Hippocratic Oath, which, parenthetically, medical students still take, even in this commercial and secular age, and you have an amazingly helpful set of rules, fundamental to the practice of the healing arts. Over the centuries, this code has served as a useful guide to our personal behavior toward our patients, both for their protection and ours.

Although the oath is somewhat dated in its language, the general principles shine through. I quote only the parts of the oath that are especially useful to the psychotherapist. Start with the rule, "I will not cut for stone even for patients in whom the disease is manifest; I will leave this operation to be performed by specialists in this art." Today we would say, "I will not try to treat something beyond my competence and will refer such cases to someone who can handle them." Further, "In every house where I come I will enter only for the good of my patients, keeping myself from all intentional ill-doing and all seduction, and especially from the pleasures of love with women or with men. . . . All that will come to my knowledge in the exercise of my profession, which ought not be spread abroad, I will keep secret and will never reveal. If I keep this oath faithfully, may I enjoy my life and practice my art, but if I swerve from it or violate it, may the reverse be my lot."

In short, (1) keep yourself from getting involved in sexual relations with patients, or seducing them in any way, and (2) preserve the confidentiality of the patient with the utmost care.

There are two situations with affective disorders in which confidence can appropriately be breached: First, if the patient is psychotic and not responsible for his or her own behavior, and, second, if the patient is suicidal and needs protection which he or she refuses. It amounts to malpractice not to protect the obviously psychotic or suicidal patient. Of course, if it is not possible to get a true picture, if the patient denies danger, unless you have some other source of information, you have to believe him or her, in most cases, provided the patient is not psychotic.

Medical-legal considerations can be troublesome. A rule of thumb that is very useful is to be as professional as you can be, be ethical, true, considerate, and compassionate. With these preliminaries, we are ready to describe meeting with the patient and preparing to diagnose and treat.

INTERVIEWING THE PATIENT

General Principles

No matter where you see the patient, there are some basic and important principles to observe.

Privacy

This means a relatively quiet place, free from observation, outside the visual and listening range of others. A separate and quite room or private office is ideal, especially if you are not invaded by the voices of others, and others cannot hear what you say. Some matters come out in a confidential situation that are suppressed when others can hear and see—crying, guilt, shame, despair, confidences, and so on. Professionals should arrange their offices so that a person going out of a private office does not have to go through the waiting room where others might be sitting.

Respect for Patient's Time

Do not take phone calls or talk to your secretary. Interruptions are very disturbing most of the time and are to be avoided. Also, be on time, and, although you should not appear eager to be through with the appointment, don't run too long. Fatigue sets in; usually 50–60 minutes is enough.

Respect for Patient's Confidentiality

It can be very disturbing to a hospital patient to see you talking at great length to a nurse immediately after your interview with him. Take the nurse aside for any discussions in the hospital setting.

Initial Interview

You know that this is a troubled person who now confronts you, as you greet and welcome him into your office, but his complaints do not usually include announcing to you that he has a certain diagnosis, for example, depression, and requires a certain kind of treatment. He has something on his mind, possibly that someone else advised him to get help. He may not even appear to be particularly unhappy; on the other hand, he may look very sad and down in the dumps; he may be agitated, or he may be very quiet. He may be well-controlled emotionally, or he may cry, but the chances are he will begin by telling you the story of his troubles and you are the one who will have to make the decision as to whether or not he has a depression. Then, if you are a physician seeing him for vague complaints and he starts telling some of his personal troubles, you listen at least long enough to make a preliminary diagnosis. His appearance may give this away—a depressed, sad, or unhappy face and body language, or in extreme cases a tendency to neglect personal care. An effort to keep up good appearances may sometimes be rather obvious.

Slow, monotonous speech characterizes a few depressed people (and this is an ominous sign), but our patient may appear bright and alert and may talk rapidly. It may only later begin to dawn on you, as you digest what he is telling you, that he is indeed a depressed person who is struggling very hard to keep up appearances. He has partly buried the depressive symptoms such as guilt, insomnia, loss of self-esteem, difficulty in making decisions, and inability to enjoy anything, but they are there. As he sits there and talks, you may find yourself, not because he expresses his pain, but by virtue of your own empathy, recognizing and feeling his suffering. Empathy is of great help with this group of people because they tend to understate their complaints, and you have to know by the little verbalization of suffering how much indeed this person is going through and how hard it is for him to keep going.

Often patients have been suffering for months without seeking help, because they have not considered themselves to be sick, but instead merely thought they were behaving badly and that they themselves were to blame and should try harder, so that they come to you only as a last resort when all else fails. Thus, many people who seek help for depressions are already in advanced stages, and you may have to make the decisions about treatment promptly.

The very first session may be extremely important, because sometimes many important things come out then, if the patient can be encouraged to tell freely what is in his or her mind. Under the initial stimulus, ideas about relationships and problems and fears, worries, and anxieties and pieces of history from his or her entire life may be verbalized in such a way in this first interview that they will not come back into the discussion again for a long time, possibly only after a long period of therapy. Therefore, it is a good idea to pay extremely close attention in the first interview and to be tuned in to all of the potentially significant ideas that come out, along with pieces of history, fantasies, fears, and symptoms, which could give a picture of the nature of the problem. Making notes afterward helps also, because later you may be able to use this information to advance your insight, by following up on the clues.

Because of this tendency for a great deal to come out in the first session, it is sometimes possible that one can predict what the later therapy will be. However, do not be surprised if the second and third times you see the patient, and even later, new issues arise that change your ideas. Often it is necessary to institute some kind of treatment very early, and a discussion with the patient at the first interview as to what he or she can expect may be very important. It is also important to cement the relationship some- what and let the patient know that you are interested and that attention to the details he or she has described has given you some insight into what is the nature of his or her trouble.

It is never too early to be responsive, to be frankly sympa- thetic, to say to patients that you recognize how much they must be going through, how much suffering they must be experiencing, because these are patients who need that feeling of security that comes from knowing that someone else is aware of their troubles. It may go a long way toward preventing the sufferer from getting deeper into a depression if you state unequivocally quite early that you recognize how troubled he or she is and that you will try to help him or her as quickly as possible. Medically oriented thera- pists are probably prone to institute treatment with medication almost immediately upon receiving a thorough account of the genuine depression. This is probably all right and proper, because the patients who go to medical people for their depressions very often are suffering from the physical symptoms—vegetative and somatic—that require relief, such as intractable insomnia, weight loss, loss of appetite, and inability to concentrate, with fatigue and lack of energy, which is sometimes disabling.

Patients who go to nonmedical psychotherapists are much more likely to talk about personal problems, such as some trou- blesome relationship—a marital problem or a similar personal relationship. For people who present themselves in this way and do not have very much in the way of treatable somatic symptoms, it is not necessary to start off with medications. Instead, you try to gain their confidence and show an understanding and interest so that they will be able to go on and tell more of their story in the next visit.

Seldom does one visit suffice with a depressed person, because depressions tend to be prolonged. The ordinary, usual course of a depression is several months, with a range anywhere from several weeks to several years, and therapy often has to be continuous during this period. This is to speak only of the acute depressive attack and not of the underlying tendency toward depression, that is, the neurosis or personality problem, which may result eventually in a recurrence, so that we have to consider psychotherapy also for prevention between attacks or after the acute attack has been resolved.

To prepare oneself to appraise the problem correctly, one must have a grasp of the theoretical basis of depressions. Here I refer not only to the psychogenetic aspects of depression, including the sociological, interpersonal, and intrapersonal phenomena on which the psychotherapy is based, but also to the illness and syndromes as described in the diagnostic categories that constitute the basic medical psychiatric model currently in use.

6

DIAGNOSIS AND EVALUATION

Diagnosis is needed for the specific clinical disorder, if any, as described in the diagnostic manuals. It should be augmented by psychodynamic diagnosis, diagnosis of disorders and trends of personality, medical diagnosis, and by evaluation of psychosocial stresses. Differential diagnosis is considered here also.

ACCOUNTABILITY

The practice of psychotherapy today is hedged around with controls, both public and private, partly resulting from third-party payments by government and private insurance companies. These pressures influence your practice in some very distracting and time-consuming ways. The therapist may have to deal with insurance claim forms, periodic reports, restrictions on hospital care, freezes of fees, and lost time because of paperwork. Nevertheless, insurance makes treatment accessible to a large number of people who otherwise could not manage it. The practitioner working within the system should try in the interest of the patient to make it as effective and efficient as possible. One way of expediting the process of payment and support for your patients is to adhere to a reasonably accurate and acceptable diagnostic system.

PLANNING TREATMENT

In addition to these administrative reasons for diagnosis, there are some sound scientific and medical reasons also, particularly for treatment planning. Diagnosis has practical functions. Of course, you will see and work with the patient's personal problems, suffering, conflicts, fears, predicament, and struggles. The diagnosis underlies the treatment plan; a formal diagnosis is necessary.

LIMITATIONS OF DIAGNOSIS

Fortunately, psychiatry has a long history of the descriptive medical approach for disorders that have a biological base, and can provide diagnostic tools of workable reliability. The less biologically based disorders, such as the depressive character and the depressive neurosis, are gradually falling into place, under the combined influence of the work of Freud, Meyer, Bibring, Mahler, and others. There is not yet a definite consensus, and the classifications reflect this lack of agreement. One thing that seems apparent is that a descriptive model does not apply as well with the less biological forms as it does with bipolar and unipolar forms, and psychodynamic and developmental models will have to be used.

Framework

The framework for collecting the diagnostic data may or may not be formal and structural, but it is always understood. It consists of the following basic parts:

    1. Interview. A one-to-one conference with patients allowing them to tell their story as they see it. It is sometimes very unstructured.

    2. History or anamnesis. Supplementing the patient's story, one goes further and takes a sufficiently detailed history of the complaints, the symptoms, and the psychosocial situation, the past history, and the family history.

    3. Mental status. This entails a comprehensive mental examination.

    4. Physical examination and/or laboratory tests. These are

performed when indicated by the kind of symptoms. Many patients with affective disorders have symptoms resembling those that could have a physical basis. Therefore, a medical examination is required for such symptoms as headache, backaches, fatigue, tiredness, weakness, weight loss, anorexia, anxiety attacks, constipation, loss of menses, impotence, and frigidity.

CLINICAL HISTORY

The patient is likely to be an adult between the ages of 18 and 80, a woman in two-thirds of the cases, and very often reports some kind of previous episode. Careful attention should be given to some important issues in the patient's past history, described in the following paragraphs.

The story of similar symptoms in the past, going back to early adolescence or even childhood, whether called by the same name or covered up as a medical illness, fatigue states, or episode of crankiness. It is common to find that depressed persons, in their thirties or forties, had at age 18 or 20 years, an episode in which they dropped out of school for a semester or had a long unhappy period because of a disappointment in a love relationship or possibly an adolescent fatigue state treated as a hypothyroidism. Early episodes of depression often mask as neuroses also, but if they were definitive and ran a course with recovery they are likely to have been depressive episodes, similar to the current one for which the patient seeks help.

Episodes of emotional disturbances of some kind in the near blood relatives suggest a family history that is positive for affective disorders. Ask about the relatives individually, siblings, parents, aunts, uncles, and anyone in the blood line. There is some specificity in the type also. When bipolar disorder occurs in a mother, and her daughter develops a mental illness, the chances are it will be bipolar, although possibly different in degree. One of the important issues is the likelihood that both mother and daughter will respond to the same medication, although this is not a hard and fast rule. Alcoholism may mask depression also, and should be looked for in the family history.

In childhood, unless a careful study was made by skilled specialists (child psychiatrist or psychologist), the episodes are likely to have been missed or called by various other names. Personality development throughout childhood may have shown various characteristic symptoms, including passive trends and a tendency to repress affects (stoicism). Apparent dependent tendencies are often covered up by an overly independent crust. Depressive neurosis starting in childhood may show up as a tendency to fatigue, retreat, silence, and lack of communication on issues of emotional importance.

Interpersonal relationships are often characterized by the presence of another singularly important person, usually the mother, father, spouse, or friend, to whom the relationship has been passive, dependent, sadomasochistic, or submissive, with or without rebellion. A variety of personality tendencies, including histrionic, masochistic, overconscientious, guilty, and compulsive behaviors suggest defenses against aggression and ways of handling aggression. Lastly, there may be difficulty in communicating feelings to persons in close relationship and sensitivity to rejection when criticism is expressed by others.

MENTAL STATUS

The conventional mental examination learned by all psychiatric residents (and physicians, one hopes) is a method of assessing the condition of a patient at the time of the examination. In hospital records the mental status goes along with the physical examination and the patient's complaints, that is, symptoms and history, to provide the information for making a diagnosis and, of course, to plan treatment. The psychiatrist initially also tries to get some impression of the personality of the patients, their family relationships, degree of dysfunction, social (i.e., personal) situation, meaningful personal stresses, traumas, and intimate personal relationships. In the affective disorders, which are by no means all identical, one has to be prepared for a range of symptoms and complaints.

Keep in mind the usual areas of examination even as you

follow the patient's story and hear what personal things he or she has to tell you. The following areas give a current assessment of the patient's mental status.

Appearance, General Behavior, and Speech

Facial expression, speech, and body movements can reveal a great deal. The expression may be very sad and downcast, the patient may not be able to smile or to show animation. Sometimes one sees a "smiling depression." Crying is not uncommon, but some people, especially those with more advanced depressions, complain that they cannot cry. Neglect of personal appearance — uncombed hair, untidy dress — are signs of more advanced, severe depression, although someone who is overwhelmed by personal and family problems, at the end of his or her rope, may show a similar neglect temporarily (i.e., for a few days). Body movements and voice may be hesitant and delayed. There is poverty of speech. It can be astonishing in an interview with a severely slowed, depressed person, how long it takes the patient to get anything said, and how little really comes out. In anxious or agitated depressions, patients may show restlessness, hand wringing, and various other signs of tension, such as scratching and picking at the skin.

Bodily and mental activity may be quite slowed, including speech, and initiation of speech may be very sparse or not occur at all. Long pauses are characteristic of more severe depression. This is *psychomotor retardation*, a definitive symptom for identifying a major depression and the depressed phase of unipolar and bipolar depression. When you see genuine psychomotor retardation, you are seeing a major depression with biological changes. Certain physical illnesses can cause some of these symptoms, but without the mental depression. Examples are hypothyroidism, myxedema, myxedema psychosis, frontal lobe tumors, and parkinsonism.

Withdrawal from contact either at home or in groups is common, and the patient has trouble initiating contact with others because of the difficulty experienced in thinking, concentrating, and communicating. *Insomnia* is usual, although there may be atypically excessive sleeping (hypersomnia) as well.

Apparently there is nothing more difficult for a slowed, depressed person to do than initiate or maintain conversation. You know your patient is getting better when he or she starts telling you things voluntarily.

Bizarre behavior suggests delusional thinking, which on exploration turns out to be appropriate to the mood of nihilism, depression, hopelessness, or guilt, unlike the bizarre behavior of schizophrenia, or cerebral disease. For example, failure to eat may be caused by the characteristic lack of appetite or may be a form of *suicidal behavior*. So also, *self-mutilation* may be a gesture of self-punishment for one's supposed sins.

Of course, the manic or hypomanic person is the opposite of all this: he is overactive, quick, talkative, euphoric, overly happy, overly self-confident, brash, and also irritable when questioned or interfered with.

These descriptions obviously do not apply to most depressed patients seen by psychotherapists. In the first place, patients usually go to a psychotherapist because of some problem they want to talk about, and only in the course of the story do you perceive the depressive symptoms—*trouble concentrating, slowness,* and *sadness*. It may be early in the course of a major depression or it may be a depressive neurosis which does not cause the relentless, persistent slowing of a major depression. Or it may be a depression that affects the thinking and attitude most obviously and has very little in the way of overt expression of depressed mood, crying, etc.

The complaints of *fatigue, tiredness, lack of drive or energy* may be accompanied by passivity in behavior and a desire to rest and retreat. Or, as is sometimes seen, a defense against this inertia takes the form of hyperalertness, pushing one's self and putting on the appearance of well-being, that is, a "smiling depression."

Mood and Affect

Look for *sadness*, either expressed or unexpressed. Very little laughter and no pleasure in things (*anhedonia*) are common.

Food, sex, play—nothing gives pleasure. The mood of depression may be expressed as *boredom, apathy, nostalgia, alienation,* or indirectly, as *irritability* with everyone. You may have to *infer* a depression by the cognitive picture, that is, by the depressive ideas expressed.

With manic or hypomanic mood there are the opposite signs of elation, euphoria, a sense of well-being, and power. "I never felt better in my life." Irritability if questioned or crossed is typical, and some manics, if out of control, can be aggressive, hostile, paranoid, and assaultive.

Ideation, Preoccupation, and Content of Thought

The feeling tone—the low, depressed mood—gives depression its name, but the depressed state is much more complex than simply a feeling. There are characteristic thoughts, ideas, concepts, and fantasies, that is, a special kind of thinking. These cognitive characteristics may be subtle but are specific, indeed, pathognomonic, of the depressed state, whether it occurs in a major psychotic depression, a depressive neurosis, or simply a lifelong tendency (viz. depressive personality).

The most obvious ideas are expressed in one or more of four areas:

1. Pessimism (i.e., a tendency to look at the negative side of everything). "Things always go wrong."
2. Low self-esteem, expressed, for example, as "I have never done anything right" or "I can't do anything right."
3. Expecting the worst—negative expectations. "Things can't get any better." "Things won't go well for me." The tendency to expect that "everything will turn out badly, so "What's the use?" There is an attitude of defeat, a giving up of hope. "You can't help me, can you?" "Things are hopeless, aren't they?" Of course, it must be obvious that this is a delusion, when expressed so badly.
4. Self-blame. "It's all my fault." Generally, depressed persons find some way to make it appear as if they have caused all the problems. Sometimes this amounts to dwelling on or becoming

obsessed with a particular idea of guilt. "I'm a burden" or "I don't deserve to live."

The presence of these depressive cognitions or patterns of thought constitutes a thinking disorder, which, when present, can acquire delusional intensity, in which case the patient is clearly psychotic and may act on his or her ideas with suicidal intent. If he or she thinks "The family (or the world) would be better off without me," he or she may also think, "I might as well be dead."

Depressive cognitions can be the focus of psychotherapy when they represent characterological symptoms. They may require analysis to determine their origin and eliminate them. Paradoxically, there are some patients, such as those with major depressions, in which treatment with medication or electroconvulsive treatment changes the outlook, so that the depressive way of thinking simply vanishes, to be replaced by more normal optimism. If, after recovery from any acute depression, the depressive cognitions persist, they should become the focus of treatment.

Cognition and the Depressive Personality

There are persons with depressive personality traits as well as an acute depressive spell. They have a life-long tendency, acquired in childhood, to look at the gloomy side of things, to lack a feeling of self-worth, and to expect the worst; when the depressive episode is over they require psychotherapy to eliminate such depressive thinking, because, if unchanged, it shows a vulnerability to unhappiness and to recurrences and relapses.

Stating this from a psychodynamic point of view, depressive personalities can be said to spend their lives under the influence of fantasies of a pessimistic, often self-punishing nature, or of fantasies of rejection. Helping the patient identify and analyze the origin of these fantasies can be the focus to psychotherapy. Usually it can be demonstrated that they have started in a relationship with a parent that is frustrating and defeating.

For example, a young depressed man said that he had always been pessimistic, and in the next breath, in talking about his mother, said, "My mother never said she loved me," and added that it was impossible to please her. He gave examples of trying to win her, but it never seemed to work. It seems likely that this pessimism originated in the idea that pleasing mother was impossible.

Delusions of somatic disease are not rare. "I've got some serious illness the doctors have missed. I deserve it."

Sometimes in paranoid people who get depressed the imagined "badness" is projected on the world. "The world is a lousy place." "I've been let down and betrayed." When these ideas of guilt, disease, or hopelessness are present and fixed, by definition the patient is psychotic.

The thread of pessimism runs through the ideas of the nonpsychotic depressed person also, with a tendency to expect the worst possible outcome of things. It may also be expressed by statements like "nothing ever works well for me." Feelings of hopelessness and helplessness, not always expressed in less obvious cases, may be elicited.

The self-image is likewise poor in periods of depression in these less grossly sick people. "People don't really like me." "I'm not very good at things." "I've never amounted to much." These depressive cognitions may surface only during a depression, but in some people one can elicit a history going back to childhood. "I've always been a pessimist."

There may be a kind of hypertrophy of memories, with the past coming through in fantasies and dreams, suggesting a prepsychotic state with the return of the repressed, and possibly an oncoming breakdown of repressive abilities. Be alert for a possible psychosis when this happens.

The presence of *suicidal preoccupations*, ideas, or even plans must be carefully noted. Sometimes these are indirect, "I'm no good." "The world, and my family, would be better off without me," are examples. A preoccupation with death is not rare and represents warded-off or frankly expressed death wishes, "Is this all there is?" or "Life doesn't hold much for me."

Sensorium and Intellectual Functions

The affective disorders do not affect memory or orientation (i.e., retention, recall, or recent or remote memory). However, many patients, especially older ones, complain of poor memory, which, on testing, turns out to be difficulty in concentrating or focusing on things, rather than memory loss. The depressive person may have to read things over and over because he or she cannot concentrate, but not because of a loss of the memory function itself.

In elderly patients a kind of *pseudodementia* is not rare. These elderly depressed patients complain anxiously of memory loss, but when given test phrases remember them readily. In patients with organic brain disease, such as arteriosclerosis or Alzheimer's disease, by contrast, there may be no awareness of a deficit in the presence of definite memory loss and inability to retain, especially for recent memory, although remote memory may be intact. If both a depression and some chronic cerebral deterioration are present, which is not unusual, you may find an improvement in memory when the depression is gone.

Similarly, orientation as to person and place are intact. Patients in a psychotic depression may say that they are in a prison as punishment, but upon questioning they usually admit it is a hospital.

Insight and Judgment

The depressive outlook affects judgment by putting a pessimistic appearance on things. Depressed people should not make important decisions when very depressed because they tend to make a depressed decision rather than a realistic one. If you think everything is bad, and will turn out badly, your judgment and behavior tend to be influenced by this attitude, and you will make pessimistic decisions. Making any decision is difficult for depressed people, whereas manics make quick, impulsive, and impatient judgments. Of course, the person who is manic or hypomanic makes overly optimistic decisions and sometimes gets into business deals and love affairs that are totally unrealistic and inappropriate.

Insight, judged by how well patients understand their symptoms, must be appraised also. Do they verbalize their insights? Manics do not know they are sick. Depressives, on the other hand, may know that something is wrong with them, but they have a distorted view of it. If they have had previous depressions, they may realize they are again getting sick, but their insight may be still colored by depressed ideas. With manic patients, the lack of insight into the nature and influence of their overly optimistic ideas may create severe problems, and it is important to prevent patients from getting into inappropriate business deals or affairs.

INTEGRATION OF HISTORY AND MENTAL STATUS

Integrating these observations into a feeling for the whole person gives a view of the depth of their illness, how much they are suffering, how driven and how burdened they are, how well or badly they are functioning, and how much they are at risk for suicide. You get an appraisal of their needs, especially their need for relief, and how urgent it is. Can they work, and how much can they manage at home or should they be hospitalized? Do they need medication? Are they so burdened that even talking is an additional burden, or does it relieve them? Are they becoming exhausted because of lack of sleep?

The mental status and the history, together, allow you to make an evaluation and at least a working diagnosis, so that you are now prepared to think of the next step. It is a good idea to make careful notes after the examination for future use.

Also remember that a skilled psychiatrist or therapist does not go at the patient "hammer and tongs" to elicit all this in an insistent, rigid manner. We have a structure in mind and an awareness of the need to gather the data, but we should never forget that our patients are human beings and deserve, indeed, require, a chance to express themselves and tell their story. We should not let the interview become so formal that the patient is intimidated or becomes resistant. An understanding and sympathetic, quiet listener who knows how to interview will learn more than one who is too aggressive.

DISGUISES OF DEPRESSION
(THE STRUGGLE AGAINST PAIN)

Because depression is one of the most painful of human experiences, persons threatened with it find themselves trying to reduce the pain by any of several methods of defense. As a result of these efforts, the depressed state may be covered up so well that no one can tell by outward appearance that this is really a depressed person. It may be disguised unconsciously by any one of several common mechanisms of self-deception that people employ, automatically, to ward off depression. It is less painful to become preoccupied with something that is merely a mask of the illness — for example, such diverse things as a physical symptom or a financial worry. The following paragraphs discuss the principal disguises commonly seen.

Physical Illnesses or Preoccupations

Depressions affect bodily functions. Consequently, some patients have symptoms of fatigue, aches and pains, or various complaints that take them to a physician, yet may never mention the depressed mood to the physician.

It is sometimes up to the family to alert the physician to the whole picture of the patient's depressive symptoms because he or she may hide them, being ashamed of having mental symptoms. The physician should be called before the examination and told the story, or a family member should insist that the patient tell the physician how much he or she is really affected. Best of all, a family member should go along with the patient and ask the physician for a psychiatric consultation.

Physicians should be careful to assess the depressive factor in patients with somatic (bodily) complaints for which no physical changes are found, especially with psychosomatic, hypochondriacal, or hysterical symptoms. About a third of depressed patients who see psychiatrists have some localized or medical complaint as their presenting symptom. Symptoms in the head, such as full feeling or headaches, as well as urinary and intestinal complaints, are common, as is weakness and fatigability. The most difficult patients to treat are those with hypochondriacal symptoms who are obsessed with the idea of some mysterious malady that no one can find. In the pursuit of and insistence on this nonexistent disease, they are able to defend themselves against the true, unbearable problem. In addition, it reveals the enormous anxiety based on fantasy that patients have about themselves. One sees patients with psychogenic pain who become suicidal when told by their physicians that there is no medical illness. The conversion symptom had covered up a serious depression.

Rationalization and Other Defenses

Patients may say they are getting lazy or that they are doing things wrong or in some way explain away their low mood, loss of energy, and concentration. The family may agree and may push them and say they are self-centered and aren't trying hard enough. Employers or associates may just observe that they aren't getting their work done and are not being active or outgoing enough and may criticize them for it. Enlightened, observant employers or co-workers may enquire if something is bothering them and whether they have seen a physician.

College students who are depressed cover it up with intellectual explanations such as "I can't get it together," to explain their loss of efficiency. They are likely to be scolded by teachers and family for "not trying hard enough." They may project also on the environment. "That class," or "that job," is "no good." "It's getting me down."

Alcohol and Drugs

Very often those who suffer seek relief by using alcohol or other drugs, and they may become dependent. The depression may be so well disguised that it can be recognized only when the alcohol or drugs are stopped. This cover-up is seen often in the young adults who easily turn to drugs for a lift or for relief. Those who have increased their alcohol intake or have started to take drugs are always suspects for depression. Many alcoholics who give up drinking turn out to be so depressed as to require treatment, usually for a depressive neurosis.

Marital or Business Preoccupations

After a separation or divorce, where one of the couple is unable to accept the loss or break in the relationship, he (usually the man) tries to pursue the lost one, threaten, hound, cajole, chase. He can be obsessed with it and needs to talk about it. Often this is an effort to ward off and avoid the pain, grief, and anger of the loss. If the divorce or separation becomes final, anger may then be greatly increased. There are people who are very sensitive to rejection; some of them are prone to violence as well as self-destruction; many of the murder–suicide stories of couples seen in newspapers are of this type. They may be avoided if some outside help is brought to the couple, especially to the one who seems least able to accept the change. Too often people increase the guilt of suffering persons by telling them to straighten up, rather than by being understanding. If the rejected person seems more obsessed or preoccupied with the issue than makes sense, the possibility of an oncoming depression should always be considered.

The same kind of story occurs when the traumatic event is loss of a job that means a great deal to the person. He or she may be unable to tolerate the loss and tries to ward off accepting it by becoming angry with his or her former employer. Murders have resulted, as have suicides. Students with this personality type who have a sense of failure in school are prone either to rebellion or to blame themselves and turn to suicide.

There are numerous other disguises and defenses against depression which will be taken up as the diagnostic problems are detailed. This summary serves as a short introduction to the next two chapters, on diagnosis.

7

FORMAL DIAGNOSTIC CLASSIFICATIONS

Although there are numerous affective states, there are fundamentally only three types of actual affective illness: major depressive, bipolar, and dysthymic disorders. The first two have definitive biological changes. Major depressive disorder has been called by various other names over the last few decades: melancholia, endogenous depression, and primary depression. The other biologically based type, bipolar, can be either manic or depressive. Dysthymic disorder (*DSM-III*) is without clear-cut biological changes. It is also called depressive neurosis (*ICD-9-CM*), reactive depression (*DSM-II*), characterological depression, depressive personality (*ICD-9-CM*), and dysthymia (*DSM-III-R*).

Although the three types overlap and sometimes feed into or follow each other, the distinction is clearly there. The major depressions and bipolar types generally respond to medication, whereas the depressive neurosis usually does not. The situation is complicated by the varieties of these three types and by the existence of partial forms and coexisting illnesses, so that a systematic classification becomes necessary.

There are two classification systems in current use in the United States, *DSM* and *ICD*. Both are accepted by institutions and third-party payers, some preferring one and some the other. *DSM-III-R*, published in 1987, is the latest edition of the *Diagnostic and Statistical Manual of Mental Disorders* of the American Psychiatric Association, and is preferred by researchers in the United States.

The World Health Organization also issues a series of classifications of mental disorders as a section of its *International Classification of Diseases*. The appropriate section of the latest edition, the ninth *(ICD-9-CM)*, appears as Appendix E to *DSM-III-R*.

The classifications agree in most areas, but differ in a few. For example, the international classification groups all neuroses together, as a separate class of disorders, whereas the *DSM-III-R* adheres to the idea that all mood disorders should be listed together, including depressive neurosis (called dysthymia). Even though it is called dysthymia in *DSM-III-R*, the term *depressive neurosis* is included in parentheses in *DSM-III* and *DSM-III-R*, and has the same code number, 300.4, used for depressive neurosis listed in *ICD-9-CM*.

Both classifications use code numbers for the disorders, with the same numbers when the disorder is identical, making the two classifications compatible. One great advantage of a code number for each diagnosis is in the preservation of confidentiality. In place of a named diagnosis, the code number can be inserted so that a casual observer cannot read personal information as the form passes through the insurance system. Psychiatrists use the code numbers for this reason.

In the United States what are now the "disorders" of *DSM-III* were the "reactions" of *DSM-II*. The descriptive concepts of *DSM-III* and *DSM-III-R* are well established, and in general use. The comparative diagnoses for affective disorders of *DSM-III-R* and *ICD-9-CM* are listed in the Appendix to Chapter 7 for those who wish to use *ICD-9-CM*.

The authors of *DSM-III* and *DSM-III-R* acknowledge the fluid nature of some of these disorders, the manner in which the person can go from one stage of illness to another and have a change in diagnosis, for example, from a cyclothymic personality to a bipolar disorder and back again on resolution of the bipolar illness. It is spelled out in *DSM-III* that when a major depression is in partial remission, the patient may also show the symptoms of depressive neurosis. Nevertheless, the diagnostic labels are useful to identify where the patient is at a particular time.

DSM-III-R

There are some differences between *DSM-III* and *DSM-III-R*. In summary:

- Although the name is now "mood disorders" with "affective" in parentheses, there is no actual change in the clinical disorders themselves. The same entities are to be diagnosed. The changes are simply in the grouping, now reduced from three major groups to two.

- Cyclothymic disorder is now called cyclothymia and is grouped under bipolar disorders.

- Dysthymia was dysthymic disorder (depressive neurosis) in *DSM-III*. It is now an equal partner with major depression under depressive disorders.

- The category of atypical disorders is eliminated. Atypical bipolar disorder (e.g., bipolar II) is called bipolar disorder NOS (not otherwise specified) and is included under bipolar disorders. Atypical depressive disorder is called depressive disorder NOS and is included under depressive disorders.

The new arrangement simplies diagnostic thinking. It reduces the possibly artificial distinction between typical and atypical disorders and groups them together. This is reasonable and appropriate, since, for example, the two tend to respond to the same medications and overlap genetically.

The descriptions are sharpened somewhat also in *DSM-III-R*. In *DSM-III-R* the compulsive disorder category is obsessive compulsive. Personality Disorder NOS is used instead of the term *atypical*, mixed or other.

Axis V of *DSM-III-R* is called global assessment of functioning and has an added refinement: in addition to rating social and occupational functioning, the axis rates psychological functioning. A nine-point scale having specific criteria is used to make the assessment.

Treatments depend on how well patients are functioning, how much they are below their normal state, and how hard it is for them to keep going. This scale is a rough but thorough way to evaluate this important aspect of the examination.

DIAGNOSIS IN PRACTICE

DSM-III-R Axes

The diagnostic categories of *DSM-III-R* make for specificity of classification by virtue of the detailed descriptions. The manual advises diagnosis in five axes:

> Axis I. The clinical disorder. In the present discussion, this means the kind of mood disorder or disorders, because there may be more than one at a time. Certain nonmental conditions go here also, such as bereavement and phase of life problems which are the focus of attention or treatment.
>
> Axis II. Personality disorder in adults or developmental disorder in children. Passive-aggressive, compulsive, anxious, dependent, and depressive personalities are common and may be the focus of later treatment of these disorders.
>
> Axis III. Physical disorders. Never treat a seriously depressed person without a physical examination, including blood chemistries, blood counts, thyroid tests and urine examination.
>
> Axis IV. Psychosocial stresses on a scale of one to six. Important because the environment needs treatment, too, in many cases.
>
> Axis V. Global assessment of functioning on a scale of nine steps. Helpful to evaluate the degree of disability and lowering of function.

The last four axes are an acknowledgment of the influence of personality, physical, and psychosocial factors, and are of special interest to the psychotherapist. Very often after the depressive or manic attack has subsided there are personality or psychosocial problems that require treatment.

Clinical Syndromes (Axis I of DSM-III-R)

Specific diagnosis is sometimes very quickly made. For example, a history of cycles of depression and excitement over weeks, months, or years is almost certainly a bipolar disorder, especially if there is a strong family history of the same thing. Early in an attack it may not be so easy, because of the various disguises; time and close watching for two or more visits may be needed.

Sometimes two clinical disorders are present, such as major depression and dysthymia (depressive neurosis). You should diagnose both. An enormous improvement in the new system is the use of more than one diagnosis and a way of describing the degree of recovery. We have always known, and Kraepelin (1921) described it well, that depressive attacks occur against a background of a personality disturbance and often leave unresolved symptoms in their wake, after recovery. The classification takes this into account by allowing you to make the diagnosis, for example, of a major depression, and simultaneously of a dysthymia and of a personality disorder, compulsive-obsessive type. Then, to make the picture more clear, the degree of severity or recovery may be coded also.

Personality Disorders and Trends (Axis II of DSM-III-R)

Have in mind not only the clinical disorders, but also the personality problems, whether a full-blown disorder such as major depression or dysthymia is present or not. Many persons have personality trends that interfere with the quality of life, not perhaps a complete disorder as described in the manual, but personality trends for which psychotherapy is helpful. Bipolar patients tend to be compulsive, detailed collectors, or obsessive and perfectionistic. Depressed people tend to suppress aggression. They may be irritable or angry people, but cannot easily and comfortably assert themselves and tend to be passive-aggressive. There is unconscious masochism in some. Sexual problems, mainly inhibitions, abound in this group to a remarkable degree, far beyond the extent expected from the inhibiting effect of an acute depression. The sexual problem often precedes the illness by many years.

Since many have suffered losses early in life which required repression of painful affects, they tend to defend against emotions and may appear stoic or may displace the affects to hypochondriacal or other preoccupations. All this should be noted for future use and present diagnosis.

Distinction between Axes I and II

The distinction between clinical disorders and personality disorders is, to some extent and in some cases, an unclear distinction for the following reasons:

1. The clinical disorders may be simply an episodic and temporary development of the personality disorder.
2. After the resolution of a clinical disorder the residuals commonly seen may, in some cases, simply be a continuation of the preexisting personality disorder.
3. The relationship of biography, or development, to the disorders themselves is not taken into account here. This is a purely descriptive classification. (For details on personality development see Chapter 8 on psychodynamic diagnosis.)

Therefore, the use of two axes provides a working model for the collection of authentic data, provided this model does not close the door on other models, especially a developmentally, biographically oriented one.

DSM-III-R is very useful for a broad acknowledgment of all vectors. Although the manual specifically eliminates an etiological consideration, such as psychodynamic diagnostic formulation, it provides a framework in which to develop psychosocial and psychodynamic appraisal and treatment. It is necessary to read the manual to get a full appreciation of the rich descriptive material there.

My criticism of *DSM-III-R* is not that it is not psychodynamic enough, although it does not pretend to be, but that it is so structured in its descriptions that it can become overly concrete and cookbookish and may create myths about the disorders which do not allow for the fluidity and development of new ideas. Also, that the major depression and dysthymia categories are mixtures and will need to be made more specific, perhaps by some biological tests. The classification may create the myth that all depressions which fit the description are the same, which they are really not. However, as it is now structured, psychodynamic formulations can be fitted in where they are indicated.

Some people prefer *ICD-9-CM* because of its greater degree of flexibility, that is, a closer relation to the variety one sees clinically. There are more categories into which the patients can be placed, making for a more satisfactory fit in some instances. The following pages contain a comparison of the two classifications for the various categories pertaining to depression.

DIAGNOSTIC CATEGORIES AND CLINICAL DESCRIPTIONS

There are four major groups of categories in both *ICD-9-CM* and *DSM-III-R* that one needs to be able to recognize. In practice they overlap, merge into one another, and complicate treatment. In *DSM-III-R* they are:

1. Mood (affective) disorders, including major depressive disorders; bipolar disorder; cyclothymia; and dysthymia (depressive neurosis and personality).

2. Personality disorders, and various depressive affects which precede, modulate into, accompany, and follow major disorders.

3. Normal grief states ("uncomplicated bereavement") and adjustment disorders with depressed mood (i.e., transitory reactions to stress and loss).

4. Depressions secondary to organic disease, most common in the elderly: organic mood disorder; primary degenerative dementia with depression; and multiinfarct dementia with depression.

CLINICAL SYNDROMES: TYPES OF AFFECTIVE DISORDERS

The affective disorders are presented here in the order of frequency usually seen by nonmedical psychotherapists.

Adjustment Disorder with Depressed Mood

DSM-III and DSM-III-R use the same term, adjustment disorder with depressed mood (code number 309.0). In ICD-9-CM it is called brief depressive reaction (309.0) and prolonged depressive reaction (309.1). This is a diagnosis nonmedical psychotherapists make most frequently. The picture can progress and become one of the major depressive types.

This group includes people who seek help with personal problems to which they are understandably reacting, but with a depressive mood that seems too severe and possibly out of proportion to the problem. Furthermore, there is an accompanying maladaptive effect and some loss of ability to cope. In the official description in DSM-III there is either impairment in social or occupational functioning or the symptoms are in excess of the "normal and expected reaction to the stresses." The specific differential is that it is assumed that the depression will remit after the stressor stops or that a new level of adaptation will occur, meaning that there is an improvement in coping abilities.

Patients who fit this description may turn out to have a depressive neurosis if the symptoms persist when the stressor ceases. Furthermore, many major depressions begin with the same story, and one must be alert for progression into a major depression in these early stages. Understanding, support, and relief from the stressors can go a long way in preventing this more serious development.

Dysthymia

Dysthymia (DSM-III-R, 300.40) is also called dysthymic disorder (depressive neurosis) (DSM-III), neurotic depression (ICD-9-CM, 300.4), and chronic depressive personality disorder (ICD-9-CM, 301.12).

Dysthymia is an old, very general, born-again term for mental depression or melancholia, which is popular in the Meyerian school. It is not a clearly defined single class, but rather a mixture of several chronic states.

The definition in *DSM-III* establishes it as roughly equivalent to the concept of depressive personality and depressive neurosis. Persons with this disorder do not have the complete affective syndrome, which means that they do not have a full-blown major depression. It applies to a wide variety of the milder, usually ambulatory cases of depression, but is not to be confused with milder cases of major depression, which have the full syndrome, however mild in degree, including psychomotor retardation.

Persons with a depressive neurosis also do not always come with overt depression. They often come with problems or complaints of unhappiness about themselves, their jobs, or some personal relationship. The problem presented may be alcohol or drug addiction or a medical problem. As they describe the particular thing troubling them, one notes a characteristic theme running through the discourse: pessimism and a generally gloomy attitude, sometimes to the extent of defeatism. This is depressive thinking. These people expect the worst, they have a low self-esteem and negative attitudes toward themselves. There is also a loss of pleasure in things, not consistent, but readily mobilized when there are reverses or frustrations. Some people describe a sense of emptiness, boredom, or sudden spells of sadness that can go away quickly with good news. Though some tend to be submissive, they can be easily irritated; that is, they tend to have passive-aggressive personalities. Although it may seem surprising, because they do not seem generally desperate, they can be preoccupied with death and/or suicide, which may be long-standing (since childhood or adolescence). The whole "down" mood usually seems greater than justified by the circumstances.

The group overlaps considerably with major depression of the milder sort, but in practice the patients turn out to have more fluctuations of symptoms, and do not progress into a major depression at least "for two years" according to the manual.

To use the descriptive criteria of *DSM-III-R*, the diagnosis is made if the patient, when depressed, has any two of the six listed symptoms: insomnia (or hypersomnia); low energy or fatigue; poor appetite (or overeating); feelings of inadequacy, low self-esteem; poor concentration or difficulty making decisions; feelings of hopelessness.

One can see that this mixture allows for a variety of possible clinical pictures. Some of these symptoms can also be found in physical illness such as hypothyroidism, early myxedema, or some other metabolic disorder, including early Addison's disease (adrenal cortical insufficiency). Medical examinations are imperative when you see this somatic element, for example, people with low potassium levels from diuretics administered for hypertension can have symptoms that come close to this picture.

In my series of patients who were originally diagnosed for chronic depression, all diagnoses were changed to dysthymia when the official language was changed. Under this category, four overlapping groups of patients remained after careful physical assessment had removed those with the side effects of drugs or other medical illness which in a small number of cases accounted for the symptoms. The four groups were:

1. Longstanding, pure depressive neurosis (called early onset, and specified as primary type in *DSM-III-R*).
2. Depressive neurosis in the setting of other serious neurotic symptoms.
3. Depressive neurosis in the setting of impulsive or borderline characters, and alcohol and drug abusers. In *DSM-III-R* called secondary type.
4. Depressive neurosis in some kind of relationship with major depression, either chronically persisting after a depressive spell or occurring in conjunction with a major depression or preceding a major depression by a number of years. If the symptoms preceded or followed the definitive attack by only a short time, they are considered preliminary or residual symptoms of the depression and not necessarily diagnostic of a chronic neurosis. They can also be called dysthymia secondary to major depression.

One of the most important aspects of this syndrome is its specificity for psychotherapy as the form of treatment. Furthermore, it can merge with chronic depressive disorder and follow major depressions that have partially recovered. Many people who have gone through a major depressive episode are left with irritability, anger, difficulties in verbalizing feelings and ideas—in short, with the kinds of symptoms for which psychotherapy is specifically required, particularly intensive insight therapy.

Depressive neurosis and the early stages of a slowly evolving major depression may look very much alike, so you must not be surprised if you find that a patient who seems to have a depressive neurosis gets worse and develops a severe depression while in therapy, or even has a sudden manic attack, indicating a bipolar disorder. These things happen occasionally, to the consternation of everyone involved. If there is a history of previous clear-cut depressive spells, you may be seeing the early stages of another major depression.

It is somewhat arbitrary when a chronic major depression merges into a long-term dysthymic disorder, but this should not interfere with the course of psychotherapy undertaken, because at this stage psychotherapy is indicated in both types, but of a special supportive type. Until the danger of breakdown is past, you protect, you do not put on pressure or analyze deeply. That comes later.

Note, in the next section, on the diagnosis of major depression, how similar the early stages of major depression are to some of the cases of dysthymic disorder, but with the diurnal relentlessness that is not seen in dysthymic disorder. Also, the sleeping pattern of major depression with its early waking, differs from the pattern of dysthymic disorder in which, usually, the problem is in getting to sleep.

Do not think, simply because the depressive neurosis or depressive personality is overtly milder, on the whole, than major depressive disorder, that it is not to be taken seriously. It can, in fact, produce serious limitations in the development of the personality, such as withdrawal from life's challenges, lowered efficiency, and the absence of pleasure. Parents with this disorder pass it on to their children, who learn to think the same way, and acquire the guilt of feeling responsible for parental unhappiness. Moreover, persons with the depressive neurosis are prone to major depressive disorders and can have suicidal tendencies, which can be acted out.

Not uncommonly, depressive neurosis can occur along with other serious neurotic symptoms: anxiety in various forms, hypochondriasis, conversion, somatization, phobia, and compulsive-obsessive symptoms.

Depressive neurosis can also occur in the setting of impulsive or borderline individuals, including those who act out with impulsive behavior, aggressiveness, rebellion, and those who become alcohol or drug abusers. In all these forms there is an underlying depressive complex that can surface and take charge when other defenses fail, as in the case, for example, of a rebellious adolescent who is jailed for drunken driving and hangs himself in his cell.

This group bridges the descriptive psychiatry and psychodynamic psychiatry, by way of those cases in which childhood experiences have created a life-long vulnerability to certain kinds of stresses, resulting in a depressive personality trait.

When depressive neurosis occurs in the setting of a major depression, biological treatment is indicated. It is not unusual to see persons who do not get relief from their seemingly neurotic depression with psychotherapy alone, but with proper medication do experience considerable relief. Monoamine oxidase (MAO) inhibitors in particular seem to give a favorable response, but other antidepressants may also be effective.

Major Depression

Major depression (*DSM-III* and *DSM-III-R*), given the same code (296.2 and 296.3) in both *DSM* and *ICD*, is also known as major depressive disorder (*ICD-9-CM*), involutional melancholia, psychotic depressive reaction, etc. *(DSM-II)*, involutional melancholia, monopolar depression, and psychotic depression.

This important class is the basic definitive depression. It is the label and concept applied to all those depressions, episodic or chronic, in all stages of severity, if they have the features that are particularly responsive to somatic therapy. It has been conventionally called "endogenous," a term now in poor repute. It includes single attack and recurrent depressions (i.e., unipolar), and also what has been called involutional melancholia, (*ICD-9-CM*) and psychotic depression. These are the disorders most psychiatrists deal with, but psychotherapists of all types see many of them, especially milder cases and in early stages. It may require great patience and skill to make the diagnosis in some cases because of the slow development of the full picture. Be alert to physiological and mental slowing, particularly dry mouth, slow digestion, head symptoms, nausea, inability to concentrate, and slowed speech.

To make a diagnosis of an attack of major depression remember (1) that depressions go through stages of onset, development, and decline, (2) that the individual attack may be arrested at any one of these stages, and (3) that the treatment depends on the stage at which the patient is seen.

There is a stage of onset, a stage of full development, and recovery stages. The illness may then go into partial or complete remission or may become chronic in about 10–15 percent of cases. In my series on affective disorders (Badal 1981), made up of the more difficult patients mostly referred from other physicians or psychiatrists, about one-third had become chronic or had frequent remissions. Fortunately, under long-term eclectic treatment most of these went into some degree of remission. To identify major depressive illness one has to take into account the stages of development and decline.

Early Stages

It is sometimes difficult to tell, in the early stages of a depression, whether the sufferer is simply unhappy or worried in a normal way over some loss or bad experience, such as loss of a job or a lover, or from business reverses. A lack of pleasure in things (anhedonia) and a general lack of energy and drive characterize the majority of minor cases seen by general practitioners.

Families often think persons affected are just sulking or feeling sorry for themselves. Indeed, they may themselves say they are "lazy" or "good-for-nothing" because they find it difficult to get things done. Whenever you hear this kind of self-blame, be alerted to a serious depression in the speaker, who may, on the other hand, cover up feelings and try to appear cheerful and push himself or herself harder to overcome the loss of energy and concentration. The opposite can occur, that is, depressions in the people who have always complained may be overlooked because they are thought always to be "complainers." In either case the following symptoms identify the early stages:

- Low mood. May be covered up and not obvious, or expressed as fatigue or loss of energy, or by pessimism and negative thinking, as in "Nothing ever turns out right."

- Trouble getting things done due to this fatigue, loss of concentration, or slowed-down thinking. Especially hard to get started in the morning. "I can't get going."

- A sense of guilt or self-blame ("I don't do things right").

- Sleeping difficulty—most waking early, having trouble getting back to sleep. Sometimes tired and sleepy all the time and sleeping a great deal. "I tire too easily."

- A loss of pleasure in usual activities (anhedonia). Lowering of appetite and sexual drive. "Nothing interests me." There may be a weight loss.

- A desire to withdraw and be left alone. Sometimes irritability with people.

- A general overall pervasive feeling of depression may come and go at this stage and may be relieved temporarily by activity or by good news.

- Persistence of at least four of these symptoms for more than a few days.

Moderately Severe Stage

At this point, the depression is well established and persistent. There are all the above symptoms, plus:

- Suicidal thoughts, sometimes acted on. Sometimes spoken but often not voiced aloud.

- Marked loss of efficiency in daily activities.

- Tendency to withdraw. Stays by himself or herself a good deal.

- Feelings of guilt, failure, and helplessness. "I'm no good."

- Indecisiveness. Tends to become despondent.

- Inability to concentrate. Relentlessness. Usually worse in mornings and better in evenings. People wonder if person is sick or angry.

- Distortions of body image; feelings of changes in body.

- The return of the repressed. Memories and associations, usually unpleasant, come spontaneously.

Severe Stage (Melancholia)

All of the above symptoms can occur, plus:

- Marked slowing down of thinking and action (psycho-motor retardation). Can't read or think (the pathognomonic, specific, unmistakable diagnostic sign).

- Inability to function. Can't take care of daily tasks at all. May stay in bed or just wander around. In extreme cases a complete paralysis of will.

- Sometimes marked restlessness and agitation.

- Suicidal and self-destructive actions. "The world would be better off without me" (psychosis).

- Delusions of sin, crimes, bodily disease, and poverty (psychosis).

- Feelings and convictions of hopelessness (psychosis).

- Physical somatic symptoms: can't eat, loss of weight, slowing of digestion, loss of sexual drive, cessation of menses.

In all three stages it is important to observe whether or not the specific pathognomonic diagnostic signs of biological change are present, because even in mild forms they identify the somatic element that separates these depressions from the purely neurotic. Whatever the name, the somatic element is an identifiable core in all those depressions, mild or severe, that require biological treatment.

Longitudinal Diagnosis

The descriptions just given make up the cross-sectional diagnosis of the individual attack at three points in the course of the illness. A longitudinal diagnosis is necessary also, based on the pattern of occurrence (whether recurrent, single attack, or chronic), whether in partial or complete remission, and whether the patient also has manic or milder hypomanic attacks (both indicating a bipolar disorder). The type with typical manic spells is known unofficially as "bipolar I," and that with only mild hypomanic spells as "bipolar II" (atypical affective disorder, *DSM-III*; bipolar disorder, NOS, *DSM-III-R*; or (bipolar affective disorder or manic-depressive psychosis, *ICD-9-CM*).

Apropos the longitudinal diagnosis, several items of history are of major importance:

1. A history of previous spells lasting weeks or months at crucial times of life—leaving home, childbirth, moving to a new area, or loss of job. There may have been no treatment or even acknowledgment that the previous spell was a depression, but a

careful history elicits the story of a let-down period of lowered efficiency lasting a few months to a year or more.

2. Occurrence of spells of enthusiasm and success lasting for weeks or months followed by a period of relatively lower energy, suggestive of hypomanic attack, or, the history of an acute manic attack with treatment.

3. Family history of depressions or of manic attacks. Here again the description of the attack may be characteristic or atypical without an actual diagnosis having been made.

Spells occurring in late adolescence and early adult life may look like situational or neurotic depressions, but if a high school or college student has a persistent lowering of efficiency and considers dropping out of school, there may be a major depression.

The rate of chronicity and recurrence depends on the group you are working with. Psychiatrists are likely to see patients who have more severe illness with recurrences.

Prolonged cases of midlife depression, which constitute about 10 percent of cases, can generally be treated effectively enough to be kept functional and out of the hospital. This is the traditional involutional melancholia which, before modern treatment, disabled its victims for 2 to 10 years. Now, with support, with adequate biological treatment, most persons with this illness remain functional most of the time. Electroconvulsant treatment is indicated in cases that do not respond to medication, as is the case with many psychotic depressives.

Bipolar Disorders

Bipolar disorders (*DSM-III-R*, 296.4–296.6) are also variously called bipolar disorder and atypical bipolar disorder (*DSM-III*), manic-depressive psychosis (*ICD-9-CM*, other and unspecified, four types, 296.8), and affective psychoses (*ICD-9-CM*, listed with eight clinical pictures, 296.0–296.7).

Anyone who treats depressions will eventually discover the existence of the manic state and certain aspects of it in particular, because a manic attack can develop suddenly—within 24 hours—

in a depressed person, whether under treatment or not, and can cause a good deal of damage before getting under control.

As the term *manic-depressive*, with its dramatic aura, has worked its way into common usage, its drama has begun to exceed its usefulness and applicability. There are at least two and possibly three different disorders in this group, and we tend to discard the term *manic-depressive* in its old inclusive global sense. If used at all, its use should be strictly limited to the more severe cases of what we now call bipolar disorder. Actually, the implications of "manic" are not appropriate either because the speeded up, euphoric state is not clearly psychotic in all cases.

Bipolar disorder seems to be a distinct entity constituting about 15 percent of the cases of major affective disorders. Although it has a genetic basis, its course can be influenced by environmental stresses and biochemical means. Three studies indicated a concordance of 50–96 percent in identical-twin studies, as opposed to 5–26 percent in fraternal twins. In twelve monozygotic twins reared apart, eight of the twelve were concordant. In unipolar disorder (recurrent depressions without manic attacks), of nine pairs of twins reared apart, four (44 percent) were concordant (Gershon 1983).

Clinical Aspects and Varieties of Bipolar Disorder

Hypomania. This mild form of excitement can occur in typical bipolar patients where the attack is spontaneously mild, as for example, in a young adult who later becomes severely depressed or severely excited. Often in the history of patients with severe spells of depression or excitement the story comes out that he or she previously experienced a spell of unusual efficiency and energy lasting weeks or months. There are actually persons of great accomplishment in whom a hypomanic state is chronic — high achievers, people who get along on very little rest and seem always to be vigorous and busy, sometimes called hypomanic personality disorder (or chronic hypomanic personality disorder, *ICD-9-CM*, 301.11).

Sometimes hypomania replaces the formerly severe attacks after the establishment of effective treatment with lithium, which may not completely eliminate but may soften and moderate the formerly severe attacks.

Because the hypomanic attacks vary in severity and in their effect on judgment, the hypomanic person should be monitored carefully for impulsive acts of poor judgment, generally involving overambitious business deals or schemes bordering on the grandiose, and also for excessive buying and spending of money. Inappropriate erotic adventures and attachments may occur also. The diagnostic issue that separates hypomanic from manic is the issue of judgment and control; you can reason effectively with a hypomanic, but not with the manic.

Bipolar II (bipolar disorder, NOS, 296.70, *DSM-III-R*). Bipolar is a recently accepted term for the cyclical form of illness in which there are mild hypomanic spells, never severe ones. It occurs in a person whose illness over the years is mainly depressive. These spells of mild excitement may occur spontaneously or upon receipt of good news, or they may only occur when precipitated by electroconvulsant or drug treatment. The antidepressant drugs occasionally bring this kind of mild spell of elation. Usually lowering the dose is advisable, although most of these spells are short lived, never going on into a major excitement. The diagnostic term most appropriate is recurrent major depression in the setting of cyclothymia.

Clinical Course and Symptoms

To condense the myriad forms, symptoms, disguises, and problems of the bipolar illness in a short comprehensive description is no easy task and cannot be wholly successful. Any professional dealing with potentially bipolar patients might start with reading the description in *DSM-III-R* and, to get more background, Kraepelin's book (1921). For breadth of view and to bring it up to date read the book edited by Wolpert (1977). Meanwhile, the following should be useful and practical.

Onset

The beginning may be insidious and slow, developing over a period of weeks, or may start suddenly and dramatically within 24 hours. There are persons who are under treatment for a depression who come out of the depression gradually and, suddenly one morning, wake up and feel well, or excited, with thoughts racing, augering the beginning of a spell of excitement. This switch phenomenon is as yet unexplained, but occurs not infrequently and can go from manic to depressive also.

If the person is not under treatment by a professional, the onset may be disguised by family conflicts precipitated by a subtle preliminary change in the personality, for example, increased activity, less sleeping, a desire for more sex, increase in drinking alcohol, a greater talkativeness, new business schemes, or a tendency to invest or spend excessive amounts of money.

If this is a relatively young person who has never had a manic attack, watch out! It is, early on, unpredictable as to whether these mild beginnings tell of an on-coming severe attack, or how soon this may happen. Sometimes it happens so suddenly that there is no time to establish lithium therapy, or the patient and his or her family may be resistant to it. To prevent the occasional occurrence of an out-of-control manic attack, it is well at this point to hospitalize the patient at once and start lithium therapy. If the patient has already had two or three depressive spells it would have been well to establish preventive measures by getting him or her into a regimen of lithium prophylaxis. Frank communication with patient and family are important at this stage. (See section on emergencies [mania] in Chapter 12.)

The Established Manic Attack

In a well-established spell there is an enormous variation in severity, but mild and severe attacks have in common (1) elevation of mood, (2) psychomotor acceleration (speeded up thinking, talking, and moving with a lessened need for rest), and (3) boundless energy.

The elevated mood is characterized by euphoria. "I never felt better in my life." There is a boundless optimism and a denial of adversity. Patients can also be very irritable if contradicted or faced with opposition to their actions or plans. In psychotic cases, there are grandiose delusions of great influence or power, sometimes resembling the megalomanic delusions of the schizophrenic, but always mood appropriate, that is, grandiose and positive, unlike the schizophrenic in whom the ideas tend to be paranoid and negative.

Course and Outcome

The manic patient should be hospitalized. Hypomania can usually be managed outside the hospital. Before lithium and electroconvulsant treatment were available, the natural history of the disease was exhaustively studied, and several typical patterns of occurrence were seen. The duration of the manic attack was anywhere from three weeks up to a year, with the usual attack being three to six months, then followed either by a well period or a depression. Those who cycled regularly tended to have one or two spells a year alternating with depressive spells. After a series of cycles over a period of several years there might be a free period of several years, followed by another series of cycles. Others had long periods between spells, depending on the amount of stress involved.

With the use of electroconvulsant treatment for severe spells plus major antipsychotic drugs with lithium, the usual course has become much less incapacitating and severe under treatment. Most patients are in the hospital only three to five weeks, while lithium therapy is being established. About one-fourth of the patients do not respond as quickly and have to be watched even after the three- to five-week period.

Much more important, prevention with lithium is possible in 60–80 percent of the patients, and with most of the other patients, the attacks are moderated enough to permit ambulatory care, although in some of those, the spells can approach severe proportions.

One pattern rarely seen is the person with recurrent manic

attacks and no depressions. If the patient is followed long enough, eventually a depression will be seen because in this bipolar disease all victims have both manic attacks and depressions.

Another pattern seen sometimes is the occurrence of frequent manic attacks and only occasional depression. Other patterns are occasional manic attacks and frequent depressions. Lithium prophylaxis is appropriate for all types and moderates depressions as well as manic attacks.

The importance of the bipolar disorder to the psychotherapist is twofold: First, during treatment of what looks like a neurotic depression one suddenly has a patient who comes rapidly out of his or her depression, gets well, then proceeds into a manic attack, to the consternation of the therapist. You have to be aware that the depressions must have had certain somatic symptoms— slowing down, difficulty concentrating, persistence of symptoms, early waking—which could have warned you that this was a major depression, however mild.

Second, the psychological aspects of bipolar disorder concern us. During the attack, conflicts sometimes come out and will need to be dealt with later. For example, marital problems, neurotic symptoms, characterological symptoms, and disorders are such problems which may, indeed, have fed into the disease in some way. Particularly one sees obsessive-compulsive symptoms requiring psychotherapy upon recovery. Deficits in self-esteem and difficulties in asserting one's rights are among the personality problems that may require an intensive psychotherapeutic program later on, after the attack is moderated. Sexual problems requiring therapy abound in the marriages of patients with bipolar disorder, sometimes preceding the attack by years. Asexual marriages are not unusual.

In addition, there is the impact on the patient's life and the family of having a genetically based disease that can disable the victim for long periods. A great deal of work is being done with families by social workers, nurses, and psychologists, as well as by psychiatrists, for these problems. As one example of family problems, the influence on an infant of having a manic-depressive mother is an important one.

Some studies (Cytryn et al. 1984, Decina et al. 1983) of

children of parents with bipolar disorder reveal a clear tendency to certain early disturbances in the infants, namely:

1. Insecure ambivalent attachments to the mother.
2. Lesser capacity to regulate emotional equilibrium—anger, fear, aggression, and impaired social behavior.
3. Only rare actual depressed mood.
4. An increase in these symptoms with age over the year of observation, so that at age 2, the children have difficulty handling hostility and sharing with others. This problem is similar to the problems the parents have in their interpersonal relationships.

Also observed in the parents were:

1. A tendency to rejection of the children.
2. Disorganization of parental lives.
3. Lack of effectiveness in dealing with the children.

These findings indicate that mixed hereditary and environmental influences are at work as early as the first year, shaping the personalities of the children. Parental guidance, therapy of the child later on, and whatever intervention is necessary at as early a time as possible are indicated for preventive purposes.

Psychology of the Bipolar Disorders

Although the genetic basis of bipolar disorder is clearly established, it is not the sole cause of attacks. In some cases it makes the patients vulnerable to the impact of stressors. In brief, it is a necessary, but not exclusive, condition for the illness to develop in all cases. It must be remembered, however, that mania cannot be considered identical with a neurosis, but is a psychosis, in which a neurochemical change like a toxic state weakens the controls the individual would normally have over his or her pleasure-seeking self. This neurochemical change can be brought about by some kind of stimulus, generally one which is designed to overcome some feelings of lessened self-esteem. A dependent woman suddenly wants to be independent when her therapist is out of town and buys huge quantities of clothes she doesn't need to show the therapist that she doesn't need him, but can buy her own clothes. There is denial of realities, overoptimism, and acting out of pleasure-seeking impulses.

In some cases it looks as though depression is the surrender to overwhelming odds, whereas mania is overcoming and triumphing over the same problem. Thus, you would expect that losses might trigger a manic attack as well as depression. This is actually the case.

Persons with bipolar illness depend for their self-esteem on great success and high achievement. Often in a family, the one who breaks down has felt, not necessarily correctly, that he or she carries the responsibility of representing the family and achieving prominence, so feels driven to achieve. Depression occurs when this achievement seems hopeless, and mania occurs when, by fantasy, he or she overcomes his or her doubts and claims the success. Anger and irritability occur when they feel that someone opposes them, which means that their long-dreamed of success is being taken away from them.

Of course, some of this kind of pathological thinking will be forgotten after electroconvulsant or lithium treatment, when the euphoric mood disappears, but meanwhile the expression of it has revealed a potential unconscious problem which can be the object of psychotherapy upon recovery under biological treatment.

Cyclothymia

Cyclothymic disorder (*DSM-III*), cyclothymia (*DSM-III-R*, 301.13), cyclothymic personality disorder (*DSM-II*), and cyclothymic disorder (*ICD-9* and *ICD-9-CM*, 301.13) are the equivalent descriptive terms used. Sometimes one sees merging into the bipolar illness a milder state in which cycling mild hypomanic and mild depressive states alternate, not severe enough to be called bipolar disorder, but is instead a personality attribute that can precede or follow a spell of mania or depression. Sometimes the treated patient with bipolar illness recovers from the major spell but continues to cycle at a very mild level, in which case we would be inclined to consider it a cyclothymic personality that did not reveal itself until after a breakdown with only partial restitution.

The depressed periods and periods of elation are not of sufficient degree to fulfill the criteria of a major disorder. Instead of painful dejection during a depression, patients are likely to feel inadequate and to lack the drive to tackle challenges. They become indecisive, conservative, thrifty, and a little bit slowed; enjoyment of their usual pleasures is lessened, and they tend to withdraw and become passive. The degree of elation is hypomanic rather than manic, but they may, indeed, tend to become unduly active, manifest bad judgment, and make hasty decisions.

There is a tendency in both manic and depressive phases to look for excitement or relief by using alcohol or drugs, such as stimulants and sedatives. It is not rare to discover in an alcoholic or drug-dependent person that the tendency to cycle preceded the dependency on drugs.

Psychodynamics of Cyclothymia

In my study (Badal 1981), persons with cyclothymic personality have all been to some degree troubled by personal problems to which they have had to make painful compromises – a loveless marriage, a tyrannical spouse, an uncompromising financial situation. The data are empirical and await more scientific corroboration, but in some cases the conclusion seems quite valid, that is, that a cyclothymic pattern emerges clinically out of a combination of a genetic background with a powerfully frustrating life situation. A necessary corollary to the concept of a frustrating life situation is an inability to cope with the frustration effectively, responding instead with a defensive and symptomatic reaction.

In some cyclothymic persons there is a looseness of controls over impulses, a characteristic resembling that of the borderline personality. This characteristic personality deficit, combined with impulsiveness, plus a tendency to become accelerated, causes these persons to create self-defeating situations and frustrating relationships, for which they blame others.

Discovering the psychodynamics of the cyclothymic personality may also be helpful in long-term therapy of the patient whose recovery from bipolar illness under treatment and with medicines is only partial. When the cycles are dampened by the chemotherapy, patients are often able to say what they are experiencing and thus really get to the psychological problems in a way they could not follow during the more severe untreated depression or manic spells.

An example is a man married to a very compulsive woman of high character and a great sense of responsibility who infuriates him with her compulsive-phobic traits because he finds himself very limited by her neurosis, yet is pleased with her devotion and kindness. He alternates between attraction and helpless frustration. The sexual activity tends often to become sparse because of the anger he cannot express. Insight therapy and marriage counseling have helped greatly to cut this Gordian knot, and the cycling of the moods, although present, is much less severe.

SUBTYPES OF MAJOR MOOD DISORDERS

An interesting development in recent years has been the research on two subtypes of the major mood disorders. These two syndromes are called *Seasonal Affective Disorders* and *Atypical Depression*.

Seasonal Affective Disorders

Although it has long been observed that some people who are subject to recurrent depressions tend to have their attacks during certain seasons, usually the fall and winter, the physiological importance of this occurrence was not studied energetically until Lewy and colleagues (1980) observed that light suppresses melatonin secretion in humans. A report followed (Lewy et al. 1980) on the bright light treatment of a manic-depressive patient with a seasonal mood cycle. Since that time there has been a great deal of research on the treatment of these seasonal depressions with light of various types. In addition, considerable research has gone into the relation of the circadian (sleep-waking) cycle to mood disorders and their physiology.

Of the various types of persons with seasonal mood disorders, Rosenthal and his colleagues (1984) have identified a special group, rather narrowly defined, as seasonal affective disorder (SAD) and characterized by fall–winter depression followed by a well period in the spring and summer. These patients had no other major psychiatric disorder, eliminating manics, and no psychosocial variables accounting for the mood change, eliminating those who might have personal stress in their lives, which are the more difficult, serious cases. This group turned out to be mostly women (83 percent) whose illness began in their 20s, with depressions averaging 5.1 months in duration, from October or November to March or April. According to Rosenthal (Rosenthal and Wehr 1987) 83 percent of the patients report that they have had hypomanic spells earlier, usually in the spring or summer. These researchers report that only 6 percent of their patients had been hospitalized and only 1 percent have had to have electroconvulsant treatment. Obviously this group is the milder end of the bipolar spectrum, with no manic attacks and relatively mild depressions.

Nevertheless, their depressions were serious enough that the patients exhibited decreased activity, sadness, irritability, anxiety, difficulties at work, and interpersonal difficulties. They differed from most depressives in some very striking ways: they had an increased appetite, they craved carbohydrates (most depressives crave no food), they gained weight (most depressives lose weight), and they slept more than usual (most depressives sleep badly). The most striking thing the patients reported was that the farther north they lived the more severe and prolonged their depressions, and that if they traveled south to a brighter climate they improved in a few days. As one might expect, exposure to bright light simulating daylight for two or more hours a day can bring about a remission. A discussion of the parameters of this treatment can be found in Chapter 13.

A seasonal occurrence is sometimes seen in more severe cases of mood disorder, as reported by Bick (1986), who described cases of both bipolar and melancholic disorder.

This subtype of relatively mild cases has considerable significance for the psychotherapist for two reasons. First, sometimes a patient who is not as responsive to psychotherapy as one might expect or who has recurrences despite insight may have a physiological burden that works against recovery and that may require biological treatment. These patients respond well to phototherapy and drugs, making psychotherapy more productive. Second, and equally important, the physiological changes that characterize any bipolar, major depressive, or cyclothymic disorder do not work in a vacuum. Although these patients have been reported not to have psychosocial stresses, the kind of cycling they report is usually seen in the setting of some interpersonal or intrapsychic problem, and therefore a more intensive psychotherapy is needed than just attention to some obvious traumatic situation.

The situation is not as simple as it seems, judging by a report on seasonal affective disorder in the Southern Hemisphere (Boyce and Parker 1988). This research team found that their group of patients with seasonal attacks of depression consisted of two subgroups, one of fall-winter depressives, almost identical with that reported by Rosenthal and colleagues (1987), and another, of equal number, of spring-summer depressives.

Despite these complications, we are now entering a new phase in research in the biological basis of affective disorders dealing with possibilities of therapy concerned with the basic biological sleep-waking cycle. This area is coming to be known as chronobiology (Lewy 1987), and its possibilities include not only the use of light therapy, as described in the chapter of this book on Biological Treatment, but also the methods of rearranging the circadian rhythm, such as by sleep disruption. These methods may be used as supplements to medications, psychotherapy, and environmental intervention.

Atypical Depression

This is another subtype of mood disorder that has received a great deal of attention and research in the last several years. There is no category for the syndrome in *DSM-III-R*, although some re-searchers think a separate category is justified because of a consistently better response to treatment with monoamine oxi-dase inhibitors than to tricyclic antidepressants, and because of a different descriptive identification of the group (Quitkin et al. 1988).

The criteria for the identification of the group are similar to those used for hysterical depression a generation ago, thus sug-gesting that this is a new name for an old condition. The criteria used by most investigators (Quitkin et al. 1988) are: the presence of a definite depression according to standard criteria, mood reac-tivity (the mood is not completely fixed but fluctuates in response to situations, especially to rejection), increased appetite and weight gain, consistently oversleeping, and severe fatigue often described as heaviness. It has been found that patients with this collection of symptoms tend to respond to medication with antidepressant drugs, and are considerably more likely to respond to MAO inhibitors than to tricyclics. The response rate is in the range of 19 percent for placebo at 12 weeks, 39 percent for imipramine, and 71 percent for phenelzine (Quitkin et al. 1988). Although the borders of the syndrome are not clear in that symptoms tend to merge with those of neurotic depression and hysteroid panic, it should be kept in mind because this group of patients often come to the psychotherapist for their sensitivity to rejection and their excessive emotionality.

FREQUENCY OF DIAGNOSTIC TYPES

The diagnoses in a study of ambulatory patients in a psychiatric clinic (Weissman and Paykel 1974) with definite depressive spells were heavily skewed toward neurotic depression (dysthymic dis-order in *DSM-III*), as one would expect in an ambulatory group. Of the forty patients, thirty-one (77.5 percent) were diagnosed neurotic depressive and 9 (22.5 percent) were diagnosed in the major depressive category. The nine were further classified as two bipolar, two involutional, and five psychotic depressives. It is likely that persons sick enough to go to a psychiatric clinic, even though considered only mildy depressed, probably have a higher number of major depressions than those who consult nonmedical therapists. However, even so, nonmedical therapists may have to expect that as much as one-fourth or one-fifth of their depressed patients may turn out to have major depressions, and a small number may have a subsequent manic attack (bipolar disorder).

Among my series of sixty-five patients with severe enough spells to be hospitalized, the figures were reversed, that is, 20 percent had a depressive neurosis, 27.69 percent bipolar disorder, 24.6 percent recurring major depressions, 10.77 percent a single attack of major depression, and 9.2 percent adjustment disorder with depressed mood, which would probably have been considered a depressive neurosis by some. However, about one-third of those with major depressions *also* had an underlying depressive neurosis (Badal 1981).

ORGANIC MOOD (AFFECTIVE) DISORDERS

Diagnostic Groups

Depressions and elations of various kinds may occur as a result of organic disease. A convenient classification of the causes most commonly seen is that of the *DSM-III-R* schedule, which lists four categories:

1. Primary degenerative dementia of the Alzheimer type, presenile onset, with depression.
2. Primary degenerative dementia of the Alzheimer type, senile onset (after age 65), with depression.
3. Multiinfarct dementia, with depression (in *ICD-9-CM* called arteriosclerotic dementia, with depression). This condition usually results from repeated small or large thromboses or hemorrhages in the cerebral cortex, caused by arteriosclerosis.
4. Organic mood disorder (organic affective syndrome in *ICD-9-CM*). An affective disorder, either manic, depressive, or

mixed, resulting from a specific organic factor, toxic, or metabolic, but not brain disease, so that it lacks the clouding of consciousness of a delirium or the loss of intellectual faculties of a dementia. It is often seen in general hospitals.

Practical Clinical Issues

The above classification makes diagnosis look very simple, but the situation for the practitioner is much more complicated than it looks. The symptoms of depression and medical illness overlap, especially the somatic symptoms, so that it is not rare for the psychotherapist to treat people who turn out to have an underlying physical illness which has been unrecognized. Consequently, the psychotherapist learns to recognize some situations which come up not infrequently, especially in dealing with an older clientele. Some of these situations follow:

- Unrecognized physical illness; for example, a depressed patient turns out to have a large cancer of the pancreas, or a large brain tumor in a silent area, or an insidious drug effect.

- Unrecognized psychiatric illness in medical patients; for example, a patient with chronic gastrointestinal complaints turns out to have a severe suicidal depression.

- The typical syndrome of an affective disorder associated with organic disorders; for example, a mixed manic-depressive attack is precipitated by ingestion of prescribed steroids, given for a skin disease or for cancer.

These disorders may be depressions or elations. They belong in either of two categories: (1) primary classical affective (mood) disorder in a susceptible person, precipitated by the intercurrent illness, or (2) secondary affective (mood) disorder, which also may be depression or elation or mixed. This is known as the organic (mood) affective disorder in the *DSM-III* and *DSM-III-R* classifications, but has historically been called a symptomatic psychosis (depression or elation) which can be expected to subside when the underlying medical illness is cured. This is the feature that differentiates a secondary from a primary disorder.

The following is a clinical example of the primary classical disorder. A 70-year-old woman with an eczematous rash was treated with steroid injections. She developed an agitated depression of the same type as the several she had experienced over her adult life, requiring hospitalization and antipsychotic medication, and lasting four months. Although steroids are known to precipitate attacks in persons with a history of bipolar disease, since she had not had an attack for a number of years, and the skin disease was severe, the risk was taken of giving her the drug.

An example of the secondary type of depression resulting from medical conditions is of a man of late middle age who was referred by a general practitioner to a psychiatrist for depression. His depression was not typical in that he lacked feelings of guilt, but he had many other typical symptoms, particularly fatigue. It was discovered that he was suffering from early parkinsonism, so mild that it had been missed. When some of the symptoms of the neurological illness were relieved by treatment, his depression was greatly improved.

This kind of secondary depression can occur in various neurological diseases. Physicians and psychotherapists should be especially alert to this possibility in persons whose depressions seem to be accompanied by unusual physical symptoms.

Depressions are seen with drugs including sedatives and hypnotics, such as the benzodiazepines and barbiturates; reserpine derivatives; alcohol; steroids; and birth control pills. It can also be precipitated by methylphenidate, or alcohol.

Illnesses that may induce depression include hypothyroidism; hidden or massive cancer (e.g., of liver, stomach, head, or pancreas); and infections, such as influenza and pneumonia. Postinfluenzal depression has been observed but not proven to occur without some predisposition to depression. Neurological diseases of some magnitude, such as multiple sclerosis, brain tumor, Parkinson's disease, and early cerebral degeneration, can also induce depression. Depression may also follow massive strokes or head injuries with residual defects, or after massive surgical procedures, such as cardiac surgery.

Manic attacks, either typical or mixed, are sometimes seen with cocaine, methylphenidate, alcohol, steroids, amphetamines, and antidepressants. Hyperthyroidism, multiple sclerosis, and strokes may be accompanied by manic attacks. An example is seen in the case of a man who came complaining of impotence. He seemed to have many of the symptoms of hypomnia: joking, sexual remarks, poor judgment evidenced by getting into a variety of businesses he could not handle, carelessness in driving his car, and overtalkativeness. After a few months it became evident that he also had signs of dementia, which was found to be caused by Alzheimer's disease.

Other Affective Reactions to Illness

Psychological reactions to serious disease and disability, such as cancer or a poor result from an operation, can precipitate an affective disorder. For example, a woman who had a hip replacement had to give up a large number of her favorite activities; she became despondent and seriously contemplated suicide. Another example, a middle-aged man is told that he has a cancer of the lung and should have a lobectomy. Acute depression, sometimes suicidal, can be precipitated by such bad news. Mixtures of grief, anger, self-blame, hopelessness, and fear enter the picture suddenly and overwhelmingly. These are not the simple adjustment reactions to external events, which, no matter how traumatic, do not threaten life or one's person with damage and deformity. Here grief is complicated by damage to one's self, sometimes with genuine severe disability and pain. Despair and grief to which you can see no resolution are then very hard to separate from the classical depressive disorder with its hopelessness, unless the defense of denial can operate effectively or hope can be nurtured for relief or cure.

Treatment with antidepressant drugs can restore sleep, relieve fatigue and depression, restore energy, and bring about considerable relief, even in the presence of quite severe physical illness. Psychiatric oncology is a fairly new field, but gives promise of being very much worthwhile, now that treatment of cancer can prolong life, which may be filled with anxiety and depressive disabilities.

Dementia and Depression

Dementia and other signs of brain damage, such as aphasia, paralysis, and transient ischemic attacks (TIAs) should be kept in mind when dealing with depression in older persons or those with neurological disease. It can make a great deal of difference in treatment and planning to know whether a spell of confusion is temporary or permanent. An example: a woman of 75 years, active, running her household, which consists of herself and her grown son. She has had depressions, recurrent but not disabling, which were relieved by amitriptyline. However, at one point, she got an attack of confusion that was severe enough to require hospitalization. In the hospital, she remained somewhat disoriented for circumstances, did not know why she was there, had a somewhat elated affect, was restless, and slept badly. Because there was a mild amount of cortical atrophy on the brain scan, it looked as though this was the beginning of a chronic dementia. However, it developed that she had a low sodium concentration in the blood and also a low potassium level. When the balance was restored in a few days she recovered, became clear and oriented, with a normal affect. She was able to go home and again run her house, resuming a normal active life. The only change was a reduction in her dose of diuretic, which was the drug which had created the electrolyte imbalance in the first place.

In contrast to this, look at the example of another woman, also in her seventies, who had had recurrent depressions most of her adult life, not disabling enough to keep her from raising a family and running a successful business. She went into an attack of what looked like her usual depression, but did not respond to medication, and over a period of months, she became more and more forgetful, finally becoming incontinent of urine. Her brain scan showed marked cerebral atrophy, suggesting a poor prognosis, which has been borne out in subsequent months, during which she has not responded favorably to the rehabilitation program in an active therapeutic nursing home. The diagnosis here is primary degenerative dementia, with depression.

Dementia and Pseudodementia

The differential diagnosis of true dementia from what may appear to be dementia in a depressed person comes up frequently, and it is essential for anyone who tries to do therapy with older persons to be able to tell the difference. This is not always easy, particularly because persons with dementia are very often depressed, and depressed people have a great deal of difficulty concentrating and remembering, which makes them appear to have dementia. Usually, depressed persons complain of memory loss, feel that something is wrong with their brain, and feel hopeless about it, whereas those with true dementia do not complain of memory loss and yet, upon testing, may have gross memory and retention defects. The person who is simply depressed, on the other hand, and complains of a bad memory, can perform very well on tests of retention and memory.

The depressed person is much more likely to have guilt, suicidal ideas, and to think the world would be much better off without him or her than is the person with dementia. Sadness may be present in both, but the depressed person is much more apt to cry, while the person with dementia may actually be apathetic. Irritability is much more likely to be seen in the depressed person, rather than the apathy of one with dementia.

If the patient falls in the borderland between the two conditions and has both, then he or she deserves a trial on antidepressant therapy, which would be a combination of drugs, psychotherapy, and attention to the support systems.

The best approach generally with the organic affective disorders is to be sure the patient has had a carefully worked out diagnosis of whatever physical basis is there. Some of the under lying causes are reversible with appropriate medical care, so that referral for medical evaluation is justified when the patient presents symptoms and behavior that do not fit clearly into a typical picture of affective disease.

DIAGNOSIS OF PERSONALITY DISORDERS AND TRENDS

In this way, the postdepressive personality discloses the scope and possibilities for an effective therapy for depressive patients, including psychotherapy for endogenous patients. Focal points, such as uncovering psychological vulnerability and dysfunctional coping, can be established. Therapy goals can be formulated, such as replacing dysfunctional by functional coping. Such a therapy must pursue the goals of both reducing the residual depressive symptoms and of preventing the occurrence of new depressive episodes.
—P. Matussek and W. B. Feil, "Personality Attributes of Depressive Patients"

PERSONALITY DISORDERS: *DSM-III-R*, AXIS II, DIAGNOSIS OF PERSONALITY DISORDERS, AND MALADAPTIVE PERSONALITY TRENDS

In affective disorders, the personality disorder itself may require treatment when the affective illness recedes. A manic patient, upon recovery, may turn out to have a crippling obsessive-compulsive neurosis (this older term was revised in *DSM-III-R* to obsessive-compulsive personality disorder). Or a depressed patient, when relieved of the depression, may have a serious passive-aggressive personality disorder. Another factor in dealing with the personality problem is that it may feed into the illness itself and nurture it. As a result, the illness may remain only partially resolved with medication until the personality disorder is dealt with.

In the more seriously ill patients, that is, those who are hospitalized, there is a high incidence of personality disorders or of personality trends of a serious nature. In my study, the most common were compulsive and passive-aggressive disorders, occurring in twenty (ten each) of sixty-five cases as a primary feature. Table 7–1 shows the findings in my series of long-term cases ($N = 65$), using the diagnoses of *DSM-III-R*.

Ambulatory patients have similar personality problems. In a very careful study of a small group of depressed women treated on an ambulatory basis, Weissman and Paykel (1974) describe a group of their patients upon recovery as being passive and aggressive, although they do not use the terminology. Their descriptions point out serious personality defects following the depression, especially in communication of feelings and needs. There were particular difficulties in the handling of aggression and anger, the patients tending to be irritable and hostile.

In one careful and thorough study of 119 treatment-responsive ambulatory patients (Pilkonis et al. 1988) with recurrent unipolar depression nearly half, 48 percent, showed some

Table 7–1

Personality Types and Disorders Found in Depressed Patients ($N = 65$)

Personality disorder or prominent feature[a]	Number of occurrences	
	As primary feature	As secondary feature
Compulsive	10	1
Passive-aggressive	10	8
Dependent	8	17
Avoidant	8	2
Introverted	8	1
Histrionic	3	3
Borderline	2	0
Masochistic	2	7
Narcissistic	2	0
Paranoid	2	2
Somatization	2	1
Schizotypal	1	0
Total	58	42

[a]This summarizes both clear-cut disorders and trends severe enough to handicap the patient.

Note: No clear-cut disorder = 7 (11.3 percent)

Source: D. W. Badal (1981). Treatment combinations in long term depressions. Summary. *Continuing Medical Education Syllabus and Scientific Proceedings in Summary Form: The One Hundred and Thirty-Fourth Annual Meeting of the American Psychiatric Association,* pp. 229–230. Washington, DC: American Psychiatric Association.

personality disturbance: avoidant 30.4 percent, compulsive 18.6 percent, and dependent 15.7 percent. The proportion with a personality disturbance is not as great as in my series of hospitalized patients, who are more severely ill on the average than ambulatory patients. The three principal types of disturbance are the same in both groups, but the distribution is different, possibly representing a difference in the patients, or possibly representing a difference in diagnostic method. Nevertheless, avoidant, dependent, and compulsive personality disorders abound in any treated group of depressed persons.

Furthermore, in his study Pilkonis was able to demonstrate statistically that the presence of a personality disorder slowed recovery significantly. His group were all treated the same, with a combination of an antidepresssant (imipramine) in adequate doses and interpersonal psychotherapy.

AGGRESSION

No aspect of the mechanisms of depression is more discussed and less understood than the place of suppressed aggression. Most misunderstood is the psychoanalytic theory, which started with the early observations by Abraham (1949) and Freud (1917) that the depressed patient is ambivalent toward loved ones and has a repressed rage that cannot be expressed appropriately. These observations have incorrectly given rise to the idea that if people can be persuaded or taught to express aggression freely the depression is relieved. This idea is seldom correct, but nevertheless this is considered popularly and incorrectly to be the psychoanalytic view, and sick people are wrongly treated by being taught to let their anger out in an unbridled way. The psychoanalytic view is really the opposite.

Actually, patients are helped to experience their feelings, but to see that they are in part transferences from early relationships to current ones. When they can experience their anger, they then can deal with it in a rational way, rather than giving way to irrational anger or to be simply irritable in an undirected way, as many depressed people are.

PROBLEMS AND SUGGESTIONS FOR SOLUTION IN DIAGNOSIS OF PERSONALITY DISORDERS

The categories of personality disorder in *DSM-III-R* overlap considerably, so that clear distinctions are often not possible (Gunderson 1983, p. 31). Clinically this does not matter a great deal, as the therapist is most concerned with the degree of discomfort or interference with functioning and not so much with specificity. In real life, personality symptoms often overlap.

Interrater reliability of these categories was not impressively high, and the therapist may feel a lack of conviction as to where to place the patient, even when he or she knows some maladaptive trend is present. This is a problem with purely descriptive diagnoses and can be surmounted by using a psychodynamic diagnosis.

There is not a clear-cut differentiation clinically between personality trends and the more florid disorders. The solution in deciding upon therapy is to evaluate the importance of the symptom in terms of its interference with functioning and comfort, rather than in terms of how well it fits into a specific category.

APPENDIX
ICD-9-CM* AND DSM-III-R†
COMPARED

Both *DSM-III-R* and *ICD-9-CM* terms are listed here with their code numbers, which in most cases are identical, but not in all. The comments in brackets on their use and meaning are mine.

MOOD DISORDERS

In *DSM-III-R* the specific clinical syndromes are called mood disorders. In *ICD-9-CM* they are called affective disorders and are listed under the affective psychoses, but with the same code numbers.

Bipolar Disorder

Bipolar disorder is the modern and more appropriate term for what historically has been called manic-depressive disease. In *ICD-9-CM* it is called bipolar affective disorder with the same code numbers for each of the following types:

---

*American Psychiatric Association. Task Force on Nomenclature and Statistics (1987). *Diagnostic and Statistical Manual of Mental Disorders.* 4th ed. *(DSM-III-R)*. Washington, DC: American Psychiatric Association.

†*International Classification of Diseases. 9th revision. Clinical Modification (ICD-9-CM)* (1978). 3 vols. Ann Arbor, MI: Commission on Professional and Hospital Activities.

- Bipolar disorder, manic, coded 296.4x. The typical elated, speeded-up state. In *ICD-9-CM* called bipolar affective disorder, manic, with the same code number.

- Bipolar disorder, depressed, code 296.5x. The typically slowed-down, dejected state. The same code in *ICD-9-CM* but called bipolar affective disorder, depressed.

- Bipolar disorder, mixed. This type has both depressive and manic features, an occasional occurrence. Called bipolar affective disorder, mixed, in *ICD-9-CM*, with the same code, 296.6.

- Bipolar disorder, not otherwise specified (NOS). In *ICD-9-CM* called bipolar affective disorder, unspecified, with the same code, 296.70. Includes those cases without any manic attacks, but with rarely or only occasional hypomanic spells, sometimes called Bipolar II.

ICD-9-CM has the following codes *not* listed in *DSM-III-R*:

- Manic disorder, single episode, 296.00

- Manic disorder, recurrent episode, 296.10

- Manic-depressive psychosis, other and unspecified, 296.80

- Manic depressive psychosis, unspecified, 296.80

- Atypical manic disorder, 296.81

- Atypical depressive disorder, 296.82

- Other (manic depressive psychosis, mixed type), 296.89

- Other and unspecified affective psychosis, 296.90

- Unspecified affective psychosis, 296.90

- Other specified affective psychoses, 296.99

Major Depression

Major depression is the classical depressive illness, also called primary or endogenous. In *ICD-9-CM* it is called major depressive disorder with the same code numbers.

- Single episode, 296.2x. (Includes a wide variety of types, course, length and severity. Use fifth-digit codes also for completeness as listed below.) In *ICD-9-CM* called major depressive disorder, single episode (296.2).

- Recurrent, 296.3x. (If there is a history of previous spells.) In *ICD-9-CM* called major depressive disorder, recurrent (296.3).

Cyclothymia 301.13

In *ICD-9-CM*, cyclothymic disorder is listed under personality disorders with the same code number.

Dysthymia 300.40

This is dysthymic disorder in *DSM-III* or depressive neurosis in *ICD-9-CM*. It is a very common second diagnosis in other major depressions. It merges with chronic depression and depressive personality of *ICD-9-CM*. In *DSM-III-R*, specify whether of early or late onset and whether primary (before age 18) or secondary (after age 18).

Depressive Disorders (NOS) 311.00

The same listing and code number are found in *ICD-9-CM* for states of depression without manic-depressive or psychotic features, not associated with stressful events and not depressive neurosis. It is a heterogeneous group composed of definitive episodes that do not meet the full criteria for major depression. Occurs in some with quiescent depressive neurosis, or in schizophrenia in remission. Often these are initial attacks in young persons who later have more typical spells.

Other Axis I Conditions Related to Affective Disorders

V Codes: Conditions Not Attributable to Mental Disorder That Are a Focus of Attention or Treatment

- Uncomplicated bereavement, V 62.82. (If persistent beyond a reasonable time or if guilt is excessive, consider depression.) In *ICD-9-CM* this is listed under adjustment reaction and is diagnosed as brief depressive reaction, grief reaction, and is coded as 309.0. *ICD-9-CM* also lists a prolonged depressive reaction, coded 309.1.

- Phase of life problem or other life circumstance problem, V 62.89. Marital problems belong here.

- Adjustment Disorder, with depressed mood, 309.00. In addition, *ICD-9-CM* has a prolonged adjustment reaction with depressive mood, coded 309.1. You may have some trouble separating this from the early stages of a major depression which follows some crisis, such as a major move or loss of job. When the stress is relieved, the symptoms cease, in the adjustment disorder.

ORGANIC MENTAL DISORDERS

The organic mental disorders cause or influence mood disorders.

- Primary degenerative dementia of the Alzheimer type includes two types:

  presenile onset, with depression, 290.13. (In *ICD-9-CM* it is called presenile dementia with depressive features, with the same code number.)

  senile onset, with depression, 290.21. (In *ICD-9-CM* it is called senile dementia with depressive features, with the same code number.)

- Organic mood disorder (293.83). Specify manic, depressed, or mixed. Called organic affective syndrome in *ICD-9-CM* (293.83).

- Multiinfarct dementia with depression (290.43) is called arteriosclerotic dementia in *ICD-9-CM* (290.43).

- Substance-induced mood disorder of *DSM-III-R* is called drug-induced organic affective syndrome in *ICD-9-CM*. Both are coded 292.84.

- Schizoaffective disorder, 295.70. (Patients with affective illness, either manic or depressed, but with mood-irrelevant delusions. Some young adults show this picture in their early attacks of what later in life turns out to be classical bipolar disorder.) In *ICD-9-CM* classified under schizophrenic disorders. However, *ICD-9-CM* also lists manic depressive psychosis, other, and unspecified (296.8). This includes manic-depressive psychosis, unspecified (296.80). Atypical manic disorder (296.81) is probably meant for those types called schizoaffective in *DSM-III-R* and listed under mood disorders. Also atypical depressive disorder (296.82) and other (296.89).

PERSONALITY AND DEVELOPMENTAL DISORDERS

Axis II of *DSM-III-R* includes personality disorder and developmental disorders. It is recommended that both axes be used; that is, if there is both a clinical syndrome and a personality disorder, both should be noted.

Personality Disorders (Axis II)

The comparable *ICD-9-CM* term is listed in parentheses if it is different from *DSM-III-R*. Those most likely to be found in affective disorders are listed under *Cluster C* in *DSM-III-R*.

The criteria for all these diagnostic categories are fully described in *DSM-III-R*.

- Avoidant, 301.82

- Dependent, 301.60

- Obsessive-compulsive, 301.40 (compulsive personality disorder, 301.40)

- Passive-aggressive, 301.84

- Personality disorder, NOS, 301.90 (unspecified personality disorder, 301.90)

Cluster A

Paranoid (301.00), schizoid (301.2), and schizotypal (301.22) are not often present with mood disorders. When they are present, the treatment is complicated.

Cluster B

Antisocial (301.70), borderline (301.83), histrionic (301.50), and narcissistic (301.81), likewise, are uncommon in primary depressions. When present they complicate the treatment. However, depressions and depressive moods are often present in these personalities.

Affective and Introverted Personality Disorder

ICD-9-CM, in addition, has a listing for affective personality disorder (301.1), which includes affective personality disorder, unspecified (301.10), chronic hypomanic personality disorder (301.11), chronic depressive personality disorder (301.12) [which would be diagnosed dysthymia, early onset (300.40) in *DSM-III-R*]. *ICD-9-CM* also lists an introverted type (301.21) of personality disorder.

CLINICAL VARIATIONS: FIFTH-DIGIT SUBCLASSIFICATIONS

In using *DSM-III* or *DSM-III-R* for the variations in major mood disorders both bipolar and depressions, there are special numbers to be inserted in the fifth digit of the code in place of the letter x, as follows: If the illness is in full remission, insert the number 6 in the fifth digit and the complete code has 5 digits, for example, 296.26. In partial remission, insert the number 5, for example, 296.25. Similarly, if the depression is psychotic, for major depression, single episode, in full remission, insert the number 4 as the fifth digit and the code is 296.24; if it is severe but nonpsychotic insert the number 3 and the code is 296.23; and if it is moderately severe insert the number 2 and the code is 296.22. If mild, insert the number 1, and the code is 296.21.

CHILDREN

You will note that there is no separate classification of mood disorders for children in *DSM-III-R*. According to the manual, the adult diagnosis should be used when the picture of an affective disorder is seen in a child. This works well for many adolescents, and a few children, but most depressed children have to be diagnosed under one or another symptom disorder, depending on what the child presents as the chief symptom. For example, the *ICD-9-CM* classification: Disturbances of emotions specific to childhood and adolescence, "misery and unhappiness disorder" (coded 313.1), fits many children who might be considered depressed. Of course, if the symptoms fit any full classification in the manual, the correct diagnosis is in that class.

8

PSYCHODYNAMICS AND PSYCHOPATHOLOGY

It is necessary to go beyond descriptive categories to identify significant human conflicts and work with interpersonal and psychodynamic issues (Perry et al. 1987). In the management and treatment of simpler cases, chemotherapy and attention to the "here and now," that is, immediate conflicts, is enough to resolve a depression, but one-fourth to one-third of the cases (depending on the selection process and the group selected) are recurrent or tend to become chronic.

In addition, many attacks of depression leave residual symptoms that interfere with the quality of life. In such cases, some of which are mild, some severe, the quality of life can be so diminished that long-term therapies are needed. Some patients, superficially well enough and apparently functioning, nevertheless lead lives of private misery because of the symptoms described here. This private misery must be acknowledged.

Long-term psychodynamic therapy directed at character traits and patterns, that is, intrapsychic phenomena, can be very successful at improving the quality of life and interpersonal relations.

A psychodynamic diagnostic appraisal is of great practical value to the psychotherapist because formal clinical diagnosis alone does not give enough practical information to manage and treat the vulnerabilities of the patients, their conflicts, and their handling of stress. Psychodynamic appraisal is also valuable for planning treatment and management of short-term patients.

The principal characterological, psychodynamic, and developmental vulnerabilities which are likely to require long-term psychotherapy or psychoanalysis are identifiable under several categories:

1. Ambivalence, dependency, and other problems in interpersonal relationships, love relationships, and object relations in general, including passivity and masochistic trends such as are seen in persons who submit to intolerable relationships in marriage, at work, or in any intimate relationship. This includes hypersensitivity to rejection.
2. Deficits in self-esteem and damage to self-esteem. Usually these deficits are manifested directly by "I'm no good," or indirectly by failure to attempt obvious new ventures. An inability to defend oneself in confrontations belongs here.
3. Pathological identifications, for example, with depressed parents. Narcissistic love relations, that is, those in which the object is used as a part of the self to make up for deficiencies felt in the self. Sadomasochistic tendencies belong here.
4. Early fixations, oral and anal, with feelings of helplessness and hopelessness. Such fixations may foster the early development of depressive thinking, including chronic pessimism, poor self-esteem, and excessive hunger for love.
5. Difficulties in experiencing or expressing affects, such as problems in handling aggression, sexuality, and sadness. One common symptom is a serious lack of assertiveness.
6. The use of pathological defenses. These include projection, repression, and denial. Sometimes depression is used as defense. A mechanism of projective identification is seen in those who have some characteristics of borderline personality.
7. Inability to mourn. Unresolved losses and uncompleted mourning are seen in some depressed patients.
8. Early development of a punishing superego, an overdemanding conscience, and intense guilt in various forms. This important mechanism is a motivation for suicide in some persons and leads to conflicts with reality and intrapersonal conflicts.
9. A preoccupation with death and a desire to kill or kill oneself, consciously and sometimes unconsciously, or

warded off, revealing its presence by a pessimistic, nihilistic attitude.

EARLY DEVELOPMENT

Identification plays a large part in the process of building self-esteem. Growing children tend to identify with the attitude of those who take care of them. If they are considered to have rights, to have value as individuals, then they will be able to regard themselves thusly. If they are treated as though they have no rights, they are likely to identify with that attitude. But the process is more complicated than this because individuals have to take into account whatever the caretakers regard as "good" and "bad," and they have to find themselves in that scheme of things.

Source of Depressive Cognitions

A predepressive kind of experience can occur in the first year or two of life out of the interaction between mother and child, when the child's expectations of the mother are disappointed to such an extent that the child does not begin to master disappointments such as separation, loss, hunger, and frustration. This deficit occurs during a separation–individuation phase of the infant's development. If these deficiencies are severe enough and re-peated enough, the child acquires a basic depressive tendency, which may or may not persist throughout life, in the form of a negative affective response to future disappointments and losses. Concomitantly, the child may not learn to deal with his or her own anger over these disappointments — a deficit which can also persist in the form of personality tendencies of the passive-aggressive type.

For the prevention of depression, such a deficiency occur-ring early in childhood may well have to be treated intensively in the growing child, directly or through the parents.

Another factor enters here in the child's development of

self-esteem, namely the question of power and competence. Children who feel impotent to win approval and love may not only feel "not good enough," but may also develop feelings of helplessness and hopelessness, which then lessen their sense of power and competence to control and master their environment, as well as to control and master their own instinctual drives. These issues are first addressed in the arena of feeding, early verbalization, and toilet training.

The tendency to think pessimistically may arise from feelings that it is impossible to be good enough to win the love and approval of their parents or to achieve the ideal they have developed as their fantasied and wished-for self. Hopelessness in future disappointments in themselves can bring about a regression to this earlier hopeless state.

A very important source of trouble in some patients is the feeling of being assigned, in the family "plans," to the role of the savior, the rescuer, or the exceptional one in the family who is supposed to make everything right for the family. A classical study by Cohen and colleagues (1954) identified this unconscious myth in a number of patients who suffered from manic-depressive disorder. Most depressives do not, or cannot, verbalize their supposed life tasks consciously, but they take their supposed assignments seriously. They are "driven" people.

THE PERSON IN CRISIS

The unfavorable combination of an overwhelming circumstance and a personality problem is present in a significant number of those whose depressions persist and become a long-term problem (see Table 7-1 on page 113). The passive-aggressive personality disorder, dependency problems, and masochistic trends are present in people who have trouble throwing off depressions or who do not respond well to chemotherapy and short-term psychotherapy.

In people with affective disorders, the therapist should look at those interactions involving dependency that have a powerful impact on their lives. They may be especially sensitive to changes in the climate of their love relationships. Those whose moods are most vulnerable to the behavior and moods of their loved ones can be plunged into a depression by a seeming rejection or a scolding that causes guilt. They live on approval, although they can take responsibility and perform responsibily; they are people sensitive to narcissistic wounds, that is, wounds of self-esteem.

Persons with poor self-esteem tend to be overly dependent on others for approval and love. They need "supplies" of love, can be unreasonably demanding of their love objects, or they can devote their lives to the justification of their existence by self-sacrificing service, always needing that sustaining approval from someone. The independent person with a healthy self-esteem and strong self-image does the same thing, but while enjoying approval, does not depend on it so much for sustenance.

Breakdown and Restitution

Once there is a breakdown of self-esteem, especially with little or no hope for restitution, depressive affect occurs, with or without depressive illness. Restitution is a process of recovery and can be spontaneous in many cases. Often depression and depressive illness recover and remit spontaneously. Treatment takes into account needs that are beyond the power of individuals to supply themselves: nurturance and protection against being further overwhelmed by their own excessive self-expectations or by the demands of the world.

A very important diagnostic evaluation to include is an overall integrative view of the patient's character or ego strength. This is an evaluation of patients' capacity to deal with their troubles, whether they are depressive symptoms, personality symptoms, internal libidinous pleasures, or external realities such as stressful relationships and situations. Observation of the following often supplies enough information.

1. How well they can experience affects, that is, how well can they tolerate depression, anxiety, frustration, and grief.
2. How much capacity they have for introspection, which

includes the ability to distance themselves from their symptoms enough to look at them and evaluate their own depression, anger, and pain. Can they mourn?

3. How much they can feel for others, that is, their capacity for sympathy, empathy, and identification.
4. How much value they see in themselves and how quickly they see that it appears they do not set a high value on themselves.
5. How much self-defeating defensiveness is there—punitive, masochistic trends or paranoid tendencies. What are their basic defenses?
6. To what extent are patients motivated by fantasy as contrasted to reality. How strong and necessary is their denial?
7. How well do they deal with a powerful libido, with its pressures and demands for outlet and satisfaction?

When depression is a defense, it has to be a defense against something very powerful, something that seriously threatens the person's control, such as a flooding of aggression and hostility to an uncomfortable degree. Also, as is sometimes seen in the long-term treatment of depressions through any uncovering technique, a reservoir of sexual frustration can be found, usually taking the form of oral fantasies, dreams, and occasional acting out.

Many persons with cyclical, recurrent, and/or chronic affective disorders live in a state of chronic sexual frustration, either brought about by an unsatisfactory marriage or by intrapsychic prohibitions. Sometimes depression, in the form of giving up, is the only way some people know to deal with these pressures.

SELF PSYCHOLOGY

The literature of the psychology of the self has developed enormously in the past two decades. There have been two general directions of the studies and two general themes: one, that the self-psychology dominates everything, and two, that it is, although powerful, only one of the dynamisms affecting the mental life.

The first theme is illustrated by the formulations of Kohut

(1971, 1977), who, from his studies of narcissistic personality disorders, described a type of person who has a maintenance relationship with a sustaining other person, the self-object. When that person, the self-object, is unavailable, the narcissistic personality becomes depressed, because without his or her mirroring or idealized object he or she feels empty and dead. Inasmuch as persons of this type quite often become depressed, it is postulated that this formulation may apply to depressions in general, although data bearing on this conclusion are lacking.

In this view of depression, the preeminent cause is a loss or failure of support of self-objects, that is, those persons with whom one has a relationship similar to that of a baby and its mother—a necessary, sustaining, nurturing relationship.

It is clear that this view has application in certain cases of depression in which the unavailability of some important other person through death, separation, loss of regard, and so forth, has precipitated the depression.

Although this is often the case, what one finds in practice is quite a good deal more complex than this formulation would lead one to expect. Fantasies, identification, anger, and sexual frustrations still have to be dealt with for their part in the breakdown, before a new self can emerge independent of the self-object or until a new relationship has been established.

The other direction taken in studies of the psychology of the self is toward integration of self-images and their conflicts over sexual and aggressive drives, emphasizing the defensive structures against repressed drives and the libidinal functions of the self structures as dynamisms, rather than emphasizing the defects in the personality, as in the direction described in previous paragraphs, according to the Kohutian model.

Both directions emphasize that patients with such pathology, and this includes many depressed patients, require somewhat different techniques in therapy than do ordinary neurotic persons, because of the low tolerance for frustration or rejection and because of the generally poor self-image. In therapy they lean on and tax the strength of therapists to tolerate both anger and clinging dependence and tax their patience for resistance to therapy.

The following example illustrates the usefulness of the

second view. A young man of 30 years, who has had four definite unipolar depressions since the age of 18, has been in psychoanalytic psychotherapy for four years. He is going through a crisis and finds himself first becoming depressed, then almost totally overwhelmed by depression. "I was a person with a depression, but now I have become the depression." This is a new self who has emerged. It had been a repressed part of the whole person, but it now becomes the whole person—angry, depressed, suicidal, hopeless, irrational, and regressed to the original childhood state from which this archaic self was derived. This self also is able, through projections and projective identification, to mold the therapist to match its archaic relationships. Thus, transferences become massive projections of childhood images, and the therapist may be forced to some extent to play the role of the parent if the therapy is to go on. Interpretation is essential.

In therapy it was necessary for him to experience the excitement he got out of his aggression toward the therapist, to be able to describe it, and to acknowledge his fantasies of a homosexual attack on the therapist before he was able to give up his infantile self and move on to a new self that had control over his aggressive and sexual feelings. At this point he also became aware of the infantile satisfaction he got out of the protective setting of the therapy and the soothing presence of the therapist—a satisfaction marred suddenly by his aggressive and sexual feelings. This working-through process was necessary; understanding the self-structure was not enough on its own.

SUMMARY

Simple psychosocial stresses and interpersonal conflicts do not explain the variety of problems seen in the patients; individual vulnerability also needs to be evaluated. A psychodynamic appraisal makes it possible to work with the special dependency needs and to give the special handling and empathy required with depressed patients.

A large number of patients have psychological problems requiring treatment even after their immediate symptoms have been treated.

The psychological issues often found include dependency and low self-esteem, difficulty in experiencing and handling affects, especially aggression, cognitive (thinking) defects, excessive guilt, and excessive need for reassurance and love supplies. Working-through processes may be needed for the treatment of self-defeating patterns.

9

DIFFERENTIAL DIAGNOSIS

There are a number of other psychiatric disorders and medical illnesses that symptomatically overlap with affective disorders. Differentiating one from the other requires strict attention to specific diagnostic possibilities. The various possible differential diagnostic problems are described in this chapter. Although the list is not complete, the principal areas of potential confusion are here, and this chapter will alert the psychotherapist to the necessity of accurate diagnosis at all times.

MEDICAL ILLNESS AND EFFECTS OF MEDICATION

Some medical illnesses without depression have symptoms of fatigue, weight loss, anorexia, nausea, and anxiety over health. The presence of depression is indicated by the more specific symptoms: work inhibition, early morning waking, loss of interest in sex, anhedonia, diurnal rhythm of severity in the morning with improvement in the evening. Certain cognitive symptoms also indicate depression: guilt, low self-esteem, pessimism, and loss of hope. Sometimes a medical illness precipitates a depression. The cognitive symptoms have the greatest specificity for affective disorders.

The incidence of hypothyroidism in hospitalized depressed patients is quite significant (one study has reported it as 10 percent), suggesting that one should be on the lookout for it in depressed patients who tire easily, appear slowed, or have any of the other signs suggestive of hypothyroidism. Occasionally, a patient with myxedema may appear on the psychiatric service, the diagnosis having been missed by the referring agency. An advanced, untreated case of myxedema may cause myxedema psychosis, which resembles dementia. A thorough medical history, physical examination, and appropriate laboratory tests are recommended whenever there is a question of one of these illnesses.

Major depression, with or without delusions, can be confused with brain tumors, especially of the frontal lobes. Medical and neurological examination, electroencephalogram, X-ray of the skull, and CAT scan may be needed to make the correct diagnosis.

Pituitary tumors that affect hormonal secretions can cause fatigue and depression, much like hypothyroidism and hypoadrenalism, and may go on for months, causing depressionlike symptoms before any more definitive signs of tumor develop. Here again, one must be on the alert for what looks superficially like depression, but lacks the guilt, low self-esteem, and pessimism of the genuine depression.

Medicines can sometimes cause secondary depressions, especially if one is dealing with an older person, who may be taking a variety of drugs routinely without giving it much thought. For example, quite a few people take diuretics for hypertension and do not mention it. These drugs deplete potassium, a lack of which can cause fatigue and slowing down, and the appearance of depression. If one sees a patient who is taking diuretics, such as hydrochlorothiazide, and not taking replacement potassium, especially if the symptoms are mainly somatic, one should communicate with the physician and raise the question of potassium level, citing the atypical nature of the depression as the reason for suspicion. A number of other medicines can cause similar symptoms, and one's index of suspicion should be high when a variety of drugs is being used. Steroids can actually precipitate typical major depressions or manic attacks in someone who is subject to recurrent affective disorders.

Reserpine, a drug once used to calm and sedate psychotic patients, is now used extensively for hypertension. This drug can precipitate depression in depression-prone persons and should never be given to anyone with a history of depression.

DEPRESSION MISDIAGNOSED AS MEDICAL ILLNESS

Misdiagnoses commonly made are of hypothyroidism, anxiety states, anorexia nervosa, migraine and tension headaches, gastro-intestinal disorders, chronic low back pain, premenstrual tension, and mitral valve prolapse. Here again, some people have both.

A common misdiagnosis among the elderly is a dementia, such as that of arteriosclerotic brain disease, or Alzheimer's disease. Often depressed people complain of trouble with memory. Usually, in depressions, upon close questioning, one finds that there is no actual loss of memory, but instead some difficulty in concentrating on anything requiring intellectual effort, so that the patient has trouble retaining things he would ordinarily remember. Simple testing with a mental status examination can demonstrate the difference. Depressed people say, "I'm losing my mind," or "There is something wrong with my brain," but on testing show no loss of retention or memory. It is simply difficulty in concentrating.

Patients with dementia, on the other hand, sometimes are not aware of their defect, or deny it, even when it is obvious on simple psychological testing. Also, the electroencephalogram and the CAT scan both show changes in the patient with dementia, but are normal in the depressed person.

OTHER PSYCHIATRIC ILLNESSES

Among psychiatric illnesses with symptoms in common are anxiety and depression. It is to be expected that these two affects overlap since in both states the patient is dealing with unconscious drives and conflicts that threaten to break through into disturbing action. Indeed, one can see all ranges of severity of anxiety in depressed states, from mild tension to overwhelming panic. Some depressed people are so agitated and restless as a result of their anxiety that it can be a dominant symptom. Agitated depression is not rare. Therapists should be alert for the presence of depressive illness whenever they see an anxious patient. The anxiety may be generalized or directed to a particular idea, such as the fear of losing control or to fears of suicide and death. In some cases, there is phobic and obsessional anxiety that either heralds an oncoming depression or disguises it.

A differential point of great importance is the cognitive area, especially helpful in diagnosis when patients can verbalize what they are anxious about. Parenthetically, what they say they are anxious about is usually a displacement from something unconscious, but nevertheless the conscious ideas and fantasies around which their anxiety is centered are very helpful as diagnostic markers. In depression, these ideas are centered around guilt, often from the remote past, around bad things they have done or thought. Guilt and punishment for bad deeds may be verbalized by such statements as "I brought it on myself," or "It's my own fault." Depression is also marked by pessimistic ideas, such as, "No one can help me," "The situation is hopeless," or "I have an incurable disease." In milder cases these ideas are watered down or disguised, but are still there in less dramatic form, such as "I've been very foolish," or "Can you help me?" or "Do you think I can get well?" The patient in such cases seems on the verge of feeling hopeless, but is still able to negotiate and receive some reassurance. The sicker patients whose guilt, self-condemnation, and ideas of doom are so fixed that they amount to delusions, are psychotic. Anxiety, agitation, delusion of bodily disease, and guilt characterize the group of middle- and late-life depressions with the picture called "involutional melancholia" in DSM-II and ICD-9, seen in anxious, obsessive persons and called major depressive episode, with melancholia in DSM-III and DSM-III-R.

There are anxious patients whose depression seems relatively minor, where the dominating symptom is anxiety, yet the patient's concerns seem excessive for the circumstances. Some of these are early stages of depression. This is the time in the development of a depression where the primary-care physician is often consulted if the concerns are physical, or, if they are not physical, the nonmedical therapist is consulted—the clergyman, psychologist, social worker, or marriage counselor. Here there is the opportunity to catch an early case which can be treated, so that a major episode is avoided. Reassurance, support, rest, and sometimes removal from other troublesome problems, supplemented by the use of medication, can help avert a major breakdown. If the patient has a history of previous episodes, one is alerted to the danger of another and must be prepared to use preventive measures.

In depressions, sometimes the anxiety is caused by the struggle with suicidal impulses or with anger. Looking behind the symptoms to the psychological causes may be important. Psychodynamically, what is indicated by the presence of anxiety is a threatened person, struggling with an inner conflict, which is actually triangular. He or she is struggling to control the breakthrough into consciousness of instinctual impulses, on the one hand, and to escape the punishment of a punitive superego on the other. Consequently, at this stage, the therapist has to be very careful not to increase the guilt by enabling unwelcome and feared impulses to rise to the surface, because this awareness on the patient's part can be a confirmation that he or she is really bad and is being accused. The danger of suicide is increased thereby. If rumination appears excessive, do not encourage it.

In those with incipient psychotic depressions, anxiety may indicate the loss of feeling intact. These persons begin to sense bad parts of themselves, resembling old internalized enemies. They cannot accept these bad parts and would like to contain them before they take over and destroy them, even if they destroy themselves in the bargain.

During the course of long-term dynamic psychotherapy and in psychoanalysis, an important differential from neurosis must be kept in mind, namely, the vulnerability to breakdown of the depression-prone person. The anxiety of depressed persons may be used as an indicator of the extent to which they are threatened by overwhelming drives in the direction of loss of control, either of aggressive impulses or aggression toward themselves. Early in a depression that is not full blown these may be diagnostic signs of depressions or manic states that are not present in simple anxiety states. Sudden bursts of memories are such an indicator.

The return of the repressed as a prepsychotic symptom in both schizophrenia and depression is an interesting diagnostic point of occasional importance, ordinarily overlooked in textbooks. Remote memories, feelings, and their associations come spontaneously as dreams or daydreams, or as conscious memories in the prepsychotic stages of psychotic depressions. They may herald an oncoming melancholia. These memories do not come slowly, with great resistance, as they do during psychotherapy or psychoanalysis, but come quickly, without much warning. The content of the ideas is usually unpleasant, dealing with painful things: death, losses, and frustrations. Memory hypertrophy of this kind also occurs in schizophrenia, with excessive rumination.

A similar phenomenon occurs in the prepsychotic stage of schizophrenia, but the differential here is based on other specific schizophrenic symptoms: blocking, delusion of a persecutory nature, bizarre behavior, etc. The history is very helpful in differential diagnosis. If the individual has a history of previous attacks of anxiety, but not of depression, it is very likely that the present anxiety does not indicate an oncoming depression.

On the other hand, if there has been previous depression, it is likely that the present anxiety is the beginning of an attack of depression, and preventive measures should be taken. However, persons with depressive illnesses are not immune to the ordinary stresses of life which make everyone anxious or unhappy. Their reactions can be normal.

The chief differential for affective disorders is *schizophrenia*, although the depressive spells are less likely to cause diagnostic problems than the acute attacks of mania. In cases of schizophrenia with increased psychomotor activity, the symptoms that identify mania are elation, flight of ideas, and mood-relevant delusions. Symptoms that indicate schizophrenia are blocking of speech, bizarre ideas, persecutory ideas, and a mood inappropriate to the ideas.

Because criteria for schizophrenia in the United States are becoming more specific, the disease is diagnosed less freely than it was a decade or two ago, so that many people are now being labeled bipolar disorder who just a few years ago would have been considered schizophrenic. As a result, we are seeing more and more bipolar patients, some of them rather bizarre and atypical, and the category of schizoaffective disorder probably will also be used more frequently. This is appropriate, according to long-term follow-up, because many of those persons called schizophrenic a few years ago, upon long-term follow-up have turned out to be typical bipolar patients. Early attacks of bipolar illness in adolescence and young adults often have confused pictures, with paranoid ideas, and early on they resemble schizophrenia, but later show typical bipolar cycling, with clear, free intervals. Lithium trials and appropriate neuroleptic or antidepressant drugs may tell the difference.

The dexamethazone suppression test may help differentiate depression from schizophrenia. It is positive in 50 percent of depressives and negative in schizophrenics, so that a positive test clearly diagnoses depression, while a negative test does not differentiate them.

Occasionally in a young psychotic adult, it is impossible to tell what the future holds because a person who appears to demonstrate bizarre atypical schizophrenic excitement may eventually be seen to be a manic-depressive. The original differentiation of Kraepelin was based on the relatively benign nature of the manic-depressive, but we know that some schizophrenic attacks are benign also and have no residual deficit.

Schizoaffective Disorder

Ocassionally a mixed state, with the circular form of bipolar illness and the content of thought of schizophrenia, may occur. The diagnosis of schizoaffective psychosis is appropriate for these cases.

A small number of cases have the symptoms of both mood disorders and schizophrenia, a surprising fact in the face of considerable evidence that families very rarely have both (manic depressive disorders run in some families and schizophrenia in others, without cross occurrence). There exists the possibility that this is a separate disorder, and it is often so diagnosed, although it is listed in *ICD-9-CM* under schizophrenia. It is far from uniform in its clinical manifestations. Some cases appear in early adult life with the picture predominently of schizophrenia, but later on in midlife, follow the pattern of bipolar disease. Some cases continue to show mixed symptoms throughout their entire course, which may follow the course of either bipolar or of schizophrenic disease.

The basic pattern is one of episodic attacks with clear intervals as in bipolar disorder, but with the content of the attack resembling schizophrenia, with mood-inappropriate delusions or hallucinations and with blocking and dissociative symptoms. The mood may be manic or depressed during the attack, or mixed, and the behavior may be aggressive and overactive, even assaultive with paranoid ideas, or it may be withdrawn and quiet.

An example is of a 17-year-old young man who had a long period of anxiety manifested by worries about his body, self-consciousness, and inability to function. This period was followed by one of excitement and aggressive, assaultive behavior requiring hospitalization and sometimes restraints, and paranoid delusions. This lasted two years, and was followed by a period of retreat and withdrawal lasting a year, with paranoid ideas continuing. He was in and out of mental hospitals for the next thirty years, but with well periods in which he was able to do some work, such as driving a cab, although he had many fights with people because of the paranoid ideas, and often lost his job because of his disagreeable, rigid attitude. At about the age of 50 he had an attack in which he appeared obviously and typically manic, with elation, hyperactivity, grandiosity, flight of ideas, and so on. Gradually his attacks took on the appearance of the bipolar illness, and in addition, responded very well to lithium. This is an example of a person whose bipolar disease, when it started in adolescence, had a mixed clinical picture, with paranoid ideas, and was considered to be schizophrenic.

In contrast, there are patients with a similar cycling, with the acute blocking, dissociation, and paranoid thinking of schizophrenics during attacks, who continue with the same clinical picture throughout life. This is the schizoaffective disorder now viewed as a separate illness. It is usually not controlled with lithium.

Schizophrenia

In addition, there are patients with clear-cut schizophrenia who have definitive depressions that respond to antidepressants. Electroconvulsant treatment is effective with all those in these groups, but relapses and recurrences are common. Lithium should be given a trial in these mixed cases.

Post-psychotic depressions have been observed in 25 percent of schizophrenics upon recovery from the acute attack. Of these, about one-fourth were major depressions and three-fourths were minor. Such a significant occurrence requires one to be on the alert for suicidal danger in discharged schizophrenic patients, as well as a need to employ antidepressants when possible.

This occurrence suggests that the underlying psychological stresses and psychodynamic factors have not been worked through during the episode. The psychosis has been symptomatically relieved, but the cause remains. At this point a thorough appraisal of psychosocial stresses and psychodynamic factors is needed, so that whatever psychotherapeutic techniques are indicated may be applied, whether individual, group, couples, family, intervention, or combinations.

Panic and Depression

The occurrence of either depression or anxiety does not automatically exclude the other. In fact, anxious depressions are as common as those without obvious anxiety. Anxiety may reach the panic state, especially in persons of anxious personality or those with a histrionic type of personality (i.e., the hysterical person). When the panic is treated (and treatment is usually rapidly successful), the depression may remain, requiring standard antidepressive methods, usually a combination of drugs and psychological methods. The early depression with panic in a middle-aged or elderly person, usually a woman, can look very much like a severe major agitated depression, but there are surprising situations in which this picture resolves so quickly with reassurance and small doses of tricyclic antidepressants that it becomes obvious that the picture was misleading and that the panic was everything. Do not be satisfied with a quick cure. The underlying issues need to be addressed, and the patient's personal predicament must be identified in order to prevent recurrence.

Anorexia Nervosa and Bulimia

These disorders, which seem to be more and more common, relate to affective disorders in some significant ways. For one thing, a depressed person who has no appetite and has lost quite a lot of weight may look like an anorexic person, and, similarly, a person with anorexia nervosa may be quite depressed. There are more persons with affective disorders in the families of anorexic patients than in the general population, suggesting a familial factor and some biological or environmental connection. Some persons with anorexia have definite major depressions with typical signs of psychomotor retardation, anhedonia, depressed or hopeless mood, guilt, and suicidal ideas, and they respond to antidepressant drugs if they are willing to take them. They make particularly difficult patients to treat because of their resistance to oral medications and to interference with their own compulsions.

Anorexia seems to be related to a compulsive personality disorder, and the depression to a genetic factor. For example, a woman, aged 30, has had both anorexia nervosa and unipolar, recurrent, almost yearly depressions since age 19 and has made three serious suicidal attempts. Her mother has chronic depressive disorder, relieved by long-term medication with amitriptyline. Her father has had some depressive attacks, quite mild, treated successfully with psychotherapy. Finally, the patient herself was persuaded to try amitriptyline, with remarkably successful results; the depressions have been almost entirely relieved, and she has been making inroads with the anorexia now for five years.

Bulimia is also seen in the history of depressive patients and may persist into the fifth and sixth decades of life if untreated. In one case, combined treatment with antidepressant drugs and analytic treatment has brought about a resolution of both the depression and the bulimia. Combined therapy is usually essential.

ORGANIC AFFECTIVE SYNDROMES

See the section "Organic Mood (Affective) Disorders" in Chapter 7.

Delirium

Manic states with paranoid ideas or other thinking disorders can be confused with *delirium* due to medical illness, alcoholic delirium, or drug effects of cocaine or hallucinogens or amphetamines. Sometimes heavy marijuana smokers also have depressionlike states, although the usual differential with marijuana is schizophrenia. Look for euphoria, elation, irritability, psychomotor acceleration, and mood-relevant ideas, such as delusions of power, in the manic. In the delirious patient, look for somatic symptoms: fever, rapid pulse, excessive perspiration, flushing, and so on. Occasionally one sees a manic patient who is also an alcoholic and has delirium tremens. Alcohol abuse and bipolar illness are not a rare combination.

10

BORDERLANDS OF AFFECTIVE DISORDERS

Patients often come with complaints in the predepressive and proto-depressive category—precursors, pieces or remnants of depression—rather than florid, full-blown clinical illness. This chapter discusses normal depression and depressive affects associated with such conditions as sadness, fatigue, grief, boredom, loneliness, and loss of self-esteem.

Since these complaints may be symptoms that indicate depression-proneness, defenses against depression, or a covered-up depression, they may be considered psychological *markers*. These "borderlands of affective disorders" can be called proto-depressive, that is, they may precede, follow, or cover up a more serious spell, or they may have a normal resolution. In either case they present an opportunity for treatment and prevention, for this is the very street the psychotherapist works, even though the psychopharmacologist may be just around the corner. The prefix pre can be used also because these symptoms may be the first outward indication of depression.

NORMAL DEPRESSION AND DEPRESSIVE AFFECTS

An example of one of these everyday moods is described by a nonmedical writer, a drama critic (Kerr 1962):

> I am going to start out by assuming that you are approx-
> imately as unhappy as I am. Neither of us may be

submitting ourselves to psychiatrists, neither of us may take an excessive number of tranquilizers each day, neither of us may have married three times in an effort to find someone who will make us happier. We are not desperate, but we are, vaguely, dissatisfied. [p. 11]

This is one kind of dysphoric mood.

When, in the course of psychotherapy, feelings and ideas of this nature come up, they can be understood and worked through. This chapter is a summary of both the important everyday affects and dysphoric moods one finds in working with patients and their role as *markers* in the definitive mood disorders.

Moods and Affects as Signals

Normal unhappiness and sadness are probably necessary and fundamental responses for adapting to reality, measuring the meaning of experience to the individual. These moods perform a function in the personal life that physical pain does for physical experience. "By being unpleasant, sadness seems to have a function—its own elimination" (Arieti 1977, p. 864). The quantity of pain or unhappiness is an indicator of the strength of the stimulus (or the importance of the event). The intensity of the response to pain or unhappiness is therefore an appropriate measure of reality for the organism. A person not capable of feeling pain has a handicap toward the experience of reality of life. Those who are not capable of feeling unhappiness or sadness similarly have a handicap in their ability to respond effectively and to measure the value of experience for themselves. Sometimes, when a depressed person is getting better, he or she can cry and can experience normal grief and sadness.

There is an infinite variety of moods and emotions, the common human experiences that psychotherapists encounter in themselves and their patients. The moods considered here occur in normal depressed states as well as in the illness of depression. Like affects in general, such feelings have structure, containing not only a sensation (mood), but an idea (cognition).

What is called happiness in its narrowest sense comes from the satisfaction – most often instantaneous – of pent-up needs which have reached great intensity, and by its very nature can only be a transitory experience. When any condition desired by the pleasure-principle is protracted, it results in a feeling only of mild comfort; we are so constituted that we can only intensely enjoy contrasts, much less intensely states in themselves. Our possibilities of happiness are thus limited from the start by our very constitution. It is much less difficult to be unhappy. Suffering comes from three quarters: from our own body, which is destined to decay and dissolution, and cannot even dispense with anxiety and pain as danger-signals; from the outer world, which can rage against us with the most powerful and pitiless forces of destruction; and finally from our relations with other men. [Freud 1930, pp. 27–28]

It is not always easy to distinguish the ordinary unhappiness of life from depressive illness. The seriously depressed person, especially at the earlier stages of depression, seems very much like anyone else who is troubled or does not feel quite well. He or she may appear to be worried about the ordinary concerns of life: health, job, family, money. It is the purpose of this chapter to describe some of the normal depressions of life, to compare them with what happens in the illness depression.

FATIGUE

Be alert to fatigue as a symptom. When we are exhausted from work and great mental concentration, we want to withdraw from everything, repair ourselves, sleep, and try to rest until strength and interest return. Depressed patients do not repair with a night's sleep; they feel just as bad, or worse, the next morning.

In contrast to normal fatigue, there is the feeling of exhaustion and fatigue seen in depressions where the feeling of fatigue and easy fatiguability on effort is common enough to be a classical symptom of major depression, usually indicating that the somatic elements of endogenous depression are present.

This is the psychosomatic fatigue formerly referred to as neurasthenia—the representation of an unconscious conflict. For example, a young man in treatment for proneness to depression and inhibitions that interfered with his functioning reported that at work the night before one of his colleagues had challenged him suddenly in an insulting way. Taken by surprise, he was unable to reply. Later, he was overtaken by an overwhelming sense of fatigue, which persisted until the next day. In his therapy session that day he was irritable and picked a fight with the therapist. When the situation was clarified and he realized that he was fighting the therapist instead of his colleague, the fatigue lifted. His life story was filled with incidents of this sort, some of them precipitating attacks of serious depression lasting months.

REJECTION

A common story is of a rejection; that is, there are those who have been slighted, perhaps by a spouse or boss. They may be angry, or feel hurt and rejected. They toss and turn at night, thinking about it. In a couple of days they feel it was not so bad, feel better, and may talk to the person, consider it a misunderstanding, and the problem seems solved.

However, the situation is not that simple. They pay a price if they do not talk it over or somehow get satisfaction for the slight; the price includes a persistent, although unconscious, sense of injustice. If a series of such incidents occurs, the sense of injustice persists and increases, requiring increasing energy to keep the hurt and rebellion unconscious. Meanwhile, self-esteem is being lowered, and general unhappiness is increasing. It is easy to see that this may be an unhealthy way to handle feelings of rejection and is, therefore, a marker of depression proneness.

Depression-prone persons, because of their need for love and reassurance, tend to react to rejection more massively than others who are not so dependent on emotional supplies. Therapists may find, to their consternation, that innocent remarks are taken as a rejection or criticism by depressed patients in therapy. This may be a sign of a transference reaction, indicating that the therapist is now the "significant other."

LOSS, GRIEF, AND MOURNING

One of the important functions of the psychotherapist is helping people deal with loss and grief, and assisting with the process of mourning, a function that may turn out to be complicated because, unlike the grief after a death, the losses and griefs of the depressed person may be unconscious. There is a great deal of literature on the subject of grief for the death of a loved one, which provides a starting point.

Loss and Its Importance

Any separation from or alteration of a significant situation, object, or relationship creates the sense of loss. The intensity of the reaction depends on a number of factors: (1) the reversibility or irreversibility of the loss and (2) the value and significance of what is lost, which is determined, for one thing, by the amount of "life space" occupied by the lost object. (3) Also important is the amount of change required by the absence of that which has been lost. Here are examples of things of importance which may be lost: jobs, homes, money, security, hopes, ideals, and expectations. Certain changes also cause feelings of loss for example of seasons, of location, and of age. Also seen are losses of people, such as close loved ones and friends, and personal traumas, such as the birth of a defective baby, divorce, or separations of all kinds.

Acute Grief after a Death

In his classic paper, Lindemann (1944) sums up his observations in four points: (1) Acute grief is a definite syndrome with some specific psychological and somatic symptoms. (2) This syndrome may appear immediately or it may be delayed and may be apparently absent or exaggerated. (3) Distorted pictures may appear in place of the typical syndrome, but each represents an aspect of the syndrome. (4) By appropriate technical work these distorted pictures can be successfully changed into a normal grief reaction with resolution.

The symptomatology of acute grief is important as an indicator of how well the survivor is going to adjust. Normal reactions to an unexpected death include such somatic features as severe anxiety attacks occurring in waves; weakness; and a generalized feeling of mental pain. All of these reactions are so severe as to lead the sufferer to avoid reminders and mention of the deceased, or any show of sympathy. Lack of appetite, strange feelings of unreality, and sometimes a feeling of fear of insanity occur. Feelings of guilt, a strong preoccupation with images of the deceased, to the point of pseudo-hallucinations, even denial of the death, are not rare. There can be coldness, anger, irritability, and accusations of neglect toward the caretakers of the deceased. One woman, who had shown no particular affection toward her mother who died in a nursing home, shouted "murderers" at the attending physician when he informed her of her mother's death, which had been expected for a long time.

This illustrates another reaction common in acute grief, namely a change in the normal patterns of conduct, as this woman had not demonstrated such unreasonable behavior in the past. She apparently was projecting her own guilt on others, the care-givers of her mother.

The duration of the normal *acute* grief reaction, that is, recovery from this acute stage, when the survivor has an opportunity to talk it out and receives moral support, has been described as about four to six weeks (Lindemann 1944).

Lindemann (1944) also lists symptoms that appeared "morbid," but that responded to intervention. A delay in reaction to the news of the death may be brief, but may, through the use of denial, be prolonged if the survivor is not in a position to react to it or is unable to tolerate the reality of the loss. Some of these delays can go on for years, and a reaction may surface at a later time if stimulated by some current reminder. For example, a man commits suicide on the anniversary of his mother's suicide.

There are also some distorted reactions that require special attention, such as overactivity without a sense of loss. Other reactions include the development of symptoms belonging to the deceased, or a sudden outbreak of a severe psychosomatic reaction, such as a bleeding peptic ulcer. One sometimes sees social isolation, the development of suspicions of a paranoid nature about the physicians, signs of suppressed hostility, or a loss of normal patterns of activity. For example, a normally conservative widow becomes daring in her investments or treats her friends in such a way as to antagonize them. Finally, there are occasionally persons who develop a clear-cut agitated depression.

There are special situations at the time of acute grief that are a cause for concern. One of these is when the survivor has a history of depressive reactions or outright depressive illness. Another is when the survivor is a mother who has lost her young child. Another situation for concern is one in which the survivor was in an extremely dependent relationship with the deceased, whether affectionate or not, or where the death causes a particularly drastic change in the survivor's life.

Mourning and Bereavement

Although we know that after such a loss the acute state of mourning will subside, we also know we shall remain inconsolable and will never find a substitute. No matter what may fill the gap, even if it be filled completely, it nevertheless remains something else. And actually this is how it should be. It is the one way of perpetuating that love which we do not want to relinquish. [Freud 1960, p. 386]

Bowlby (1961b) described the stages of grief that have become the basis for the most current view of the process of mourning, namely, the stages of shock, suffering, and recovery.

Of course it must be understood that these stages overlap and the transition from one to the other is not even, but has a back-and-forth movement. For example, as indicated by Freud's letter, even after recovery, the sense of loss can be very great. Life is never really entirely the same.

It is in the later two stages that the work of the psychotherapist really begins and is something more than first aid, which it often is in the first, the acute stage, the stage of shock. A most important issue at all stages is differentiating mourning from depression, although at the outset it should be stated that the two affective states have a great deal in common, as described by Freud in the paper, "Mourning and Melancholia" (1917). Table 10–1 shows some of the similarities and differences between depression and mourning.

Grief Work

The process of mourning requires work on the part of the bereaved in order for the stage of suffering to proceed to recovery. This work includes the pain of acknowledgment of the loss and, in time, facing the feelings of loss, anger, sorrow, fear, and guilt, as well as recollection of the good things that allow one to hang on to the memory of the deceased. In depressions, a similar process takes place as one learns to face the griefs and losses of life and learns how to mourn. The psychotherapist can help here, because after the acute stage, patients learn that the world is not particularly interested in hearing about their troubles, while at the same time they still need someone to talk to who won't tell them to "stop grieving and face life," which they are already trying to do. In more troubled persons, such as those vulnerable to depression, medication may be necessary, as well as paramedical methods of group therapy, occupational therapy, and family support services.

Almost every religious and social agency in western countries now has support groups run by professionals for the benefit of those who are grieving. Society has become very much interested in death and mourning, and a great deal of literature is available,

Table 10-1
Comparison Between Similarities and Differences of Depression and Mourning

Symptom	Depression	Mourning
Sadness, sorrow, pain	Yes	Yes
Insomnia	Yes	Yes
Crying	Yes	Yes
Anhedonia	Yes	Yes
Inconsolable early on	Yes	Yes
Anxiety	Yes	Yes
Somatic symptoms	Yes	At first
Weight loss	Yes, often	No
Hypochondriacal ideas	Yes	Occasionally
Psychomotor retardation	Yes	No
Anorexia	Constant	Early only
Guilt, early	Usual	Sometimes
Guilt, late	Unresolved	Resolved
Anger	Against oneself	Against the world
Inconsolable	Constant	Eventually recovers
Family history of depression	Yes	No
Object of mourning	For an abstraction or for the past	For a loved one
Chief preoccupation	Guilt, failure	Loss
Loss	May be fantasized	Real

technical, lay, and self-help. A reading list is given at the end of this chapter.

Clinical Applications

Grief differs from depression in that it is a necessary process of adjusting to the loss of a loved one and, as such, must be experienced in some degree in order to go on with life. Symptoms may be very much like depression except there is less guilt and less persistent loss of function. Also, in grief the loss is real, but in depression it is often fantasied. If there is much guilt or if the grieving extends beyond a normal period of mourning, then a depression has occurred which must be treated. There can be grief for other losses, too, as well as from a death. Grief requires a process of mourning which is a painful experience that sometimes overtly resembles depression. Unlike the situation with depression, however, it is not generally wise to interfere with the work of mourning which must be done to detach the bereaved from the lost object.

There are those who are unable to grieve because they are not able to express emotions, or even to experience them consciously and work them through. Often one sees this problem among those who tend to become depressed and withdrawn. Also, if there is a loss, but it is not expressed and worked through, it may leave a wound or may be displaced and become expressed in some other less healthy way than with grief. For example, anger, guilt, and physical complaints are areas to which unexpressed grief may be displaced.

Losses are hard for children to work through and recover from because they do not have the language to express their feelings. Often children may seem to be indifferent when losses occur, such as a move to a new home, loss of friends and security, sickness of a parent, or even death. At such times, with such children, you may be sure that a displacement will occur. Schoolwork suddenly suffers, anger or temper tantrums supervene, or there is moodiness or other symptoms. Even asocial or antisocial behavior in a child can result from an inability to mourn or a need for comfort and understanding. The "bad" child can be a misunderstood child.

In the early stages of grief and the mourning process, loneliness may be an important indication to sufferers that they must be with someone to compensate for the loss. Another important aspect of loneliness is that it has a normal function for the personality in respect to a person's relationship to love objects. It helps people know the value of those from whom they feel isolated and separated, and they come to see themselves as separate persons. The experiences of all these normal depressive signal affects—sadness, loneliness, nostalgia, boredom—all have an impact on the individual and induce reactions which may go two directions, either toward correcting the loss of the unpleasant affect or toward withdrawal and retreat.

Unresolved Grief

There is considerable evidence that unresolved grief, that is, failure to work through a serious loss, can have a profound effect on the personality, especially of growing children, but also adults. This unresolved feeling can be shown to influence future behavior in serious ways, and with serious consequences, for example, in anniversary reactions such as holiday depressions. An example given earlier is pertinent here, which is of a man who committed suicide on the anniversary of his mother's suicide.

Perhaps the most important area for the psychotherapist for understanding and treating mourning is not in the treatment of those who have just lost a loved one through death, but rather in the treatment of depressed and depression-prone patients whose griefs are unconscious, are defended against, or have influenced personality and behaviors in such a way as to interfere with the quality of life. In his book *Depressive States and Their Treatment*, Volkan (1985) has assembled a group of very pertinent papers on the importance and the vicissitudes of mourning in depressive states, written by therapists who have studied the dynamics of mourning and depression according to the nature of the experience at different stages of life—childhood, adolescence, adult life, and old age.

An example of unresolved grief is of a 40-year-old man who experienced excessive grief at the thought of terminating his analysis and said that it reminded him of the loss of both of his parents, for whom he had never grieved for different reasons: In the case of his father, it was because he had felt that his father was aloof, though very kind, and he had never been able to come to terms with him and establish their relationship satisfactorily. In the case of his mother, it was because she became permanently psychotic when he was 14, and he went back to live with his divorced father, hardly seeing his mother again and never grieving for her. The effect of this failure to grieve had been that he had devoted himself faithfully to bosses who had taken advantage of his loyalty and had never been able to extricate himself from these relationships because he needed to have the bosses as substitute fathers. He also had put up with his wife's alcoholism and delinquencies because he needed her as a mother.

SEPARATION AND NOSTALGIA

The experience of nostalgia borders on the normal, but can become pathological. It resembles grief in that a loss is involved. The classical example is of college students away from home for the first time, facing the world alone, missing all they hold dear, and perhaps lacking the self-confidence to cope with the challenge. They are too ashamed of their feelings to complain and consequently never unburden themselves. Some of these cases may get worse and progress into a silent depression, with inability to function and difficulty in studying or making friends. The length of the separation has particular importance. People on long trips, such as salespeople away from home on prolonged business, may have the same depressive reaction as people in prison, who are separated from home for long periods. Any of these separations can lead to suicide.

Werman (1977), writing of normal and pathological nostalgia, describes the relationship of nostalgia and homesickness to the painful aspects of depression. The modern meaning of nostalgia has separated it somewhat from its former synonym, homesickness. Nostalgia, Werman says, is now defined as it is in Webster's New World Dictionary of 1966 as "a longing for something far away or long ago" (Werman 1977, p. 388). Sometimes it is difficult to distinguish nostalgia from homesickness.

A certain amount of nostalgia can be considered to be normal wherein there is a healthy surrender to a homing tendency to return to the past, to childhood, to sleep, and to the unconscious. This conception of Werner's agrees with the observation that one cannot go through life without experiencing a normal nostalgia, the pain of the loss of the past; it is in this sense that nostalgia can be the symptom of a normal existential depression. Even to the extent that sometimes the past "massively" intrudes into the present uninvited and sometimes unwanted, even to this extent it can be a normal experience.

Werman also quotes Freud, "Actually, we can never give anything up; we can only exchange one thing for another" (p. 393). What appears to be a renunciation is really the formation of a substitute or a surrogate.

Kleiner (1970) points out that nostalgia can be a serious symptom. It can prevent the nostalgic person from a normal relinquishing of infantile objects. In the case he reports, the patient showed spontaneous return of nostalgic early memories which kept her from being able to mourn the loss of the past. Through analysis of this problem she was able to go to a more satisfactory relationship with the present.

Some depressives, by contrast, tend to be preoccupied or even obsessed with the past—events, relationships, places, and failures—usually with a painful feeling. Sometimes past events dominate their thinking in a very painful way as something never mastered and left unsatisfied. One question for the psychotherapist is whether to encourage this and how to use it in the therapy.

Compare normal ways of handling lost objects, such as images from the past, with the way depressives handle such things. A normal way is through nostalgia, which, unless it becomes severe homesickness, can be pleasant. There is good evidence that depressed people have suffered more than the usual amount of massive traumata—death of parents, major moves, and losses. The remembrance of things past in such cases is too painful.

RETURN OF THE REPRESSED IN MELANCHOLIA

Here is an example of how different is this kind of bittersweet, sometimes very pleasant, nostalgia from the pathological return of memories in the seriously depressed person. An example is a woman in her sixties who is in the early stages of a psychotic depression, a severe melancholia, and at the time was in the hospital. She kept thinking of the hallway in her father's home of years ago. She tried to get it out of her mind because it came totally uninvited and forced itself on her; she tried to think of the hallway of her own home, to push the other memory out of her mind. When asked for associations on the hallway of her father's home, she immediately said, "His casket lying there after his death." She had been an only child, a great favorite of her father's, and had a poor relationship with her mother, who had recurrent depressions and was seldom available. His death was a severe blow because now she was alone with her unloving mother. Thus, in the beginning of her melancholia she was reviewing a traumatic experience of her youth: the loss of her father, the most painful thing in her life. The return of the memory signified an overwhelming loss to which she had never adjusted.

BOREDOM AND APATHY

Boredom and apathy are normal experiences, but can represent depression. Some depressed people complain of boredom. The question, "Is this all there is to life?" should alert the therapist to a depressed state of mind.

Boredom can be more than a casual state of temporary indifference, as it has come colloquially to mean. Rather, in its older sense of tedium, ennui, weariness, it is used in both colloquial speech and in traditional grammar. It can progress to mean a lowering of spirits and even to a melancholy mood. The feeling apparently results in a withdrawal of emotional importance from what is going on around, so that one becomes indifferent to what is going on. Cathexis (emotional charge) is withdrawn into the self, and what is being experienced outside one's own self ceases to be of interest (Greenson 1953).

Surprisingly, one also comes across this boredom in persons who have had severe depression and unfortunately are vulnerable to becoming depressed again.

A very attractive, intelligent woman, in her fifties, in sound health, cheerfuly announces that she is bored, but to her this means, "I'm just marking time until death. My life is over." These remarks were made after she had recovered from her fourth suicidal depression in as many years. It represented her feelings in a relatively well period; one can only account for the cheerfulness and good spirits with which the statement was made by a decathexis of the idea of death under the influence of a splitting mechanism.

As we inquire further, we find that she has always been appalled at the idea of growing old and losing her feminine charms. She is a very attractive woman in her 50s, but recently her husband developed a cardiac arrhythmia and became suddenly impotent, so that the couple's love life has been almost completely lacking in sexual gratification, whereas prior to her husband's illness they enjoyed a very satisfying sex life. For her, "Life is finished" means, "I've lost my sexual attractiveness."

It becomes obvious that there has been a serious loss for her, not only the loss of gratification and sexual release, but the loss of self-esteem from feeling less loved by her husband and the loss of power to attract him. She is forced to think about the changes of age suddenly, rather than gracefully and slowly. The loss was more important for her than for others because of the high value she always put on her own sexual attractiveness. She feels angry and then becomes enormously guilty; all the ingredients for a profound depression are there. No wonder, then, with this mixture of feelings, that she loses hope and sometimes gets to the end of her rope and cannot restrain herself from the impulse to suicide. Her description of this mood as "boredom" brings out how intense the suffering of boredom can become.

Boredom has a function in her mental economy, namely, to act as a defense against temptation to give in to her impulses. As long as she can feel bored and empty she is not aware of the inner pressure to rebel, sexual frustrations, or feelings of anger. When the boredom fails and she becomes aware of her feelings, her solution is to destroy herself by suicide. Her boredom had the function of warding off or covering up drives and feelings. Past history revealed also that she missed her long-deceased father, who meant so much to her and was a friend.

AFFECTS RESULTING FROM LOSS OF DEFENSES

A number of affective states may follow losses, even in the normal person. Some become nostalgic or may develop homesickness for the lost place, home, or a loved one. Then sorrow and misery and grief may set in, to the point of despair; a chronic state of despondency may occur. Naturally the sufferer would like to overcome this situation and emerge victorious, but may feel helpless to solve the predicament. Thus, we have to deal with the concept of *helplessness*. If it looks as though it were impossible to get out of the predicament, they may develop a feeling of *hopelessness*.

One effect of this feeling of hopelessness is that individuals may withdraw from the situation and nurse their grievances; they may become moody and hurt, hostile, or irritable; they may develop a prolonged pessimism, meaning that they think nothing can be done about their predicament; they feel powerless.

Here, "predicament" means that the situation which precipitates this sequence of events is not always some loss or death or loss of a job or some ideal. It may, instead, be that individuals find themselves in some kind of complex predicament from which they see no escape, even if they attempt to solve the problem in some way and to relieve the distress.

Another common symptom in connection with this kind of experience of loss is *disillusionment*. Usually, disillusionment means what the word literally says, the loss of illusion, which is a loss of a dream or fantasy of oneself or of the world. An example is given in a book review of T. H. White's *America in Search of Itself: The Making of the President, 1965–1980*. Referring to the author, the reviewer wrote: "In recent years, however, his spirits have hit bottom, and now, feeling frustrated and inadequate to the task, he declares that this book will be 'my last story of an election' " (Sherrill 1982, p. 1).

The article goes on, "But he is wise to quit. He is so thoroughly depressed that he can no longer be trusted to see things clearly, and he knows it. *America in Search of Itself* . . . is an extraordinary expression of disenchantment" (p. 1).

There are some other interesting clinical applications of the phenomenon of helplessness as it has been observed in depressed persons. For one, a whole school of thought has arisen of those who regard depression as an example of "learned helplessness," with the implication that it can be unlearned. This concept does indeed apply to that relatively small group of persons who are chronically depressed as a character trait, or who have recovered from a depressive illness but are left with the chronic symptom of a helpless outlook on life. It does not apply to those who are acutely ill with a depressive illness, in which the sufferer is genuinely unable to function and requires help to be rescued from this state.

LONELINESS

Like boredom, loneliness is a complex affect; it is a feeling that has content, that is to say, there are ideas, some of them unconscious, concurrent with the surface mood of loneliness. The environmental situations that bring about loneliness are often obvious. Everyone has experienced loneliness as a result of absence of the persons who are important, the love objects. For example, in homesickness, which has already been discussed, there is often painful loneliness. Loneliness is such an intense feature of the mourning reaction that it perhaps is not a strong enough term for the kind of loneliness that is present during acute grief.

There is a normal function to loneliness, in that it alerts one to the value of those from whom one feels isolated and separated. In college students away from home for the first time, loneliness is often the motivation for making new relationships and finding new sources of satisfaction to replace those left behind.

BIOLOGICAL FUNCTIONS OF AFFECTS

Unhappiness, like other painful experiences, may be a signal that individuals have to observe in order to be alerted to the presence of something that should be dealt with. Unhappiness and sadness certainly can be viewed as biological signal mechanisms in this context.

Schmale and Engel (1975) call this the "conservation-withdrawal state." They speak of the relationship of depression to human existence, that is to say, how depression and depression-like moods fit in with our need to adapt not only to our environment, but to our inner needs. Schmale and Engel go on to say, "The hallmark of the conservation–withdrawal state is relative immobility, quiescence, and unresponsiveness to external environment input" (p. 183). This is a state of disengagement and inactivity. It has a defensive purpose in that it allows for repair, but it can also be a response to hopelessness, fatigue, and helplessness. To withdraw from something because it is beyond the organism's ability to cope with it is one of the basic human reactions. It allows for repair, such as one gets in sleep, and perhaps sleep is one of the primitive withdrawal reactions which are necessary for the maintenance of biological stability. It is a primitive defense reaction.

The organism has limits. We all should learn to withdraw from stimuli and repair ourselves; there are limits to what can be tolerated in the way of unusual stimuli. There is some kind of depletion of stores or reserves of energy-giving materials in the body which requires a certain length of time to reestablish. The psychotherapist can often help patients to recognize this depletion and get some needed rest and relief.

SIGNS OF WITHDRAWAL, ALIENATION, OR RETREAT

Moodiness and sullenness are descriptive terms and do not give a clear indication of what the person experiencing them feels. They are terms that might be used by a mother in describing a hurt or angry child, and, to be sure, the underlying meaning of these to the acute observer is that sullenness generally means anger and moodiness generally means a period of *withdrawal* and *unresponsiveness* to the contact with other people. Such a preoccupied person, unable to handle his or her feelings or acknowledge them, may well be in the early stages of depression.

LOSS OF SELF-ESTEEM AND THE SELF-IMAGE

The loss of self-esteem associated with depression goes beyond the normal amount of pain at having failed in some endeavor; judging by the apparent realities, it is an overreaction. In order to understand this reaction one has to examine the origins of self-esteem. This simple popular concept of self-confidence and the loss of self-confidence is not enough to explain the sweeping denigration of the self which is possible in depression-prone people. For example, a 45-year-old man, speaking of his deceased father, said, "He was a good man. I'm not fit to polish his shoes." Soon after this the man was found dead by suicide. This is much more than a lack of self-confidence; this is a complete and unrealistic denigration to himself. An overwhelming and unjustified sense of unworthiness, of worthlessness, a sweeping condemnation of himself led him to destroy his own life. This is not normal depression; it is delusion—psychotic depressive illness. At the time of his suicide this man was coming out of a deep depression; what was merely a low self-esteem during his well period became a delusional fixed idea during his illness. One important difference between normal depression and the illness depression is a delusional fixation on guilt, self-blame, self-castigation, and unworthiness. It is indeed illness when such an idea dominates one's thinking. Sometimes psychotic ideas persist after recovery.

In contrast to this sickness with its total immersion of the personality, the normal depressive states and affects and the early states of depression that have been discussed here all involve only a portion of the personality and do not overwhelm or completely interfere with the ability to test reality at this stage. The person involved can still say that he has some distance from his feelings, some objectivity. Normal sadness, unhappiness, and even severer forms such as despair and hopelessness may be transitory states that anyone could experience in a reaction to some kind of loss. Their transitory nature, the recovery by resting a reasonable length of time, all differentiate these states from a true depression. It should be added that the loss and separation from a love object are the principal sources not only of these states but of depressions themselves. Another important difference is the ready improvement when the loss is restored. The genuine depressive does not respond so readily when the stress in the environment is corrected, because the intrapsychic stress continues to operate and an intrapsychic loss continues to exist.

DEPRESSIVE EQUIVALENTS: THE INABILITY TO PERCEIVE AFFECTS

Some persons with depressive character and some who eventually suffer a depressive breakdown share with obsessive and compulsive individuals a remarkable inability to experience conscious affects, a condition that Sifneos (1972) has called "alexithymia." This characteristic is also present in persons who develop psychosomatic symptoms (Nemiah 1978) in which a physical symptom comes in place of a feeling. For example, instead of becoming angry, the alexithymic person has an elevation of blood pressure or a headache. In depression-prone persons, when a situation arises in which one would expect anger, or at least some self assertion, the depression-prone person might experience fatigue or apathy, that is, a lack of feeling.

It is to be expected that if a person is unable to experience affects, the emotions associated with depression may also be experienced in a repressed or inhibited way. This turns out to be true in quite a number of cases and in a variety of ways. People who cannot experience sadness or grief or longing, nor deal with the emotion in a healthy and rational way, tend to have symptoms rather than affects and cannot consciously tell why they do not feel well.

Persons with this inability to perceive their own affects tend to become depressed without knowing why or they may defend themselves against painful affects by a variety of defenses and maneuvers, creating a clinical picture of something entirely different from depression. These disguises have been called "depressive equivalents," and they are many and varied. In a volume entitled *Masked Depression*, Lesse (1974) has collected a group of highly informative essays by a number of authors on the general subject of the clinical and theoretical basis of the concept of depressive equivalents. Among the dozens of common symptoms named in that volume, the principal and most common are hypochondriasis; acting out (especially in adolescents and children); drug addiction and alcoholism; obesity; anorexia nervosa; delinquency; and psychosomatic symptoms such as chronic pain; and, not surprisingly, accidents. Each period of life has its own age-related methods of warding off depression and other painful affects.

The use of alcohol to ward off depression is a well-known method. Its importance can be well substantiated; for example a much higher percentage of alcoholics who give up drinking develop serious, disabling depressions than a comparable group recovering from any other illness.

Somatization is also commonly used as a mechanism of defense against anxiety and depressive moods. The patient with atypical pain, such as atypical facial pain, pelvic pain, or strange somatic sensations which seem undiagnosable, may be quite depressed and not know it. If one takes away the pain, the depression may become manifest. Physicians have to be mindful of this because it needs special handling. One doesn't say to the patient, "There is nothing wrong with you," and close the conversation. One explains that emotions such as depression or anxiety can cause physical symptoms and that the next step is a consultation with a psychiatrist. In the same spirit, patients have to be willing to accept that something may be going on in their lives that they do not fully understand, that it is in their best interest to look into it with professional help, and that a psychiatrist or psychotherapist can help them do that.

SUMMARY

There are certain prevailing dysphoric emotional states that are depressive equivalents or predepressive states; they bring suffering and require attention. They may be minor or, on the contrary, may disguise and yet indicate the presence of an underlying serious depression. The common denominator of these affective states is a sense of loss, and, indeed, they often occur after a serious personal or threatened loss. Grief, nostalgia, frustration, hopelessness, despair, helplessness, and defeat are states of mind that have to be considered. When these moods come up in the course of therapy, they show a need to work through the underlying cause. For the practicing psychotherapist, dysphoric moods serve as markers for both the trait of depression-proneness and the state of depression.

11

SUICIDE AND THE MOOD DISORDERS

The psychotherapist who treats persons with affective disorders sees a substantial number with suicidal potential, because there is a close relationship of suicide with depression of all kinds, even in seemingly mild cases. The therapist's job is complex; it starts with the evaluation of the danger, both immediate and long-range, and then demands taking steps for prevention when needed. In addition, one must use one's awareness of the nature of the suicidal ideation to help patients understand themselves and get at the underlying cause.

EPIDEMIOLOGY

Of *completed* suicides, over 90 percent suffer from a psychiatric disorder, of which depression is by far the most common, accounting for about 50–75 percent of the cases. The remainder can be ascribed to alcohol or drug abuse, personality disorders, a few with schizophrenia, and a small number to physical disease such as delirium. In completed suicides, men outnumber women three to one, and the rate of those over 40 years of age is considerably higher than the rate for those under 40.

About 15 percent of persons with diagnosed depressions ultimately commit suicide, about one out of every six, a very high mortality and preventable in most cases.

Attempted suicides outnumber completed suicides by eight-fold, but carry a risk of future completed attempts about 25–30 times the risk in the general population, so that one must take very seriously a failed attempt. Women outnumber men when only attempted suicide is considered, and those under 40 years of age are more evenly represented in this population. Diagnoses of those attempting suicide include a higher percentage of personality disorders, life situation reactions, and drug and alcohol abusers, but depression still ranks highest among causes in the group. As to age and sex distribution, women make more suicidal attempts than men in the younger white adult group, but men, especially in the older decades of life, are more likely to complete the attempt. Another important fact is that in the three decades after 1950 the death rate of young adult and late adolescent males, both white and black, has tripled. If the rate from accidents and homicides in this age group is added, the figures become even more devastating, and one would certainly have a right to consider many of these deaths as suicidal, because often a disregard for one's own life caused the accident.

Suicide is the ninth cause of death among all causes in the United States. It is the second most common on college campuses, the first being accidents, of which a goodly number could be ascribed to disregard of one's own life. Among medical students, suicide is the most common cause of death, and it is the third highest cause among those still in their teens.

AGE-RELATED CONSIDERATIONS

The time of life of the person at risk of suicide influences both the predisposing and the precipitating factors which have to be considered in diagnosis and in planning treatment and prevention. Youth has its special, poignant concerns as does mid-life; old age with its problems of decline and loss can be painful beyond endurance.

Farberow and Shneidman (1983) have made some important observations:

Younger males tend to have more highly charged motives of the wish to die; they are more angry, but also more depressed and guilt-ridden than the older group. Older males tend to have more chronic feelings of discouragement, illness, fatigue, and exhaustion. The middle-aged group shows gradually lessening guilt and self-blame.

With women the trends are similar. The active, more violent wish to kill or to be killed predominates over the wish to die by more than two to one in the younger women, whereas in the older women the pattern is dramatically reversed, by more than three to one.

Older women, like older men, tend to show more discouragement, despair, feelings of being a burden, and depressed feelings about pain and illness. Age 60 seems to be the age at which pain and discouragement increase dramatically.

Implications for Treatment and Management

In the younger group, once the emergency is passed, attention should be directed toward working out and gaining insight into the intense feelings involved in the interpersonal relationships through the use of specific psychotherapy, as well as making changes in the environment.

In the older age group, there is a greater need to bring about the relief of chronic stresses and sources of pain through environmental changes, treatment of illnesses, and provision of supports to increase morale and diminish the feelings of uselessness.

These generalizations only provide a background. Each individual patient has a special situation that must be treated on its own merits. There are many older persons who can profit by insight therapy and need this kind of help with their interpersonal relations and, sometimes, with characterological symptoms.

RISK FACTORS

The most common risk factors, statistically are:

1. Diagnosis of depression.
2. History of previous attempts.

3. History of suicide in immediate family.
4. Alcohol or drug abuse.
5. Over 40 years of age, single or widowed, white male.
6. Young adult male alone or away from home.
7. Presence of a physical illness.
8. Recent separation, loss, or illness.
9. Lack of emotionally supportive personal relationships or groups.

Precautions

Depressed persons can be so expert at concealing their feelings that they may be "at the end of their rope" without anyone being aware that they are overwhelmed. Unusual silence in persons who are having a hard time just keeping up their daily activities may conceal the fact that they are brooding about something and are on the verge of suicide. At the extreme opposite pole there are those who talk a great deal, not convincingly but perhaps threateningly, of suicide. In this case one is tempted to scold them and not think they mean it. But one should not be misled; the person can appear not to mean a word of it, and yet may indeed end up killing himself or herself.

The psychotically depressed, that is, persons in advanced depressions, especially those who show delusions of guilt and also are slowed down, are *always* in danger of suicide. When there is danger, you do, of course, discuss it with the sufferer, who may be greatly relieved to be in the hospital where the fear of self-destruction is less intense.

If you decide that the danger is not so great and that ambulatory treatment is safe, at least be sure you have discussed it with the patient and family, so that they know that the family and the patient can call you any time, day or night, if the impulse is too threatening or the suffering unbearable.

If you are notified that the patient has indeed taken an overdose, speedy action is essential to get him or her to a hospital where his or her stomach can be washed out and supportive treatment given. In this day of intensive care units in hospitals, any patient who is still breathing upon admission should survive.

A time to be especially careful is the time during treatment at which psychotic or slowed-down patients begin to become active; they still have depressive ideas, but now have the energy to carry them out. Another time for this group is during the first two years after seeming recovery, when depressive ideation may persist.

There are other symptomatic considerations one must be aware of. These apply not only in full-blown depressive disorders but are indications of someone at risk in general.

Evaluating the Risk

Suicidal thoughts occur frequently in the general population, possibly over 50 percent of the people in one study admitted to having had the thought at least cross their minds. Therefore, the depressed group whom the psychotherapist sees will contain many to whom the thought of suicide has occurred, making it obviously important to find out who is actually in danger. The statistically important risk factors listed above give some background, but applying statistics to the individual is hazardous. The situation is more complex, because therapists have to evaluate this risk not only in those who speak of suicide but also in those who they suspect are suicidal, but who do not mention it—a sizable group.

Two steps are advised: taking a history and evaluating the mental status.

In taking a history, note previous attempts, history of depression, suicide in the family, depression in the family, and recent losses and traumas. Evaluating the mental status can be done in an informal way, but one should end up by making a diagnosis. The presence of major depressive symptoms increases the risk considerably, especially if psychosis is present, with its delusions of guilt, with psychomotor retardation, and inability to function. If depression is present, then one must surely question the patient about death wishes, hopelessness, and suicidal thoughts. This can be done in a very tactful and appropriate way. The following ideas must be investigated:

First, is the idea present at all? Ask such questions as, "Have you had morbid (or painful) thoughts? " or "Have you felt that life isn't worthwhile? " or even, "Have you been troubled by thoughts of suicide, or of harming yourself?" Each therapist will work out his or her own language, and then the nature of the idea (i.e., is it a fear, a wish or desire, or a passing thought?). How strong is it? Is it an overwhelming desire, or not a desire, and how frequent? Is there a real wish for death or does the person want to live?

What are the defenses against the idea, the resistances, the deterrents (e.g., religion, family, future)? One man whose lover had died was very depressed and thought continually of suicide, but said that he was not going to kill himself because it would leave his business in such a mess. That means less immediate danger, but sounds an ominous note for the future.

Is there a plan, and by what method? All this information is used to evaluate the danger.

Special Situations

The Despairing and Overwhelmed Person

There exists the experience of feeling overwhelmed that goes beyond the normal in both degree and persistence. It is so painful that all one wants is relief. The signs of giving up may be an obvious emotional exhaustion, a sense of defeat and desperation, or simply unresponsiveness and apathy. Such persons are suicidal risks. Fawcett and colleagues (1987) report data from a group followed for four years differentiating twenty-five patients who committed suicide from 929 patients who did not. Half of the suicides occurred within one year of the patient's entry into the study. The most important features differentiating the suicide group were hopelessness, loss of pleasure or interest, and mood cycling. Diagnostic subcategories, suicidal ideation at the entry into the study, suicide attempts, and severity of the attempts could not be differentiated.

The Exhausted Person

A constellation of fatigue, defeat, guilt, depression, or melancholy can occur in a variety of people, with or without full-blown depressive disorders. It can occur in relatively well persons who are overwhelmed by some catastrophe, some experience. By contrast, it can occur in people who are very mentally ill, for example, persons with schizophrenia, or who are at an early stage of a major psychotic depression. When exhaustion occurs with despair, even though it may not be the dominating presence, it should be treated with respect, because this complex can lead to self-destruction or, at best, to loss of effectiveness and bad decisions.

The Angry Person

Sometimes ill-concealed or openly experienced anger after a great loss, real, fantasied, or symbolic, is the only clue to an oncoming impulsive act. A recent death, a divorce or separation, an impending move, jealousy, loss of job, or the like, may precede and stimulate the anger.

The Guilty Person

The guilt of the depressed person is unrealistic. First, it is exaggerated beyond a degree appropriate to the supposed transgressions. In fact, it can be so extreme as to be delusional. For example, the person may feel responsible for all the ills of the world. Second, unlike genuine shame, patients advertise and announce, indeed insist, that they are bad persons. They neither make nor look for excuses.

Guilt may be masked behind the plausible self-blame one expects from those who are very conscientious, but you know they are sick by the insistence and persistence of the attitude. After all, really bad people do not go around filling the air with mea culpas; nor do the really bad ones threaten or commit suicide. Excessive guilt is a definite warning that the danger of suicide exists.

The anxiety and pain of the guilty person, under the influence of fantasies or delusions of sins or wrong-doings, is often a potent factor in the motivation for suicide. This guilt may be expressed in a direct fashion, such as "I'm no good," or "The world would be better off without me," or "I'm a burden to my family," or "I'm a sinner." It may also be concealed and not expressed, so that one may have to ask patients about their ideas toward themselves. This must be done tactfully in order not to suggest that you think they should be guilty, by making a general statement such as, "Depressed people sometimes seem to blame themselves unnecessarily. Do you tend to blame yourself a good deal?"

Those with Recurrent Depressions

Persons formerly hospitalized for depressive psychosis are twenty-five times more likely to commit suicide than the general population. Recent hospitalization increases risk; for example, in one study 66 percent of all suicides in formerly hospitalized patients took place within nine months of discharge, and in another study 74 percent took place within a year.

Those with a History of Suicide in the Immediate Family

If a mother or a father has committed suicide, there is an increased risk. This influence is especially important because it operates at the level of identification and is unconscious. There is likely to be no discussion of the force impelling the victim toward self-destruction, and denial may cover up the danger, as well. By uncovering the risk under appropriate psychological conditions, we temporarily increase it. Therefore, patients in intensive therapy should be watched. The long-term effect of working through the complex should be to relieve it, but, even so, this is a powerful repetitive tendency and may return into the patient's life despite therapy. Anniversaries of suicides are important periods of risk.

The Medically Ill Person, Especially the Delirious Person

Medical illness, which lowers the strength of normal controls and is accompanied by severe anxiety and possible delusions, can allow desperate impulses to take over. The most common cause of suicide in general hospitals is *delirium*, a physiological reaction with multiple causes, including postoperative changes in fluid balance, fever, toxic states of all kinds including alcohol (delirium tremens) and drugs (drug delirium), head injury, and primary cerebral disease, such as encephalitis or brain tumor.

Delirious persons should be constantly watched to guard against impulsive acts, including suicide, which should be completely preventable in this group.

Persons Jailed for Criminal Acts

Jails are notoriously fertile breeding grounds for suicide. People often commit crimes because they are not mentally well, or because they are desperate, so that the prison population has a proportion of persons who are vulnerable to suicidal acts. There also are persons who tend to be impulsive, to act out, and to have poor controls generally over instinctual drives; one could well expect impulsive suicidal acts from this group in jail or prison. The convicted criminal is known in prison as a "loser," and the sense of loss and defeat is at times overwhelming.

In an article on police aspects of suicide, Litman (1983b) gives several circumstances that should alert the police to the danger of suicide: when a "respectable" citizen is arrested for something he is ashamed of; when the prisoner is known to have suicidal ideas or has made an attempt and is still depressed; when the prisoner is known to have or have had a mental illness and has talked of suicide; when the prisoner has suffered a recent rejection by a spouse or sweetheart. These cases should all be seen by a specialist, either a psychiatrist, psychologist, or social worker, or another specialist in suicide.

The police are often called to see or rescue someone who is threatening suicide with a gun or by jumping from a building. Heroics usually are not productive, and the best course to take is one of patience; communicate with the suffer and try to reason with him or her.

Once the person is confined, especially if for a long term,

there are the powerful forces of separation, loneliness, loss, and sexual frustration to contend with. Here, preventive measures for the vulnerable personality can be employed—psychotherapy for example. Education of personnel is vital, as is the availability of professionals who can perform diagnostic and treatment services.

Persons Referred for Consultation and Patients in Therapy

There are three critical periods involving the therapist directly: (1) immediately after referral, before the initial contact, (2) after consultation, and (3) during the course of therapy.

By the time patients are referred to therapists for consultation, their feelings may well have become so intense that the danger of suicide is critical, and, indeed, actual suicides have occurred during the period of waiting for the appointment or the consultation. For that reason, it is vital that consultants see patients right away, even if the patient, referring physician or agency, and family minimize the danger. It is the job of the consultant—not of the referring person—to make this evaluation.

Another period of great risk is after contact with the consultant, when the patient has brought out the problems and the feelings of self-destruction and may actually be more overwhelmed than earlier, and has not yet formed a relationship of trust with the therapist. This is a time to be especially careful to protect the patient from his or her own impulses, to consider getting the cooperation of the family, and to hospitalize the patient if there is risk. Later on in therapy, after a trusting relationship is established, the therapist is in a better position to take some risk with certain patients.

Another period of intensified risk is during long-term intensive therapy when a negative transference occurs. Persons with affective disorders tend to have strongly ambivalent relationships; it is not to be expected that the therapist will be spared such a reaction. One of the special risks of intensive therapy with this group is that their transferences may take the form of a recurrence of the illness, and one must evaluate the tolerance of individual patients, how much they can bear in the way of therapy, and when they need relief. Here again medication, getting a consultation, involving the family, and hospitalization should be considered.

PSYCHOLOGY AND MOTIVATION

Pain and Suffering

In describing the specific symptoms of depression — sadness, guilt, boredom, disillusionment, insomnia, and so forth — one can make the fatal error of overlooking a most important symptom, which is the degree of human pain felt in depression. According to sufferers from the illness, words do not convey the severity of a mental anguish severe enough to make somebody suicidal. While it is true that in many people with depression the idea of suicide originates in low self-esteem in ambivalence toward love objects, and in the inability to express aggression in a healthy way, and while it is also true that suicide often represents a murderous, destructive impulse toward someone else turned upon oneself, nevertheless the act itself is often brought about by the *degree* of suffering, from which the sufferer cannot see any relief. The intensity of feeling becomes so great that it makes the sufferer act on his or her ideas, which otherwise might not be carried out.

Those who say that the only time they get any relief is when they go to sleep, and that they cannot really sleep very well, are in danger. When they get up in the morning and hate to face the day because there will be no moment when they do not have a feeling of misery, then we know that we are dealing with serious depression. How does somebody who has never felt this way picture what it must be like? It is very difficult to identify with somebody who has that kind of suffering, because it is so far outside one's healthy experience. How can one identify the feeling that turning to work, to recreation, or to some other distraction is unsuccessful, and that the suffering continues relentlessly throughout the day and night regardless of any effort to ward it off? One can talk intelligently about ideas that bother the patient and about guilt, self-blame, and loss of self-esteem, but these are empty words unless one really knows how painful the feeling of depression can become. That there is agony from which there is no escape is perhaps too hard for the nonsufferer to accept. Even after somebody has made a suicidal attempt, successfully or not, one has trouble realizing that it was because the pain was too great to endure.

It is much less difficult to be unhappy than to be happy; unhappiness and misery are universal. However, the kind of unhappiness that is suffered in a depression when it has become an illness is not of this nature. It is, in a seriously depressed person, a uniquely painful thing.

The Need for Relief

There are times when the need for relief transcends all other considerations in the treatment of depression. Relief may be obtained by rest, reassurance, and, of course, moral support. When individuals are depressed, there is usually another person, the one person upon whom they depend, who is the important vehicle of therapy, so that the conservation-withdrawal reaction of individuals that allow them to repair themselves, restore their energies, and undo the damage of loss, is much more likely to be successful if it is done with the aid of that caring person. Perhaps it is similar to the condition of children who are exhausted and go to bed at night; but if the parents are not at home, they cannot sleep.

Similarly, depressed patients are not likely to get the rebuilding and reassurance and recovery if they do it entirely on their own, but are more likely to be reassured if there is some caring person looking after them and acting as a parent surrogate while they sleep and rest. There are human limits; we all have to learn to withdraw from stimuli and repair ourselves. There are limits to what can be tolerated in the way of unusual and exhausting stimuli. There is something biological about the conservation–withdrawal reaction and the need to repair oneself, which can be seen even in animals who have been exhausted. The biological substrate of the moods is apparently involved here.

Loneliness and Suicide

Possibly the power of the other person, the caring person, is in direct proportion to the amount of loneliness and isolation that is felt by the depressed person. To perceive the pain of the loneliness and isolation is an extremely imporant function of the therapist. This loneliness sometimes indicates the early stages of withdrawal from the environment. The person may not be out of contact physically, but may be pulling back from emotional contact, so that there is almost no overt indication except perhaps apathy, indifference, or simply some degree of unresponsiveness. Persons experiencing loneliness may not be aware that they are withdrawing, or that they are actually out of contact; they may simply be preoccupied. To all external appearances, they may be going about their business in a normal fashion and reacting normally. They may be lonely in a crowd while participating in the activities of the crowd.

Helplessness and Hopelessness

To understand the pain of depression one has to take into account the feeling of helplessness. Helplessness is a term that covers a wide variety of feelings; helplessness and hopelessness can be so painful that the only possible escape and relief is through suicide, or so the individual thinks. The important aspect of the mood of helplessness is that it can be motivated from either direction, outside from the environment or inside, from the drives and purposes and motivations of the individual. However, even though not in the setting of a complete clinically observable depressive disorder, these affects are capable of producing such misery that they lead to suicide. This is why sometimes individuals who have committed suicide cannot be said to have been sick in the ordinary sense of the word prior to their suicide. For example, if they feel helpless in satisfying their own desires to prove themselves to the world, to be good persons, they may not be sick, but they are in as much danger of suicide as those who are in an advanced endogenous depression.

It should be a surprise to no one to hear that studies have shown that the most specific and predictable risk factor for suicide is the presence of the feeling and idea of hopelessness. One should always inquire of potentially suicidal patients how the future looks to them and whether they think they can be helped.

PERSONALITY AND PSYCHODYNAMICS

There are risk factors for persons who do not have a depression that overlap with symptoms of persons who do. These risk factors represent personality characteristics of nondepressed persons and may account for the danger of suicide in those individuals. These factors cut across diagnostic lines, are present in certain depressed persons, and may account for the difference between those depressed persons who are seriously at risk of suicide and those who are not.

Low Self-esteem and Excessive Dependency

Those whose self-esteem is fragile and who depend excessively on the esteem and love of others are at risk. When a relationship has been based on this kind of need, which arises from a deficit of narcissism, any threat of loss of the important supporting person causes severe anxiety. If the relationship does break off, there results a wound in the already fragile system. The pain of the wound demands relief of some kind. Some persons with this kind of pain project their own guilt on the other person and attack. Murders and wife-beatings can result. However, if those who have been rejected or suffer the loss do not project, but tend to introject, then they are likely to feel guilt and be at risk for suicide. The suicidal act represents destruction of their bad self or the bad part of themselves.

If self-esteem is dependent on fantasies of power and competence, then losses of position of power, money, and control of others can create unbearable pain. One example is that of a person who becomes medically ill and thereby dependent on others. Because of the disability he or she suffers a wound of self-esteem. It is important with such persons, through psychotherapy, to help them feel better about themselves and to tide them over the most painful period of loss of functioning.

Instinctual Drives as Risk Factors

Anger and jealousy play a part in the murder-suicide cases which are so often dramatically written up in the newspapers, especially in the love triangle cases. The psychotherapist who is doing marital counseling should be in a position to do preventive work in cases in which one of the pair shows certain signs which give a forewarning of danger. The history of poor control over impulses, with outbursts, or drug or alcohol abuse are ominous signs.

Intolerable sexual excitement in the presence of guilt feelings can also be seen, especially in those persons who tend to respond to their own feelings with an unusual amount of disturbance and seem unable to tolerate the amount of frustration and excitement that everyone faces in everyday life. This lability of affect can turn what might be a pleasant occasion for most people, such as a birthday party, into a miserable painful occasion. Masochistic drives, either disguised or even nearly conscious, can be detected in some people, motivating them to manipulate occasions to derive suffering from pleasure, and with some, to cause actual bodily injury. Look for danger in those who give a history of not being able to handle drives successfully. Paradoxically, those who tolerate extreme frustration without a whimper may also be at risk, because of the guilt which follows when instinctual drives threaten to become conscious.

Physical Illness and Self-esteem

Suicides occur in those with incurable illness, such as painful debilitating cancer, where an inevitable downhill course is expected. However, depressed people have pessimistic fantasies, ideas, and even delusions of bodily disease and may have a much more pessimistic outlook on a situation than is justified by the realities. One should be on the lookout for this kind of depressive coloring when a physical disease is present. Such vulnerable persons need protection, with reassurance, close watching, and specific treatment of the depression. Antidepressant drugs, sometimes in small doses, can be very helpful here, in conjunction with psychotherapy.

Even a less than serious physical illness can disturb the maintenance of self-esteem and precipitate self-destructive urges in a vulnerable person. Deformities, defects, and other damages to the body image can cause a desire to get rid of the unwanted part of the self.

SUICIDE AND TREATMENT

The basis of treatment of suicidal persons can be considered as tripartite: prevention, intervention, and "postvention" (Shneidman 1976). All three are important for the prevention of tragedy and the restoration of the suicidal individual to a healthy life. Treatment is based on the identification of the risk factors and on the actual diagnosis of the underlying illness, and on the immediate situation in which the patient is seen.

The Suicidal Crisis

Suicidal urges tend to appear as crises that may occur periodically in the individual patient and may last anywhere from hours to years, surfacing at times of illness, loss, or disappointment. Once the crisis is passed, one can be reasonably safe until another trauma activates the urge at a later date. During a crisis, the function of the therapist is two-fold: (1) to help the patient survive the crisis and work out a satisfactory control over the precipitating causes and (2) to identify and treat the long-term predisposing causes, in order to prevent recurrences.

In the office of the psychotherapist a most important chain of preventive maneuvers is initiated. If the patient is not considered to be at risk, then the question of suicide can be handled within the framework of the therapy and is a matter between patient and therapist. If there is the possibility of treatment with medicines, then arrangements should be made immediately, before the patient leaves the office. Every psychotherapist should have access to a physician, preferably a psychiatrist, for such a contingency, so that the patient does not have to go begging for treatment and thereby fail to get it. If the risk is seen to be great, hospitalization is in order and should be arranged before the patient leaves the office, and the patient should be accompanied to the hospital or emergency room.

The cooperation of the family members is usually necessary in this kind of emergency, and they should certainly be involved as soon as it is evident that the patient needs prevention and intervention. In this way also the contact with the family opens the way to the later care which may be necessary to help them and the patient after the crisis is over. The therapist should be prepared to have family conferences and sometimes may find it helpful to make house calls when indicated, for example, if the family is frightened and the patient refuses to come to the office or to a hospital. With one's own patients, the crisis may be an occasion for using and cementing the therapeutic alliance. A therapist who has remained at the side of his patient through a suicidal crisis, and possibly saved his or her life, finds that their relationship is strengthened so that further help with the underlying problems is made possible.

One cannot emphasize too much the importance of the relationship with a caring person in the prevention of suicide. One suicidal patient said that, "I wouldn't do that to old Dave" (his physician), but, when Dave left town on a trip, he did make a suicidal move that took his life. One also cannot emphasize too much the need for attending the suicidal patient at all times, in order to prevent impulsive action on his part. Even on the emergency ward, one may find it necessary to supplement the care given there, by the emphasis of the therapist and family on vigilance.

The Suicide Prevention Center

This subject is discussed in Chapter 18 but it also merits mention here for its specific bearing on the management of suicidal risk in general. Because of the public health aspects of suicide prevention, and because it seemed apparent that the standard facilities— hospital emergency rooms, physicians, clergypeople, social agencies, and even psychiatric emergency centers—were not enough, a number of centers were established in major cities with 24-hour suicide hotline telephone numbers. In the two or three decades since the establishment of these centers, it has become apparent that they have served a very useful purpose in the prevention of suicidal acts, although statistics to this end are very difficult to come by. Moreover, they continue to be a source of both direct help and referral to other agencies for more extended help to the potentially suicidal persons who have no one else to turn to. A comprehensive discussion of the experience of one such center is given by Shneidman and Farberow (1983).

The Emergency Room and Aftercare

Emergency room care should include protection, proper diagnosis, and arrangements for treatment, with follow-through, nothing being left to chance. If hospitalization is indicated, it should be instituted at once and carried out. Some patients disappear between the emergency room and the hospital ward to which they were to be sent.

Follow-up and aftercare are vital. If possible, the therapist should follow the patient through the hospital stay and plan to continue therapy for the treatment of residual symptoms that are often present and continue to trouble the patient after the crisis is over. Crisis intervention, understanding, relief, and support go a long way toward preventing suicide, but when there has been a long-standing struggle with self-destructive impulses, long-term therapy is needed. If self-destructive trends are present, based on narcissistic injuries, masochistic tendencies, and depressive ideation and fantasies, as well as other personality symptoms, the treatment of choice is psychoanalysis or intensive psychotherapy, because they deal with underlying causes.

The family should not be left out, either during the crisis or in the aftercare, as suicidal crises may cause wounds that need healing (Lukas and Seiden 1987). They may bring to the surface conflicts that need to be dealt with not only by the patient but by the family or the important loved ones with whom the patient has close relationships. Family involvement may mean family conferences, couple's therapy, treatment for children, or individual therapy for spouse or parents. Further details of special handling for adolescents and children will be presented in the chapter covering the special problems of these ages.

The following illustrates a clinical application. A recurrently suicidal woman of late middle age with bipolar II disorder was treated with lithium and antidepressant drugs, plus close monitoring, supportive therapy, and psychotherapy with insight into current problems and personality development. Sexual frustrations from her husband's loss of libido following a heart attack had caused self-hatred and guilt in her. A hospitalization, with group therapy, gave her education into the nature of her experience. In addition, her spouse was found to have a severe enough characterological depression that it required treatment, which helped improve the patient's morale. Through a strong positive relationship, the development of sublimating activities was made possible, and the passage of time brought about a resolution of the patient's suicidal potential and control of her underlying illness. The whole process required several years. She still needs lithium, but is independent and functioning.

This treatment process, aimed at the basic suicidal tendency is characteristic of the long-term process required in more complex situations with patients who suffer from recurrent affective disorders and have recurrent suicidal crises.

MEDICAL-LEGAL CONSIDERATIONS

Responsibility for Suicide

Formerly suicide was considered a crime, but society and the courts increasingly recognize it as the symptom of an illness in which protection of the patient, by a physician–psychiatrist, a hospital, a psychologist, a social worker, or an institution of some sort, is part of the treatment for which a professional is responsible.

However, it is neither an accepted by-product nor the acceptable symptom of an illness, but is a preventable outcome for which professionals are responsible and for which they can expect to be punished. In the last two decades there has been a dramatic increase in liability suits of all kinds, among them malpractice suits, with the result that anyone responsible for the care of patients is much more likely to be sued in cases of accidents or deaths than in the past. It has become difficult at times to get malpractice insurance; rates have increased greatly, institutions are demanding that their staffs be protected by high insurance limits, and all those who take care of patients – physicians, nurses, social workers, psychologists, clergypersons – know that they can become defendants in lawsuits even when they exercise normal precautions. No one who does psychotherapy is immune.

The Law

The law now demands reasonable care in foreseeable circumstances. Generally, if there was no way of knowing that the patient was suicidal and if the responsible person took precautions to find out if he or she were suicidal, no negligence is found – that is, if adequate diagnostic procedures and treatment methods were employed and the patient was then not known to be suicidal, no negligence is found. However, if a hospital staff knows that a patient is suicidal and uses precautions, but these precautions are inadequate, the hospital may be found liable. Standards of care prevailing in similar institutions are used as guidelines by the courts.

Some suits have been lost when physicians did not take the time or make the effort to evaluate the patient adequately. Thus, it would seem that the conscientious practitioner should have no trouble because he or she will, by definition, take the time and trouble to find out if the patient is suicidal and take suitable precautions. There are some warnings that experts give (Litman 1983). On an emergency service of a hospital, if a suicidal patient is not admitted, the record should explain very carefully the reason for not admitting him or her. If a patient is discharged prematurely from the hospital, it should be clearly documented that every effort was made to persuade him or her to stay, which would include a refusal to discharge the person without the family taking the responsibility.

If patients are really suicidal and the physician or therapist thinks they are not responsible for their own behavior, then the question of confidentiality changes, and the responsible therapist or physician should talk to the family. A psychotic patient should not be responsible for this decision.

Psychiatrists sometimes are trapped by their own rules in regard to confidentiality, but the rules change if patients are too sick to be responsible for their own behavior. If a patient is suicidal, one talks to the responsible members of the family, enlists their cooperation, and advises them as to how best to deal with their responsibility in the matter. Open communication will go a long way to prevent lawsuits and to save the patient's life. At the same time, the therapist's attitude of caring and sincerity can help establish a trusting relationship with the patient, which may also help save his or her life and, incidentally, prevent a lawsuit. Insurance people say that people seldom sue physicians who demonstrate their compassion and show a conscientious and devoted attitude.

The prescription of drugs deserves a great deal of care when the patient is clearly, or even possibly, suicidal. Nonrefillable prescriptions of small amounts should be given. Communications with the pharmacist may be helpful if there is some question as to the manner in which the medicine is being used, for example, if one suspects that the patient is hoarding drugs, in which case the family might help also. One should always calculate whether the prescription contains enough medicine to kill the patient, and, if it does, the amount should be cut down to a safe level.

One more precaution should be observed. If there is any doubt or hesitation on the part of the therapist about suicide, a consultation should be insisted upon, not simply for medico-legal reasons, but because the consultation may help in a practical way to solve the problem. This holds true to a large extent for all questionable situations, whether suicide is involved or not. Another opinion, a fresh point of view, may be very helpful.

The Ambulatory Patient

The law recognizes that psychiatrists have little control over ambulatory patients, but there are still lawsuits in cases of suicide of ambulatory patients if the responsible professionals did not take reasonable precautions. If a relationship of trust exists with the patient, that is, if the patient is well enough to form a positive relationship, then one makes a bargain with the patient to be available if needed, and the patient knows he or she can call day or night. If an open discussion takes place about the danger of suicide and the patient and therapist both feel that the admittedly present suicidal thoughts are controllable on an outpatient basis, then the patient need not be admitted.

Exceptions

Angry patients, who seem unreasonable, even though not overtly psychotic, are at risk, especially if they want revenge for some real or supposed injustice or affront or has had genuine losses in their love-relations, such as a threatened divorce or the discovery that the spouse is having an affair or prefers another person. Evaluating this kind of a patient can be difficult, but it is better to err on the side of caution and admit the patient to the hospital if one is very uneasy about the outcome.

The professional's job is more difficult nowadays because of the present-day policies of shorter hospital stays, open hospitals with less careful watching of the patients, less restraint of the patient's movements, and the encouragement of patients to take more responsibility for themselves. These policies give the patient more leeway to commit impulsive acts than in the days of stricter supervision and longer hospital stays. To compensate for these greater dangers, a greater degree of control is needed with the ambulatory patients who are at risk, such as frank communication about the dangers with the family, who should feel free to call the therapist if they see ominous signs. There are times to be especially alert: vacations of the therapist, holidays, anniversaries, separations, and times of loss.

In cases where part of the patient's problem is the presence of long-standing self-destructive ideas, these will eventually enter the discussion and possibly be experienced by the patient as genuine suicidal urges. Although the resurgence of these urges in therapy can create some apprehension on the part of both patient and therapist, there is a positive side, namely, that it is now possible to work through the psychodynamics and possibly to eliminate the suicidal wish once and for all; at least, an increased understanding of the death wishes and an increased control may result.

PART III

TREATMENT AND MANAGEMENT

12

STRATEGY

Since the specific mood disorders are a heterogeneous group, no single treatment can be expected to have exclusive and universal application. The hope that either psychotherapy alone or chemotherapy alone could cure all the diverse types has generally been abandoned; one has to look to both methods in most cases, integrating them in the treatment program and giving appropriate emphasis to one or the other, according to the need of each individual.

GEOGRAPHICAL SETTING FOR THERAPY

We work where we happen to be—in private practice, in a clinic, in a hospital, in a social agency, and the like. We should, however, always be mindful that our particular workplace may not be right for individual patients in their present state, or the time at which they bring their problems. The following discusses certain specific situations that require attention in regard to the physical setting of therapy.

Therapist's Office

Many patients with milder mood disorders can be seen in the therapist's office. Privacy, uninterrupted time, and a quiet confidential setting are vital. It is important not to have interruptions, such as telephone calls.

Patient's Home

Occasionally one encounters a patient who is so resistant to treatment or so immobilized by depression that it is necessary to make a house call. Such a home visit provides an opportunity to get a different perspective on the patient, although it may be a great inconvenience to one's schedule. Professionally trained therapists usually compulsively adhere to their schedules not only for practical reasons, but because their training makes them uncomfortable without familiar surroundings in which they are "lord and master, or mistress." You can learn a great deal about a person by observing his or her home setting and family in their home.

An example is of a middle-aged man with long-standing bipolar disorder of the classical manic-depressive type, not well controlled, who was seen for the first time in his apartment because he lived alone and was so immobilized by depression that he could not get into his car and come to the therapist's office. Not one of the persons giving his story and referring him had prepared the therapist for what he was to see. As expected, he was very slowed down and depressed. But his apartment! It was stacked with pictures, books, newspapers, magazines, dishes, cameras, which were all lying on chairs, sofas, tables, and all over the floor everywhere, so that one had to pick one's way through the chaos. He was a compulsive collector—a hoarder—to a pathological degree. In addition to his bipolar illness, he obviously suffered from a severe obsessive-compulsive neurosis that handicapped him severely in life, a neurosis he rationalized by various means so that it never entered his discussion, and one would not have discovered it so quickly had not a home visit been made.

Also requiring a home visit are the occasional manics, out of control, who refuse consultation because their mania tells them they don't need it. Here you may have to go in force, with their family physician or clergyperson and persuade them to come to the hospital. On rare occasions, one has to write a formal commitment paper and take the police to persuade such persons to come to the hospital for treatment.

In psychotherapy with less sick patients, there is usually no reason why they should not come to the therapist's workplace. In fact, it probably is healthy for the patient to get out and away from home and family, to get insight and the kind of objectivity often needed to bring the situation into perspective.

The home may bring out some of the patients' symptoms, because that is where they let down their guard, and their family may be able to supply insight into their behavior that the patients cannot or do not offer. For example, a family may reveal that the patient has suicidal ideas—a point the patient may have suppressed in an interview. A wife may reveal that her hypomanic husband is making impulsive and grandiose business moves, which, when he rationalizes them in his way, are made to appear sensible.

Patient's Workplace

Clinics and dispensaries may be good for case-finding, but usually not for therapy. The employers and colleagues may be very helpful and concerned about those people, for example, who have trouble keeping up with their work. It is not rare to find persons who have spared their family anxiety, but who have spoken of their problems at work. Usually such patients should be referred away for actual treatment.

Daycare Hospitals

The integrated approach in a daycare setting, with social workers, group therapists, and nurses available, is very helpful for people who are ready to leave the hospital, but not ready to be at home alone. It can save the patient from relapses and recurrences.

Psychiatric Hospital

Fewer patients need to be hospitalized than before because of our increased ability to use medication effectively and because in psychotherapy we are more and more aware of how to get the necessary support at home.

However, hospitalization can be necessary and advisable. If one can continue the therapy right through the hospital stay, it may be very helpful, even though sometimes hospitals are not convenient places to do individual psychotherapy.

Daycare hospitals, psychiatric hospitals, and private or public centers for ambulatory care now tend to be organized around a staff that can do family and group therapy, recreational and occupational therapy, and sometimes the psychiatric services of individual psychotherapy and chemotherapy. Integrating the appropriate therapies can be lifesaving for a certain group of more severely ill patients who are under stress and in fairly difficult situations. If one does not have this organization at hand geographically, for example, to see a spouse or children, it is necessary to have them available for referral because many situations call for an integrated approach.

Sometimes an integrated approach in an active hospital can be very helpful to people, not only for the relief of an acute depression or manic disorder, but also with a long-term problem by providing the insight gained by observing others with the same illness while, at the same time, having family involved in family group sessions—in short, involving the patient on all significant levels. An inpatient program can sometimes do a great deal for a patient in a relatively short time because of the intensive and integrated approach.

For example, a 60-year-old woman, who was married to a physician, had a recurrence of suicidal ideas. She had had five or six previous severe depressions, now controlled with lithium and antidepressants, but her underlying personality problem of guilt and shame and low self-image continued to keep her vulnerable to repeated breakdowns, although these were usually aborted by treatment.

In the hospital, in addition to her usual treatment of psychotherapy and drugs, she had group therapy and joined a class in sewing, and her husband participated in the family sessions. It was helpful to her to discover that others had the same problem and to be able to talk to them. Her husband was helped in his insight into how families handle the problems, and the communication between husband and wife improved.

After her discharge, she felt that the intensive hospital experience had helped her more than any other single therapeutic device, other than individual psychotherapy. It had been a very good experience because she had been able to find other people who had similar problems which they had accepted and could discuss. The nurses had concentrated on helping her to observe her depressive cognitions and pessimism and helped supplement the insights gained in psychotherapy. Her shame diminished considerably in this setting, which was a benefit she carried home with her.

General Principles

The management and treatment of the hospitalized patient deserves much more space than can be given in this book. However, some general principles can be emphasized:

1. Neither the psychiatrist nor the psychotherapist should allow patients to become patients of an organization. Rather, they should make frequent visits and observations, be in charge, know what is going on with their patients through frequent contacts with the staff, letting staff know their ideas and purposes, and the rationale of the treatment program. They also should participate in the carrying out of this program, as in writing notes and orders.
2. Psychiatrists should keep in touch with the psychotherapists and with any consultants whose opinions are needed, such as the patients' personal physicians.
3. Therapists and psychiatrists both should have expertise in the various treatment modalities that may be required, including chemotherapy, and should have an understanding of other therapies and their place in the hospital armamentarium, such as group therapy and occupational therapy.
4. Therapists and psychiatrists both should take into account

the patients' relationships and their environment, including family relationships. If any environmental manipulation is needed before patients leave the hospital, therapists themselves or with the aid of the social worker make some effort to change or influence the patients' home environment in such a way that the very problems which brought on their illness are dealt with before the patient leaves the hospital.

Patients can be shocked by sudden hospitalization, by admission procedures, by the attitudes of those who first greet them in the hospital, and by the very fact of having to make the dramatic move of being sent to a psychiatric hospital. If possible, they should be spared the actual procedures of an admissions office and go directly to the ward, accompanied by their family, who then can take care of the formal procedures.

The therapist should meet the patient there as soon as possible, thereby lessening the impact of the dramatic and strange surroundings and lessening the sense of abandonment some patients feel. At this time the therapist can also help the staff begin the patient's therapy in an appropriate way, without loss of time.

PROCESS OF TREATMENT

The treatment of mood disorders is not an isolated, single event; it is a dynamic process in which a number of variables are at work. There is short-term treatment for acute depressions and long-term for chronic and recurrent types. There is psychological treatment of several types, directed toward the patient, and also treatment of the environment to influence the milieu of the patient. There is medical treatment, specifically, chemotherapy (pharmacotherapy), now especially effective with major depressions and bipolar types. All these variables have to be coordinated and integrated in the process of treatment.

The specific treatment at a particular time depends on (1) the stage of the illness, (2) the severity of the depression or manic state, (3) the amount of suffering, (4) the weighing of pressures and stresses on the patient, (5) the danger of recurrences, because depressions and manias tend to relapse and recur, and (6) deficits in the quality of life.

Table 12-1 shows the variables in the treatment plan.

STAGES OF TREATMENT

Treatment varies a great deal according to the point in the course of the illness at which the patient is being seen. This section describes the usual sequence.

First Contact

The first meeting may be an emergency, in which cases crisis intervention is required. A preliminary working diagnosis is made,

Table 12-1
Variables in Treatment Plan

Focus	Aim	Location	Timing
On patient	Relief of symptoms	Ambulatory	Emergency
Individual psychotherapy	Treatment of the illness	Hospital	Early, middle, or late stage of illness
Electrotherapy		Half-way house	
Chemotherapy	Prevention of recurrences and relapses	Day care hospital	Recovery or follow-up
Physical therapies			
Group	Improvement of quality, of life		
Occupational			
On environment: Crisis intervention			
Psychosocial intervention: couples, family, children			

and relief from suffering takes precedence, through hospitalization, medication, relief from work, and so forth. Included in the first meeting are:

- Protection from excessive stress and demands of the environment

- Protection from self and self-demands

- Rest from emotional fatigue

- A chance to regroup and restore resources

- Evaluation of need for various types of therapy, including medication, education, and reassurance

- Psychological catharsis of immediate problems. A chance for the patient to unburden himself and be heard

- Attention to family and other relationships, as needed in a crisis

Early, Middle, and Late Stages of Illness

Treatment for these stages include the above steps as well as the following:

- Assessment of whatever predicament led to the depression, by making a careful evaluation of outside causes, such as personal relationships and stresses, and also evaluation of personality disorders and problems

- Monitoring the medication and adjusting dose

- Brief psychotherapy and the beginning of intensive psychotherapy, when needed

Follow-up

Following recovery, there remains the problem of treating the longer-term personality problems left in the wake of the illness. There is also the need to prevent recurrences and relapses, which are frequent. The methods used are:

- Medication.

- Support by therapist, family, workplace, organizations, groups, therapy support group, etc.

- Treatment of psychosocial problems. Involvement of family and spouse, when needed, and the use of family and couples therapy.

- Individual psychotherapy. Treatment of personality disorders and trends which may have contributed to the breakdown or have been found to interfere with relationships or otherwise lower the quality of life. Analytic psychotherapy and psychoanalysis belong here. Psychotherapy has been demonstrated to improve the response to medicines and to diminish the need for medication in some patients.

EMERGENCY SITUATIONS

There are five situations in which the need for help is urgent enough to constitute an emergency. These are discussed here more or less in the order of their urgency, but any of them can be serious enough to require immediate action.

Suicidal Risk

When the patient is first seen, whether at home, in the therapist's office, or in the emergency room, the danger of suicide should be evaluated, even though it does not come up spontaneously.

Suicide is important enough in the context of mood disorders that Chapter 11 is devoted to it. Here its place in the initial evaluation is outlined.

Whether at the initial contact or later, one is alerted to the risk of suicide by any one of the following:

1. *Suicidal preoccupations.* References, especially if repeated, to such ideas as, "I'd be better off dead," or "If I had the nerve I'd kill myself," or a seeming preoccupation with death or the hereafter.

2. *Ideas or delusions of loss of control.* "I'm losing my mind" is a common example, or "I can't stand it any more."

3. *Delusions of guilt or wrong-doing.* Assertions such as "I'm no good," or "I don't deserve to live," or "Everyone would be better off without me." "I've done wrong" or "I'm a criminal" are also heard. Related delusions of somatic disease, sometimes viewed by the patient as punishment, are important, such as "I have cancer, and the doctor can't find it."

4. *Sudden withdrawal.* The person who is obviously suffering and becomes quiet and uncommunicative. He has a depressed appearance, but says little or nothing, sometimes moving through the day as if in a trance.

5. *Inability to function.* The person who suddenly or gradually loses the ability to get through the day's work or perform his or her regular tasks.

Any one of these symptoms requires immediate investigation, evaluation, and possibly intervention, in order to prevent a tragedy. When patients are unable to get help by their own efforts, someone has to step in and see that they get into a protected situation very soon. If you are convinced that there is real suicidal danger and the patient shows one or more of these symptoms, showing that he or she is probably psychotic or potentially unable to control the suicidal urge, the patient should not be allowed out of your sight or that of a responsible person until he or she is in an emergency service or a psychiatric ward. The patient should continue to be watched even there. Suicide prevention centers can be helpful in suggesting available facilities in the community. Acting through the family physician sometimes helps, but might occasion some delay, so one is generally better off to go straight to a psychiatric facility. Suicide prevention centers and hospitals are listed in the local telephone directory and are prepared to pick up the problem, provided someone takes the responsibility to get the patient into safe hands.

Diagnosis of the patient's immediate problem is essential to evaluating the risk, as there are several situations which in themselves convey a high risk. These are discussed in Chapter 11.

Hospitalization should be insisted upon if there is real risk, especially when patients are so sick that they would not be able to exercise responsibility for their own behavior. If there is no immediate danger, but it might become a problem, then the relationship with the patient should be developed so that the therapists can depend on their patients' calling them if they feel endangered. "Call me any time, if you feel the danger threatening you," is a good way to ensure preventive contact. Also, the family should be alerted and brought into the discussion. In the hospital, the physicians and the nursing staff, especially those who are in daily and hourly contact with the patient, should be included in the preventive effort and should report what they hear and see to the responsible therapist.

The Suicidal Act

When an actual suicidal act has occurred, whether completed or not, first aid is needed for the family, in addition to whatever treatment the patient needs. Therapists or psychiatric consultants may be in the best position to give this first aid, especially if they have been acquainted with the patient or the family. This may be a very difficult task, but has to be done by someone, because the situation is much more complicated than in the case of a natural death. Guilt, anger, accusations, perplexity, shock—all these may come out. Although it is important for the responsible therapist to be completely honest, he or she should beware of playing God and taking on the complete responsibility for the patient's act. Sometimes a conscientious therapist gives the family the impression that he or she feels at fault for the patient's suicide, when he or she really was not. Because of the danger of malpractice suits, we should not risk exaggerating our mistakes because of excessive guilt.

The family, also, should not be allowed to suffer excessively from guilt, if it can be avoided. One of the most painful experiences a therapist can have is to face the family of a patient who has committed suicide while in therapy. Even in those cases where neither the family nor the therapist had any warning, both parties can experience guilt at not preventing the death, and sometimes each blames the other. Understanding and sympathy are essential for the open communication of these feelings, so that they can be dealt with. If necessary, the therapist should go to the home, call on the family, and participate to whatever extent is appropriate, in order to help the family understand and cope with the tragedy.

The therapist has suffered a loss, too, and has a right to acknowledge it, without damage to his or her reputation or self-esteem. We are forced to admit that, although we work very hard to prevent suicide, and we are defeated when we fail, no one can prevent all suicides when dealing with such a high-risk group.

The children pose an especially difficult problem in the case of any unexpected death of a parent, and they are often not considered in the immediate crisis. Someone skilled in helping children grieve should take on this task, because the children often do not have the language or the ability to work it through by themselves. In her book *A Child's Parent Dies* (1974), Erna Furman describes the methods employed by the skilled child therapist. In addition to taking the child's feelings into account at the time, the therapist should also, if necessary, give the responsible adults any assistance they need later on to help the children grieve in their own way.

Acute Depression

Sometimes the acutely depressed patient, even when not suicidal, requires emergency management and may have to be hospitalized at once or at least given immediate treatment to provide relief from overwhelming symptoms. This may happen on the first visit or later in therapy, when the patient may become worse and require special attention, such as extra, unscheduled visits, medicines, and so forth, sometimes even at night or on weekends.

If such a crisis comes up unexpectedly in the course of a busy day, it can take some time to do the special things needed. We have to expect that occasionally we will have to interrupt our schedule to call the family or arrange for hospitalization. It is best to have an available hospital and a psychiatrist to refer to.

Explaining the matter to the patients may also be difficult, especially if they are psychotic, in which case they may not be able to make the judgment, and the family will have to be consulted and used to expedite the hospitalization. In extreme cases, a formal temporary commitment procedure may have to be followed, but most of the time patients can be persuaded that the course of action is in their best interest, or they may be suffering enough that they can accept your recommendations in order to get relief. The hospital can turn out to be a haven and a comfort as well as a source of special treatment procedures. It may be necessary to accompany the patient to the hospital; however, if the family is available, it works well to have them act as escort. A prompt visit by the therapist to the hospital later may go a long way toward helping the patient accept hospitalization and adjust to it.

Helping Families in Emergencies

Hospitalization, especially if urgent or unexpected, can be very upsetting to the family as well. It is within the function of the responsible therapist to help relieve the family's distress as much as possible for humane reasons as well as to ensure the cooperation of the important persons concerned with the patient and to improve communication and understanding from the very outset. Talking to parents, spouse, and grown-up children can be very helpful, indeed essential, if the patient is so severely depressed or manic that his or her judgment is affected and not to be trusted. For example, a severely depressed widow, 60 years old, accepted hospitalization, but did not want her three grown-up children, all of whom lived in another city, to know about it, "for fear of worrying them." Since they all usually call her frequently and would obviously be very concerned not to find her at home, it did not make sense not to let them know where she was. Needless to say, the psychiatrist overruled the patient on this request. The children were very grateful for the information and gave additional information that was helpful in the evaluation and planning.

Another consideration is what to do with younger children when a parent has suddenly left the home to be confined in a hospital. Here the adults in the family, properly guided by the therapist, usually have to do the explaining and fill in the gap left by the parent's absence, and the therapist should check on what is actually done in order to make sure that the children's emotional needs are met.

Emergencies in Hospitalized Medical and Surgical Patients

Consultations in hospitals should be answered promptly, especially if it is suspected that the patient has a mood disorder. They should never be allowed to go overnight without investigating the extent of the emergency by talking with the responsible persons. Rarely can a depressed or manic patient safely be allowed to go overnight without being seen and evaluated by a responsible psychiatrist.

If, on examination, the consultant sees danger of suicide or loss of control, she should try to form a close enough relationship with the patient to get his or her trust and evaluate the degree of control the patient can be trusted to exert. If there is danger, the staff should be alerted and special watch set up until the patient can be transferred to a psychiatric service; there, certain precautions are standard, and the consultant should be sure that they are properly set in motion.

Families must be informed and involved, also, so that certain potential dangers are avoided, such as the patient walking out against advice, unauthorized medicines being brought in, or the family opposing treatment because of lack of information.

Hospitalizing Patients

Occasionally a mania or hypomania occurs during the course of psychotherapy in a patient who was not considered to be bipolar because the depression was mild, speech was normal, and there were no striking somatic signs. Anyone who treats depressed patients has to be prepared for this and should recognize the early signs: a sudden lifting of a pervasive depression, a sudden surge of a feeling of well-being, remarkable insight, or the return of re-pressed memories in an unexpected way. All this can happen in a day or two, and, when it does, the therapist should be alerted to the possibility that the patient may go on to a fullblown manic attack.

It is important to try to persuade patients with symptoms of early mania to come into the hospital while they are still rational, because in a very short time they may be too irrational to manage. The combined efforts of family and physicians may be necessary to overcome the resistance of a manic patient even in the early stages of an attack. Persuasion, arguments, and explanations all help.

Therapists in charge may have to participate in the procedure actively. They may have to go to the residence if patients refuse to come to them and use their and the family's influence to get the patient into the hospital. With manic patients, it is necessary to take a firm stand and insist that your professional judgment be carried out.

If force is necessary, one has to call the police, who can then transport the patient, usually without much resistance, to a psy-chiatric facility with the authority of a commitment paper signed by a physician. The alternative, letting the manic person be free to race around, making numerous annoying and disastrous phone calls, getting into serious trouble, and *not* getting treatment, is to be avoided energetically.

Patients admitted to the hospital belong to one of the fol-lowing groups:

1. Severely depressed, possibly psychotic, brought in for their protection, for diagnosis, and for treatment.

2. Manic patients, admitted for the same reasons.

3. Less severely depressed patients where the possibility of suicide exists, and it is not clear whether the patient can manage outside the hospital.

4. Diagnostic problems, when the actual diagnosis is not clear and the patient may need relief as well as evaluation.

5. Adolescents who are quite disturbed, although not psychotic, and need relief as well as appraisal of the problem and an evaluation of the circumstances, especially when some kind of acting out is occurring, such as running away, delinquency, drug or alcohol abuse, or somatic complaints which may be covering up a depression or manic attack.

It can be a great relief to family, patient, and therapist to have one of these patients safely admitted to a good facility, but the work does not stop there. Some functions are required of the therapist while his patient is in the hospital, namely:

The family may need help in a number of ways, help which the psychiatrist in charge may not be in a position to give. Therefore, it is important that the therapist keep in touch with the medical staff and follow the patient in the hospital.

The actual process of psychotherapy may continue in the hospital. In some cases, important issues come up during a breakdown that can be either worked into the therapy immediately or remembered and later found useful. Issues such as what led to the breakdown can be more obvious and useful for gaining insight. Of course, in psychotic patients there is a limit to the usefulness of insight during a breakdown, as the retention and recall of significant material is seriously interfered with during a psychotic break.

Preparation for discharge involves the therapist who will be following the patient afterward, in such matters as frequency and timing of follow-up visits, arranging for day care, home care, when to go back to school or work, how the medicines are going to be handled, if any. All these matters are important in the prevention of recurrences, which are frequent in mood disorders.

The details of the actual hospital treatment, with diagnostic appraisal, drug or electroconvulsant treatment, group therapy, occupational therapy, physical and recreational therapy are in the charge of the psychiatrist and staff, but it can be helpful in ensuring continuity if the therapist keeps in touch.

ROLE OF FAMILIES IN TREATMENT AND PATIENT'S RESPONSIBILITY

The appalling misunderstanding people can have of members of their own families never ceases to be amazing. It is more than mere ignorance when people are unable to recognize the existence of a depressive illness after it has been carefully described and explained. Moreover, some people have their own explanation of the relative's symptoms, their own attitude, and seem unable to give that up. "He wants sympathy" or "He is trying to get attention" are some of the things you hear. Or, as one wife said, "I've got more troubles than he has, and I'm not depressed."

Another singularly impressive phenomenon in families is not so obvious, yet it is so powerful that it is at the very heart of the causes of affective disorder. That is the profound influence, totally unconscious and unintentional, that two people can have on each other's illness. It has been demonstrated that, in families where more than one member has an affective disorder, when one gets sick others are likely to get sick also, or may recover. An example is of an elderly woman whose depression kept getting worse despite treatment. One weekend she suddenly called her psychiatrist to say that her 35-year-old daughter, living with her, had to be admitted to a psychiatric service. She had an acute manic spell, which had evidently been getting more and more obvious for several weeks. Although she had talked somewhat complainingly about the daughter's messy house habits, she never mentioned the increasing sleeplessness, the speeding-up, the irritability, which would have alerted me to the fact that the daughter was advancing into a manic attack. Perhaps the manic attack of the daughter was an effort to cope with the mother's depression.

The significance of this story lies in the patient's becoming more and more depressed without being aware of the overwhelming influence her daughter had been having on her burgeoning depression and, equally important, her influence on the daughter's increasingly severe manic state.

An acknowledgment of these powerful interpersonal forces lies in the increasing number of psychiatric facilities that have organized group family meetings for therapeutic purposes. No modern, progressive psychiatric hospital or clinic can afford to omit family work from its armamentarium for both therapeutic and preventive purposes. Both inpatient and ambulatory patients need this service.

There are other examples, involving husband and wife, where the wife recovers from a depression and the husband becomes depressed. Sometimes the wife becomes more assertive and active after treatment for her passive dependent submissiveness and is much harder to live with. The dominating husband finds himself unable to dominate as easily and is troubled; he may eventually feel defeated and depressed. Sometimes the roles are reversed, and the original patient is the husband and the dominating wife has to cope with his new-found assertiveness.

What this means is that intervention may be needed in the form of couples therapy, or joint family meetings, or individual therapy, in order to make changes in the pathological relationship which brought on the illness. These techniques are applicable not only in cases of simple maladjustments and depressive neurosis but also in cases of genuine major disorders, including the bipolar. One must acknowledge, of course, that patients with major disorders need biological treatment, but they are also heavily influenced by the psychological and interpersonal climate.

Of course, depressed persons with their excessive guilt are very likely to accept blame for all the wrongs of the world. Moreover, when they find so much fault with themselves, sometimes their family is inclined to agree that they are not much good. They have failed to recognize that, even if they are right in their self-blame, it means that they are sick, because well people do not attempt to advertise their sins, but rather try to conceal them.

ADVICE TO FAMILIES

1. Don't push. Patients are already driven to their limit by their own conscience. Depressed people are usually overcon-

scientious and have an exaggerated sense of their own responsibility.

2. Don't shame the patient. Patients already have too much guilt. Don't say things, directly or indirectly, that will tell them you think they are lazy or not trying hard enough. It will make them more depressed and add to their feelings that they are worthless and the world would be better off without them.

3. Do encourage them to rest when they need to restore their energies.

4. Do appreciate their suffering and misery.

5. Do believe them when they say anything about suicide, directly or indirectly. There are some direct and indirect hints: "I'm a failure." "I'm no good." "I can't go on." "I'm hopeless." "Things look hopeless." "I can't manage." "You would be better off without me," and so on. Without mentioning suicide, they tell you they are contemplating it. Nonverbal clues can be revealing—a firmer handshake or embrace than usual, an extra goodbye wave of the hand.

6. Do get them to accept treatment, to accept hospitalization if necessary, to take medicine, to accept a slower work pace, to continue treatment. Remember, 40 percent of people who have an attack of depression have a recurrence within a few years.

7. Do participate in the therapy that is directed at improving their relationships with their family and environment. This may mean couples therapy, it may mean family therapy, and it may mean individual counseling or therapy for you.

LIVING WITH A MANIC PATIENT

If patients are not obviously sick enough to be sent immediately to the hospital, it may be necessary to monitor and control their activity nevertheless, because their judgment may be faulty; for example, they are prone to spend money recklessly, to get into inappropriate love affairs, and to make inappropriate phone calls or business deals. It is necessary to have an understanding with the patient, between family, patients, and psychiatrist, that someone will monitor these activities and help them control their behavior when necessary. It is no favor to patients to allow them to make fools of themselves or to damage their personal life or reputation when, by stopping them, you can prevent these disastrous consequences. This means daily contact with someone while the lithium and/or tranquilizers are taking hold. Meanwhile, the psychiatrist should also see the patient regularly, probably every day, in order to monitor his or her behavior and to inject realistic thinking into the scene.

Manic and hypomanic persons do not really like to lose that pleasant "high" and tend to resist medications or restraints that slow them down. You have to explain, even to mildly manic persons, that it is not good for them to neglect their medication. Living with a manic or hypomanic person is one of the most difficult things in the world; when it becomes too difficult, *that* in itself is a sure indication that the patient should be in the hospital.

LIVING WITH A DEPRESSED PERSON

It is true that one of the most difficult things to manage is living with a manic patient, but be assured that living with a depressed person, especially early in the treatment, can be a very, very great challenge too. If these persons are quiet and unaggressive it may seem easy on the surface, but then there is always the worry that they may be contemplating suicide. And if they have the usual inability to get going in the morning and seem to want to be around a great deal, doing very little, it can be very worrisome, or even annoying, because you may not grasp that they are really ill.

Sometimes it helps to encourage them to get started in the morning, even if it is only getting dressed. Don't expect them to be able to manage all the usual activities; when they do that, they will be well. Also, many people with moderately severe depressions, who can still function at work, should be encouraged to do so, but do not be surprised if that is all they can do, because they may be able to do nothing at home afterward, or on weekends. It is sometimes good for those who can work to do so, even if they cannot function well at home.

If the slowing down is so great that none of these activities is possible, then medication and possibly hospitalization are in order. The family should not be expected to function as full-time nurses with a sicker patient; that is a job for the professionals.

During a depression, major decisions such as job change, marital change, moving, and so forth, should be deferred. Decisions made during a depression are usually depressed decisions, overly pessimistic and not realistic. By the same token, decisions made during a manic phase suffer similarly from a lack of reality, but toward the overly optimistic side.

ADVICE TO PATIENTS

1. Accept your illness as an illness. It is not your fault.
2. Don't blame yourself. Depressions result from a combination of circumstances and from a depletion of the body energies. The processes that give the nervous system its drive and energy are at a lowered level and need to be restored by rest and by special antidepressant medications.
3. Take the treatment prescribed, whether hospital, medicines, rest, psychotherapy, or other. Be willing to examine the possibility that your own evaluation of the problem may not be correct. The most difficult patients to treat are those who are obsessed with certain of their own ideas (e.g., that something they did wrong years ago is the problem). The easiest person to deceive is yourself. Believe the therapist if you can. If you cannot believe him or her this may be a symptom of your illness, that is, of your pessimism and loss of hope. You should discuss your ideas frankly. Although therapists are not infallible, they are usually correct and will make every effort to clear the air for your recovery.
4. Progress can be very slow and you may need hospitalization. However, treatment is invariably successful, although it may take time.
5. You will recover. Do not believe the hopeless, pessimistic feelings you have. These negative feelings are a part of your illness. It is like looking at everything through dark glasses. When you recover things will look normal and bright again.

6. Once the immediate pain is relieved, you may need to look at your situation and try to identify your predicament. There may be things you will want to change by means of counseling or psychotherapy.

7. If you are or have been depressive, learn to recognize the signs of getting sick and learn to cooperate with the physician about adjusting the dose of medication up or down to arrest a major depression. Learn when it is time to rest and spare yourself stress, but also learn when it is time to get out of bed and get going. Most of the time it is healthy to get up in the morning, even if you feel low. It can be demoralizing to stay in bed. Also, learn when an oncoming depression can be averted by talking out some problems with your therapist. The tendency of the depressive is to be passive and inactive. That is all right for rest and restitution, but also remember to get help. If you have suicidal ideas, discuss them with a professional even before you begin to believe that things are hopeless and desperate.

8. If you are or have been manic or hypomanic, learn to recognize when you are beginning to speed up—the early waking, the increased energy, lack of fatigue, the talking, the numerous phone calls, the optimism, the buying, and so forth. Call your psychiatrist at once. Cut down your activities at once. Don't drink. Don't buy anything. Don't make a lot of phone calls. Don't get embroiled in love affairs—they are usually inappropriate. Don't make any major decisions without consultation, such as job change, trips, marital changes, or business deals.

If you follow these rules and get under treatment at once, even if it requires hospitalization, you will save yourself a lot of trouble and painful regrets. People have ruined careers, financial security, and marriages as a result of unrecognized manic spells. Don't let it happen.

Of course, in the elated, speeded-up state, you "never felt better in your life," and you do not want to think of that glorious intoxicated feeling as an illness. But it is, and the earlier in its course that you recognize it the better.

13

BIOLOGICAL THERAPY

DEFINITION

Biological therapy is treatment by any mechanical, chemical, or physical means. The use of medicines, known as chemotherapy or pharmacotherapy, is by far the most common biological method in use today. Psychopharmacology is the science and practice of the use of medicines that alter mental functioning, used mainly for the treatment of mental illness.

Another biological therapy in use is electroconvulsant therapy (ECT) or electroshock, as it was formerly called. Light therapy, physical therapy, exercise therapy, and sleep deprivation are new experimental methods that have not yet been proven effective.

CLINICAL BASIS FOR BIOLOGICAL THERAPY

People who have cycling bipolar disorders (manic-depressives) or established major depressions appear, to the trained observer, as though some impersonal, that is, bodily, force is affecting them — perhaps a toxic substance or a nervous system change totally outside their voluntary control. If they are manic, they appear to have an excess of some chemical stimulant; when they are depressed they appear to have a depletion of it. Victims themselves feel the depression or mania sweeping over them like an outside force, much the way a fever sweeps over their body.

The clear-cut sleep disturbances in which early waking is so regular and so consistent, the loss of appetite, the loss of taste, the slowing down of all bodily processes, including salivation, lowering of blood pressure, lowering of heart rate, the cessation of menses, the lack of sexual excitement, the disappearance of erections and nocturnal emissions, a great many such physiological symptoms give the appearance of biological changes in depression. If they have had such spells previously, the victims may say that they are "getting sick again." They recognize it.

Because of the physical nature of this process, certain of the affective disorders are not treatable by psychotherapy alone. Patients become victims of biochemical processes over which they have no voluntary control; for example, the person with a bipolar depression or a manic attack cannot respond to psychotherapy until the overwhelming physical changes are controlled.

Psychotherapy will not relieve the symptoms of a psychotic major depression or a nonpsychotic major depression with melancholia. Once the symptoms are moderated by medication so that the patient can respond effectively, psychotherapy can be used and can be very effective in relieving the important psychosocial and personality problems which often give rise to the illness.

Beside this unresponsiveness to psychotherapy, there is an expected and predictable response, in certain classes of depression, to drugs or to electroconvulsant treatment; there is a failure to respond to simulated treatment, shown in experiments which were done decades ago. With a biological cure such as electroconvulsant treatment, it seems reasonable to postulate a biological basis. The similarity and consistency of some types of depression, the manic-depressive and the psychotic, paranoid involutional depressions, over the ages, in all cultures, also suggest some biological basis.

The psychotherapist working with depressed patients may notice a persistence of symptoms despite seeming insight. The physical signs may be mild, such as early waking or excessive sleeping, but without severe insomnia; fatigue or easy fatigability; a lack of initiative; or mildly lowered efficiency without definite psychomotor retardation. This mild, somatic, vegetative slowing down may not seem severe enough to interfere with psychotherapy, but when it is evident that there is some additional impoverishment of thought, a persistence of a few poorly developed recurrent themes of a pessimistic content, one should seriously consider medicines, via a consultation with a psychiatrist.

PSYCHOSOMATIC PROCESSES – THE SOMATIC BASIS

To complicate matters, cerebral functions can eventually involve hormone systems, through the hypophysis and the pituitary, causing changes in other glands of internal secretion (e.g., the adrenals) which secrete hormones, thus modifying body chemistry. There are not only mood changes but also changes in steroid balance, thyroid function, menses, and so on; an ongoing state is created that becomes independent of voluntary interference. In the early stages of this process, before the problems become fixed, successful intervention can be inserted anywhere, from the point of the psychological stimulus or to the end point, the symptom complex. However, if the process has become self-perpetuating, resonating and independent of the original stimulus, for intervention to be successful it has to be done at the neuronal (i.e., cellular) level, by physical and chemical means. This is where drugs, electroconvulsant treatment, and other biological methods are indicated.

MEDICINE AND RESPONSIBILITY

Psychotherapists should know certain practical things about psychopharmacology, as should the patients themselves and their families. At the very least, anyone involved with the degree of closeness and responsibility of a therapist should know what obvious symptoms call for medication, and should also be aware that there is specificity in the prescription of drugs. Psychotherapists need to know the relationship of their own work to the effect and use of the drugs, the complications in management involved for patients who are involved in both forms of treatment, cases where either medication or psychotherapy is preferable, and those where a combination is best.

Since medication is also useful in prevention, it is essential to be aware of the dangers and benefits of long-term use of drugs as well as the need for supervision and the continuous monitoring of effects and potential side effects, including signs of overdose, sensitivity, or failure to respond.

The spectrum, particularly of depressions, is so wide that often the range of cases seen in any one therapeutic setting may give the therapist too narrow a view of drug usage. Those who see only children know that one has to be very sparing of medication with children, but still must be alert to the rare child who has an affective disorder and needs medication as well as psychotherapy and environmental intervention. People who care for the elderly are going to see many physically related depressions, but the use of medicines in the elderly requires special care and special techniques.

Therapists who see mostly ambulatory, functioning patients probably do not see many who have more severe major disorders, possibly one or two in ten. Therefore, they have the impression that drugs are not important.

On the other hand, therapists working in hospitals with more severely ill patients, whether nonpsychotic, prepsychotic, or psychotic, may perhaps have the impression that everyone treated by psychiatrists is or should be given medication, which is not true.

The use of medication for ambulatory patients raises many questions, and one should know fairly exact indications, because this is a group from which major disorders may eventually arise and the use of drugs early in the course of the episode can be very effective in prevention. A comprehensive review by Rifkin (1988) of nine studies comparing imipramine with electroconvulsant treatment of inpatients reports somewhat higher figures for imipramine, a tricyclic antidepressant, than those reported by Baldessarini, especially when higher doses are used. Improvement ranged from 72 to 80 percent with imipramine treatment and slightly but significantly higher with electroconvulsant treatment.

THE PATIENT AND PSYCHOPHARMACOLOGY

One of the most common questions patients' families ask is, "What does the medicine do?" or, "How does it act?" Leaving aside any phobic significance to this question, one has to answer directly, leaving the analysis of the question for later.

One can safely say that the antidepressant drugs used today are not stimulants in the amphetamine sense, but operate to assist the body's own mechanisms to work better and can be discontinued upon recovery without dependency or addiction. This statement probably answers the unspoken questions. Depressed persons do fear drugs; they fear dependency, and they don't like what they call "crutches." Submission to medicines may threaten to increase their already overblown guilt and increase anxiety.

Numerous studies have been done comparing the effectiveness of antidepressant drugs to placebos, using foolproof double-blind designs (Baldessarini 1983, p. 102), leaving no doubt that these drugs are effective medicines. The figures for measurable relief of symptoms generally are in the range of 66–75 percent of cases or more, compared with placebos, which have a range of 20–40 percent, depending on selection.

The monamine oxidase inhibitors (MAOs) give similar results with nonpsychotic depression in hospitalized patients, with about two-thirds of the group responding favorably to the drug in a study (Janicak et al. 1988) comparing the effect of phenelzine on psychotic and nonpsychotic patients. The response to MAO inhibitors in this study of depressed inpatients differed according to whether the patient was psychotic or nonpsychotic. Of the group who were nonpsychotic 68 percent were responders. Of those probably psychotic 43 percent were responders, and of the definitely psychotic only 21 percent were responders. Such studies confirm our belief that drugs are the first choice for nonpsychotic depression, but that many of the psychotic group will require ECT because they do not respond to medication. With milder major depressions and depressive neuroses, responses both to drugs and placebos are higher than with severe major depressions. Although the drugs are not perfect, most of the time, if properly selected, they do the job; when they do not, there are other options, as described in the section on combined treatment in Chapter 15.

Chemotherapy and Types of Depression

The specific types of depression in which medication may suitably be employed are classified in *DSM-III-R* as follows:

1. Major mood disorders. Medication is almost always required for:
- Bipolar affective disorders, both manic and depressive attacks.
- Major depressions, both single episode and recurrent.

2. Other mood disorders. The second large group, those without obvious physiological basis, have depressive symptomatology, but without somatic changes; the principal one is dysthymia (depressive neurosis), which often does not require medicines and is treatable by psychotherapy. Cyclothymic disorder is actually an attenuated form of bipolar disorder and is so classified in *DSM-III-R*. If pronounced, it is sometimes treated with lithium, although it can be seen as a psychogenic reaction to stress and can be helped by means of psychotherapy and psychological intervention also.

Schizoaffective disorders also respond to medication. This group is not in as great danger of being overlooked as some of those in the next three classifications, which are *secondary* depressions—those due to substance abuse, those due to use of various kinds of medication such as reserpine, and, of course, those which follow physical disease, the organic affective syndrome. Another large category, probably to be seen in the offices of social workers, psychologists, clergypersons, and in clinics for medically ill people (because sometimes physical symptoms result) is the "adjustment disorder with depressed mood" (*DSM-III-R*). This class includes some depressions that we might call "existential," including, nostalgia, separation syndromes, and so on. Another group, perhaps not seen as frequently as the adjustment disorders, should be put in the classification "not attributable to a mental disorder," specifically, "phase of life problems" or uncomplicated bereavement.

For all these secondary depressions, medication may sometimes be very helpful, both for relief of suffering and to prevent a major depression. However, the underlying condition must be taken into account and treated also.

PURPOSES AND FUNCTIONS OF MEDICATION

Medication has multiple functions, namely, to resolve the illness, or to relieve some of the more severe symptoms of suffering, such as insomnia, anxiety, and agitation, and to expediate psychotherapy. Medicines are also useful in preventing breakdown in functioning, suicide, and recurrences.

The first function of medicine is to bring about a resolution of the illness, which can be expected in 65–80 percent of appropriately selected cases. It takes from one to several weeks to achieve this result; 20–35 percent do not get much relief easily.

It is necessary to recognize the need for relief of symptoms that are unbearable. Those who need such relief include severely suicidal patients, patients in whom insomnia is severe enough that it is leading to exhaustion, or severe depressives with enormous fatigue and inability to function, sometimes to the extent that they are unable to get out of bed.

When symptoms are not as severe, chronicity or periodicity, which prevents functioning, justifies medicine; it can save time for the patient, sometimes months of disability. There is also the question of anxiety, which can be severe enough to require relief. Relief of symptoms expedites psychotherapy by making the patient more accessible to psychological change. Before given medication, patients may be so slowed down that they cannot talk or so sick that talking about their problems makes them worse. Psychotherapy then becomes possible largely through the use of medication.

A major reason for using medication is for prevention of breakdown, suicides, and recurrence. For example, it is possible, in the early stages of depression, to ward off an oncoming depression if the exhausted person can be helped to obtain rest by the use of medication given to improve sleep and/or tranquilizers to induce rest. In the onset period, where personal issues arise that create considerable stress, a depression can sometimes be prevented by the use of antidepressants, tranquilizers, and/or hypnotics.

Medication can prevent both cycling and breakdown during therapy. For example, a young man with a history of four previous depressive episodes originally broke down during intensive psychotherapy, but is now undergoing an intensive psychoanalytic psychotherapy while taking lithium for prophylaxis. He has had fluctuations in functioning and mood, but has weathered them without a major breakdown or loss of ability to function.

PSYCHOPHARMACOLOGY

Some psychotropic drugs have specific antianxiety, antidepressant, antipsychotic, and antimanic effects. There are cellular mechanisms whereby medicines, such as the benzodiazepines, for example, diazepam (Valium), are addictive. The study and application of drug–behavior relationships has become the science of psychopharmacology. The principal discoveries in the treatment of affective disorders include the monoamine oxidase inhibitors (MAOs) and the tricyclic antidepressants.

MAOs relieve depression. Since these drugs inhibit the neurohormones (monoamine oxidase) which break down the biogenic amines which act as neurotransmitters (norepinephrine, serotonin, and dopamine), the assumption is that this allows the available transmitters to do more work. This action implies, at least for working purposes, since it relieves depression, that there is some kind of malfunction of neurotransmitters in depression; this is not necessarily a correct assumption. This theory is the basis of the biogenic amine theory.

Another class of drugs, the tricyclic antidepressants, also relieves depression. These drugs operate, at least in part, by preventing the reuptake (binding of neurotransmitters and thereby neutralizing them), once they are used, thus enabling them also to do more of the work of transmitting nerve impulses across the synapses. There are now classes of these drugs that work on the different neurotransmitters, so that if a patient is not helped by the class that effects norepinephrine activity, he or she may be helped by drugs that affect serotonin. Research in this field has developed fifteen or twenty of these drugs to date, all of them effective.

DRUGS CURRENTLY USED IN AFFECTIVE DISORDERS

Once it is decided that the patient should be given medication, there is the problem of deciding on the correct drug or drugs (combinations of antidepressants and tranquilizers are often necessary). There is some specificity in the use of antidepressants; one drug does not do for everybody. Table 13-1 describes the seven classes of drugs used for affective disorders. The table also rates their effectiveness on the four groups of target symptoms present in affective disorders, with an added column on schizophrenia for comparison (*AMA Drug Evaluations* 1983; Baldessarini 1977; *Compendium of Drug Therapy*, 1985–1986; *Goodman and Gilman's The Pharmacological Basis of Therapeutics* 1985; *Physician's Desk Reference* 1988; Roy et al. 1984).

Anxiety

Many drugs are in use today for anxiety, principally the benzodiazepines and phenothiazines, and also meprobamate and buspirone (Buspar). The anxiolytics are described in Tables 13-2 and 13-3. The effective working time for most benzodiazepines is 5–8 hours. Metabolites linger for 8–200 hours. Hangovers are common because of slow elimination. Metabolic products of many are the same. The benzodiazepines have a tendency to accumulate. Tolerance develops and dependency is common in prolonged use. Addiction can follow. *The benzodiazepines should be tapered off, not stopped abruptly.* They are not to be used in children or first trimester of pregnancy. Start with small doses,

Table 13-1

Drug Use According to Target Symptoms

Class of drugs	Target symptoms				
	Anxiety	Insomnia	Depression	Mania	Schizophrenia
Anxiolytics Benzodiazepines	++++ ++++	++++ +++	++ ++	++ ++	+ +
Miscellaneous	++-++++	++-++++	+	+	0-+++
Antidepressants, tricyclic	+++	++	++++	May aggravate	Not used except for depressive psychoses and some depressed schizophrenics
Imipramine	++	+	+++	May aggravate	
Desipramine	++	++	+++	May aggravate	
Doxepine, amitriptyline, and others	+++	++	+++	May aggravate	
Antidepressants, MAO inhibitors	+*	+	++++	May aggravate	Not used except for depressive psychoses and some depressed schizophrenics

Antidepressants, others	Varies with drug	Varies with drug	Varies with drug	Aggravates	Varies with drug
Antipsychotics	+++	+	+	+++	++++
Antimanics					
Lithium	0	0	Treatment † and prevention, +++	Treatment and prevention, +++	No effect except those with concomitant mania or depressive cycling 0
Carbamazepine (Tegretol)	0	0	0	++++	0
Stimulants					
Amphetamines	Aggravates	Aggravates	Temporary benefit, ++	May aggravate	Intensifies psychosis
Methylphen-idate	Aggravates	Aggravates	Temporary benefit, ++	May aggravate	May precipitate psychosis
Beta blockers* (e.g., propanolol)	Relieves physical symptoms	+	May aggravate	0	0
Sedatives and hypnotics (e.g., barbiturates)	+++	+++	For sleep, +++	For rest and sleep, +++	For rest and sleep, +++

*Helpful in panic states.
†Variable effects. May relieve, have no effect, or make slightly worse.
0 No effect; not useful.
+ to ++++ Degress of benefit.

Table 13–2

Anxiolytics: Benzodiazepines

Generic name	Proprietary name	Elimination (half-life, in hours)	Duration of action	How supplied (mg)	Starting dose for anxiety (mg)
Alprazolam	Xanax	12–15	Intermediate	Tablets: 0.25, 0.5, 1	0.25–0.5, 3 times per day
Chlordiazepoxide HCl	Librium Libritabs	5–30	Longer	Capsules: 5, 10, 25	5–10, 2–3 times per day
Chlorazepate di-potassium	Tranxene Tranxene-SD Azene	36–200	Longer	Capsules and tablets: 3.75, 7.5, 15	3.75–7.5, 2–3 times per day
Diazepam	Valium Val-release	20–50	Longer	Tablets: 2, 5, 10	2–10, 2–3 times per day
Halazepam	Paxipam	14–100	Intermediate	Tablets: 20, 40	20–40, 3–4 times per day
Lorazepam	Ativan	10–20	Intermediate	Tablets: 0.5, 1, 2	0.5–2.0, 3 times per day
Oxazepam	Serax	5–10	Shorter	Capsules: 10, 15, 30; Tablets: 15	10–15, 3 times per day
Prazepam	Centrax Verstan	36–200	Longer	Tablets: 5, 10, 20	30–60, per day

Table 13-3
Miscellaneous Anxiolytics

Generic name	Trade name	How supplied (mg)
Chlormezanone	Trancopal	Capsules: 100, 200
Hydroxyzine HCl	Atarax	Capsules: 10, 25, 50
	Atarax 100	Capsules: 100
	Vistaril	Capsules: 25, 50, 100
Hydroxazine pamoate	Vistaril-IM	Capsules: 400
Meprobamate	Equinal	Tablets: 200, 400
	Miltown	Tablets: 200, 400
	Miltown 600	Tablets: 600
Tybamate	Tybatran	
	Salacen	
Buspirone	Buspar	Tablets: 5 and 10

tailor to need. Overdose potential for the anxiolytics listed in Table 13-3 is somewhat greater than for benzodiazepines because of a narrower margin between therapeutic and toxic doses. These drugs have been very useful and are still useful as alternatives to currently popular benzodiazepines. Buspirone, an anxiolytic released in 1987, is said to be unique in that it has no addicting properties, does not cause motor impairment, or an increase in alcohol impairment. It does have cross-tolerance with benzodiazepines and hypnotic drugs. Although time is needed for proper evaluation, it looks promising.

Insomnia

Various anxiolytic and hypnotic and some antidepressant drugs are useful for insomnia. It is important to relieve this symptom enough to allow rest and relaxation. Table 13-4 gives information on sedative hypnotics. The drugs listed in Tables 13-2 and 13-3 are useful for insomnia, particularly meprobamate in doses of 200-600 mg.

Table 13–4

Sedatives/Hypnotics (Sleeping Pills)

				Target Symptoms			
Drug class	Generic name	Trade name	Anxiety	Insomnia	Mania	Depression
Barbiturates*	Amobarbital	Amytal	Not used	+ + +	Rarely used	Given to improve sleep
	Amobarbital sodium	Sodium amytal	Not used	+ + +	For sleep and sedation	Given to improve sleep
	Aprobarbital	Alurate	Not used	+ + +	Rarely used	Given to improve sleep
	Butabarbital sodium	Buticaps, Butisol sodium	Not used	+ + +	Rarely used	Given to improve sleep
	Mephobarbital	Mebaral	Not used	+ + +	Rarely used	Given to improve sleep
	Pentobarbital	Nembutal, Nembutal elixir	Not used	+ + +	Rarely used	Given to improve sleep
	Phenobarbital	(Various)	Useful in some cases	+ + +	Rarely used	Given to improve sleep

	Phenobarbital sodium	(Various)	Useful in some cases	+ + +	Rarely used	Given to improve sleep
	Secobarbital	Seconal	Not used	+ + +	Rarely used	Given to improve sleep
	Secobarbital + amobarbital sodium	Tuinal	Not used	+ + +	Rarely used	Given to improve sleep
Non-barbiturates	Ethchlorynol*	Placidyl	Not recommended	+ + +	For sleep only	Given to improve sleep
	Ethinamate*	Valmid	Not recommended	+ + +	For sleep only	Given to improve sleep
	Methyprylon*	Noludar	Not recommended	+ + +	For sleep only	Given to improve sleep

Table continued on next page

231

Table 13-4 continued

Drug class	Generic name	Trade name	Target Symptoms				
			Anxiety	Insomnia	Mania	Depression
	Flurazepam*	Dalmane	Not recommended	+++	For sleep only	Given to improve sleep
	Temazepam†	Restoril	Not recommended	+++	For sleep only	Given to improve sleep
	Triazolam†	Halcion	Not recommended	+++	For sleep only	Given to improve sleep
	Chloral hydrate‡	Noctec and others	Not recommended	+++	For sleep only	Given to improve sleep

*Drugs usually not recommended except for persons for whom benzodiazepines, phenothiazines, other antianxiety, antipsychotic, or hypnotic drugs do not work well. Use should be temporary because of the danger of addiction.
†Benzodiazepines used entirely as hypnotics. For benzodiazepines used for sedation see Table 13–2.
‡Much cheaper than other nonbarbiturate hypnotics because the generic is available. There is also less hangover because of rapid elimination. Tolerance develops fairly rapidly.

Mania

Antipsychotics (see Table 13-5) are used frequently, often along with lithium. The drugs listed in Table 13-5 are very useful in psychotic depressions and particularly in mania, to help control agitation, restlessness, severe anxiety, insomnia, and destructiveness, and to bring about rest in the hospitalized manic patient in the 1-3 weeks before lithium has produced its therapeutic effect. Sometimes small doses have a quieting and antidepressant effect on major depressions also.

These drugs are known as neuroleptics because of the frequent neurological complications: pseudoparkinsonism, acute dystonia, akathisia, and tardive dyskinesia, which have to be treated with antiparkinson agents. They have anticholinergic side effects: drying of mouth, reduction of accommodation, slowing of bowel activity and secretion, and slowing of bladder function. They also lower the threshold to seizures, and sometimes cause hypotension and restlessness. Many have antiemetic effects and also may aggravate glaucoma.

Carbamazepine (Tegretol) was recently found to relieve manic symptoms. See Table 13-6. The following are still experimental, but promising antimanic drugs: valproic acid (Depakene), clonazepam (Clonapin), and various calcium channel blockers.

Depression

Tricyclics and Similar Compounds

Tricyclics have been preferred, but newer drugs have been added (see Table 13-7). The drugs listed in Table 13-7 all have a half-life of 15-30 hours. They require 1-6 weeks to build up an adequate therapeutic level, which can be measured by a blood test. Best results are obtained by starting with a modest dose, 10-50 mg, all given at bedtime to minimize side effects of drowsiness and to help sleeping. The dose is increased over a week or two to an effective level. Top doses vary from 125 mg to 300 mg

Table 13-5
Antipsychotics (Neuroleptics)

Drug class	Generic name	Trade name	Mania	Psychotic depression	Schizophrenia
Phenothiazines*			+++	+++	+++
Thioxanthenes†			+	++	+++
Dibenzodiaze-pines	Loxapine succi-nate	Loxitane	+	+	+++
Indolenes	Molindone HCl	Moban	+	+	+++
Butyrophenones	Haloperidol	Haldol	+++	+++	+++

*Phenothiazines include chlorpromazine HCl (Thorazine), prochlorperazine (Compazine), thioridazine HCl (Mellaril), fluphenazine HCl (Permitil), carphenazine maleate (Proketazine), piperacetazine (Quide), mesoridazine (Serentil), promazine HCl (Sparine), trifluoperazine HCl (Stelazine), acetophenazine maleate (Tindal), perphenazine (Trilafon), and triflupromazine (Vesprin).
†Thioxanthenes include thiothixine (Navane) and chlorprothixene (Taractan).

Table 13-6
Specific Antimanic Drugs

Generic name	Trade name	How supplied (mg)	Dose for the acute attack (mg/day)	Dose for prevention of cycles (mg/day)	Blood levels	Value
Lithium carbonate	Lithium carbonate Lithane Lithobid Eskalith Lithotabs Lithonate	Capsules and tablets: 300	600–1800	300–1500	0.9–1.2/m Eq/L for the acute attack 0.7–1.0/m Eq/L for prevention	Very useful in both acute attack and prevention
Carbamazepine	Tegretol	Tablets: 200 Chewable tablets: 100	200–1200	200–1000	Not needed; check rbc and wbc regularly	Very useful in cases; resistant to lithium

Table 13-7
Tricyclic Antidepressants

Generic name	Trade name	How supplied (mg)	Therapeutic dose range (mg)
Amitriptyline	Elavil, Emitrip, Endep, Amitid, Amitril	Tablets: 10, 25, 50, 75, 100, 150	50–300
Desipramine	Norpramin, Pertofrane	Tablets and capsules: 25, 50	75–200
Doxepin	Sineqan, Adapin	Capsules: 10, 25, 100	75–300
Imipramine hydrochloride	Tofranil	Tablets: 10, 25, 50 Ampules for IM injection: 25 in 2 cc	10–300
	SK-Pramine	Tablets: 10, 25, 50	
	Janimine	Filmtabs: 10, 25, 50	
Imipramine pamoate	Tofranil-PM	Capsules: 75, 100, 125, 150	75–300
Nortriptyline	Aventyl Pamelor	Capsules: 10, 25	50–100
Protriptyline	Vivactil	Tablets: 5, 10	15–60
Trimipramine	Surmontil	Tablets: 25, 50	50–150

(for imipramine). Maintenance dose ranges are at the lower end of the dose range. Side effects may require lowering the dose.

Monoamine Oxidase Inhibitors

MAO inhibitors are used only occasionally, but can be very effective. These are listed in Table 13-8. There are potential complications that limit their use. MAO inhibitors are used for people who are refractory to tricyclics or cannot take them. They require the patient to avoid tyramine-producing foods (see Table 13-9), as well as other stimulants (amphetamines) and antidepressant drugs (tricyclics) until 10 days after discontinuing MAO inhibitors. They are generally very effective, especially with atypical depressions, but because of the danger of hypertensive crises in the presence of tyramine-producing foods are usually employed only if other drugs have failed. Dietary restrictions required with use of MAO inhibitors are delineated in Table 13-9.

Other Antidepressants

Table 13-10 lists other antidepressants. They are used for depression of all kinds, especially with insomnia. Two of the most recent are trazodone HCl (Desyrel) and fluoxetine (Prozac). They are very welcome additions because they cause less disturbing anticholinergic side effects of tricyclics. These drugs (or similar new ones) may be used more and more because of its freedom from those sometimes unacceptable side effects.

Stimulants

Caffeine, amphetamines, methylphenidate (Ritalin) are stimulants and are used only occasionally, in special circumstances (see Table 13-11). These stimulants are very seldom used because of the rapid development of tolerance and dependency. Occasionally, in a resistant depression, any of them may be used for a

Table 13–8

Monoamine Oxidase (MAO) Inhibitors

Generic name	Trade name	How sup- plied (mg)	Dose (mg/day)
Isocarboxide	Marplan	Tablets: 10	10–30
Phenelzine sulfate	Nardil	Tablets: 15	30–60, reduced to 15 for maintenance
Tranylcypromine sulfate	Parnate	Tablets: 10	10–60

Table 13-9
Dietary Restrictions with MAO Inhibitors: Tyramine-Producing Foods

Foodstuffs to avoid	Comments
Cheese	Cottage and cream cheese permitted
Beer, red wine, sherry, and liqueurs	Clear spirits and white wine permitted
Yeast and protein extracts	Includes some packet soups and yeast vitamin supplements (Brewer's yeast)
Fava or broad bean pods (Italian green beans)	Shelled beans or other legumes permitted
Smoked or pickled fish (herring)	Includes caviar
Beef or chicken liver	
Fermented sausage (bologna, pepperoni, salami, summer sausage)	Untreated, unspiced sandwich meats permitted
Canned or overripe figs	
Stewed whole bananas, banana peels	Banana pulp permitted

Table 13-10
Miscellaneous Antidepressants

Generic name	Trade name	How supplied (mg)	Dose (mg/day)
Trazodone HCl	Desyrel	Tablets: 50, 100	50–400
Amoxapine	Asendin	Tablets: 50, 100, 150	50–100
Maprotiline	Ludiomil	Tablets: 25, 50, 75	50–150
Fluoxetine	Prozac	Tablets: 20	20–60

few days, sometimes very effectively but always under strict supervision. Caffeine may be very useful in helping a sloweddown depressed person get started in the morning.

Criteria for Selection

Criteria are clinical symptoms and physiological measurements. Measurements include the use of biological markers, particularly the dexamethasone suppressive test (DST). DST has recently become available as a test for melancholia (endogenous depression), that is, those depressions in which a definite chemical physiological change has taken place. A positive test indicates the presence of major depression or melancholia with 90–95 percent accuracy, but a negative test is only 50–60 percent accurate, and therefore does not eliminate major depression. A test dose of dexamethasone (Decadron, Hexadrol) of 1 mg is given by mouth at 4:00 P.M., and the plasma cortisol is measured at 4:00 P.M. the next day. A postdexamethasone value of greater than 5 μg/dl indicates major depression or melancholia.

Fundamentally, clinical symptoms are the most reliable guide in deciding which medication to use. For people who have a good deal of restlessness, agitation, and anxiety, antidepressants with sedating effects usually are tried first (amitriptyline, doxepin, trazodone). For those with less anxiety, who evidence mainly slowing down and fatigue, the nonsedating drugs should be used (imipramine, desipramine, trimipramine). Most of the time, the clinical criteria point to the right drug without recourse to the dexamethasone suppression test.

Table 13–11
Stimulants

Generic name	Trade name	How supplied (mg)	Dose (mg/day)
Aphetamine	Benzedrine	Tablets: 5, 10 Slow-release capsules: 15	5, 10, 15
Dextroamphetamine	Dexedrine	Tablets: 5 Slow-release capsules: 5, 10, 15	5, 10, 15
Methamphetamine	Desoxyn	Tablets: 2.5, 5 Slow-release capsules: 5, 10, 15	2.5, 5, 10, 15
Methylphenidate	Ritalin	Tablets: 5, 10, 20	5, 10, 20
Caffeine	No Doz, etc.	Tablets: 100	100
	Coffee	60–100 per cup	
	Tea	25–35 per cup	

TRICYCLICS AND OTHER ANTIDEPRESSANTS

Administration

In most cases, the best way to administer the medication is to start with a small dose, in order to minimize side effects, and gradually increase the dose until improvement occurs. The usual starting dose is 25–75 mg per day for all drugs except trazodone, for which the starting dose is 50–100 mg, and protriptyline, which is 10–15 mg. The entire daily dose may be given once at bedtime to minimize side effects and to get the benefit of the sedative effect at night, a maneuver which also relieves insomnia. The maximum daily dose usually required is 100–200 mg, sometimes as high as 300 mg, reached after about two or three weeks, for all drugs except trazodone, which is usually achieved with 200–400 mg, and protriptyline, which is 50–60 mg.

A steady-state plasma concentration is achieved at any one level in one–three weeks. The level that will result in improvement may take one–six weeks if one uses three weeks to build up the dose. Laboratory assay of blood levels is helpful when improvement does not take place at higher doses, usually 150–175 mg for most tricyclics, before going to the highest doses. The test finding may be low, and higher doses are needed, or one may have gone above the therapeutic level and must lower the dose. Values of plasma concentrations are available for optimal results in some of the drugs, namely imipramine, desipramine, nortriptyline, and amitriptyline (American Psychiatric Association. Task Force on the Use of Laboratory Tests in Psychiatry 1985; Glassman et al. 1977; Risch et al. 1979). However, most of the time these are not needed because clinical judgment is usually effective enough.

Results of Treatment

If the expected medication does not work, then others are tried after tapering off the first drug over a one- or two-week period. Ultimately, although one can expect relief in a majority of cases, there are four groups that can be identified according to response:

Quick Responders

This is a fairly large group of patients with dysthymic disorder, or very early or mild major depression, who respond quickly in one–seven days or so to small doses of as little as 25–100 mg of imipramine or amitriptyline. They are rather mildly depressed without much somatic symptomatology; that is, they are sad, discouraged, feel guilty, have trouble sleeping, and are anxious and troubled, but do not have psychomotor retardation and are still able to function. It is remarkable how quickly these patients respond. One gets the impression that something else is at work for which the drug acts as a trigger, such as the catharsis of unburdening themselves of their troubles or the feeling of having help with an otherwise lonely problem. This brings up the question of psychotherapy, which is discussed in the next chapter. Our experience with people who are in an early stage of major depression, especially if there is a history of a previous spell of major depression, is that it is possible to abort an oncoming spell at this stage.

Slow Responders

Most persons with established major depressions typically take one–six weeks to respond to medication. With these persons it is necessary to build up a steady-state plasma level by gradually increasing the dose range of 125–300+ mg daily for most tricyclics (250–400 mg for trazodone; 40–60 mg for protriptyline). In case of doubt, blood studies for plasma levels should be done to ascertain that the level is within the therapeutic range. Blood levels require individual interpretation because of individual idiosyncrasy of response. Also, the standards vary somewhat according to laboratory. If the level is above the therapeutic "window," the dose should be lowered; if below the "window," the dose should be raised.

Nonresponders

The proportion of persons who become disabled over a long period of time or have frequent relapses, or who only partially recover, depends on selection, that is, the type of clientele in the therapist's practice. In a general practice, it is safe to say that 10 percent of those with all affective disorders have a major disorder, and probably one-third of these are difficult, chronic, or relapsing types. Difficult cases are more frequent in psychiatric practice, where probably two-thirds are major disorders and about 30–35 percent of the cases are prolonged or nonresponders. Most patients do not have to be hospitalized because drugs and psychotherapy keep them out of the hospital, unlike the situation that existed before effective medication was available, when a high percentage needed hospitalization. With these cases one triesvarious drugs, checks blood levels, supplements the drugs with L-tryptophan or triiodothyronine, and occasionally obtains good results. Some more nonresponsive patients benefit by periodic or maintenance electroconvulsant treatment. It is often necessary also to correct adverse psychosocial situations, which are usually present in such cases and sometimes are overwhelming and constitute an important obstacle to recovery until removed.

Side Effects

Tricyclic antidepressant drugs have side effects, some of which are unpleasant (see Table 13–12). The side effects most of them have, with the exception of trazodone, are anticholinergic, (i.e., drying of the mouth, occasional blurring of vision, constipation, and sometimes urinary hesitancy or even retention). The intensity of these effects is dose-related and most of the time does not prevent using the medication, but they can become serious if neglected. Another side effect, principally of amitriptyline, doxepin, protriptyline, nortriptyline, and trazodone is drowsiness, which can be useful in relieving insomnia if the medication is taken at bedtime. It is important to prevent constipation, particularly, by prescribing stool softeners and bulk laxatives prophylactically, and by keeping doses as low as possible without sacrificing effectiveness.

Tricyclic and other antidepressants, even trazodone, can cause cardiac arrhythmias in some susceptible people. It is necessary, if someone has heart disease, to be extremely careful in administering these drugs. Some cardiac patients cannot take them at all. If there is any question, the cardiologist should make the decision.

It is essential to use these drugs to their optimum effect. Side effects can be unpleasant, but it may be necessary to put up with them to get relief.

PSYCHIC ENERGIZERS AND STIMULANTS

Amphetamines (dextroamphetamine) and methylphenidate (Ritalin) can be very useful transiently in certain rare depressions which are not responding well to other drugs, particularly the tricyclics. The combination accentuates the effect of each so that extreme care should be used. Combination with MAO inhibitors should be avoided. Sometimes, perhaps one time in a hundred, a few days of treatment with 10 mg of methylphenidate or 5 mg of dextroamphetamine in the morning can be enough to trigger the recovery process from a long depression.

TRANQUILIZERS

Since many depressions are characterized by varying amounts of anxiety, agitation, restlessness, and insomnia, the tranquilizers can be very important in relieving symptoms. Minor tranquilizers, including, the benzodiazepines, diazepam (Valium) lorazepam (Ativan), chlorazepate (Tranxene), chlordiazepoxide (Librium), or meprobamate (Miltown, Equanil), can help a good deal. For extreme agitation, major tranquilizers (e.g., phenothiazines) are helpful. Sometimes an oncoming depression can be aborted successfully by insuring adequate rest and sleep. Judicious use of hypnotics at bedtime for a few days may keep an early depression from getting worse. This may require anything from minor tranquilizers to major hypnotic drugs.

LITHIUM

Lithium carbonate has become one of the most helpful treatments used today in psychiatric disorders. Not only does it dramatically improve the treatment of manic attacks (the excitement spells of bipolar disorder) but it is useful in *preventing* both manic spells and the depressed phase. Anyone who has had two or more recurrences of depressions should have an opportunity to try lithium as a preventive for a suitable trial period, a minimum of 1 or 2 years, depending on the frequency of cycling in the individual's history.

Lithium should not be given without proper medical approval and clearance; specifically, kidney function should be checked by a creatinine clearance test, liver function should be tested, the heart should be normal, and blood count and blood electrolytes should be normal. Thyroid function tests should also be done as lithium tends, in women particularly, to cause a diminution in some patients of thyroid function over a period of years. If the function is low, thyroid replacement is given. Renal functions, especially in men, may be lowered and should be checked yearly by creatinine clearance.

It may take lithium 2 or 3 weeks to bring down the hyperactivity of a manic patient to normal; meanwhile the patient may need a major tranquilizer (neuroleptic), such as haloperidol or a phenothiazine, to control the psychosis, and hospitalization may be required. In exceptionally hyperactive patients, electroconvulsant therapy may be required to bring the attack under control so that the patient can rest and accept medication. Recently it has been reported that large doses of lorazepam (Ativan) either by mouth or intramuscularly can be used instead of major tranquilizers in the early management before lithium takes effect. This drug avoids the extrapyramidal side effects of neuroleptics. The dosage of lithium used for maintenance can be monitored by the use of blood levels, initially weekly levels for several weeks until a pattern is seen and a satisfactory level maintained, then monthly until the pattern and level are secured and stabilized, then 1–4 times yearly. It is important that the blood levels be kept at a level for prevention between 0.7 and 1.1 mEq/L. Levels above this are probably not safe, and levels below this are probably not effective, except for prevention.

If another attack of depression begins while the patient is receiving an adequate dose of lithium, then usually an antidepressant should be added. Characteristically, under lithium prophylaxis, the response to antidepressant and antimanic treatment is more rapid and the attacks of depression and mania are less severe than without lithium.

Side Effects

Discontinue the drug immediately and have a blood level done when these occur:

- Tremor of hands severe enough to interfere with writing and other fine movements

- Nausea for more than a day or two, with or without cramps and indigestion

- Diarrhea for more than a day or two

- Interference with consciousness, for example, excessive drowsiness or coma

There are some safe side effects: (1) A fine tremor which does not interfere with function is often present at normal therapeutic levels. (2) Sometimes loose stools which are only occasional and not daily are safe. (3) Some indigestion, intestinal cramps, or gastric distress which results from taking the lithium on an empty stomach can be prevented by taking it with meals or with a small amount of food.

Effects of Prolonged Administration

Reported occasional or rare effects after years of use include loss of hair, skin discolorations, weight gain, and psoriasis (in predisposed persons). Lowering of thyroid or kidney functions occurs in a few patients. The latter may be an indication for stopping the medication. Renal function should be checked yearly, at least. Thyroid function should be checked if hypothyroid symptoms develop.

Effect of Stress on Response

Response to lithium and lithium prophylaxis can be influenced by stress. One report described three cases in which failure to respond can be caused by psychological stress (Benson 1976). If your patient is a nonresponder, look carefully at the psychosocial situation for stressors, and be prepared to deal with them.

It should be said here also that the onset of manic attacks can be influenced by emotional crises in the intimate family relationships. Sometimes close members of families become depressed and sometimes manic when the other member of the pair gets sick.

Lithium is not 100 percent effective either in cure or prevention of all cases.

CARBAMAZEPINE (TEGRETOL) FOR BIPOLAR ILLNESS AND AS AN ANTIDEPRESSANT

Between 20 and 30 percent of bipolar patients and a smaller number of unipolar depressives do not respond well or are intolerant to lithium. It has been discovered (Post, 1983) that a substantial number of these patients do well with carbamazepine, a drug which has been used for a number of years for epilepsy and is marketed in the United States under the name of Tegretol. At this writing it has not yet been approved by the Food and Drug Administration for bipolar disorder, but it seems likely that it will be, although with caution because of some side effects, particularly its potential for causing aplastic anemia, hepatitis, or exfoliative dermatitis. Therefore, the drug should not be the first choice for the treatment of mania or depression, but should be reserved for those cases in which lithium cannot be given or is ineffective. Before starting the drug, it is imperative to have baseline blood counts done, as well as liver function tests, since there have been a few cases of jaundice and hepatitis reported (Physician's Desk Reference 1988).

When properly used, the drug is very effective, especially with more severely ill patients, that is, those who cycle rapidly or continuously and the severely manic. Such severely ill patients should be in the hospital for the beginning of treatment.

The method is to start with low doses, in the 200-mg to 400-mg range, and increase slowly at 4- or 5-day intervals by adding 200 mg at a time, to a maximum of 1,400 mg per day. A few patients may require higher doses, up to 2,200 mg per day, but only if they have shown some evidence of beneficial effect at lower doses. Of course, at every step of the way the patient should be monitored for distressing symptoms, such as skin rash, sedation, and dizziness. Also important is monitoring for anemia and leucopenia by frequent blood counts, twice weekly in the first weeks, weekly for several months, and monthly for 2 or 3 years after that. A recent review (*International Drug Therapy Newsletter* 1986) states that the drug should be discontinued under the following conditions: red cells less than 4 million/mm^3, hematocrit less than 32 percent, hemoglobin less than 11 g per 100 ml, leucocytes less than 4,000/mm^3, platelets less than 100,000/mm^3, reticulocytes less than 0.3 percent, and serum iron greater than 150 μg per 100 ml.

A low white cell count is fairly common, but it returns to normal when the drug is discontinued. If the patient complains of sore throat, feeling sick, fever, bleeding gums, or has petechiae, the blood counts should be checked immediately before any additional doses are given.

Certain drug interactions should also be kept in mind, and the following drugs should be avoided when the patient is taking carbamazepine: the antibiotic erythromycin, the MAO inhibitor isoniazide, warfarin, doxycycline, phenatoin, desipramine, and possibly some neuroleptics. A reversible hypothyroidism has been reported (loc. cit.). It is also wise to stop the drug if a skin rash occurs, as it is reported that a few of those with rashes go on to the more serious complications named above (loc. cit.).

In summary, it is wise to start with low doses and increase gradually, monitoring the patient carefully. Blood levels of the drug are not as helpful as the occurrence of side effects in deciding whether or not to continue.

A lessening of the symptoms of hyperactivity and aggressiveness may be seen in the first week or two, and substantial improvement in the third and fourth week. Thus, it is seen to act at about the speed of lithium, and neuroleptics may be required to control the patient in the first week or so. This fact complicates matters somewhat as there are interactions between carbamazepine and neuroleptics, particularly haloperidol, which is often a drug of choice with acute manic psychosis. For example, the drug may increase the metabolism of the neuroleptic, lowering its efficiency, so that if carbamazepine is discontinued the haloperidol concentration rises, causing extrapyramidal symptoms.

It is surprising, with these dangers, that many persons can take the drug, but it turns out that many can, and it has been a very useful drug to add to the armamentarium. It has been used for years for epilepsy, and with suitable precautions it should be very useful for those cases who do not respond to lithium. The amount of chronic disability should guide one's choice of treatments. For those who are chronically disabled, with repeated hospital admissions, the drug may restore them to functioning and, despite the risk, it can be very much worthwhile.

CHRONIC DISABILITY

There is always a group, however, of about 15 percent (half of the nonresponders) who remain pretty much disabled a good part of the time regardless of how intense the drug treatment. These can be divided into types:

- Patients with early onset bipolar or unipolar disease, starting in adolescence, that interfered with education, personality development, and the development of adult skills and coping abilities.

- Persons with neurological defects, such as cerebral arteriosclerosis or any deteriorating cerebral disease. These are usually the elderly with a long history of major affective disorder.

- Those with very difficult psychosocial problems which cannot be solved, such as are seen in an elderly dependent widow, spinster, or bachelor with no family.

- Combinations of above three groups. These complicated cases are very difficult to help unless some environmental changes can be engineered to bring relief from an otherwise intolerable situation. Bringing a nurse to help with an aged mother, getting supportive sitters, transferring to an adequately supportive environment, all may help bring relief. Daycare hospitals are very useful, as is organized group therapy, in keeping the chronically ill persons functioning and out of hospitals.

Society is becoming much more aware of these needs than it was a generation ago, and supportive facilities are more available. However, there is plenty of room for improvement in both public and private sectors, so that insistence may be necessary on the part of the therapist on finding and using facilities that make the difference between success and failure of therapy.

TIMING OF MEDICATION ACCORDING TO STAGE OF DEVELOPMENT OF DEPRESSION

There are stages in the clinical course of typical major depressions that influence the use of medication.

Stage I. The Well Stage

In Stage I, in which a predisposed person who is vulnerable to depression comes with some personal problem or with some psychosomatic symptom, the important thing is to identify the vulnerability and the underlying tendency to depression. This is evidenced by the patient's poor self-esteem, a tendency to self-debasement, to take losses hard, toward pessimism, to downgrade his or her own achievements, and perhaps a tendency not to enjoy life very much—an anhedonia. One can add guilt feelings to this list, usually greater than seem reasonable. In addition, there may be a marital or family problem characterized by ambivalence in the love relationships, although it is quite likely that the ambivalence is unconscious. At this stage the patient uses repression as a defense, has trouble expressing his or her aggression directly, and tends to express it in a passive-aggressive way.

Somatization may be a successful defense at this stage, and there may be psychosomatic symptoms, such as migraine or ulcer, or a depressive equivalent (e.g., alcoholism). If the patient has a past history of breakdown of a clear-cut depressive nature he or she actually belongs in Stage VI (well stage after recovery) and is treated differently from the person who comes for the first time with no history of depression and no family history of depression. In the cases in Stage I (the well stage, with no previous history), one should then try to identify frustrating situations and personality problems which, combined, create a seemingly insolvable predicament. At this point it is likely that one give no drug treatment at all. Most patients whom one sees in this category do not at any time need medication. Some of them later on may require some sleeping medication with hypnotic drugs, such as benzodiazepine in modest doses, possibly barbiturates, and possibly a mild tranquilizer such as diazepam or lorazepam in small doses. But for the most part one can deal with people at this stage on a purely psychological basis. The nonmedical psychotherapist, of course, needs to have a physician, preferably a psychiatrist, to prescribe the drugs.

Stage II. Preliminary Changes

In Stage II, there is a definite loss of enjoyment and zest for life, coupled with a tendency to withdraw and perhaps the emergence of definite depressive symptoms such as feelings of being "blue" or "downhearted." Withdrawal from contact is perhaps the most important and should be acknowledged as vital to successful defense. Sleep begins to become disturbed, appetite may be decreased, and more defenses such as projection or conversion may be needed, the old defenses of repression being insufficient. Somatization is still in effect, but may not suffice.

The beginnings of anxiety breaking through the defenses may require the patients to look restlessly or compulsively for things that will help ward off depression, such as activity, drinking, the use of cocaine (in the young adult), acting-out behavior such as wanting to change jobs or spouses, wanting to look for other types of enjoyment in life, a love affair, a desire to escape. Some sort of change in behavior may be noted, especially in children or adolescents, where the depression may not have the usual adult picture; these behavioral changes betray that the person is troubled. At this stage it is easy to overlook the underlying depression. Sometimes old somatic symptoms may be present. Besides ordinary headaches, as mentioned in the "well" stage, there may be unusual head pains or anxiety about physical health.

In this stage, medication can be useful, particularly if there is enough sleep disturbance that rest is essential. In this case one gives a hypnotic to help with sleep, such as a benzodiazopine, barbiturates, or chloral hydrate, or, if the insomnia is mild, one can use only tricyclic antidepressants. At this stage, which tricyclic should be used? If there is a clear-cut need to help the patient sleep, one uses amitriptyline, protriptyline, doxepin, or trazodone, or others, giving the whole dose at bedtime because the side effect of drowsiness is helpful at this point. If there is no trouble sleeping or there is hypersomnia, and the depressive symptoms are quite clear-cut, one starts out with a nonsedative tricyclic such as imipramine in small doses, 50 mg at bedtime, gradually increasing over a period of 2–3 weeks until some response is elicited, up to 300 mg per day.

Stage III. Prebreakdown

Stage III is a stage in which something serious and out of the ordinary is obviously happening. Sleeping disturbance is worse, sometimes with the pattern of early waking, at 3:00 or 4:00 or 5:00 A.M., with an inability to get back to sleep, and sleep may not be restful. As one man put it, "I have a thin veil of sleep." There also may be hypersomnia at this stage. Other common symptoms are a loss of sexual desire, fatigue, and a nonspecific anxiety. "Am I losing my mind?" is not a rare question. Distinct depressive ideas occur, such as feelings of helplessness, hopelessness, and suicidal thoughts. Concentration becomes difficult, decisiveness is lost, and indecision tends to predominate.

This is the type of depression one sees perhaps the most often, and it is not only the most common but it is the stage at which most depressions stay throughout their course. If certain other changes take place that indicate a coming breakdown, it may signal the onset of a psychotic phase. Such changes occur as the loss of repression and the breaking through of suicidal ideas and impulses into consciousness and their acting out; fantasies of repressed ideas and memories may return. If this happens, it suggests the return of the repressed, and breakdown of reality testing is likely to occur.

At this stage, treatment should be preceded by a medical evaluation, and the patient who seems to be overwhelmed or under enormous stress may need relief by being hospitalized. At this stage, supportive psychotherapy is by far the best psychological treatment, and anything such as analysis that accentuates the return of the repressed is to be avoided. One should not probe too deeply, but one should listen to patients who are under pressure to get something off their chest.

Drug treatment at Stage III resembles that of Stage II. If the patient shows signs of slowing down and definitely has psychomotor retardation, one gives a tricyclic antidepressant with stimulating properties, such as imipramine or norpramine. Again, start with lower doses and increase until the desired effect is obtained. If no improvement occurs, it is possible to do blood levels of the tricyclics, but it is rarely necessary, as you give the drug to maximum effect anyway. However, there are standards which may be observed if you are able to get tricyclic blood levels.

If the nonsedating (noradrenergic) group does not produce improvement within 3–4 weeks, one of the sedating (serotonergic) group of tricyclics should be given. Sometimes the drugs produce rapid effects; improvement may start within a week; however, often patients do not begin to get well for a month, and one tends to wait that long, or even 6 weeks if it is at all possible, judging by the patient's ability to tolerate the drug. In the case of those who are more restless or verge on agitation, one uses a serotonergic drug, either amitriptyline or doxepin, perhaps the latter by preference because of a somewhat greater sedative effect. Start with doses of the range of 50–75 mg a day, given at bedtime, and work up to 150–200 mg; occasionally 250–300 mg may be necessary.

The tricyclic antidepressants are sometimes troublesome because of anticholinergic side effects (see Table 13–12). It may be necessary to cut back on the dose or to stop the drug for a time in certain patients who develop constipation or urinary retention. It is wise to warn the patients in advance to report any such symptoms and to use vigorous preventive measures. The drying of the mouth and blurring of vision which occur routinely with these drugs are sometimes a problem, but generally we ask the patient to tolerate these relatively minor side effects. Constipation can routinely be controlled by the use of laxative substances such as bulk additives and/or stool softeners taken regularly in order to prevent what can sometimes become quite serious obstipation. Desipramine is the least anticholinergic. A switch to trazadone (Desyrel) may be necessary.

Occasionally a patient comes along for whom one of the MAO inhibitors is extremely helpful. An example is of a married woman, aged 50, with a series of depressions persisting over a period of more than 2 years despite energetic biological treatments, including tricyclic antidepressants and one series of eight electroconvulsant treatments. Tranylcypromine, an MAO inhibitor, was very effective in reversing her depression, dramatically, within 2 weeks. Parenthetically, this chemotherapy was integrated into the total treatment program, which included addressing a troublesome marital situation with couples therapy. Her own rather severe compulsive manner also ameliorated enough so that she was able to return to normal functioning. The MAO inhibitor seemed to give enough symptomatic relief that the total program became effective after two very difficult years of lack of progress. Table 13–9 lists the restricted foods to be avoided while on MAO inhibitors.

Stage IV. Breakdown Stage

Stage IV (melancholia) does not occur in all patients, but in those in whom it does occur a psychotic depression supervenes, following a gradual development from the previous stage. Sometimes this stage is not identified until a suicidal attempt takes place, showing loss of control over the suicidal drive. Other changes signify psychosis, such as guilt to a delusional degree in addition to feelings of hopelessness, which may be nihilistic and delusional, (e.g., with somatic delusions). Loss of reality testing occurs, characterized by inability to distinguish between fantasies of worthlessness and reality. Concentration is poor, sleep seriously disturbed, and ability to function has been lost. In this stage the drug therapy is much the same as in previous stages, but hospitalization is almost always necessary.

At Stage IV failure to respond to drugs is more common, probably with a failure rate of 75–80 percent. Electroconvulsive therapy is then necessary and, indeed, lifesaving. It may also prevent a long-lasting depression which might have gone on for years.

Stage V. Recovery Stage

Stage V is a stage of considerable vulnerability. Relapses are frequent, up to 40–60 percent within the first 2 years. The patient may or may not have a lack of confidence, although depressive symptoms are relieved, and sometimes an amnesia for the depressed period, especially if electroconvulsant treatment was given. During this time support, reassurance, and a nurturing psychotherapy are the correct methods of treatment. Rehabilitation may be necessary, that is, a gradual introduction of various functioning aspects of the person's life—chores, reading, visits home, etc.

Medication at this stage helps prevent recurrence and relapses. Whatever drug or combination of drugs found effective in bringing the depression to this stage should be continued, although many patients, if unsupervised, tend to stop them. The odds are approximately 2 to 1 in favor of prevention of relapses when medication is used, over those cases in which it is not.

Stage VI. Well Stage After Recovery

Stage VI is much like Stage I except that one hopes the patient has learned something and has developed greater protection against

Table 13–12

Side Effects of Antidepressants

Drug	Side effects		Contraindication
	Mild	Severe	
Lithium	Slight tremor, bad taste, weight gain, loss of hair, aggravation of preexisting psoriasis, hypothyroidism	Tremor, diarrhea, abdominal cramps, seizures, collapse	Diuretics, kidney disease, low kidney function, cardiac arrhythmia, severe psoriasis
MAO inhibitors	Mild tremor	Tremor, hypertensive rises	Hypotension or hypertension, coincident treatment with thyroid hormone or with tricyclics, eating foods yielding tyramine, inability to follow diet
Tricyclics	Dizziness, constipation, dry mouth, blurring of vision, mild delay of micturition, sedation	Obstipation, urinary retention, cardiac arrhythmias, postural hypotension, fainting, collapse	MAO inhibitor treatment, glaucoma, cardiac disease, especially with arrhythmia. Patients over 60 need lower doses, close monitoring

Other antidepressants (e.g., trazadone)	Sedation, drowsiness, amenorrhea	Cardiac arrhythmias, hypersensitivity, myocardial infarction, elective surgery, electroconvulsant therapy
	Cardiac arrhythmias, priapism, nausea	See tricyclics
Amoxapine (Asendin)	Amenorrhea, galactorrhea, extrapyramidal reactions	Cardiac arrhythmias, priapism, nausea
Maprotylin (Ludiomil)	See tricyclics	Seizures MAO inhibitor therapy within 10 days, seizure disorder
Bupropion (Wellbutrin)	Stimulation	Seizures Seizure Disorder

Note: All drugs can cause skin rashes insensitive people. Overdoses can cause death. All these drugs are toxic in overdose quantities. Combination drugs, including perphenazine and amitriptyline HCl (Etrafon) and chlordiazepoxide and amitriptyline HCl (Limbitrol) have effects and contraindications of the component substances.

breakdown by having gone through the depression with psychotherapeutic help and intervention for the relief of psychosocial stressors. If any personal predicament has been identified, work should be continued on this; problems in the family that have been identified should be treated by intervention, family therapy, couples therapy, etc., and problems in the patient's character should be treated by psychotherapy. Any troublesome frustrating personal situation should not be allowed to go on without some attempt at intervention; it is asking for trouble to send patients back into situations that brought on their depression in the first place, unless some changes are made.

For prevention in recurrent types, lithium may be helpful. There are good reasons to think that lithium, though not a very effective antidepressant against the acute attack, may protect against the occurrence of further depressions, particularly if the depressions tend to be episodic and not chronic.

CLUSTERS OF SYMPTOMS AND DRUG TREATMENT

There are several current trends in the use of medicines which should be noted here. Certain aspects of mood, for example, are highly indicative of the need for biological therapy. For example, the cluster of symptoms—hopelessness, suicidal rumination, and unreactiveness to usual psychological alleviators—is an indication for tricyclic antidepressants, and suicidal rumination or attempt is an indication for convulsive therapy. The presence of psychomotor retardation and the cluster of somatic symptoms that go with it—slowing of bowel function, fatigue, early morning waking—are likely to be an indication for biological therapy, including convulsive therapy. However, in all cases tricyclics are used before convulsive therapy.

Anxiety and other neurotic symptomatology are likely to eliminate convulsive therapy, cut down on the use of tricyclic antidepressants, and increase the number of cases in which MAO inhibitors are given. Delusions and hallucinations are likely to reduce very much the use of tricyclics and monoamine oxidase inhibitors, yet the number of those receiving electroconvulsive therapy is much the same as in the group with psychomotor retardation. In addition, certain personality features contraindicate convulsive therapy or tricyclics. These are generally what we would consider to be hysterical symptoms—the histrionic or dramatic personality.

The presence or absence of precipitants, external or internal, is apparently looked upon generally as important in the choice of medicines. Tricyclics are generally given where there is no obvious internal environmental precipitant but when there is some physiological or internal physical precipitant, or when there is an internal intrapsychic precipitant, such as a feeling or sense of object loss or disappointment. Vegetative features are indications also: insomnia, anorexia, and weight loss are likely to be indications for tricyclics. The sleep cycle of early waking is a very clear-cut indication for tricyclic antidepressants.

The history of a clinical course of repeated attacks with episodic clear periods is also a routine indication for the use of biological therapy, particularly if there is no other diagnosable psychiatric illness.

DRUGS AND PREVENTION

Medication should be continued until one is convinced there is not going to be a major relapse, which may be months. It is a very individual matter, depending on the patient's own history and the amount of stress he or she is under which might bring on a relapse or recurrence. Sometimes a small maintenance dose will suffice to keep the patient in balance, such as 50 mg a day (for tricyclic antidepressants). Occasionally one sees someone who requires 150 mg per day or more indefinitely to stay well. The treatment must be tailored to individual needs. There is a small group of chronic and long-term patients who have to continue medication indefinitely. Another group have less frequent recurrences if the drug is discontinued gradually between spells during the well interval.

NONCOMPLIANCE

Patients do not always take the prescribed medicines. It would be naive to expect that people who are full of fears and have their own fantasies or delusions about what their problems are can comply with instructions in every case. Some patients resist medication altogether, and some take too little or resist taking it regularly. People who do not, or cannot, follow instructions fall into several groups.

The Severely Depressed

Those who have such severe depressions that they cannot function in any responsible way or have no initiative, cannot be expected to concentrate on taking a certain amount of medicine at a certain time every day. Anyone this sick should be in the hospital; if hospitalization is not possible, someone at home should be responsible for administering the drugs.

Manic Patients

Those who are so euphoric and speeded up, in a manic state, that they are too scattered in their purpose and actions to be responsible. This group also should either be hospitalized or have someone else be responsible.

The most common cause of resistance to lithium in manics is their resistance to losing that euphoria which characterizes the manic state. They are also afraid that they will be less self-confident and creative. Most of the time their fears are groundless; they will become less active, but will be more productive because better organized and less scattered. Of course, without treatment patients are probably in for bad depressions later on, if they have bipolar disease, and with lithium prophylaxis they are less likely to have a depression.

Those Suffering Severe Side Effects

There are those in whom the side effects seem worse than the disease. Tricyclic antidepressants can cause severe constipation, even impactions requiring manual removal, although prevention by routine use of stool softeners and bulk formers can forestall much of this complication. Tricyclic antidepressants have an exaggerated effect in those not uncommon persons in whom the depression itself is accompanied by a slowing of bowel activity, dry mouth due to diminished salivation, and slowing of peristalsis. Particularly if these signs are present, by all means routinely give preventive doses of stool softeners and bulk laxatives. Avoid cathartics on a chronic regimen, although laxatives, cathartics, and enemas are sometimes necessary for the acute constipation. Milder drugs, such as milk of magnesia, are preferred if they are effective.

Blurring of vision in rare cases, though not serious, can cause anxiety and noncompliance.

Urinary retention in middle-aged men or elderly with enlarged prostates can be serious enough to warrant lowering doses or even stopping the drug. If there is a history of difficulty in urinating, be very careful; start with small doses and increase gradually.

Lithium is notorious for noncompliance because of the tremor it may induce even at therapeutic levels. Of course, if the tremor occurs only at higher doses, it is easy enough to lower the dose and still be within the therapeutic range. Another occasional reason for noncompliance is the thinning of hair which may occur in some people.

Other Noncompliant Groups

Those whose anxiety is increased or who feel sedated by the particular effects of the specific drug may stop their medication. Antidepressants such as imipramine, by adrenergic effects, can cause an increase in pulse, tremulousness, and apprehension which, in some persons, plays into the anxiety already there. The sedative effect of the serotoninergic tricyclic drugs such as doxepin, trazodone, and amitriptyline also can cause feelings of relaxation which are threatening to a personality to whom passivity and lack of energy are frightening.

The compulsive anxious person will read about all the side effects and immediately interpret the worst possible outcome. As one would expect with depressed people, this kind of fantasy is not unusual. Reasonable explanations or arguments are needed to convince certain patients that side effects have to be disregarded at times.

Suggestable persons of hysterical character may have heard from friends, or from popular articles, that medication is dangerous or, in the opposite direction, may have heard of a particular drug that helped a friend and will take no other.

Some patients have certain unrealistic fantasies and ideas, for example, that they are not ill and do not need a medicine. This includes the group who are psychotic and have the delusion that no one can help them and that there is no use taking medication. Another group are those who, although not overtly psychotic, seem to have ideas of their own about their condition and do not want to acquiesce to anyone's control. For them, taking medicine is a defeat which they cannot accept.

Another group are those to whom *any* medication is a threat, either because it alters their feelings or because it affects bodily processes and creates anxiety, or because of a paranoid attitude that is based on a lack of trust in general and a fear of being poisoned in particular, in which case a medicine is a foreign body that penetrates their defenses and takes control out of their hands. This is a phobia rather than a delusion but just as effectively prevents compliance.

Overmedicators and Hoarders

There are people who take more than is prescribed, either in an attempt to get relief or for suicidal purposes. To prevent this eventuality, know the patient's intentions in advance. Or, if you cannot be sure that you are safe with the particular patient, at least give him an amount that will not kill him in case he takes it all.

This discussion does not exhaust the subject of noncompliance. One could also mention the hoarders of hypnotic drugs (popularly known as sleeping pills), who want a big enough supply hidden away to make that eventual self-destruction possible, if they choose that route. If you are a prescriber of drugs, try to keep track carefully of the amounts prescribed, and check the numbers against the amount used. Talking to the pharmacist occasionally helps in the monitoring process; pharmacists are generally very anxious to share responsibility with dangerous drugs.

Reducing Noncompliance

Dealing with noncompliance is not easy. What is important is to prepare for it in advance and give a preliminary explanation covering the rationale of the medicine, explaining the side effects, using reassurance, and especially evaluating the patient's mental state and capacity for cooperation. If you fail to do this you may be in for a hard time.

If you are a nonmedical therapist and someone else is giving the medication, you must try to work on your own antimedication prejudices, an attempt which is not always successful. If you are not prejudiced against chemistry, but uneasy about the possibility that medication is not right for this patient, you must at least communicate your questions to the prescriber of the drug who should (I hope!) be glad to discuss your doubts with you. As a professional, he or she has an obligation to do this.

No matter what you do or say, some people simply end up by not complying. You have to accept this as part of their problems, their illness, and live with it somehow. In cases where medication is vital, such as controlling a manic patient, the cooperation of the family should be enlisted.

As in other aspects of the care of patients, trust and compliance are likely to be greatest when the physician is genuinely concerned, takes enough time, and shows enough interest in the patient to be really involved. Sometimes patients know or sense something about themselves that we don't know. They may feel that they need to keep their autonomy and to work through and attempt to solve their problems psychologically. Although professional pride may be somewhat offended by this rejection of the magic remedies, do not give up. The patient may need time to accept the treatment offered and keep his or her autonomy and dignity at the same time. "I don't like a crutch," some persons say to you. This kind of denial is unrealistic, but perhaps the patient needs it to keep his self-image intact.

Usually such persons will eventually take the medicines if they really need them, after they see that you are sincere and do understand them, especially if they can grasp and accept the concept that this is an illness like any other and not a personal failing on their part. In others this attitude is difficult to distinguish from a delusion because of its rigidity, and one's patience is sorely tried.

Relief of suffering is helpful in reducing noncompliance; if the medication obviously works, people are likely to be believers. However, once relief is securely established, then you find that some people stop the drug without consulting you—an eventuality to guard against by frequent enough contact with the patient.

OTHER BIOLOGICAL TREATMENTS

Light treatment (phototherapy). Some persons, especially those with mild depressions occurring in the fall and winter, have been found to improve greatly when exposed to bright light for two to four hours a day. This group is mostly women with definite depressions, many of the mild bipolar type. The condition has been identified as Seasonal Affective Disorder, and has received so much popular and professional attention as to acquire the acronym SAD. Actually, it seems to be an attenuated form of bipolar illness, generally occurring in families in which there is a good deal of depressive illness.

Exposure of the patient to 2 to 4 hours of bright artificial illumination in early morning or late afternoon lessens depression a great deal after 2 to 3 days, but a relapse occurs when daily exposure to light is stopped. Spontaneous remission can be expected in the spring. The relief comes within 2 or 3 days of daily treatment, and continues as long as the treatment goes on. Because unpleasant side effects may occur, this procedure should not be instituted without the advice of a physician who is well informed about the method.

Although the method does not work for those with more severe major depression, it is said to improve the winter mood of healthy people (Saletu 1986).

Sleep deprivation. Another experimental treatment is keeping the depressed patient awake either all night or for several hours during the night. On the day after the deprivation the patient comes out of his or her depression but soon relapses. Another side effect in depressed persons who are also bipolar is the induction of an attack of mania. As a result of these complications, it is wise to use sleep deprivation very carefully, if at all (*Psychiatric News*, 1986a).

ELECTROCONVULSANT THERAPY (ECT)

In the 1970s a very heated controversy raged as to the rationale and effectiveness of electroconvulsant therapy (ECT), a standardized treatment that had been used widely in the treatment of both depressions and schizophrenia during the years before the introduction of effective antidepressants, when no effective treatment was available for these more severely ill persons. This controversy resulted in seriously limiting the use of an effective therapy and deprived some people, especially those with psychotic depressions, of their best chance for a quick recovery. Persons with less severe depressions have generally been effectively treated through the wide use of effective antidepressant medication in the last three decades. Although these drugs do not work as rapidly as ECT, they appear to be just as effective, except in cases of psychotic depression. They have the advantage of allowing psychotherapy to go on concurrently, an advantage precluded during ECT because of the temporary amnesia (American Psychiatric Association. Task Force on Electronconvulsant Therapy 1978).

Since that time, a number of studies have established both ECT's usefulness and superiority to drug treatment in hospitalized psychotic patients (Rifkin 1988). Most research today is concerned with the question of the most effective technique of the method (Abrams et al. 1983, Sackeim et al. 1987), or with selection of those most likely to be helped (Rifkin 1988). Abrams and colleagues (1983) compared the therapeutic efficacy of ECT using bilateral placement of electrodes, with that using unilateral placement in a group of fifty-one patients with melancholia. They found that six treatments brought about an 81.1 percent improvement in the bilateral and only a 55.5 percent improvement in the unilateral group. The fact that only six treatments were given probably accounts for the fact that the overall improvement rate was less than the usual expected rate of over 90 percent; the usual number of treatments for a depression with melancholia is eight.

As a result of these and other studies, along with the almost universal experience of psychiatrists, the indications for ECT are limited to its use in severe depressions which do not respond to medication, to depressed schizophrenics who do not respond to medication, and to manic patients who are out of control.

Electroconvulsant therapy consists of giving a series, at intervals of 2 or 3 days, of electrical stimuli to the head, inducing a grand mal seizure from which the patient recovers in a few minutes. The technique is painless and is quite refined, in that it is administered under brief anesthesia with a short-acting barbiturate, and no motor seizure occurs because of simultaneous injection of a curare derivative.

After a series of six or eight treatments, there is dramatic recovery in 90 to 95 percent of patients with major depressions. The most impressive recoveries are in the sickest melancholias, especially those who are psychotic.

In modern use, with anesthesia and medication to prevent muscle contraction, there is no observable convulsion (i.e., no motor component of the seizure). The experience is of a brief anesthetic, lasting a few minutes, followed by a period of sleep of ½–1 hour.

The anesthetic used for ECT in most clinics is an intravenous short-acting barbiturate. The possibility exists of a patient having a reaction to any anesthetic, so that one should inquire ahead of time as to whether he or she has ever shown any sensitivity to barbiturates or other drugs. If so, a different anesthetic must be used. Because occasional anesthetic reactions might occur, the treatment is given by a person trained in resuscitation, and the necessary equipment or oxygen supply and breathing apparatus are right there at hand, as for any general anesthetic.

The question of brain damage is brought up by some people, but damage is actually negligible and can be avoided by careful selection of cases and by cautious administration.

USE IN DEPRESSION

The place of ECT in the treatment of depression is firmly established, although it is used more specifically and much less frequently than a decade or two ago. It is a highly effective treatment, producing total or nearly total relief from symptoms in over 90 percent of properly selected patients. The antidepressant drugs have helped in the last three decades to make ECT unnecessary in most cases of milder depression, but for that small proportion of depressed persons who do not respond favorably to drugs, it definitely gives dramatic relief and saves lives as well as the patients' time.

Some psychiatrists tended in the past, before antidepressants were available, to use the treatment in a wide variety of patients, giving the impression of indiscriminate or inappropriate use. Nowadays, psychiatrists in the United States reserve it for a narrow range of selected people. It is reserved for those who do not respond to drugs and psychotherapy or who are so disturbed that no other treatment can be used, or when the saving of time is critical, as in a patient with a past history of a long disabling depression who does not get relief from drugs, usually psychotic types with melancholia.

Use in Mania

Manic patients who are out of control are also helped by ECT. Some patients are so agitated and resistant to taking medication that it can be life-saving to administer a few treatments. The likelihood is that the patient can then be persuaded to take lithium and tranquilizers and will fairly rapidly get better.

Lithium requires 2–3 weeks to take full effect. With mild, manic, out of control patients, in danger of hurting themselves or others, ECT may fill the gap while the drug is taking hold, especially if neuroleptics such as haloperidol are not effective.

Effectiveness of ECT

Although the benefits of ECT have been documented time after time, each practitioner has his or her own experience. One study looked at forty-five depressed patients treated with ECT in which the criterion for inclusion in the study group was a diagnosis of depression by the patient's psychiatrist, confirmed by a testing scale used for checking on the depth of depression. Of the forty-five patients, forty-two (93 percent) returned to the normal range after a course of ECT. The three patients who did not return to that range showed some improvement, but remained depressed enough to stay in the hospital.

The degree of improvement was substantial (60–100 percent) in *all* of the forty-two patients who benefited. What is more significant, those with the most severe depressions showed improvement to the same levels as those with mild depressions.

A number of careful studies show similar results (Rifkin 1988, Abrams et al. 1983). In the last few years, other methods have been used more because of the availability of new drugs and the need to explore their usefulness. During this period, ECT has possibly been underutilized, and some people who have not received it would have benefited by ECT, particularly through the saving of time and the diminishing of suffering and disability. For example, in a long midlife depression lasting five or six years, with several hospital admissions, marked loss of functions at times, and considerable misery for patient and family, it might have been better to give ECT and get the patient functioning quickly, following up with work on the underlying problems. The problem with ECT is recurrences and relapses, which must be guarded against with medicines and psychotherapy to individual and environment.

Side Effects

The dangers of ECT must be kept in mind, but there is misunderstanding about this also. The following is a list of the side effects and their importance:

Transient Memory Loss

In the usual course of 6 to 10 treatments there may be temporary memory loss for recent events such as those occurring during the course of treatments and immediately preceding it; some of this may not come back. For example, patients may not remember how sick they were when they entered the hospital, and you may have to remind them of some of the things that happened. A good deal of the lost memory will come back, and usually nothing from the patient's past or present life is lost. In elderly patients, especially those with cerebral arteriosclerosis, the treatments have to be spaced out, sometimes with interruptions of a few days or a week, in order to prevent memory loss. However, usually by the time there is some transitory memory loss the patients also get relief from the agony of their depression and value the relief so much that the temporary loss of memory is relatively unimportant.

Temporary Confusion

The term *confusion* describes any irrational state of mind in which the patient is puzzled, shows misunderstanding of his or her situation, acts impulsively, possibly aggressively, or shows loss of control. There is usually, but not always, some memory loss with this state. Occasionally a patient, after a few treatments, may become confused in this manner, and the question arises as to whether he or she is getting worse. This problem is solved by waiting a few days for the confusion to subside, then continuing with the treatment. The appearance of getting worse may frighten the patient and his or her family and, indeed, may frighten inexperienced physicians and staff, but it very rarely is as serious as it looks, except in elderly patients with cerebral arteriosclerosis.

Immediate Physical Symptoms

After the treatment, most patients sleep for half an hour or so, and later in the day may feel tired and somewhat uncomfortable.

Headache is common on the day of the treatment, but is relieved readily with aspirin and is gone by the next day. In general, these symptoms are of less than a day's duration.

14

PSYCHOTHERAPY

Psychotherapy is any treatment that uses psychological means for the resolution of symptoms; it includes individual, family, couples, and group methods. The individual methods in common use for mood disorders are supportive, educational, psychodynamic, analytic, cognitive, abreactive, cathartic, interpersonal, and various combinations thereof.

EFFECTIVENESS OF PSYCHOTHERAPHY IN AFFECTIVE DISORDERS

A recent study conducted by the National Institute of Mental Health (at a cost of $10 million according to *Psychiatric News*, 1986b) has examined the effectiveness of brief psychotherapy (sixteen weeks) in the treatment of 250 nonpsychotic, nonbipolar depressed outpatients, of whom 44 percent were defined as severely depressed, with scores of 20 or more on the Hamilton scale (Hamilton 1960). The method employed in the study was the comparison of four groups of patients: a control group given a placebo, a group receiving imipramine (an established tricyclic antidepressant), a psychotherapy group treated with interpersonal therapy, and a psychotherapy group using cognitive therapy. Sixty-eight percent completed at least twelve sessions of treatment over a space of fifteen weeks. The results showed that both forms of psychotherapy were as effective as the drug, although the drug was quicker. By sixteen weeks, the psychotherapies and the imipramine were equally effective in the resolution of symptoms, and all three were more effective than the placebo.

Other studies have confirmed the effectiveness of psychotherapy, either alone or in conjunction with drug therapy. In one study the combination was shown to be more effective than either drug or psychotherapy alone.

Any experienced psychotherapist is not at all surprised by these findings, but the work had to be done in order to establish statistical validity. Such studies have enormous value for justifying psychotherapy in the minds of policymakers in academia, government, and business and insurance circles. They are, however, open also to misuse. For example, short-term therapy may be claimed to be sufficient for everyone because it works in the partial short-term relief of some symptoms, thus neglecting long-term considerations. Or drugs, being cheaper, may be said to be just as good as psychotherapy, neglecting the important factors of post-treatment functioning. The paramount danger is of failing to tailor the treatment to particular individual problems.

It is much more difficult to test the effectiveness of long-term psychodynamic treatment for several reasons, one of which is that it deals with more complex issues than the results of a short paper test of symptoms specific to depression. It deals with depression-proneness, characterological symptoms, recurrences, the quality of life, and the quality of object relations. These are not easy to measure statistically, although in practice this treatment is effective in many cases.

Like health care in general, the practice of psychotherapy is now heavily influenced by third-party payers, whose power is so enormous that it can change the goals from what is in the best interest of the patient to what is most economical or to what works for the average, which is not necessarily what works best for the individual. The scientifically trained psychotherapist has the obligation to be the advocate for the individual and for what is in his or her best interest, whether it is brief or long-term, superficial or intensive.

This chapter describes a method that is demonstrably effective, flexible enough for general application with the mood disorders, and based on what is in the best interest of the patient. It makes use of techniques contributed by analytic, interpersonal, cognitive, and other therapies.

Specific Goals of Psychotherapy

A careful study by Weissman and Paykel (1974) amply demonstrated that short-term therapy can resolve the symptoms of depression of about half the general run of ambulatory patients treated in psychiatric facilities, such as general hospital outpatient clinics. Another group, almost half, are improved but have some symptoms, while about 10 percent can be expected to be no better after a year. These results were obtained in a group in which antidepressants were given early and generously. Although the drugs had a remarkable effect on the acute depressive symptoms, there was a definite lag in the effect on social functioning, so that drug-treated patients tended to be socially impaired even when they appeared superficially well, thus possibly being vulnerable to relapses and recurrences. Many of these patients had lost confidence and feared recurrences. They often wanted and needed therapy, not only to improve the quality of life, prevent social disruptions, and reduce the impact on children, but actually to prevent recurrences.

The specific deficits found even in those with symptomatic improvement are in certain special areas of their functioning: management of aggression and hostility, interpersonal relations, communication with others, and work performance. They cannot have open and harmonious relationships, and they tend to be irritable in their dealings with intimates, corroborating the psychoanalytic observations that depressives cannot deal with aggression openly.

The conclusion reached by most clinicians is that psychotherapy is needed for affective disorders during the acute attack, in the follow-up period, and sometimes over the long term. Nevertheless, there is a need to be aware that this attitude is not universal.

Prevailing Attitudes Toward Psychotherapy

The range of attitudes of psychiatrists and psychotherapists is broad, running from those who shout from the housetops that psychotherapy is not needed at all, to those who consider the use of medication an abomination. Obviously part of the difference in attitude is due to selection; that is, people who practice chemotherapy alone have largely collected patients who have those illnesses which respond to chemicals. Patients of this group present their symptoms, often somatic, for treatment. Those who practice psychotherapy principally have practices composed largely of persons who can use psychotherapy, who present their personal and social problems rather than symptoms. However, there is a large overlap, and a substantial number of patients lie in the overlapping area. They present both symptoms and personal problems and need both drugs and psychotherapy.

As to the various attitudes about the kind and direction of psychotherapy, that too depends on the practitioner's training and orientation. Those who see large numbers of persons briefly do not have time to perceive the complexity of every person who passes rapidly through their care. They may miss key factors that made the persons depressed, such as their interpersonal relations, unhappy love life, defeated hopes, frustrations, and losses. Short-term therapy may miss the effects on the family, and the family impact on the patient. Brief therapy may not allow enough time to discover the story that is behind the symptoms.

A therapist who sees only short-term patients concentrates on the here and now—immediate problems that can be resolved quickly. If one follows the patients for more than a few weeks and gathers more experience with the long-term, repetitive nature of affective disorders, one is more and more likely to become aware of the impact of long-term personality disorders and interpersonal relationships on the genesis of the recurrent spells. With the accumulated years of follow-up, the here-and-now approach is often not enough.

Until medicines were available, patients with recurrent bipolar disease could have intensive psychotherapy only between attacks. They were not easy subjects for psychotherapy. Through the use of medicines, people with major mood disorders are accessible to psychotherapy and are found to need it. Most people with bipolar disorder and major depressions have an underlying personality disorder that needs to be treated as well as the symptoms of the bipolar disease. The relationship between the personality and bipolar disorder is still not understood, but, at least, by treating both you improve the quality of life, increase the capacity to use the effects of biological treatment, and help prevent recurrences.

Function of Psychotherapy in Mood Disorders

All persons with affective disorders need some kind of psychological help. If there are precipitating social stresses, personal problems, or personality tendencies, but also an established major depression with its typical physiological changes (i.e., persistent patterns of insomnia, anorexia, and slowing-down), then both biological therapy and psychotherapy are needed.

Types and Mechanisms of Action of Psychotherapy

Supportive Methods

These methods protect, sustain, encourage, and otherwise help a threatened or overwhelmed person through a critical period, until he or she recovers the capacity to cope. Methods include hospitalization, getting support at home (including household help), relief from a job, and lessening psychological pressures. These aids are especially indicated during those stages of major depressions when the patient has trouble functioning. Reassurance and compassion are important here. The presence of another, understanding person provides the frightened, lonely person with a parental image – a good parent.

Cathartic Methods

The expression of feelings can give immediate relief, especially for those who have been unable to express feelings or have had no one to talk to. Sometimes catharsis allows unaccustomed feelings to become conscious. The patient may be frightened of the feelings, causing either resistance or increased anxiety and depression, that is, negative therapeutic reaction. With major depressions of psychotic potential, especially in a prepsychotic stage, this is to be avoided. Yet catharsis remains important for relief in many patients.

Educational Methods

Knowing the nature of their problems can strengthen patients by strengthening the rational forces of their mental functioning. It also allows them to accept help and decrease their loneliness. Cognitive therapy, which is an educational method, helps patients recognize the specific depressive ways of thinking and their unrealistic nature, so that they are provided with a weapon against them.

Psychodynamic and Insight-Providing Methods

These methods help patients understand how their symptoms came about, and how stresses, interpersonal relationships, and their own internal forces have combined to affect their feelings and cause the symptoms. This process strengthens coping methods by showing patients where to put their efforts.

Psychodynamic and Abreactive Methods

During the process of gaining insight, feelings are aroused that are associated with the memories evoked and the experiences discussed. When insight is gained, the associated affects are reexperienced from a new perspective, and the process of working through is experienced. There is relief from feelings of guilt and aggression over repressed rage and sadism. Masochistic patterns are relieved. The patient is better able to experience normal sadness and depression. The same method can be applied to the personality trends that have led to the depression or mania.

Transference Methods

By using the person of the therapist as an authority figure, it is possible to bring about a dependency that can be therapeutic by identification with the strength of the authority figure. Many depressed persons are very emotionally needy and get temporary relief from the relationship. Certain charismatic therapists have a large following of patients who lean on them, call them up at all hours, and in general depend on their intervention in the patient's daily life. This is a two-edged sword because of the difficulties in resolving the dependency.

Combined Methods

None of these mechanisms operates in a vacuum. The therapeutic process involves the interaction of several vectors. Psychoanalytic psychotherapy and psychoanalysis belong here; this kind of intensive therapy is applied after relief is obtained from supportive, educational, and protective therapy, in order not to overwhelm patients with more feelings than they can handle.

Targets of Psychotherapy

Psychotherapy can be directed toward the following targets:

1. The disorder itself, specifically such symptoms as distortions of reality evidenced by certain ways of thinking (i.e., depressive or manic cognitions)
2. Precipitating factors (i.e., psychosocial stressors)
3. Personality traits that cause symptoms or lead to illness; this includes intrapsychic mechanisms, including defense mechanisms, which lead to symptom formation

4. Interpersonal relations, including not only the current relationships, but the early object relations from which they are derived

5. The whole personality

The purpose of psychotherapy is not only to relieve symptoms but to prevent recurrences and improve the quality of life. One does not send the patient back into the very environment that bred the illness without some improvement in the environment or the capacity to deal with it, or both. Recurrences are frequent in depressive illness, occurring in possibly 40 percent or more of the cases. Prevention is an important part of treatment, and psychotherapy is an important part of prevention.

Psychosocial stressors are conditions or circumstances that have so affected individuals that they have reacted with a depression. These may be immediate, one-time events (such as loss of a job), repeated traumata, or ongoing undramatic chronic situations with which persons cannot cope successfully because of their own particular personalities. A common example is a passive-dependent person married to a domineering, aggressive spouse; another is a parent with a grown-up, disturbed child who dominates and brow-beats the parent, who cannot rescue himself or herself because of neurotic guilt feelings. Another common example is a person in a job with an intolerably domineering employer, with whom the depressed person cannot be sufficiently assertive to have any measure of control over his or her own destiny. Such seemingly insoluble predicaments are the subject matter of psychotherapy. Interpersonal relationships are very important in both cause and cure of depression and require a good deal of treatment time.

Treatment is directed toward helping the individual to see what the more or less unconscious elements are in these circumstances, both in the circumstances themselves or in the way of dealing with them. For example, if patients are not assertive enough, one helps them work through the origin of their passivity and helps relieve them of their inhibitions in expressing anger, in being assertive, or in taking charge of their own lives. This process may require short-term or long-term psychotherapy, or may require psychoanalysis for those troublesome personality patterns that can be changed by psychological work. Those who have been so fortunate as to have had long-term intensive psychotherapy of analytic type or psychoanalysis seem to turn out better in later years than those who were treated by superficial counseling alone.

Another important burden is the failure to achieve one's aspirations and hopes. People are often not aware of their own goals and aspirations and cannot verbalize consciously what they hope to achieve at any one stage of life or with any one endeavor. Also, what might seem like a passing disappointment to one person can have the meaning to another person of a terrible loss or failure. Psychotherapy includes helping suffering persons to know what they are suffering about and helping them to cope with it.

EARLY STAGES OF THERAPY

Psychotherapy begins with the first interview, which has been described in some detail in Chapter 5 as a diagnostic interview. Although the general principles described there were oriented around a diagnostic attitude, some therapeutic principles were incorporated also. Some of these points covered included the forming of a trust by an understanding attitude, affording an opportunity for patients to be heard so that they feel less alone, the explaining of their feelings and complaints as symptoms of stress, and alleviating the sense of guilt.

Many patients are suffering silently. From the first, the therapist lets those patients know that this suffering is understood, with the result that sometimes the patient gets some relief from catharsis early in the contact. A good deal of the suffering is from the sense of guilt, but often depressed persons know only that they are miserable and have no insight into the concept of a depression or what their symptoms add up to. When the idea is explained, they get some comfort and relief out of knowing that this is a recognizable depressed state and has a cause that can be discovered and corrected.

Sophisticated patients are aware of the recent research that has demonstrated the effectiveness of psychotherapy for depression, and some of them speak about it and are reassured of the validity of using a psychological approach to their own problems.

Sometimes a simple supportive attitude may bring some relief regardless of whether this depressed person has a major depression or merely a partial depressive state. For example, a widow of 75 years of age, under treatment for carcinoma of the lung, living with a housekeeper, came to the office feeling quite depressed. She had a history of recurrent major depression, and was under prophylactic treatment with lithium. When she had mentioned that none of her family had come to see her during her recent hospital stay for chemotherapy, but that her children, who live at a distance, out of town, had called, the psychiatrist had sympathized and said, "It must be hard to go through this alone." At the end of the session she sighed and said she felt better that someone realized how she felt. Things had not changed, but she felt better about it.

Even very simple education as to what constitutes a depression can be helpful at the start. For example, a man working for a large company, who has been moved to a new town to take charge of a division, finds it difficult to get up and get going in the morning, does not sleep well, has trouble getting much done at work, yet is uncommonly fatigued. He had been successful in his previous assignment, had been happy in the former locale, and now misses his colleagues, his friends, and his familiar territory; now he has to start all over. The sense of loss has been severe, but he had been accustomed to the idea of moving and was so taken up with the arrangements and the transition that he had taken no time to grieve for his lost attachments, nor had he thought of the feelings involved.

It was some comfort to have a chance to talk about his feelings. Later, after several sessions of therapy, he recalled that when he was a child his father moved his family several times, and the patient at each move had suffered a great deal of pain and nostalgia over the lost attachments. On the occasion of one move he had stolen money and had taken a bus back to his old town in an effort to relieve his painful longing for old friends and territory. These painful memories were awakened by the recent move, giving the therapist a chance to help the patient work through his old childhood feelings as well as the recent adult experience. Then he could shed a few tears of sympathy for the child he once was and could see that the move, by reminding him of old losses, had precipitated his depression.

The Therapist in the Early Stage of Therapy

Depressed people have trouble talking, although there are the garrulous depressed who use talking as a defense against feeling their sadness. Most patients are somewhat slowed in their thinking processes, tend to be withdrawn, and, being generally of the personality type who are not in good contact with their feelings, have trouble expressing themselves. They need help from the start; they can do very little by themselves. If the therapist is passive, a stalemate is soon reached, which is an uncomfortable situation with no constructive purpose. This impasse is easily avoided by the simple method of telling the patient things he or she needs to know and things the therapist believes the patient must be experiencing.

As an example, a businessman, retired from work just the year before, accompanied his wife to her psychiatrist's office. He had no complaint, but his wife informed the psychiatrist confidentially that her husband had been very irritable for months, unlike herself, who had been in a very good mood indeed in the new retirement home in a small town in the mountains. The psychiatrist asked to see her husband, who was quite willing, but had very little to say except that he was playing more tennis than he ever had in his life. The psychiatrist then said he thought it must be hard to make a big move like that, to which the man replied, "I've lived in the city all my life. In our new place it is really country. Do you know what I miss? I miss buildings." It then became a lively discussion of how much he missed his old cronies, with whom he had fraternized for forty years and whom he no longer saw. He did not want to spoil it for his wife, and in fact he was quite surprised to find himself speaking in such a nostalgic manner. He got a good deal of relief from the discussion.

There are situations in which the therapist has to be careful early in the therapy not to be too active, especially with a new patient, because the symptoms may indicate early stages of a psychotic depression, such as the signs of spontaneous breaking down of the barriers of repression and the return of the repressed. An example often seen is rumination over remote events in the past, especially those which convey guilt. Here reassurance is in order, rather than interpretation. Another example is dreams of death or of suicide. These should be discussed on a reality basis, not as signs of aggression against someone else.

A common source of anxiety that must be handled carefully early in the contact is the fear of "losing one's mind." Usually this means that the patient is afraid of losing control and doing something impulsive, which may turn out to indicate aggressive thoughts or suicidal impulses, although sometimes sexual ideas are interwoven with aggression. Here patients must be allowed to ventilate their ideas to whatever extent they are able, and reassurance is again appropriate once the ideas are understood and evaluated as to any genuine danger. Asking carefully for the content of the fears can usually supply the necessary information.

Projection can cover up aggression in people who cannot tolerate the guilt of experiencing their own anger and hatred. For example, a depressed woman in the hospital complained that the staff did not like her. It soon developed that it was she who did not like them, because no one could look after her as well as her former psychiatrist, who had died the year before.

Early Interventions

With somewhat disorganized patients, or with those who are compulsive and tend to be obsessive about their symptoms, it may be helpful to give them something concrete to work on. Such things as keeping track of activities or being put on a simple schedule can help divert patients from their obsessive preoccupation with symptoms and depressive ideas. Often the patient's ego is restricted and impoverished by the depression, and an assignment of something constructive helps, such as keeping track of dreams, or of food intake, or of hours of sleep. If it helps fill the vacancy in their thoughts, it may reduce their painful sense of emptiness.

Early in the therapy it may be possible to see that the patients' preoccupations may, by the defense of displacement, cover up the true precipitating cause of their depressed feeling. For example, a man came for therapy stating that he had just lost a lover to another man and could not find anything to relieve his depression. It turned out that he had had a severe disappointment in his job, for which he found himself unsuited, and that the lack of success in the job had caused him to turn to the lover, whose function was to be an antidote to his loss of self-esteem. The real problem was the failure to achieve in his work at the level of success he had set for himself. The discussion then turned to the question of why he set such unrealistic goals.

Working through may start early in therapy, although certain patients who tend to become depressed are not easily brought in touch with their emotions and cannot work through the precipitating causes to their roots. For example, a woman of late middle age, very close to her mother all her life, at the time of her mother's death gradually went into a hypochondriacal agitated depression. She spoke very little of her mother unless it was brought up, talked mainly of complaints of her immediate family, and slowly got worse, until finally she was hospitalized and eventually was given electroconvulsant therapy with good results. The inability to grieve for her mother and to work through her attachment is characteristic of certain depression-prone persons who cannot cope with losses. With others, who can mourn, it is possible early in the course of therapy to assist in the mourning process and expedite recovery.

Precipitating Events

An obvious place to start therapy is with the patient's immediate problems, especially those that seem to have been involved in bringing on the symptoms. With persons who seek help for depressive symptoms, it can take several weeks or more before the nature of the stressful circumstances comes out. In the first week or two of contact, the patient often cannot elucidate the traumatic factors, which is not surprising because depressions occur most often in those who do not have this insight and tend to repress their feelings about their painful experiences.

Studies have shown, however, and therapists know from their own work, that depressions occur as a result of psychological stresses and that it is therapeutically effective to bring out the awareness of this with the patient. In one study (Leff et al. 1970), it required 4–6 weeks to elicit the stories of even such powerful experiences as a stillbirth, a severe injury to a child, or the recent death of a family member. Another study (Paykel et al. 1969) demonstrated that persons with depressions had experienced five times as many stressful events as the general population. The stressful events included loss, such as death of a close family member, separation, divorce, departure of a family member from home, marriage of a child, or a son being drafted into the army.

Early Interpersonal Intervention

Common problems, often discovered in the early stages of therapy, provided one looks for them, are in the sexual sphere. In marriages, sexual problems are common and may require joint marital sessions with the couple, although this has to be approached tactfully and at the right time. Guilt over sexuality is common, and misunderstandings are frequent. In the man, guilt may prevent him from pressing any demands, and in the woman a combination of guilt and passivity may prevent her from showing any signs of sexual desire. In one couple who had not had sexual relations for more than five years, the husband experienced recurrent depressions lasting months, requiring antidepressant medication for months at a time. The patient thought his wife was to blame, but when the subject was brought up the wife said, "Oh, I wouldn't put him under the pressure of asking that." To which the husband replied, "You were afraid of getting pregnant." Apparently the matter had never been discussed while, at the same time, his anger deepened from the feeling of rejection.

In another case in which the husband felt rejected because his wife seemed to have constant fatigue or headache, especially at bedtime, the husband reacted with depression and anger. In treatment he became aware that his anger was forcing his wife into a withdrawal. When he was able to approach his wife with affection rather than anger she was able to respond, and the marriage improved enormously.

Guilt over masturbation is common and can be relieved readily by discussion. At the same time, discussion of it provides an entree into the fantasy life of the patient.

Early identification of depressive patterns of thinking may permit early intervention. The key ideas—"I'm no good," the negative thinking, the pessimism—can come up very early in the therapy and can be shown to be the important factors in the patient's difficulty in coping with losses.

For example, a 40-year-old woman, deserted for another woman by a husband who had misused and abused her, entered the hospital in a state of depression characterized by crying, complaining, clinging to the staff, inconsolable feelings of abandonment, and profound ideas of guilt. "I brought it on myself," "I'm not very good—no one wants me," "I'll never find anyone else," were some of the statements she made. Her mood was labile, and there were no somatic signs of depression, such as slowing down, or an inability to concentrate. When it became apparent that she was no longer grieving for her husband, with whom she had had a very poor relationship, therapy consisted of helping her identify the kind of depressive thinking that dominated her, so that she was able to stop the ruminating and the compulsive, repetitive recital of the pessimistic ideas. It was clear, then, that her ideas came from her relationship to her mother, who had rejected her and abused her as a child. The focus of therapy then changed from a repetitive preoccupation with her more recent loss to a working through of the rejection by her mother. The working through and her ability to identify her depressive ideas as symptoms (rather than reality) started the recovery process, which eventually resulted in full recovery and, several years later, after much work, a job and a new husband of a much more appropriate personality.

SHORT-TERM PSYCHOTHERAPY WITHOUT MEDICATION

In the nonmedical psychotherapist's practice, most of the clients come with some problem about which they are unhappy, anxious, worried, or depressed. The focus is on the problem rather than the symptoms, unless the symptoms become so overwhelming that they become the center of the problem, in which case some symptomatic treatment such as medicines may be necessary.

The psychiatrist, too, has patients who do not require medication — persons reacting with incomplete depression or with a depressive affect to an obvious situation (the adjustment disorder with depressed mood of *DSM-III-R*) or those with a depressive neurosis (the dysthymia of *DSM-III-R*). The psychotherapy employed should be tailored to the individual need and selected to fit either the short-term treatment or the long-term needs, or both.

The following is an example of a patient treated by psychotherapy alone for the resolution of a mild depressive reaction to a loss.

She was a young black woman, well-groomed, articulate, who did not appear depressed, but smiled continuously in spite of her presenting complaint which was, "I feel depressed." The story she gave was refreshingly open, and revealing of her psychology.

Although only 32 years old, she had three children, age 15, 14, and 12, the oldest having been born when she was 16. She was now divorced. The trouble began the year before, when her family said to her, "How come you have a boyfriend 23 years old when you are over 30?" and they pressured her to get rid of him. Then the boyfriend enlisted in the army and left town. She became very depressed and took an overdose of aspirin, then called her father and told him what she had done. He came to her rescue and took her to an emergency service of a hospital, where she was treated and released, with the advice to get psychiatric treatment, which she did not do until months later when her gynecologist made the appointment for her. This now brought her here for treatment.

In addition to feeling depressed, she said that her "motivation is poor." She had no somatic symptoms, ate with appetite, and slept well, but was on a weight-reducing diet.

At age 22 she had weighed 195 pounds, but with care and diet she was able to keep her weight at 140 pounds.

Her past history, as obtained in the initial interview, poured out with much feeling. She had become pregnant at the age of 15, while still in high school, by a boy who was 17 years old. They married. As she told the story she cried freely, saying, "I never grew up at that time." Her first baby was born the next year, the second the following year, and the third the year after that. Her husband had an affair with another woman, and the couple separated, but, "He kept coming back." They were divorced seven years ago. She had been working part time, also taking courses at a community college, and "growing up."

The family atmosphere was significant. Her father was a retired public employee, her mother a teacher. Her parents never had a harmonious relationship, having separated many times in the patient's memory. The patient remembers how unhappy she was when her father left home during the separations. "And now I keep separating from my boyfriends." Her husband, the father of her children, had been her first and only boyfriend until after the divorce.

Over the next several weeks she was seen in the clinic regularly for visits of an hour, once or twice a week, gradually improving not only in her symptoms but in her attitude toward herself.

Initially she described herself as losing her temper and then being very sorry. She also said that she was very jealous because she suspected that her present boyfriend went out with another girl on a recent Saturday night. "I need someone to love me. I don't know if he loves me." She said, "I am looking for a father figure. My boyfriend is 20 years older." Her mother told her she did not have a close enough relationship with her father. "My daughter is sixteen. She doesn't have a close enough relation to *her* father; she will have the same problem."

In her second session a few days after the first she came in better dressed and appearing rather seductive. "I feel fine today." She had not been depressed and had had the family in for Sunday dinner, but her father had not come. She thought that her 16-year-old daughter was going to have the same problem, of not having a relationship with her father. "Brothers have the advantage. They can go to work and find a father there." "Even if my boyfriend calls every day, I think, 'Does he really care? Some day he is going to leave me.'"

The themes of the next few visits were: her health and her feelings about her female body, especially whether she would need a hysterectomy like her mother, who couldn't satisfy her father afterward, so he left her. "Mother is lonely and has no friends." "It's the woman's fault if she loses her husband. If she isn't good enough he will look elsewhere."

All this she said while declaring that she felt fine, and not depressed. When asked if she might be hiding her feelings she said, "Maybe so. Forgive me. You are the man."

She missed some sessions, once because she "had nothing to talk about," but then felt guilty because she knew she needed help. Since coming to the clinic she has felt better. "I don't know why."

The main themes continue. "Men want certain things. If I can't give them, it's my fault." Her mother said, of the 16-year-old daughter, "You know what's going to happen." The patient cries as she tells this. When she got pregnant at the age of 15, "That hurt me." She cries again. "I'm not used to talking much, but I think a lot." "Everybody has a dream about their life. If I didn't have the baby, my life would have been better. All my plans were ruined. I still feel it would be better if that did not happen." People say, to her younger sister, "Don't be like [your sister]." "That is me. I don't like myself. I hate myself."

Over the next few weeks she moved on to discussing her personality problems, especially how she cannot express her feelings and keeps them inside. "I let people walk on me, but I can do nothing about it." Also she discussed how she handled her children. A strong positive transference began to develop as the patient improved, and she had dreams which indirectly referred to the therapist and his wife, of whom she was jealous. The positive feelings were allowed to come out and were accepted as normal, but not analyzed.

After three months of treatment the patient had improved enough to be discharged, to return if needed.

It seems likely that it would have been better to continue to treat her over a longer term in order to deal more thoroughly with her depression-prone character. This is probably the minimum that should be done for the acute mild depression which clears up quickly. The additional basis of the symptoms, the circumstances which led to the attack, remained untouched.

LONG-TERM DEVELOPMENTS AND WORKING THROUGH

As the symptoms of depression abate during the course of short-term psychotherapy, some of the underlying problems may surface and require attention and further therapy in order to prevent recurrences and improve the ability to cope with life. Insomnia, fatigue, hopeless feelings, suicidal ideas, and panic may disappear, but certain things remain which are troublesome and do not augur well for the future.

One sees a dissatisfaction with the self, although this may be projected on someone else. For example, a young man spontaneously recovered from a depression lasting two years, which had been severe enough that he had retreated from society, had worked at a much lower level than his normal capacity, and had been so miserable that he had often contemplated suicide. Upon recovery, he became much more energetic, although not speeded up as in a manic state. He began to get involved with people, but in an adversarial way, arguing and finding fault, to the extent that it was soon apparent that his behavior had a defensive purpose, namely, to ward off any examination of himself and what he was doing with his own life.

This same mechanism is seen in those in a manic state, but he was not accelerated in his psychomotor activity, nor was he euphoric in the manic sense of the word. He was identifying with the aggressor, in the manner in which he attacked people to avoid being attacked. The mechanism of projective identification enabled him, by attacking and forcing other people into rejecting him, to maintain his sustaining fantasy, namely that the world was unfair to him; that is, he was not unfair to the world. It is quite apparent that, guided by this philosophy, he is bound to be rejected and disappointed by the world and to go into another depression eventually.

In other cases, passivity and masochistic behavior may emerge, requiring much more psychotherapeutic work. For example, a man approaching retirement comes for therapy for a recurrence of a depression after a number of months of feeling quite well. It turns out that, despite a great deal of therapy, he still tended to submit to his wife's wishes without bringing forward any of his own, so that he found himself doing rather major things without actually wanting to, nor making any protest. As a consequence, he was in a rage most of the time over the relationship. His lifelong pattern of submitting to women had not been dealt with in his therapy because it was ego-syntonic and he got a great deal of pleasure from it. Now it had pushed him to the point where the pain was too much. Specifically, he was being pushed to make a geographic move that he genuinely disliked. When he discovered what he was doing he was able to overcome his passivity, discovering at the same time, to his surprise, that his wife was quite happy to see him speaking up for a change.

This kind of problem with interpersonal relations may not resolve with short-term therapy, because intellectual insight does not change a long-standing pattern, based on infantile object relations. For example, a very talented man who worked with several partners was in a constant turmoil because he was unable to assert himself in an effective way and was so irritable with the other men that anything he suggested met with resistance. Nor was he able to leave the organization, because it would have seemed disloyal. The idea that it would be disloyal came from a childhood fantasy that, in his large family, no one should protest, and the individual welfare had to be sacrificed for the good of the whole. Nor could he run away from home, as he sometimes fantasied doing, because that would not really hurt anyone but himself, and it was important to him to hurt someone to get even for his pain. So the solution was to stay and make life miserable for the others, as well as himself, getting a good deal of satisfaction out of the arrangement until it became apparent, during the therapy, that he was defeating himself at the same time. Only in working through the childhood roots over a period of several months was he able to resolve the situation.

Vicissitudes of Aggression

The difficulties depressed patients have in handling their aggression come out in later stages of therapy. Repression and displacement are the major defenses seen. A man who is very angry with his wife may displace his anger on the children or on some innocent casual contact person. For example, a young lawyer known for his aggressive courtroom style with antagonists came for therapy because of insomnia and anxiety attacks in the night. As his therapy went on, it was apparent also that he was chronically depressed and that in his nocturnal anxiety attacks he also had suicidal fantasies. It required a considerable length of time in his therapy before it became evident that he was repressing murderous fantasies toward his wife, and another long period before he was able to work out his differences with her.

If a transference has formed, the patient's anger toward the therapist is bound to develop at times of disappointment over the results of therapy because they fall short of the patient's magical expectations. The anger may be displaced on others, so that when a patient seems to be having unnecessarily irritable reactions to others, one should look for anger with the therapist. If patients are able to learn to express anger in the therapy situation, they then no longer need to displace it on others.

Another eventuality is the surfacing of resentment and anger toward parents and other figures from childhood. This is usually anger that the patient never learned to express as a child and now actually experiences for the first time. It is important that the therapist help the patient see that the source of the anger is long in the past and that it is now not realistic to act it out on the parents or to displace it on other persons, such as spouse or children.

Sometimes the rage over the injustices of the world can be so great that it has to be warded off in one way or another. Once patients start to talk about themselves and their lives, long-buried hatred and anger tend to push to the fore, and defenses against it are threatened. Sometimes murderous dreams occur, or dreams of bombing or of destruction of the world by explosions set off by criminals or madmen, referring to the patients' view of their own unconscious selves.

As therapy goes on and these sources of anger come to light and are worked through to their roots, the irritability tends to lessen and interpersonal relations become much easier.

Fusion of aggression with sexuality can often be found in patients who are prone to depression. In men, sadistic impulses toward women may surface during long therapy, as these are often men who have been dominated by a strong need for mothering and have been suffering all their lives from a deficit in the reassurance they received from their own mothers. For such men, sex may represent a sadistic attack on the women, not in actual fact but in fantasy. When this can be acknowledged, the sexual relations improve and lose the sadistic component. In women, a sadistic attitude toward men can be seen, sometimes covered up by a seeming masochism and submissiveness. Fantasies of attacking or biting the penis, and murderous feelings toward men, are seen also. A desire to be loved, held, and looked after by a woman may lead some women to seek a woman therapist, and, indeed, in such cases, having a woman therapist may be beneficial.

Regression and Infantile Sexuality

Although ego psychology rather than infantile sexuality is now given most of the attention of those who work with the affective disorders, it is still important to remember that powerful instinctual forces are involved. In long-term therapy, in which one sees patients through cyclical periods, evidences will often be seen of regressive oral drives. Fantasies of nursing at the breast, the desire to be held, and biting fantasies can appear. In both women and men the fantasy of cutting off someone's penis may appear and can often be traced back to the father, either as a retaliation for the patient's own imagined castration or to win the mother's love and admiration. Patients who have been subjected to enemas seem to have a great deal of residual anger whenever they have to be passive and submissive under almost any circumstances, even over submitting to psychotherapy or to taking medication ordered by anyone else.

When one finds a patient who resists medication, that patient has probably had a serious childhood distrust of mothering and feeding, and probably had a feeding problem as an infant.

The self-doubts and the guilt which seem so inappropriate in patients, because their personality is usually so conscientious and their character so upright, may apply to their unconscious, which can contain unbearable pressures of infantile rage and sexuality. For example, after a suicidal patient had been in therapy for several years, he was able to say, "There is no point in killing myself. That won't hurt anyone, and the whole point is to hurt someone badly and make them suffer as I do."

Of course, this kind of material does not come up easily, and a strong relationship, in which the patient can trust the therapist's acceptance, is a requirement for getting a therapeutic benefit from working through the sources of such sadistic attitudes, which leads to a discussion of the kinds of relationships and transference necessary to long-term work with patients who have affective disorders.

Transference in Affective Disorders

Most people suffering from a depression are in such discomfort and misery that they are grateful for the attention given them and tend to be cooperative and to become dependent. Manic patients, on the other hand, do not want interference and may attack the therapist from the beginning or run away from any attempted therapy.

After the acute phase of a depression has been relieved somewhat, depressed persons still suffer and are aware enough of their problems to maintain contact with their therapist. One should respect this attitude because patients know intuitively that they still need help, even though the reasons may not be spelled out. The danger of dependency is really not great, because generally patients want to become independent once they feel that they have solved their problems.

The attitude of the therapist cannot help but be protective at first, because these are patients who are seriously threatened by life, are suffering, and need an advocate right away. The role of the therapist is to be that advocate until the ego of the patient is strong enough to sustain the forces that impinge on him or her both from the outside world and from within, in the form of anger, guilt, and frustration. As a result of this function, the therapist is seen in a very positive light by the patient and may be sufficiently idealized that the patient feels a strong support from the relationship.

The supportive role may be enough to sustain patients until they solve their life problems sufficiently well that they can go on with good functioning indefinitely, and the relationship can be tapered off. Stopping therapy too quickly can be traumatic, as these are persons who do not take losses easily; it is advisable to taper off slowly, over a considerable period of time, to allow the patient to work through the separation gradually.

In long-term therapy, in which one deals with the underlying personality problems, the transference problems become much more complex, because of the regressions that can take place. It is not unusual for depressions to develop in the therapy as a result of disappointment with the therapist, who has initially been idealized and then disappoints the patient, who wants to be loved and nurtured like a child. For example, before the therapist's vacation one patient said, "It is obscene of you to take a vacation. Why don't you stay home and take care of your patients like any responsible therapist." It turned out that her father had many absences from home when the patient was a child and that there were reasons to suspect him of having sexual affairs outside the marriage, which explains the patient's use of the term "obscene."

In the initial idealizing transference, the patient does not announce that he or she is becoming dependent, but demonstrates it by various means, such as flattering remarks indicating a positive, idealizing transference, phone calls, more complaints than usual, an increase in symptoms. These actions indicate the development of an infantile transference. Such a transference is usually ambivalent, and anger can develop quickly, out of disappointment in the therapist.

The disappointment with the therapist may be acted out with others, because the patient cannot express anger toward the therapist. If it is not acted out it may be manifested by the appearance of an actual depressive reaction, either partial or a full-blown symptomatic depression. This gives an opportunity to the therapist to help the patient to work through the original childhood depression, of which the transference depression is a repetition.

Suicidal crises occur during therapy also. If the mounting anger and disappointment are not dealt with, it is possible that they may be acted out in a self-destructive way. For example, a young woman who had been in therapy for a year began to argue with her therapist at every meeting, interrupting him at every opportunity, not letting him speak, and generally showing signs of great resistance to the therapy. She spoke of her resentment to friends, but not to her therapist, nor could she tell him what she was arguing about. This impasse went on for some days, until one day her family found her in the garage, preparing to gas herself to death.

Therapy of such regressed patients can be hazardous, because one is always at the razor's edge with them, close to a depression on one side and to unbearable rage on the other. One has to try to measure the tolerance of patients to their unconscious forces and be prepared to reassure and support them if they feel overwhelmed. It may be a great relief to the patient to learn that murderous feelings toward the therapist are acceptable and can be understood as something transferred from childhood relationships. The "negative therapeutic reaction," a worsening of the symptoms, can indicate that the patient is, indeed, overwhelmed by his or her feelings. On the other hand, it may be a healthy experiencing of sadness and grief indicating that, with the process of therapy, he or she is learning to tolerate reality.

Termination

The ultimate goal is resolution of the problem underlying the depression, leading to health and independence. Since depressions tend to be long lasting and recurrent, expect therapy with this goal to take a long time, even several years. During that time the natural tendency of the depressed person to be dependent can transfer, with relentless certainty, to the therapist. The skill and insight of even the most experienced therapist may be severely taxed, and great patience is required, because independence may be a long time coming. In fact, it is important not to stop therapy too soon or abruptly. It is like a death, in the patient's scheme of things, to give up the person whose sustaining empathy has been there for years. Given time to work through separation, the patient will profit by the separation eventually.

In short-term cases, termination is brought about when symptoms are relieved and the patient feels prepared to go on alone, which can be anywhere from one or two sessions to a few months. After this, a follow-up period of occasional visits is helpful in preventing recurrences and in establishing any need for long-term therapy or any other interventions such as couples therapy.

In longer term cases, where the goal is the therapy of personality disorders and trends which form the basis of the patient's depression-proneness, and where there are recurrences and serious intrapsychic psychopathology, therapy lasts for years before it can be tapered off. Sometimes it seems endless, but then, after five or six years, the therapist finds that he or she has ended the intense phase of treatment and has moved on to a follow-up stage.

The termination of long-term cases has to be prolonged enough to permit working through of separation, which may take a year, because it is only with threatened separation that some of the childhood losses and separations emerge enough to be worked through. When a mourning process has been completed, it is possibly the first time in the patient's life that he or she has been able to mourn for the genuinely great losses that have occurred in his or her life, as in the lives of most people. This mourning takes place without the development of a depression, indicating sufficient strength for the patient to go on in life without the therapist.

Even here, with rather thoroughly treated patients, it is well to remember that enough transference may persist that it can have a sustaining value for the patient; also, a tapering off period can have continuing value in picking up remnants of any separation process that has not been sufficiently worked through.

15

COMBINED TREATMENT: DRUGS AND PSYCHOTHERAPY

As far as I am concerned I have had great help from medical colleagues used to the administering of the modern drugs, with three patients in severe states of depression. In all of these cases the therapeutic use of drugs did not in any way interfere with the progress of the analysis, quite on the contrary it helped the analysis to maintain itself during phases when otherwise the patient might have had to be hospitalised. Only in one of these cases some difficulty was created for a short time by a somewhat excessive drug prescription, which made me feel suddenly that the patient ceased to be himself.

I think I would feel very different if drugs were used to bring material with which the patient found it difficult to deal. In cases like that the situation would be rather near to that of hypnotised patients whose resistances are overrun by an external force instead of being worked through gradually. [A. Freud 1971a, p. 1583]

For the definitive mood disorders, with the exception of depressive neurosis and characterological depressions, some combination of psychotherapy and medication is by far the most common approach used by psychiatrists today. Characterological states of depression, depressive affects, and dysthymia (depressive neurosis) are treated generally by psychotherapy in the hands of various kinds of psychotherapists, or by psychoanalysts.

ECLECTIC THERAPY

The concept of eclecticism, from the Greek word *eklegein*, means "to single out." Eclectic means "choosing or consisting of what appears to be best from diverse sources" (*American Heritage Dictionary* 1983, p. 223). In applying psychotherapy it is well to have a range of diverse sources, methods, and techniques to draw on and to choose what seems best and most appropriate, and also to have sufficient knowledge of biological therapy for choosing the correct medication. The methods chosen have to be used to their optimum potential in each case, avoiding superficial or inadequate treatments.

Integrated Treatment

Eclectic treatment means not only combining chemotherapy and psychotherapy but also combining various kinds of drugs and various kinds of psychotherapy, whenever indicated.

It is not enough to single out the treatment modalities applicable to a particular case. They must be integrated into the treatment process. When more than one influence is at work in bringing about the symptoms, as is often the case, then more than one treatment modality may need to be used both for relief and the prevention of recurrences. There are various terms for the method: integrated, multifactorial, multimodal, or pluralistic therapy.

The most common example is that of a depressed person who is receiving a tricyclic antidepressant drug such as imipramine and simultaneously is receiving some form of psychotherapy. Another common example is the depressed person with a history of recurrences who is receiving lithium for prevention, imipramine for depression, and a hypnotic drug for sleep. Chemotherapy is then integrated into the program of individual, group, couples, or family therapy, as indicated by the individual needs.

Two types of questions come up frequently:

1. *Who would make the decision about medication, such as how long should one take it and when to change dosage?* The

answer to this is that the psychiatrist makes the final decision, with input from the psychotherapist and the patient.

2. *What kind of dependency might ensue, if any? Is it psychological or is it physiological?* The answer is that both or either kind of dependency can result from anxiolytic and hypnotic drugs, but not from antidepressants or lithium.

Initiating the Process

Examples

To illustrate the process and timing of treatment, three cases are described here, the first of which is relatively mild, the kind of problem that might come to any psychotherapist, medical or nonmedical, to be referred to a psychiatrist for diagnosis and the possibility of drug therapy. The second is a rather severe case of suicidal depression that was treated by a combination of psychotherapy and drug therapy, but then later turned out to have psychosocial problems of the type requiring marital counseling. The third is a very complex case in which the problems went through a development starting with a psychotic depression and gradually, upon recovery, requiring the use of complex drug therapy, later marital counseling, still later individual psychotherapy and, in the long run, a change of the life style—truly a complex process.

Case 1

A 62-year-old man had left his executive job in a large company by way of early retirement, three years earlier. Although he had an adequate retirement income, he had gone enthusiastically into a business operated out of his home, a business that gave him an opportunity to indulge a hobby and allowed him to live in a way that he found very pleasant and much to his liking. He had always been subject to anxieties when crises occurred. In fact, one reason for his premature retirement was that the pace of the work in his former job had become so competitive and intense that he had problems with insomnia and anxiety.

The year or two preceding his coming for therapy had been difficult. His wife had been putting him under pressure to move from their large house, to sell it and to change their way of life. He was increasingly agitated about this possibility and increasingly had trouble sleeping and keeping calm. To his family physician he had presented his somatic symptoms of anxiety, but not his personal problems.

At the first meeting with the psychiatrist, he went rather quickly, after describing his symptoms, into the problem of the move suggested by his wife. This was clearly what was weighing upon him most heavily. He was given a trial dose of amitriptyline, 50 mg at bedtime, to be raised gradually to an effective dose. At this first session, his wife was brought into the discussion. The couple were cautioned against making any major move at this time because of a possible effect on his depression. His wife was conciliatory and cooperative, and they promptly agreed that there would not be any move for the present.

On his return for the second visit a few days later, he announced that the medicine was "miraculous." He was enormously relieved, he was sleeping well, and he seemed to have calmed down enough that he was able to settle down and do some work on his business papers and conduct his affairs in a much more comfortable manner.

On his third visit a week later he was continuing to take the small 50-mg dose of amytriptyline and felt that he was back to normal. He and his wife had arrived at a working arrangement that would allow him to continue in their present house so that he would not have to make a decision about moving for another year or two. The part this decision played in the relief is obvious.

At the very first visit it was clear that there were many features of the first stage of a depression. Persistent insomnia was the only somatic sign; he described feelings of depression and discouragement, feelings of low self-worth and guilt, suicidal fantasies, adding "but I would never do it." Also, he gave a history of a tendency to react to competitive situations with feelings of low self-worth and gave the impression also of a tendency to take a passive reaction to situations that might call for activity, or at least for decisions. A diagnosis of depressive neurosis (dysthymia) was made because of the presence of definitive depressive symptoms without the somatic symptoms of slowing down or psychomotor retardation. Although he might possibly be at the beginning of a serious major depression, there was a possibility that it could be turned around rather quickly. The drug chosen, amitriptyline, has some sedative effects and promotes sleep, but is primarily an antidepressant. He was a "quick responder"; a small dose was all that was needed.

The obvious presence of his wife at the first session and his account of the problems and the differences between them made it apparent that he had a passive relationship with her, but at the same time a good deal of resistance to her wishes. He needed help with her as an ally. Therefore, through a kind of educational joint session with her, by giving an objective description of his condition, it was possible to secure his wife's cooperation, so that her changed attitude apparently relieved him greatly. The next phase of the treatment after this early intervention could possibly have been the treatment of the person himself, of his longstanding depressive neurosis. However, the patient did not wish to engage in this and seemed under no immediate need to do so. The treatment ended there; someone will probably hear from him again.

Case 2

The second case illustrates the next step in the progression in therapies required to follow the fortunes of a severely ill patient upon recovery if one is to do a thorough job. That is, if you not only treat the acute depression, but try to ferret out the nature of the psychosocial situation and the personality disorder which, in combination, have produced a predicament giving rise to the depression.

A 42-year-old married woman, a high-grade secretary, came to the hospital in a severe enough depression that she was hospitalized for her own protection. There was a history of two previous suicidal depressions occurring in the fall of the year, a typical pattern for the bipolar patient or for the person with major depressions with recurrences. After a suicide attempt the year before she had recovered with no residual physical damage.

She recovered from this depression in six weeks with hospitalization and the use of amitriptyline plus the usual inpatient global therapy, including group therapy, individual psychotherapy, and some work with the family. During this hospitalization it became quite clear that she was in an intolerable situation because of her relationship with her husband. She had a rather submissive personality and was not able to fight her own battles very well. Her husband was a domineering, rather demanding man, who, though of very high character, tended to run anyone around him. He kept secretaries very busy, and the patient felt that, if she quit her job, she would become a "member of his staff." This would not work for her; she could not tolerate such close enslavement to his rather compulsive needs, so she had to insist on her own career, although it had stresses of its own.

After this hospitalization the situation became open enough to be talked about, and it was possible to explain to the husband with sufficient objectivity why she had to have her own career. Only larval depressions occurred in the four years after this change, alternating with a very mild hypomania. Also, she was under lithium prophylaxis.

The story does not end here, however. It followed that in order to maintain this separateness, she had to do things which her husband obviously found intolerable, and he gradually withdrew enough from her so that the quality of their marriage deteriorated. At this point it was necessary to bring the husband in and try to treat this new situation, in order to solve the ultimate problem.

The patient belonged to the group of persons who have prolonged depressions or whose illness tends to be recurrent and does not respond satisfactorily to chemotherapy. They also have a difficult marital relationship. Sexual problems abound in this group. Absence of sexual relations or absence of any true love life is very common, so that a good deal of effort after recovery has to be directed toward improving the quality of the marriages.

Case 3

This case is another illustration of the progression and integration of methods that one has to employ in treating the changes in the illness that takes place during the course of therapy. The patient described here had had recurrent depression and was seen first after having had a depression of 3–6 months' duration every year for four years.

She was a young married woman with two children. She had been under the care of a psychotherapist and became ill with a severe agitated depression during the course of this therapy. She had begun to get involved in a struggle with the therapist, or at least this is what appeared on the surface.

She was unable to function and was brought into the hospital for treatment in a prepsychotic state. Her controls were not good, she talked rapidly, and was in a highly erotic, flirtatious state that is common in a mixed hypomania and depressive state. After a day in the hospital she was already passionately in love with the young medical student who had examined her, and was agitated by her own erotic excitement, restless, depressed, guilty, talking rapidly with a push of speech, but in a depressed mood impervious to discussion. There was a strong element of pessimism, hopelessness, and low self-esteem. The diagnosis was bipolar II disorder, mixed. She could not respond to psychological treatment. Seven electroconvulsive treatments, over a period of 2½ weeks were followed by rapid recovery, and she was able to go home. During her initial weeks at home it was necessary to have a housekeeper because she was not able to take care of the house and the children without a good deal of help.

Over the next two years she gradually demonstrated an almost disabling compulsiveness in which she spent so much time on details that she could not get more than one household job done every day. Also, emotionally ravenous, she was hungry for support from both men and women. She brought pages of notes to the sessions of mixed interpersonal and insight-related psychotherapy. Her low self-esteem had started in her childhood where she felt that she was worthless compared to her brother.

The reality problem at first seemed to be an unresolved attachment to her father and mother who were divorced, but after months of work mainly focused on her relationships with her parents, her sibling, and her husband and children. She then became aware of the necessity of working out some conflicts with her husband. Couples therapy was commenced and the couple was seen in conjoint sessions weekly for a year. When the husband's behavior indicated that he needed therapy himself, he was sent to another therapist for his own personal problem, which consisted of personality patterns that made him fail in some of his own important professional work, so that he got into trouble and took out his resentments at home, being verbally abusive with the children and the patient. The marriage had been sexually frustrating also, which his wife could acknowledge.

She was given lithium prophylaxis and amitriptyline as needed for the short depressive spells that occurred several times a year, but were not disabling enough to prevent functioning.

Important changes occurred during the next three years. The patient gradually changed from a passive, dependent person to a much more active, outgoing, and rather ambitious woman who wanted a career. She was able to experience and discuss her idealizing transference feelings. She was able to accept the fact that her marriage would probably break up. In evaluating the treatment modalities, it seems likely that the change toward activity in her personality resulted from a partial working through of her own passive, dependent personality tendencies made possible by intervention in the marital crisis. She could fight her own battles.

The psychotherapy was of a combined nature, at first educational and cognitive, later psychodynamic with working through. She had to be educated to take her medication and to use it appropriately by being told the function of each drug in some detail. It was evident that, after the relief of the major depressive symptoms, her underlying obsessional neurosis and depressive neurosis, as well as her marital problems, persisted and required treatment for themselves.

Cognitive therapy was employed in a classical way in that her pessimism and tendency to react to events with low self-esteem was identified as a symptom. "You always take the pessimistic view of things," "It is an unhealthy way of thinking," she was told whenever the symptom appeared. Also, "This kind of thinking process is destructive, is not good for you, distorts reality, and can lead to demoralization and depression." The process of working through included trying to trace back the development of these depressive ideas out of her relationship both with her pessimistic father and a very self-centered, narcissistic mother. The competition with her brother was resolved. Eventually she attained a much better understanding of herself.

The treatment time to reach this point was 4 years following the original depression treated with electric shock. During this time she has not had a disabling depression, and the larval depressions that still occur two or three times a year respond to relatively brief changes in her therapeutic regimen, usually a moderate increase in the antidepressant drug and a short series of psychotherapeutic interviews of one or more. Lithium levels are maintained at blood levels of 0.7–0.8 mEq/l and monitored at monthly intervals in the first 6 months, later every 3 months.

There is no way in which individual psychotherapy alone could have cured the vegetative symptoms of this patient with bipolar illness when she was in her acute disabling depressions. By the same token, biological treatment alone would merely have reduced the intensity of her cycles, but would not have changed her depression-proneness based on a long-standing depressive neurosis *(ICD-9-CM)* (dysthymia disorder, *DSM-III-R*). The marital conflicts which antedated her depressive breakdowns required special attention themselves.

This is the manner in which the more chronic complex disabling depressions can be approached with combined therapies, integrating and combining not only drugs, support and psychotherapy, but also progressive combinations of psychotherapy given at appropriate places during the course of the treatment contact when needed. This kind of complex and integrated therapy program is needed for complex situations. It may take several years and often seems endless, but if properly applied usually results in a functioning patient with a good quality of life, able to face and deal with problems in a reasonably healthy, constructive way, without breaking down.

Long-term Disability: Failure to Respond, Treatment-resistant Cases and Chronic States

Some patients tend to have prolonged and chronic illnesses or to cycle over a long period of years. They present complex problems. As an example, in a group of sixty-five patients that I treated over a period of years, twenty-three were disabled over a period of 4 years (Badal 1981). This group was unselected, but had a large proportion of more severely ill patients who had been hospitalized.

Table 15–1 illustrates the variety of methods required in the treatment of this group of patients, with almost complete recovery obtained in eleven of the twenty-three patients and partial recovery in half of the others.

In this series of sixty-five cases, the twenty-three with chronic, prolonged depressions were of both bipolar and unipolar type, characterized by recurrences and chronic disability. The incidence of certain adverse clinical factors was higher in this more disabled group than in the group whose response to combined therapy was more prompt. These factors included advanced age with cerebral changes, very early (adolescent) onset of bipolar illness, the coincidence of irremediable chronically stressful life situations, and the coincidence of serious characterological, neurotic, and personality problems that either had never been treated or had received a less than thorough therapy. For example, one person with a disabling obsessional neurosis had received supportive, but not thorough, analytic psychotherapy. It

Table 15-1
Psychological Treatments in Long-Term Patients

Methods	Number of times used (N = 23)*
Support, protection	23
Individual psychotherapy; eclectic therapy	19
Cognitive, educational therapy	18
Interpersonal therapy	12
Insight: psychoanalytic or other intrapersonal therapy	7
Group therapy in hospital	7
Couples therapy (9 married)	6
Spouse treated individually	3
Family therapy	3
Group therapy, post-hospital	2
Occupational therapy, post-hospital	1
Nursing home	1
Day care hospital	1
Classical analysis	1

*Eleven eventually recovered with integrated therapy of multimodal type.

was possible through intervention directed to the ongoing stressful life situation to bring about a great improvement in more than half of these cases.

In the group of patients with chronic or recurrent disorders, there is a higher incidence of both chronic stresses and disorders of personality than in those patients whose illness did not become chronic. The most striking difference is in the number of patients in the chronic group in whom there occurred *both* a personality problem and a chronic, ongoing, serious psychosocial stress. Close to three-quarters of the chronically disabled had this combination, while less than one-quarter of the patients who did not become chronically disabled had the combination. Statistically, the findings showed a chi square of 8.97 (d.f. = 1), and $p < 0.01$.

If a patient with an acute affective disorder has both a serious ongoing psychological stress (such as disturbed marriage) and a serious personality problem, one can expect that, unless one or both of these problems is corrected, there might well be recurrences or chronicity, and possibly both. The message is clear.

Intervention is needed beyond attention merely to the immediate symptoms.

It should be remembered, of course, that this kind of intervention is never easy and is not always accepted or welcomed by the patient and the persons with whom he or she is involved. Often people, even when suffering, do not like to have their relationships questioned or altered. It is not unusual to get some resistance if you try to intervene in a long-standing sadomasochistic relationship. Nevertheless, it is a practical and useful rule of thumb not to send a person recovering from a breakdown of any kind back into the very environment that fostered the event without some attempt at altering the noxious situation. Very often successful prevention begins at this point—for example, when a recovering patient is still in the hospital and the family is involved.

Practical Issues in Treatment Combinations

Who Gives the Medicine?

A good many patients are treated today by a psychotherapist—social worker or psychologist—with medication given by a nonpsychiatric physician. This method works in some instances, but in certain more complex cases, the internist or general physician cannot possibly know the complexities of the use of the particular medications needed and should not hesitate to refer to a psychiatrist. Generalists cannot be expected to know as much about psychopharmacology, which is a small part of their practice, as do specialists who devote their entire time to it. Sometimes people are inadequately and inappropriately treated under this arrangement.

Some psychiatrists are either jealous of their prerogatives or work best alone and like both to administer medication and do the psychotherapy. This stand makes it hard sometimes for nonmedical psychotherapists to find a psychiatrist who is willing to share responsibility, but if one is found it can work out very well. The psychiatrist has to be assured that the psychotherapist is trained and competent, and the latter has to have the same confidence in the psychiatrist. One of the problems of this arrangement is the sometimes wide difference in educational backgrounds of the psychiatrist and the therapist. A frank discussion at the outset, with the patient's permission, may help to resolve these differences, if they are resolvable.

Some psychiatrists emphasize medication and are not well trained or indeed interested in more intensive psychotherapy. Psychiatrists with this orientation should have available for joint treatment programs professional therapists such as psychoanalysts, social workers, psychologists, or nurse-therapists.

One problem in doing intensive psychotherapy, including psychoanalytic psychotherapy or even psychoanalysis, is the occasional person who becomes so disturbed or suicidal that intervention, either hospitalization or medication, seems indicated. Having a psychiatrist available for patient hospitalization or medical treatment is necessary, but the question then is whether to continue psychotherapy through the acute episode. In some cases it is very useful to exploit the psychological material of the episode because sometimes personal matters surface that can be worked through. In other cases therapy has to be interrupted because the patient is too disturbed; trying to do insight psychotherapy with a disturbed manic or a psychotic depressive can be pointless and one has to wait until a firm grasp of reality returns under the influence of biological therapy.

With intensive psychotherapy, it may be useful for the therapist to refer certain patients to another therapist for medication, even though the therapist himself or herself may be capable of treating with drugs. Certainly, this is the case with patients undergoing psychoanalysis. For the therapist to prescribe the drug himself or herself introduces a parameter that complicates the transference and requires additional working through for ultimate complete independence. The patients do not always like the inconvenience of another physician, it is true, but the gain is potentially great, and some patients prefer it. Sometimes it is not possible to get a cooperative psychiatrist, and then one has to work through the dependency.

It is advantageous for the psychiatrist to prescribe medication and also to be the psychotherapist in most cases that do not go on to an intensive psychotherapy of longer duration with uncovering and working through.

Psychoanalysts are divided on this issue; one group does not hesitate to prescribe drugs, and at the other end of the spectrum are those who do not prescribe drugs and oppose it on principle. If a patient could profit by medication, those in the latter group refer the patient to a psychiatrist to prescribe the drugs.

Bipolar patients who have had thorough psychotherapy or analysis early on seem to do better than those who have not, but both still require medication of the standard type—lithium and antidepressants.

ADVICE TO THERAPISTS (SOCIAL WORKERS, PSYCHOLOGISTS, CLERGYMEN, NURSE CLINICIANS, COUNSELORS, AND PSYCHIATRISTS)

While treating people with depressive symptoms by means of psychotherapy, be sure to recognize the kinds of symptoms that require medication: relentlessness of symptoms, persistent insomnia, loss of appetite and weight, psychomotor retardation, and inability to concentrate and think. Be prepared to refer the patient to a psychiatrist to prescribe and administer medical methods that may include hospitalization, medication, or other biological therapy, such as electroconvulsive treatment.

It can be very difficult to treat some depressed patients, particularly those who do not respond or who respond slowly. There is a limit to the amount of depressed thinking one can be exposed to; if you find yourself getting impatient, watch out! The patient will pick it up and feel more guilty, increasing the danger of suicide.

Having whatever is your own unhappiness or existential depression under control is very helpful. Therapists should be able to tolerate a certain amount of loss and depression themselves; they should know what loss is. Therapists who have had psychoanalysis find it enormously valuable in helping them to understand and treat depressed people. For one thing, the tolerance for depression and the ability to recognize mourning in all its phases and disguises, which come with psychoanalysis, are invaluable.

ADVICE TO PSYCHIATRISTS AND PHYSICIANS

While administering medication, be sure to evaluate the psycho-social stressors, the personality problems, the psychodynamics, and the individual's personal relationships, where intervention and/or individual psychotherapy may be needed. Often, after a depression is initially relieved by medication and rest, the person-ality problems and the environment may have to be treated to prevent recurrences. Do not send the patient back to the very environment which bred the illness without some effort to change the situation that fostered the depression in the first place. Recog-nize those cases where relatively simple psychotherapy is not enough, where long-term psychotherapy treatment is needed. See the family, and evaluate their role; they may need help of some kind. This includes children.

In addition, consider the possibility of group therapy, which can be a very helpful supplement to the individual therapy tailored to each case. The group can give education, support, insight, and working through. Groups run by trained professionals are usually found in larger hospitals and social agencies.

As mentioned previously, do not hesitate to do a complete medical evaluation in the presence of certain somatic symptoms.

SOME INTERACTIONS OF DRUGS AND PSYCHOTHERAPY

Facilitation of Psychotherapy by Medication

If the patient's symptoms are severe enough to interfere with any attempts to get at the underlying problems, medication or elec-troconvulsant therapy may make psychotherapy possible by im-provement in ability to concentrate, relief of suffering, or restora-tion of a sense of reality. Patients with psychotic depressions or severe manic attacks simply cannot use psychotherapy in the usual sense.

Patient's Preference for Medicines

When, after using medication, patients experience enough relief, they may not want to go through the work of psychotherapy and the changes in life needed to solve the underlying psychosocial problems. Then the question is, "Should they continue to use the relief-giving medications?" Antidepressants are not addicting drugs and are very useful in both short- and long-term situations; one should not hesitate to use them where symptoms dictate. You can do only what the patient is willing to do. There are cases, however, where one has to hold the line at allowing long-term dependency on tranquilizers, which can be addicting.

What Does Intervention Do to Medication?

One should do preventive work on psychosocial and intrapsychic causes along with preventive drugs whenever possible. Don't promise that such intervention cures the illness—for example, to solve a marital problem or some other predicament—but you can promise that it makes the illness easier to manage and results in improvement in the quality of life. An example here is a woman who cycled twice a year from psychotic manic to depressive and was totally incapacitated for five years by her illness. She stopped having any spells at all when she obtained a divorce. Or a single, middle-aged woman who is cycling widely from manic to depressive with hospital admissions yearly, even though maintained on lithium and medication appropriate to the phase. When a nurse was brought in to take care of her sick, depressed (bipolar) mother her cycles were reduced to a manageable degree; much less medication was needed, and hospitalization was no longer required. Intervention can help reduce the need for medication and make an unresponsive case responsive.

Medication after Psychotherapy or Intervention

In long-term intensive psychotherapy, some patients with milder disorders are eventually able to give up medication when their neuroses are worked through. Some people who have used antidepressants and hypnotic drugs for sleep should be able, after a thorough analysis, to go without medication, unless of course there is some untreatable predicament in the environment, such as a sick spouse or some other burden. Do not expect a person with genuine bipolar disorder with a strong genetic component requiring lithium to recover entirely. It does happen, but most of the time the cycles are still there potentially, usually at a reduced and manageable level even after a thorough analysis. Most important, the quality of life has improved enormously. These cases are very individual, and each one must be treated for the complexity of factors involved.

Use of Tranquilizers

The benzodiazepines and meprobamate, and other anxiolytics, are addicting tranquilizers. The antipsychotic drugs, such as the phenothiazines and other neuroleptics, such as haloperidol, the thiothixenes, etc., are not addicting but can sometimes cause neurological side effects, most seriously tardive dyskinesia. Useful as they are for the anxiety that accompanies most depressions, there is a caution: don't let your patient continue after the acute attack at the expense of a more rational psychological approach to the underlying cause. In addition, caution patients to withdraw gradually by tapering off when stopping the drugs, especially benzodiazepines, rather than stopping abruptly. Tapering off prevents what can be uncomfortable or even dangerous withdrawal symptoms.

16

COURSE, OUTCOME, AND PROGNOSIS

The course of the individual attack of any affective disorder refers to the duration of the spell itself, outcome refers to the immediate aftermath, and prognosis to the expectation of recurrences, and the quality of life to be anticipated in the future. The traditional view of the outcome of an attack of depression or mania is that it is benign and self-limited. This favorable view turns out to be correct in about half the patients; also, there is a great diversity in the length of an acute attack, with a range of a few weeks to 2 or more years. Some melancholias may actually last five or more years, with ultimate recovery, although with intensive treatment there are usually remissions and exacerbations during the course of the long illness, so that the patient is not severely ill during the entire course of the illness. With appropriate care, most patients, even those with long-term illnesses, can be kept functioning much of the time and out of the hospital even though not completely recovered. In about 20–35 percent of initial cases, chronicity and recurrences are a problem despite intensive treatment. Percentages vary with selection.

FACTORS INFLUENCING OUTCOME

Several factors play into the wide variation in both immediate outcome and long-term prognosis, These several vectors do not operate independently, but interact with one another and have varying degrees of influence from case to case. They are:

315

(1) Diagnosis: the several distinct disorders have different natural histories and durations. (2) Severity: severe attacks, especially those occurring later in life, tend to last longer than milder spells. (3) Personality: patients with severe personality disorders tend to have poorer outcomes, with persistent disturbances in the quality of life. (4) Psychosocial stressors: concurrent environmental and interpersonal stress tends to prolong attacks and cause recurrences. (5) Physical health: poor physical health can handicap recovery and cause recurrences.

Diagnosis

A most significant determinant of course and outcome is diagnosis. Bipolar disorder, by definition, is an illness that tends to recur. The attacks vary a great deal in length, but most of them last less than six months. On the other hand, mid-life to late-life melancholia usually occurs only once or twice in a lifetime, but can last for 2–5 years or more, with remissions brought about by treatment.

Other unipolar depressions last from 2 months to 2 years, but tend to recur. One cannot predict, at the outset, how long the attack will last nor how frequent the recurrences will be. These recurrent depressions may occur once or twice a year for life or may, in another person, come as rarely as once or twice in a lifetime.

Depressive neurosis (dysthymia), on the other hand, is chronic in the sense that a depressive tendency is always there, but has wide fluctuations in the amount of depression that is present. This variation depends on how much stress the person is having to cope with and how much of an internal struggle he is having.

Personality

Personality problems, which are common in affective disorders, can cause disability in themselves, at the same time influencing the prognosis and outcome of the illness itself. A depressed person who has an accompanying compulsive neurosis is likely to be more seriously disabled and for a longer time than a person who has no serious personality problems.

An example is the case of a single man, brilliant and talented, whose bipolar illness began when he was 40 years old and continued, with alternating depressive and manic spells, until his death at seventy. His compulsive symptoms had limited his career and prevented him from accommodating to the limitations of an illness, even though he complied with lithium treatment and his cycles were dampened somewhat. He never really functioned successfully, even during the intervals between spells, because of his compulsiveness.

In contrast, there are many persons with recurrent depressions dampened or even eliminated by medication who, by virtue of excellent control of the illness and the absence of any disabling personality symptoms, can lead normal lives, have successful careers, and raise families. As an example, a man of 40 years, with a successful professional career, had his first manic attacks during his twenties. He had three spells before he was started on lithium prophylaxis, augmented by thioridazine as needed, and a program guarding against excessive loss of sleep. Supportive psychotherapy, at first weekly, then monthly, was maintained throughout these years. This high degree of functioning was made possible by the stability of his personality, his good interpersonal relations, and by his intelligent controls over his illness.

Environment

Chronic disability can result from ongoing environmental stresses, interpersonal conflicts, and traumatic experiences, especially those over which the individual has no control.

ACUTE DEPRESSION IN AMBULATORY PATIENTS

What can one generalize, in concrete terms, about the outcome of acute early depressive spells? The answer depends a great deal on selection of patients and the kind of practice one is doing. First, consider an ambulatory group. In a very careful study (Weissman and Paykel 1974) of 57 women who were treated at an outpatient clinic for an initial attack of depression, some very characteristic things were noted:

1. Five of the forty patients who completed the study (12.5 percent) had to be hospitalized for periods up to 4 weeks.

2. Of the 57 given antidepressants, 9 (15.8 percent) did not respond to the initial antidepressant in an original 4–6 weeks' treatment. Two (3.5 percent) responded in too few days to be considered to have a true drug response. Two (3.5 percent) terminated because of drug side effects. Four (7.0 percent) did not cooperate with the treatment.

3. Intensity of contact affected the relapse rate; for example, none of the patients in psychotherapy (which dealt mainly with "here-and-now" problems on a once a week basis) dropped out during 8 months of treatment, whereas two patients in low contact did. Low-contact patients relapsed within 8 months at a rate of 35 percent, as compared with 20 percent of those in psychotherapy.

4. Patients dissatisfied with drug treatment tended to go into psychotherapy or to want casework therapy.

5. Most patients improved a great deal in the first month.

6. In a 20-month follow-up study, about half of the patients were symptom free and the other half had mild to severe depressive symptoms. Difficulty communicating was present in both symptomatic and asymptomatic groups. The majority were considered asymptomatic or mildly depressed.

7. About three-fourths of the group selected in this way were diagnosed as neurotic depressive and the other one-fourth as psychotic (i.e., two bipolar, two involutional, and five psychotic depressives. The diagnosis of neurotic depression would probably be less frequent if the newer terminology of *DSM-III* or *DSM-III-R* were used. This group probably contained an assortment of patients with mild major depression and dysthymia).

8. The majority of the patients wanted to continue the contact to ensure available help should the symptoms return; that is, the depressive episode had made the patients feel vulnerable.

Also, the impairments of social functioning, marital disorder, and so forth, often required counseling.

In summary, although most people became reasonably well, there was a need for ongoing treatment programs past the initial depressive spell of a few weeks to months.

HOSPITALIZED PATIENTS

With the more severely ill hospitalized patients, one sees the same diagnostic groups, but the distribution is reversed. In a study of 65 patients, most of them hospitalized at least once, three-fourths belonged in the various severe categories of major depressions and bipolar illness and only one-fourth in the neurotic depressive (dysthymic) disorder group (Badal 1981).

Because of this difference in distribution, the outcome in the hospital population differs quantitatively from that of the group seen in an outpatient clinic in the proportions who require hospitalization, intensive treatment, and length of follow-up. Most of this group tend to get some relief early on also, but they tend to relapse, and the illness recurs or becomes chronic, requiring intensive treatment over periods of 2–4 years or more. However, better results, that is, resolution of symptoms, are eventually obtained in all but about 5–8 percent after prolonged therapy.

Chronicity

In those persons with the more severe and persistent disorders, bipolar and some unipolar types, the underlying tendency to recurrence can be cushioned by lithium and medications, but lifetime supervision by a psychiatrist is usual. On the other hand, the person with a series of recurrences over a period of several years may recover and never have another spell, if things go right. If there is an accompanying personality disorder, such as severe compulsiveness, dependency, phobias, or poor self-image, or a depressive personality, intensive psychotherapy may help individuals handle their depressive tendency so well that they can function well, leading full and satisfying lives, managing their cycles in such a way that the world around them does not see anything of their illness. One often sees such persons, successful and outstanding in their careers and happy with their personal and family lives.

The individual spell of depression or mania is benign in about one-half of the patients. One can promise most patients that they will recover and may even be better than before the spell as a result of the insight gained and the maturation of personality achieved if psychotherapy is directed toward personality problems.

A similarly positive result also can be expected in most of those who have depressive neuroses, depressive reaction to trauma, and secondary depressions. Maturation, insight, and greater strength and understanding can result from going through a depressive spell with therapy directed toward the underlying depression proneness.

Insight and better ability to cope can help in prevention of future attacks and in improving the quality of life. To achieve this kind of result can require considerable attention to both biological and psychological factors. As one patient with well-controlled, long-standing bipolar illness said years after her analysis, "I take lithium and it helps. But as far as I'm concerned, it was psycho-analysis that did it. I'll take my analysis over medicine any day. I would be in a hospital now if it were not for analysis."

Any person can have frightening scrapes with melancholy, without being sick. Recovered depressives do not escape their share of normal unhappiness. No therapy can accomplish that, but it can succeed in bringing them at least as far as the rest of humanity.

PART IV

AFFECTIVE DISORDERS AND THE LIFE CYCLE

17

CHILDHOOD

VARIATIONS IN CLINICAL SIGNS
AND SYMPTOMS WITH AGE

The affective disorders may present different appearances at different stages in the life cycle. Childhood has its special and characteristic effects on whatever mental disturbance occurs. Although young children experience affects deeply, they do not have the concept of depression or grief, nor do they have the vocabulary to express all the ideational components. They have to be taught a vocabulary before they can deal with and express their inner experiences of feelings (Katan 1961).

Moreover, the whole picture of a depression is highly influenced by the biological and cognitive developmental stage at which it occurs (Bemporad 1982). At what early developmental stages can a clinical depression, as distinguished from depressive feelings, actually occur? The scattered childhood experiences which unite in the adult personality are not sufficiently organized to provide the total massive all-encompassing experience that is an adult depression; usually depressive anlage, seeds, or potentials appropriate to the age level are all one can see in the observed child, that is, partial expression, depression-related affects, withdrawal, guilt, etc.

Not until puberty does the child's nervous system, hormone status, and general physiology reach a point where the physical/chemical changes of depressive disease are possible. What effect the child's depressive experience may have on later adult development is a vital issue also.

In adolescents and young adults, biological changes, love relations, jealousies, feelings of inadequacy, inability to face the world and leave the family, plus failures, can contribute to depression and to the high suicide rate in adolescents. The picture of depressive illness itself may be atypical in adolescents and young adults because the defenses of denial and acting out hide the problem and cover up the symptoms. Adolescents tend to disguise illness effectively by such actions or defenses as dropping out of school, anger and rebellion, sullenness, or a neglect of studies. If they seek help it will be for the personal problem, whatever it is, and not for the symptoms. Furthermore, early attacks of both mania and depression give mixed rather than pure forms, often with neurotic or psychopathic coloring.

In *mid-life*, a process of change culminates in the climacteric with the loss of childbearing, regrets, grief, guilt, and disappointment. This experience continues on into old age, with symptoms resulting from the decline of the body and preoccupation with health and genuine real losses—of career, of supports, and of physical and mental strength.

DEVELOPMENTAL STAGES: THE LIFE CYCLE

With a phase-of-life approach, one can see the individual at the tasks of each developmental phase, adapting, growing, adjusting, coping with both the inner world and the outside, or retreating, being disappointed, frustrated, and breaking down, according to his or her psychological preparation and genetic endowment. Each person must be allowed to linger at any developmental stage long enough to learn what he or she has to learn at that stage, not only of coping with the world around him or her, but of controlling and dealing with his or her instincts. In respect to the awareness of affects and acceptance of affects, early childhood is important, especially when language can be learned to communicate feelings. The failure to experience, acknowledge, and tolerate affects at the early stages can leave unresolved residues which later trauma can cause to surface in the form of helpless feelings, hopelessness, depression, pessimism, passivity, and masochistic trends.

The life-cycle approach of Erikson (1963, pp. 247–274) utilizes a schema that is task-related and directed toward adaptation. It leaves out the passion and storms of the instincts which are at the heart of the affective disorders, and it omits the agonizing internal struggles of the patients—the people who love, hate, fear and sometimes kill themselves.

The convenient symptomatic treatment methods available today (i.e., short-term therapies) may miss problems of rage and sexuality, which are common in affective disorders. The earlier observations (Abraham 1949) that manic-depressives reveal fixations at and regression to earlier stages of development (oral and anal) seem to have been buried under the more recent observations on power struggles, helplessness, and hopelessness. Yet, examples of the importance of the instincts are found at all ages. For example, one has to distinguish toddlers in early childhood because of their polymorphously perverse natures and the specific tasks of separation–individuation and the development of independency versus dependency, but also because of their need to control aggression, anger, and hate, as, for example, when a younger sibling is born. Or, another example, in adolescence or adult life, and even in old age, jealousy and loss in love life can lead to breakdown or to murder and suicide.

For convenience of presentation, specific age-related affective disorders and related problems are discussed under the four headings of childhood (this chapter), adolescence (Chapter 18), adult life (Chapter 19), and late life periods (Chapter 20). Table 17–1 schematizes in practical terms a view of the affective disorders in the life cycle.

AFFECTIVE DISORDERS IN PREADOLESCENT CHILDREN

Important practical matters involving children come up during the treatment of adults. When treatment of an adult patient includes intervention in the environment, as it often does, bringing the family under examination, studying the effect of an illness on the family, and thinking in terms of prevention of future problems, then the children become involved along with the patient.

Table 17-1

Affective Psychopathology in the Life Cycle

Period	Tasks and processes	Psychopathology (affective)	Clinical manifestations
Infancy and early childhood (birth to age 5 or 6)	To develop trust and a separate self; to be nurtured; to experience and express affects; to learn to control instincts; to play at life	Overdependence; failure to cope with affects and bodily processes; failure of separation; excessive dependency; self-doubts; self-rejection; failure to protect self; failure to play, sadness	Passivity; apathy; unhappiness; irritability; restlessness; withdrawal; sulking; fears; depressive affect; self-injury; rarely–suicidal acts; depressive illness
Latency (age 5 or 6 to puberty)	Sublimation; constructive use of intellect	Failure of sublimation; over-repression; excessive guilt; feelings of worthlessness; somatization; sleep disturbances	Poor school performance; masochistic feelings

Stage			
Early adolescence (age 10 or 11 to 15 or 16)	Experiencing instincts and a new self; control of instincts	Acting out; suppression; impulsiveness; withdrawal; guilt; self-destructive feelings and ideas; regressions to oral stages with dependency, drinking, drugs; rejections of progress; self-destructive feelings, acted out in daring acts	Adult disorders start occurring; occasional psychosis; depression and mania occasionally; pseudodelinquency
Late adolescence and young adulthood (age 15 to 25)	A more complete identity; finding a mate; control of sexuality and aggression; responsibility; ability to live with and experience affects	Rejection of adulthood (withdrawal from developmental tasks)	Adult illnesses seen; failure to function; rebellion; breakdown
Mid-life (age 35 to 55)	Responsibility in work and in parenthood	Failure; despair; illness; self-doubts; withdrawal	Typical illnesses
Late life (age 55 and on)	Satisfaction with work done; continued responsibility; ability to live with losses and sadness and cope with physical decline and illness	Anger; bitterness; despair, excessive grief; excessive dependency; loss of self-esteem; defenses against loss—paranoia, denial	Melancholia and other forms of depression Organic changes; dementia, etc.

Child psychiatrists, child therapists, child psychoanalysts, child psychologists, and social workers have been directing their attention to childhood affects and symptoms that may be precursors of adult depression. Developmental models directed toward understanding and relieving the child's symptoms have important implications for prevention as well. Sources of information are from retrospective observations on adults and from direct observation on children.

Definition of Childhood Depression

Although recent literature in child psychiatry is now full of references to childhood depression, there is far from agreement on what is being called depression. The important distinction to be made is the differentiation between definitive depressive illness, such as major depressive disorder, and various normal kinds of depressive affects ranging from normal sadness, grief, and the like, to apathy and withdrawal. The majority of patients with so-called depression do not have depressive illness, but a depressive reaction to the circumstances of their lives, or a depressive affective experience. The information from which these conclusions are drawn follows.

Information from Adults

Adults bring their childhood into their therapy with memories of losses and childhood traumata; one needs to know about this childhood to understand the adult. Also, adult therapy provides clues as to what happens to children. There is a growing interest in the importance of the childhood experience for later development of affective disorders, especially depression, along with the hope of opening the door to treatment, prevention, and preventive methods in the rearing of children. Specific precursors are now being identified.

Adults, including those not grossly neglected or abused and from stable families, when undergoing intensive psychotherapy or psychoanalysis, eventually come around to the reconstruction of several kinds of experiences from early childhood. These include the following: some hopeless situation, such as a struggle with the mother in which the child loses and feels disappointed and defeated; an irretrievable loss, either through death or separation; the unresolved and unexpressed feeling left over from this trauma; a relationship with a depressed parent, either identification or partnership. Along with these traumatic experiences, there often is also a feeling of responsibility beyond the child's years, a dedication, which carries over into the adult as a driving force so that reverses and losses are taken hard.

Such experiences in some adults, when reviewed from the perspective of adult treatment, constitute an actual early childhood experience that is reactivated when the adult is caught in a similar, seemingly hopeless situation. It is not a definitive depression in the adult sense, but a constellation of interrelated behaviors and affects that has been covered up. The adult depression includes the return of the repressed childhood experience. In adult treatment, the working through of this childhood experience becomes an important part of the therapy directed toward the patient's depression-proneness. Usually, although a definitive childhood depressive illness is not clearly retrievable in analysis, certain other anlagen or precursors of depression can be worked through—deficits in self-esteem, guilt, ambivalence, and so forth. In addition, paradoxically, the depression-prone personality may create situations which lead to breakdown, particularly by an unrealistic assumption of guilt for things beyond his or her responsibility.

If one is treating adults for depression, sooner or later one is going to hear about their children and may have to help decide something very important about those children; for example, does the child have a depression or other symptoms, does he or she need treatment, and how do the child and the parent influence one another?

Diagnosis

Clinical Manifestations Seen in Children

The clinical signs and symptoms seen in children that have to be explained and understood are in three categories: behavior, mood, and thinking. The behaviorally significant symptoms and signs are withdrawal, loss of efficiency, self-abuse or disregard of personal injury, suicidal impulses and actions, and aggressive acts toward others. In addition, hypoactivity or its opposite, restlessness and agitation, may be seen.

Mood changes seen are sadness and grief, weeping, apathy, unhappiness in a variety of expressions, anger, aggression, ambivalence, and sometimes the inability to express or even feel affects. The thoughts and ideas can express negativism, self-doubts, and loss of self-esteem, as well as general pessimism and defeatism. Suicidal ideation can be found even in preschool children. Masochistic trends are seen also.

In addition, defenses against painful depressive affects are seen, with repression, denial, apathy, running away, silence, and acting out with an effort to be good.

Significance of the Clinical Manifestations: The Controversy

There is currently a controversy as to the significance of these symptoms. One opinion, represented by those engaged in child therapy and child analysis, can be stated thusly:

As child psychiatrists, we have never emphasized diagnosis in the sense in which it is used in adult psychiatry for the simple reason that it has not been useful or significant for therapy. Instead, we emphasize from the very first the causes, the background, the family, the intrapsychic life of the child, and his environment, and try to get the persons who are involved in the situation to become actively engaged in the appraisal and the therapeutic process. [T. R. Warm. Personal communication]

Or, as stated by Anna Freud (1971b):

If symptoms are viewed merely as manifest phenomena, dealing with them remains arid so far as analytic interest is concerned. If the clinician is alerted to see opening up behind these the whole range of possible derivations, causations, and developmental affiliations, the field becomes fascinating, and scrutinizing a child's symptomatology becomes a truly analytic task. [p. 184]

To summarize, clinical child therapists do not find it necessary or even useful to make the kinds of descriptive phenomenological diagnoses that form the background of adult psychiatric practice today, because in the practice of child therapy this kind of diagnosis misses the point. The circumstances that bring on the symptoms are more important than a mere cataloging of the symptoms themselves. In adult work, specificity of diagnosis is important because it directs the treatment, particularly biological treatment, to specific methods.

However, there are now a good many active workers trained in the research methods of adult psychiatry, particularly the methods used to appraise the results of drug treatment for statistical studies in large groups. These persons are applying their techniques to the study of children, with the result that they are saying that the occurrence of depression in children is very much underdiagnosed and that they have the statistics to prove it. If the contentions of this descriptive-statistical school are correct, we are going to see a great many children getting antidepressant drugs; thus the controversy.

Special Problems of Diagnosis in Children

There is often difficulty in even observing the clinical symptoms adults complain of, which is one reason why depression in childhood is not often diagnosed. Children, even more than adults, do not tell what they actually feel until they know and trust the questioner. In a very interesting article on the formulation of a rating scale for depression in children between 6 and 12 years of age, the authors describe their experience with asking children about morbid and suicidal ideation (Poznanski et al. 1983). They discovered that virtually all the children (in their study of thirty hospitalized children) knew the word "suicide." Two of the three severely depressed children in their group denied thinking about suicide, but the authors later learned that both children had seriously discussed suicide with their ward attendants and teachers. "Thus, children who are depressed, but deny suicidal thoughts may well be suicidal, just as in the case with adults" (p. 202), the authors conclude. There are no protocols in the report, but it appears that most of the "depressions" reported were difficult to differentiate from separation reactions. "Morbid" ideas were common and the general impression is that the cases were of the situational reaction type and not adult types of depression. The critical questions, which usually are neglected, these authors found to be in the areas of "morbid ideation, suicidal ideation, sleep difficulties, and an assessment fo the child's capacity to enjoy life" (p. 203).

Children differ from adults in that nonverbal depressive affect can substitute for verbal reports of dysphoria, and social withdrawal occurs instead of the anorexia and weight loss in the adult. Those items in the rating scale used by Poznanski and colleagues (1983) with the highest correlation with a depressive profile were depressed mood, impaired school performance, anhedonia, unexpressive communication, hypoactivity, and a tendency to passivity and withdrawal.

Other observers have listed the essential clinical features of childhood depression as follows: dysphoria (persistently unhappy mood), generalized impairment in response to previously reinforcing experiences, and a reduction in self-initiated activities. Previously pleasurable activities no longer appeal (Dweck et al. 1977, p. 153).

Associated features depend on age and developmental level; for example, changes in self-esteem, guilt, personal and general pessimism, or blaming others develop as the children near adolescence. Duration for a minimum of four weeks is stipulated. Note that psychomotor retardation—the pathognomonic diagnostic sign of major endogenous depression of adults—is missing. If these signs fit any adult syndrome, it is dysthymia, or possibly the adjustment disorder with depressed mood, not a major depression.

With such an inclusive list of symptoms, one is going to assess quite a variety of children under the rubric of depression, with the result that an artificial class has been created, yet one has not actually described any children with genuine adult-type depressions. This is the error that one makes with lists and controlled interviews—an entity may be created that does not exist in reality. The use of the scale will certainly pick out unhappy children, and when it is applied in practice it does include a substantial percentage of children, many more than seems reasonable, to consider as having a clinical depression. This method of measuring depression seems to lack specificity. It has been pointed out that, with children, specificity is important:

> Sadness, apathy and guilt are quite different from feeling depressed and each represents a characteristic response to specific situations in the inner and outer world. It is a mistake to lump them all together under "depressed" which then simply means "not pleasant." But even "depressed" unto itself is not an entity. Detailed descriptions of it point to rather different affective states, e.g., "helpless and hopeless" differs from "empty and alone" or "nothing feels good" or "nothing is worth the bother." [Furman 1985, p. 6]

The conclusion Furman came to from her study of this method of assessing depression was that one is really dealing with a variety of affective states, and not with a syndrome.

Specific Disorders and Syndromes

Bipolar Disorder and Major Depressive Disorder

Definitive major depressive disorders are very occasionally reported by adult patients to have started in their childhood. It is important to distinguish symptoms that might constitute a partial syndrome from the complete syndrome; and it is important to separate preadolescent childhood from adolescence, as it is well known that adult types of disorders can start in the adolescent years.

In my series of 65 well-studied adult patients, none could actually be said to have started in childhood with the definitive syndrome. One woman with a chronic depressive neurosis (dysthymia) reported suicidal ideas at the age of 8. One man reported that his father had had depressive spells in childhood while in an orphanage and in adult years developed a bipolar disorder.

The only other example is also an indirect one, not seen by myself, but reported by a bipolar patient seen once in consultation, who said that his son, age 7, has had symptoms of hypomania, had been diagnosed as bipolar and is under lithium treatment elsewhere, at an excellent facility. In conclusion, documented attacks of major affective disorder in childhood are rare, but do occur.

Kraepelin (1921), who dealt with hospitalized patients, stated that depressions could start in childhood. In his book, *Manic-Depressive Insanity and Paranoia*, he describes adult cases from the group he classified as manic-depressives, whose symptoms began in childhood. However, he does not describe full-blown depressions in the children.

From observations on adults, it can be stated that the history of an adult disorder occasionally can be traced back to early childhood in the preadolescent years, but the adult history yields symptoms or personality characteristics which might be viewed as part-symptoms: unhappiness, feelings of rejection, low self-esteem, guilt, fatigue or withdrawal, inefficiency in school, etc., and not the definitive syndrome until adolescence.

Although it is hard to find, there is a reference to affective disorders in children in the latest official diagnostic manual (*DSM-III-R*). In a few lines under age-specific associated features under mood disorders, there is a statement to the effect that the *essential* features of a major depressive episode are similar in infants, children, adolescents, and adults, but that there are differences in the *associated* features, particularly in the presence of separation anxiety in children. In adolescents, negativistic or antisocial behavior, school difficulties, neglect of appearance, or substance abuse may occur.

In the same manual under dysthymia (depressive neurosis), the statement is made that the disorder may begin in childhood and that social interactions and school performance are affected. Also, it is stated that these children react negatively to praise or to positive relationships.

Dysthymia and Adjustment Disorder with Depressed Mood

Depressive affects, depressive lines of development, or depressive personality trends are as common in childhood as major depression is uncommon. If affective disorders of the adult type are rare, sad and unhappy children are very common. *ICD-9-CM* has a category with the code 313.1, called "disturbance of emotions specific to childhood and adolescence, with misery and unhappiness," which fits some of these children.

In *DSM-III-R*, the "adjustment disorder with depressed mood," coded 309.00, as in adults, fits some children, and, in persistent cases, possibly dysthymia, early onset (depressive neurosis), coded 300.40, of "primary type," Symptom diagnosis such as avoidant disorder, coded 313.21, may apply.

Larval early forms, and other anlagen, are possibly precursors of depression. It is in the early development that some of the most important childhood observations are made. Child analysts have made acute observations that reveal the origins of the depressive affects, depressive thinking, and depressive personality development. Studies of the development of depressive affect indicate that mourning, or the inability to mourn, are particularly important, especially in identifying the kind of ambivalent love relationship that start in childhood.

Anna Freud (1971b) has prepared a classification of symptoms based on the origin and cause of the symptom, rather than its end result. In the case of depression, the emphasis for therapeutic purposes is not that this is a depressed child, but on the meaning of the symptom of depression. In this classification, depressive states are among the symptoms resulting from alterations in the libido economy or direction of cathexis. For example, when the narcissistic cathexis of the self is "decreased unduly, the symptoms are *bodily neglect, self-derogation, inferiority feelings, depressive states, depersonalization* (in childhood)" (p. 168).

A. Freud also attributes some of the symptoms seen in depression to changes in the quality and direction of aggression, although she does not emphasize any connection with the entity of depression. Instead, she emphasizes inhibitions and failure at play, learning, and work. Also, defenses against aggression can be "responsible for the swings between *self-injurious behavior*, which corresponds to aggression turned against the self, and violent *aggressive-destructive outbursts* against animate and inanimate objects in the environment" (p. 169).

What she is referring to here are depressive affects and depressive trends, not the adult-oriented diagnosis of depression as a clinical entity, yet often these very phenomena crop up in the histories of our adult depressive patients. It may be that these childhood symptoms indicate depression-proneness and that treating them may prevent depression in adult life. Follow-up studies will have to be done to confirm or refute this theory.

The focus of treatment should not be on symptoms, but on the background causes, even in those unusual cases of clinical depression, more or less, of adult type. The focus should be on the environment, on the object relations, and on the intrapsychic pathology, to whatever extent it has developed.

In discussing the difficulties of using descriptive definitions of depression in children, Furman (1984) describes the complexity of the affects that children experience on the death of a parent. Apathy, for example, can sometimes be a defense against sadness or depression and sometimes merely all the child is able to feel at this stage of development. Furman also comments on the differences between sadness and depression:

> Perhaps the most common difficulty in assessing the patient's affect is the easy confusion between feeling sad and feeling depressed. The depressed feeling is marked by dejection, helplessness and hopelessness, and it is accompanied by lowered self-esteem. None of these are characteristic of sadness. Hence, the depressed

person feels impoverished, while the sad person feels unhappy, but relatively rich. [pp. 248–249]

Identifying Depression-Proneness

To identify early signs which may indicate depression-proneness, there are some specific symptoms, as well as personality trends, to look for.

Presenting Symptoms of Depressive Types

1. Directly expressed depressive moods and affects and cognitions: sadness, apathy, pessimism, negative attitudes, defeatism, grief, and anhedonia.
2. Indirect expressions: withdrawal, rebellion, resistance, irritability, self-denigration, excessive guilt, self-punishment, masochistic trends, poor concentration and school performance, lowering of efficiency, delinquent behavior. These are the result of depressive affect, or defenses against the pain of depressive affect.

Personality Development of Depressive Trends, Either Fully Formed or in Status Nascendi

The symptoms observed clinically include the following: deficiency in self-esteem; inability to experience or tolerate affects, especially grief and mourning; identifications with depressed parents; ambivalence in love relations; passivity, masochistic trends, and a tendency to self-punishment; and over-conscientiousness.

The following discussion is of the manner in which the most common of these arise in childhood.

Through the Experience of Loss and Grief

The experience of mourning and grief in adult life has provided a model for comparison with depression (melancholia). Recent studies of mourning in childhood, or lack of it, are providing some information applicable to the relationship of early life to later depressive development.

In her paper "Absence of Grief," Deutsch (1937) has reported cases of adults in which the failure to mourn in childhood had long-term effects of several kinds: the appearance of later depressive symptoms with suicidal potential, the later appearance of neurotic hysterical symptoms, including paradoxical compulsive weeping, the development of apathy or lack of feeling in important situations, and avoidance of love relationships. She concluded that "the process of mourning as reaction to the real loss of a loved person *must be carried to completion*. As long as the early libidinal or aggressive attachments persist, the painful affect continues to flourish, and, *vice versa*, the attachments are unresolved as long as the affective process of mourning has not been accomplished" (p. 21). How to bring this about in children is now a very practical issue.

The therapist has to be prepared to assist the mourning process. The techniques for doing this depend on the age of the child. Some practical guidelines have been outlined by Furman (1974). "We devoted special attention to crucial questions—criteria for mourning in childhood, the difference between the child's task of mourning a parent and adult bereavement, the incidence and nature of depression and apathy in bereaved children" (p. 10). In the discussion of apathy she states:

> The only factor common to all our depressed or apathetic patients was their lack of conscious awareness of sadness or of its true ideational content. In each case the treatment process had to uncover either the underlying affect or content or both, and, with the help of interpretation, assist the child in gaining conscious recognition. The patient's ability then to tolerate and express his deep sadness in relation to its real content depend not only on his conscious recognition but also on *the availability of a person who could empathize with him and maintain a relationship that could support the child in his task.* The analyst could fulfill this role with the older children. For prelatency children [up to age 6 or

so], direct help or at least "permission" from the sur-
viving parent was necessary. [pp. 196–197. Italics
added]

This task requires either a skilled therapist or a very understanding
parent or other caretaker, or a combination of these.

One can apply the same method to analyze the other
depressive anlagen and symptoms and uncover the significance of
the experience.

Through Damage to or Deficits in the Development of Self-esteem Manifested as Feelings of Inadequacy, Low Self-regard, and Unworthiness

Observations of special importance in the evolution of depression
are those concerning deficits in self-esteem. Also, a deficiency in
self-esteem can be basic to a developing suicidal tendency. Deficits in self-esteem can start very early—in first or second year—
with failure to protect oneself against damage, etc.

Development of Feelings of Pessimism and Hopelessness, Manifested Clinically as Feelings of Helplessness

The tendency to think pessimistically can start very early, for
example, in the child's feeling toward his or her mother. The child
may feel that it is hopeless to try to satisfy a rigid mother or to
attract the attention of a distraught mother or to get warmth and
love from an inhibited or compulsive or depressed mother, an
attitude manifested in later childhood as defeatism and failure.

Here is an example in an adult case in analysis. This was a
30-year-old man who has had four clinical major depressions,
who described his early childhood before the age of 7 or 8 years
as characterized by unsuccessful attempts to please his mother.
There were three siblings born with less than a year between,
certainly a handful for the most insightful mother, which his was

not. There were also three others born at longer intervals. He said of his mother, "She was very fair. She rejected all of us." At about age 6 or 7, he went into a long period of withdrawal and passivity, spending much of his time in a rocking chair, listening to the radio, as though giving up any attempt to deal with his mother. His father tried to rescue him, but was unable to do so. This defeatism, with retreat from his environment, provided a model for his later reactions when confronted with difficult tasks requiring self-esteem.

Through Depressive Identifications

The process of identification starts very early, with imitation and response. If the mother is depressed and unable to convey or express active interest, the child may not only become apathetic and unresponsive, but may identify with the mother's mood and become depressed. Patterns of response such as this persist into adult life. Patients and grown children may still respond to one another's depressed or elated state by developing the counterpart, even to a severe enough degree to have a clinical depressive or manic spell.

Through the Development of Guilt, Self-punishment, and Masochistic Trends

Children who tend to harm themselves, who neglect their personal safety, or seem to inflict damage or pain upon themselves may be identifying with a punitive parent. Also, masochistic trends may sometimes be seen where a child has had to submit to abuse or pain, mental or physical, in order to keep in contact with a parent. Here intervention and parent guidance is indicated.

Through Deficits in Formation of Object Relations

The development in the first two years of the child's sense of self and way of relating to his or her mother (primarily) can determine the paths later development will follow. Anyone interested in the field should study the child analytic work described above, including also the work of Mahler and her associates (1975), who have shown in detail among their many observations how a depressed mother can, by her failure to stimulate, respond, encourage, and approve, create a depressed child.

Early Childhood: The First Three Years

Phenomena seen in very young children sometimes contain anlagen of adult problems and require intervention. In his book *Child Psychopathology and Adult Psychoses* (1976), Freeman describes (pp. 10–18) several cases from the literature of children who had common symptoms of massive withdrawal, anxiety, and loss of contact, and were treated by different therapists (Fraiberg, Sperling, and Furman). These children seemed "passive, overwhelmed, and helpless" (p. 11). There were other symptoms also, suggesting adult borderline cases: "the easy movement from advanced levels of the ego and object relations to primitive levels . . ." (p. 15). The patients were all less than 3½ years of age, had been subjected to severe psychic trauma, including witnessing intercourse and being sexually molested. All responded to intensive therapy and intervention. To include all these affective disturbances in a discussion of affective disorders, per se, does not mean that these are forerunners of adult illness.

It is not known how far treatment and intervention at an early age will go toward preventing the development of affective disorders later in life, as there is still much to learn through long follow-up of early cases. In a recent series of papers from a collaborative study on the impact of children of having a manic-depressive parent, some important conclusions were reached. Of the parents, Davenport and colleagues (1984) wrote:

> Manic-depressive mothers, in contrast to control mothers, tend to be less attentive to their children's health needs, emphasized performance in some achievement-related areas, were more overprotective, and reported

more negative affect toward the child. They also were more disorganized, less active with their children, and more unhappy, tense and ineffective. Index parents secured lower scores in the areas of family interaction and social adjustment, and they experienced situational problems of considerable severity, including clinical depression in the well parent. [p. 230]

Of the children, Zahn-Waxler and colleagues (1984) observed:

By the age of 2 years, children with a manic-depressive parent were already found to be experiencing substantial psychiatric problems. Children with a manic-depressive parent had difficulty in sharing with their friends and in handling hostility, showing maladaptive patterns of aggression. The social and emotional problems of these children were similar to the interpersonal problems of their manic-depressive parents. [p. 236]

In an editorial in the same journal, Solnit and Leckman (1984) commented, "If replicated and elaborated, these findings, together with the findings of other investigators, could round out an emerging picture of the early life of children at high risk to develop serious affective disturbances" (p. 241–242).

Treatment in Children

There is a range of techniques available, starting with environmental manipulation and family supports, to treatment via the mother, mother guidance, and direct psychotherapy or psychoanalysis of the child. If a seriously disabling pattern is already fully established, such as withdrawal, masochism or obsessive-compulsive symptoms, an intensive program of psychotherapy or of psychoanalysis is required for the child.

Treatment of Major Disorders

As for treatment and management of the rare definitive major disorders, the available methods are just as numerous and complex as with adults. Diagnosis of the exact need then permits exact and appropriate therapy, but diagnosis has to be more than descriptive. Here one has to diagnose the nature of the traumatic situation and the inner situation of the developing personality, then select the appropriate treatment and management: environmental manipulation, treatment via the parents, group work, family therapy, individual psychotherapy, psychoanalysis, or possibly medication and combinations of these. Chemotherapy is used sometimes, but standards, side effects, and influence on personality are not understood. For example, tricyclics can cause gynecomastia and breast changes.

Antidepressants can have paradoxical effects, as well as unfortunate side effects. Controlled studies show that in preadolescent children, antidepressants are no more effective statistically than placebo in the treatment of depressions. No one has demonstrated otherwise to date.

Antidepressant drugs are not recommended for children under 6 years of age, and even in the older groups there is not enough experience to know what long-range side effects may occur. Changes in body image such as that induced by breast changes may be more harmful than any potential good effect.

Lithium is reported to have been used in the exceedingly rare clear-cut major bipolar disorder. Because the long-range effects of the drug in children are not known, it is recommended that it be used for as short a period and as low a dose as possible, perhaps just to tide over in an emergency, and that treatment of other concurrent causes be carried out simultaneously with psychotherapy or analysis, parent guidance, elimination of disturbing environmental causes, and so forth. (With full-grown adolescents, it is safe to use the drugs according to adult standards, as long as developmental considerations, family influences, and conflicts are not neglected.)

Care of Children of Depressed Mothers

Whenever a depressed nonpsychotic mother of young children is under treatment, one should try to avoid hospitalization or other separation, if there is no risk of suicide or rejection of the child. This is to prevent separation problems in the children. The mother's needs have to be considered too; she should have enough support and help that her illness can be treated successfully. Even if she has to have full-time help and be in bed, at least she will *be there* for her children, who can come to her for contact and comfort. See Morrison (1983) for more details.

18

ADOLESCENCE

Adult disorders begin to appear in their adult form during adolescence, but often differ enough from the adult form that they merit a separate description. Also, in adolescence early recognition of problems allows for preventive work that can be critical for the course of the disturbed person's entire lifetime, making it possible to correct tendencies that often cause serious trouble later if left untreated. The tremendous increase in adolescent suicides in the last two decades alone demands special attention.

Kashani and colleagues (1987) studied a community sample of 150 adolescents aged 14, 15, and 16 using a structured interview. A major depressive disorder was found in 4.7 percent of the group. All those with major depression also had dysthymia, and another 3.3 percent had dysthymia alone.

There is a wide variation in age of onset of adolescence from one individual to another and in the rate at which maturation can occur. There are three merging phases: early (puberty), middle, and late adolescence. Puberty starts a year or two earlier in most girls than in boys, so that prepubertal emotional changes can be seen in girls at age 10 or 11 that are not seen in boys until the age of 12 or 14.

Some of the symptoms of the age itself, especially early adolescence, may overlap with what in an adult might be considered symptoms of affective disorder: a tendency to withdrawal, denial of emotional response, overreaction to slights, excessive self-denigration, and others. Also, affectively disordered late adolescents are now sufficiently grown up that they may have the freedom and ability to act out depressive and manic ideas like an

345

adult, so that impulsive acts such as assaults and suicide become more frequent and more likely to be lethal. Moreover, at this critical period vital decisions are made, and changes take place which effect the entire course of adult life.

Adolescence is a period of risk for several reasons. First, the overwhelming influx of sexual drives, sometimes without adequate preparation, may threaten controls and create needs beyond the capacity either to contain or direct them. Under the influence of the awakened oedipal conflict, for example, regression may occur, characterized by rebellion against authority; or the compulsive seeking for an ideal object may prompt unacceptable, inappropriate acts causing guilt and shame. Meanwhile, the childhood ideals sometimes turn out to be very difficult to achieve, also causing guilt, especially in cases where the adolescent may have set impossible goals because of fears and fantasies of failure and rejection, based on childhood expectations not yet corrected by realistic adult conceptions. Confrontation with the larger world and realization of the relative personal powerlessness may give rise to feelings of pessimism and uselessness or other depressive affects in certain vulnerable individuals.

Today many adolescents are exposed to travel, to overwhelming experiences in the larger world, and to information beyond their ability to process, with the result that norms seem more difficult to define; alienation, meaninglessness, and loneliness are not unusual. Withdrawal and regression to earlier patterns can result; the predepressive child then becomes the depressed adolescent. Family disruption, the great increase in divorce, working mothers who are absent from the home, as well as the frequent absence of the father through divorce, death, or personal pressures all set the stage for development of adolescent depression.

PSYCHOPATHOLOGY AND CLINICAL DIAGNOSIS

Adult types of mood disorders tend to start showing up in late puberty and middle adolescence, with the appearance of occasional depressions or manic attacks in 12- and 13-year-olds. The differential diagnosis from schizophrenia can be troublesome because at this age the affective disorders are sometimes colored by immature thinking, regressions, and gross sexual pathology. By late adolescence, at age 17–20, the adult patterns are more likely to be clear-cut, and differential diagnosis is simpler, so that affective disorders are easier to diagnose.

Meanwhile, the childhood kinds of affective states continue: low self-esteem, withdrawal, masochistic trends, pessimism, passivity, inability to experience or express emotions, apathy and poor functioning, sometimes with depressive equivalents or masks of depression, such as hypochondriasis and acting out with rebellion, truancy, etc.

The work of the adolescent is to make the transition from childhood to adult life, from dependency to independence, and from needing parents to preparing for parenthood. The transition is not always easy, even in those who do not become ill, and this fact requires the therapist to be able to distinguish the normal transitional adolescent states from actual disorders and illnesses.

The danger of suicide in adolescents is of increasing importance, suicide now being the third most common cause of death during these years. Many of these deaths occur in youngsters who either have an affective disorder or some related affective state causing despair and pain.

Diagnosis and Evaluation

The same problems of diagnosis are present with the adolescent as with children: failure to communicate on the part of the child and the parent and failure on the part of the professional to look for the symptoms that act as disguises, defenses against depression, or equivalents, causing unclear clinical pictures; all these add up to missed diagnoses. In addition, there are, as in children, a great variety of depression-related affects that lead to misery and suffering, and indeed, sometimes to serious acts such as suicide. Those moods seen in adolescents vary with their age, usually tending to be less defined in early adolescence and better defined in late adolescence; affects include boredom, alienation, disillusionment, apathy, loneliness, and detachment, sometimes culminating in guilt, shame, withdrawal, and despair.

Normal Adolescent Depression

Adolescents today consider themselves to be sadder, lonelier, and more sensitive than in the 1960s, when rebellion was an acceptable life-style. In the 1980s, adolescents also search for meaning, but are often lost in their search and find themselves powerless and do not always find a secure philosophical nest in which to develop. The diagnostic problem for the psychotherapist is complicated by these normal adolescent experiences, for sometimes young people who need help in finding themselves are referred for therapy, or refer themselves, and it becomes the task of the therapist to decide important questions about the seriousness of the complaints and the depth of the affective experience, whether they represent normality or a serious problem.

Normal Moodiness versus Affective Disorder

There is a commonly held belief that adolescents are normally moody, that is, given to great fluctuations of mood from unrealistically sad and depressed to elated and joyous. To some extent this is true, and some adolescents are indeed quite emotional and labile, given to enthusiasms and also to dislikes. However, one cannot rely on this possibility clinically, as everyone is not the same, and there are many adolescents who normally are quite unemotional outwardly, and are restrained, guarded, and inhibited. In each case, one has to evaluate the symptom, if it is a symptom, as to whether it is normal, an illness, or a character trait.

In any case, it may be a method of defense, keeping painful affects from consciousness and permitting a psychological balance to be maintained. Moods can lessen tension and allow for mastery over impulses. Adolescents normally should be permitted their moods.

In the emerging clinical depression, the persistence, depth, and guilt are characteristic, along with poor self-image, especially if there is an accompanying and persistent loss of ability to experience pleasure. Persistence and chronicity are characteristic both of the clinical syndrome and the character trait; the differentiation here is made on the fact that the character trait goes back into childhood, whereas the illness has a definite recent onset, with a recent drop in functioning.

Diagnosis should conform to an accepted classification, either *DSM III-R* or *ICD-9-CM*. Preferably, it should include the five axes of diagnosis recommended and described in *DSM-III-R* as well as two other categories or lines of appraisal that are especially important in adolescence: (1) the assessment of symptoms (for example, the evaluation of definite depression-related affects, moods, ideas and behaviors, such as suicidal intent), which may be present in a goodly number of persons who do not have a clear-cut affective disorder, and (2) the diagnosis and appraisal of intrapsychic phenomena (i.e., appraisals of defenses, psychodynamic issues, instinctual development, cognitive development, and important aspects of object relations).

Definite Clinical Syndromes and Disorders

The definitive disorders are likely to be diagnosable by adult standards if one looks closely and is not led astray by some commonly seen disguises (Lesse 1974). The following paragraphs describe age-specific disguises, which color the depressive picture and distort it.

Preoccupation with Self and Body, Manifested by Hypochondriacal Physical Symptoms. Sometimes a physician is consulted, but often the adolescent covers up in one way or another, for example, by treating the symptom himself or herself with physical exercise or by excessive attention to diet or by denial. Fatigue is a common symptom and is often misdiagnosed as lowered thyroid function, hypoadrenalism, or other mythical endocrine disorder. The parents' denial of emotional problems may have a strong influence in selecting the diagnostic road taken. It is up to the physician to do a careful study of the medical symptoms and advise the appropriate treatment, sometimes against the resistance of both patient and parents. Adults with both bipolar and unipolar affective disorders tell of early spells of a hypochondriacal or psychosomatic nature. Early psychotherapeutic and pharmacological intervention might go a long way toward preventing later trouble.

Antisocial Symptoms—Withdrawal. Because adolescents can be very prone to keep their own counsel, to withdraw from communication, and be silent when with adults, it is easy to miss a depressive type of withdrawal and to mistake it either for normal reticence or for sullenness.

Adolescent Turmoil. The often seen irritability, restlessness, inability to sit still, constant seeking of companionship, and neglect of schoolwork may be an attempt to ward off loneliness, sadness, and feelings of inadequacy. Because the usual need for group identification overlaps with this behavior, it can be a disguise.

Poor Performance and Loss of Efficiency. When the typical depressive symptoms of difficulty in concentrating and slowing of mental process creates problems with attention and retention, often there is a dropping off of performance, which may easily be misdiagnosed as irresponsibility, laziness, or carelessness. When school performance drops consistently in a formerly good student one should have in mind the possibility of depression. In those persons with this symptom who do not have a genuine major depression, a consistent drop in performance probably indicates some painful preoccupation and possibly a need for intervention.

In addition to the above disguises and presenting symptoms, there are some differential diagnostic considerations in those patients who have obvious major episodes of such severity as to require hospitalization. As with young adults, the chief differential possibilities for confusion in serious cases are schizophrenia and schizoaffective psychosis.

Regressions. These are behaviors that are reversions to the behavior of a younger child, in an adolescent who has already achieved age-appropriate behavior. The regression can be relatively normal, indicating a need for attention, or it can be quite pathological, indicating an oncoming breakdown, either manic, depressive, or schizohprenic. An example of a normal regression would be that of a girl of 12 years who suddenly starts following her mother around the house after having suffered a slight from her schoolmates.

More pathological would be the case of a girl of that age who suddenly wants to stay in the parents' bedroom at night, like a frightened young child. Some pseudo-delinquent acts are regressions, such as stealing, breaking things, and vandalism (in which smearing paint on walls is common). Compulsive, uncontrolled eating has a regressive quality, as does its opposite, refusing food as a defense against sexuality. Other more gross breakthroughs of instinctual impulses are sometimes seen—loss of fastidiousness, fecal smearing, loss of modesty, or open sexual displays.

When pathological regressions occur, there is need to be careful about uncovering unconscious material, as it may further the regressive tendency or even produce a more psychotic reaction. In therapy, signs of regression may be transference reactions: child-like dependency, clinging, or rebelling in an infantile manner. In adolescent manic attacks there may be flirtatiousness and loss of sexual control, with acting out more appropriate to an older person occurring side by side with infantile, regressive behavior.

Differential Diagnosis

If delusions are present, are they mood-appropriate and relevant? In elated states and excited states are the delusions megalomanic and is the mood euphoric? If so, probably this is a manic state; even if somewhat persecutory ideas color the picture, the presence of a consistent pattern of megalomania probably indicates mania. Are the delusions self-denigrating, hypochondriacal, or guilty? If so, they probably indicate a psychotic depression.

If the illness is cyclical, with periods of consistent overactivity and excitement alternating with periods of inactivity, then likely the condition is bipolar, even when the thinking is not clearly depressive or manic. At the least, when the mental content is mixed, paranoid, or not clearly manic or depressive, if a cyclical pattern is present, we are justified in considering this a schizoaffective bipolar state, and not schizophrenic. The importance of the differential is, of course, that the schizoaffective response to lithium can be very good, whereas the schizophrenic response consistently is not. Neuroleptics are useful in both types (see Table 13–5).

Other uncommon differential diagnoses are physical causes, brain traumas, toxic conditions, and drug effects. Depressions secondary to the toxic effects of chemicals of an addicting nature must be considered. Fortunately, laboratory procedures (i.e., blood levels, plus a careful history) will often answer this question. Marijuana sometimes produces a depressive reaction, possibly indicating an underlying depressive tendency. When the reaction is confusional with paranoid delusions, it probably indicates a paranoid tendency, possibly schizophrenia. Usually such cases are best diagnosed and treated in a hospital.

The common denominator in all these related states is the depressive affect, misery, self-blame, shame, guilt, hopelessness, sometimes to the point of despair. This common core creates the risk of suicide and points to the need for help.

Bipolar Disorder

Although manic-depressive disorder, now usually called bipolar disorder, is rare, even very rare, in childhood, it occurs frequently enough in adolescence that one should be on the alert for it, especially in the children of bipolar patients or in the first-degree relatives. Akiskal and colleagues (1985) have reported on sixty-eight juvenile offspring or siblings of adult bipolar patients, showing that all but eleven had some form of affective disorder, over half having some signs of bipolarity, and the remainder either depression or dysthymia. The eleven had symptoms of substance abuse and later were classified as dysthymic or cyclothymic. Of the ten prepubertal children, four had hypomanic features, but full-blown manic psychosis did not appear until puberty. The mean age of onset was 15.9 years, with a range of 6 to 24. Recurrences were experienced in 71 percent in the follow-up study of three years. Depressive episodes were the most common, but some manic and mixed states did occur.

The presenting symptoms varied. One boy was seen by a pediatrician for abdominal cramps, but was found to have a decreased interest in schoolwork, cried often, and wished he were dead. One girl had had repeated pediatric examinations for a year of listlessness, crying, and loss of interest, and finally reached psychiatric attention when she was found unconscious in a bathtub, having cut her wrists with a razor blade. The psychosocial situation was not discussed.

The manic onset varied, sometimes showing mood-relevant, grandiose ideas, and sometimes schizoid symptoms of mood-incongruent ideas, which were paranoid or otherwise painful, unpleasant ideas or delusions. One timid, somewhat introverted boy of 13 years was arrested by the police when he was singing and dancing in heavy traffic and jokingly threatened to shoot anyone with a water gun when approached. He later responded very well to standard inpatient treatment for mania with haloperidol and lithium.

With adolescents and young adults who are destined to have long histories of affective disorder, the initial attacks of depression can be larval, relatively minor, and could easily be considered simple, situational reactions if one did not carefully observe the presence of (1) persistent lowering of efficiency and concentration; (2) psychomotor retardation (slowing of activity); and (3) persistent loss of capacity for pleasure, especially with social withdrawal.

Similarly, the initial manic attack may not be typical. It may be hypomanic, or may be mixed, with what looks like schizophrenic symptoms, but there is always speeding up of thought processes, and the content is mood-relevant, that is, megalomanic.

Even in a psychiatric hospital, the early bipolar disorder may be unrecognized, unless looked for. By using a structured interview designed to identify bipolar disorder, Gammon and colleagues (1983) demonstrated that five (29 percent) of seventeen adolescent inpatients satisfied the DSM-III criteria for bipolar and atypical bipolar disorder, although these diagnoses had not been identified.

The five patients diagnosed as having bipolar disorder, according to the criteria of DSM-III, all had classical symptoms of both mania and depression, but they were not picked out until the researchers sat down with them with a structured interview and the complete list of symptoms and took thirty minutes concentrating on that list with the patient and the patient's mother. In short, something made those florid psychoses less obvious and disguised the symptoms until someone looked specifically for them. One tends to be distracted from the correct diagnosis by a low level of suspiciousness for the diagnosis in general, particularly by the presence of the kinds of preoccupations adolescent patients have, which becomes the center of attention—"psychotic features, antisocial and impulsive behavior, and poor academic and psychosocial performance"—suggesting "adolescent turmoil" (Gammon et al. 1983, p. 546).

Unipolar Disorder

The more common form of major affective disorder at all ages is the unipolar form, either single attack or recurrent. The number of persons with this illness starting in adolescence is substantial enough that it should always be considered, especially when there is a family history of affective disorder. The form of the attack may be classical and full blown, but it may also be disguised by the predominance of one aspect of the symptom complex, as in later life. For example, a depression may be present as fatigue or other psychosomatic or even hypochondriacal preoccupation. There are others in the college age group in which rumination with plausible, distracting guilt over some misbehavior or a preoccupation with some obvious problem may so mislead the observer that the underlying depression is missed.

Adolescent and Adult Depression Compared

In a recent study and review (Strober 1985), some striking differences were tabulated. Endogenous and psychotic depressions were twice as common in adults, and psychomotor retardation almost twice as common. In addition, although subjective depres-

sion, loss of appetite, diurnal variation, and delusions were reported almost as frequently in the adolescent, other highly significant symptoms, although common, occurred much less
frequently in the adolescents. There were loss of pleasure, suicidal
thoughts, self-reproach, distinct quality of mood, nonreactivity of
mood, lack of energy, and psychomotor retardation. The conclusion one reaches from a review of these studies is that, although
there is an overlap in the adult and adolescent groups in that some
major depressions occur in both groups, nevertheless, the adolescent group that was selected by these standardized methods
contains a considerable number of those with something other
than major depression. Since protocols are not given, these may
be mainly transient depressive reactions (adjustment disorder with
depressed mood) or developmental neurotic and characterological disorders of affective type (now included in the catchall term
of dysthymia).

Dysthymia, Adjustment Disorder
with Depressed Mood, and Cyclothymia

These three disorders, although fundamentally different, can be
confused because they have in common an observable depressive
reaction beyond what the circumstances would call for. Together
they account for a large number of the affective disturbances seen
in adolescence. For example, Joan, a 15-year-old girl is unhappy
because her favorite girlfriend has suddenly taken an interest in
the patient's younger sister. She is so unhappy that she swallows
some tincture of iodine in a suicidal attempt and then tells the
family about it. When the situation is explored and explained, the
sister, the girlfriend, and the patient make up, and the patient's
depression is relieved. This is an adjustment disorder with depressed mood, that is, a depressive reaction beyond what is usually considered normal. Another example is Margery, a 13-year-
old girl who has been very unhappy because she has to go to
school dressed in clothes her mother has chosen for her which
she, the patient, considers wrong according to what she has
observed the other girls wearing. She is afraid to protest, but

instead makes an ineffectual suicidal attempt. Nothing happens; her message goes unanswered, and the family goes on as if nothing unusual had happened. The girl makes no more suicidal attempts, but soon seeks other consolations in teachers who approve of her because of her excellent intellect and achievement. She goes on to a troubled life during her adult years.

The undercurrent of a depressive tendency that can surface and take over under traumatic conditions seems to be present in these conditions, and when the symptoms occur they should signal that this is a vulnerable person who needs psychotherapy, possibly prolonged enough to get at the underlying personality trait itself with the hope of curing the depression proneness.

The true cyclothymic state is usually found in the family of bipolar persons and often makes its presence known in the adolescent. Mood cycles, often precipitated by losses, are not so severe as to be considered bipolar, but are nevertheless apparent enough that the patient gets the reputation for being unstable and overreactive, both on the euphoric high side and on the depressive down side. Sometimes these persons are misdiagnosed as having borderline personality disorder, but differ in that their instability is usually limited to mood fluctuations, without the extremes and social behaviors of the borderline. Although the condition is not sufficiently studied to make definitive generalizations, one should attempt treatment with lithium and neuroleptics. The same kind of psychotherapy used for borderline patients has been helpful in some cases, with strong controls and monitoring. In others, psychotherapy employing both educational and insight therapy can help prevent impulsive acts, school dropout, and conflicts in the family.

Depression-Related Moods and Affects

There are many sad and depressed adolescents who do not have the complete syndrome of a major or minor depression, but who nevertheless are disturbed enough to warrant attention. The affects and moods referred to here are the same as those described in the adult depressive affects (sadness, boredom, brooding, and inferiority feelings, resulting in moodiness and withdrawal, or dejection, sometimes to the point of despair. There can be insomnia and appetite disturbances or other physical symptoms without observable physical signs. Sometimes these are of such transient nature or so mild that they are indications of a transitory disappointment or loss. When accompanied by guilt and shame over some unknown or minor occurrence, they can represent the beginnings of a more serious depression. The presenting symptom may be some physical complaint such as headache, thus giving the pediatrician a chance to look for other psychological symptoms, and possibly enable a referral to a psychotherapist. A thorough evaluation may then be made.

An example is Adrian, a young college student, 18 years of age and a good student, who had become very depressed and unhappy, feeling useless and outside of things. He came for counseling, saying that he could not locate himself in the great mass of students, having gone to a smaller high school in which he was well known and popular. Although he had no thought disorder or serious guilt or self-destructive ideas, he felt that college was not meaningful in the way he had expected it to be and that he might consider dropping out because of his discomfort and unhappiness. The problem was solved, not through psychotherapy, but by advising him to make an attempt to join the activities for which he had talent and interest, namely, the music activities and organizations. He had played a trumpet in the high school band, but had not considered himself good enough for the college band and had therefore not attempted it. The counselor encouraged him to try out, which he did, finding to his surprise that he was accepted and could perform quite adequately. Also, he was well-accepted socially by the group, made friends, and lost the feelings of isolation. Follow-up during the four years of college found him well and preparing for admission to medical school.

Personality Disorders and Trends

These are important in any discussion of mood disorders for two reasons: (1) They predispose to, and accompany, the disorder and may be the central focus of therapy and prevention; and (2) they present symptoms of behavior, mood, and thinking that bring the youth to the therapist and need treatment in themselves, whether or not a definitive clinical syndrome is present.

One traditional popular view of the normal adolescent's personality is that it is unstable, labile, and unpredictable; exaggerated emotions are expected; passions are free; excesses are the order of the day. Or so we are to believe. However, if this is true of some adolescents, they represent a minority and also it seems, not surprisingly, that it is really more true of certain personality disorders, including the hysterical, the borderline, and the cyclothymic.

The standard accepted personality disorders listed in *DSM-III-R* can be applied to adolescents, as these describe character traits that have developed during childhood, continued through adolescence, and by late adolescence are in their adult form. There is value in identifying not just the full-blown disorders, but also trends that may well need treatment and are part of the general assessment of the personality. Both may require prolonged and intensive treatment in themselves, even when an acute affective disorder is symptomatically relieved, just as in adults where, for example, those with recurrent unipolar disorder may require treatment for obsessional neurosis when their depressive or manic attacks are controlled with medication.

Special Themes and Tendencies

The history of the individual may reveal important trends. An important differential diagnostic point between the serious clinical state of depression and the normal adolescent depression of an existential type is in the history of the individual (Anthony 1970). In normal adolescents who are simply making a normal adjustment to a depressing situation, the history is of a good development with good relationships to parents and peers; in the more serious types, with the implication either of breakdown or of a future of maladjustment, there is a history of pathological patterns of development: (1) those whose childhood has a history of numerous disturbances, from sleeping problems, eating problems, colic and head banging in infancy to negativism, disobedience, truancy, masochistic behavior, and running away from home in the older child; and (2) those who were ideal, well-adjusted, and even-tempered children, who were good, kind, and sympathetic, but who really did not have a wholehearted, unambivalent identification with the parent. These latter turned out to be vulnerable to traumatic happenings such as accidents, illnesses, and school problems, any of which could plunge them into a depressive development.

There are certain areas of personality that are likely to come up in the therapy of depressed and suicidal youngsters of whatever clinical diagnosis. These are:

1. Excessive orality and dependency or its opposite (i.e., independence and bravado). The abuse of drugs or food, (i.e., alcohol use and/or anorexia or bulimia) are the clinical manifestations.

2. Ambivalence or excessive dependence in love relations, resulting from a failure in nurturance and failure to form an integrated self.

3. Obsessiveness and excessive guilt over failure and over instinctual impulses.

There are difficulties in the experiencing of affects. An example is in the inability to mourn. The two contrasting personality types described above—those who have a history of much childhood difficulty and those who were always considered "good," successful children—have in common an inability to tolerate affects, including an inability to mourn in the normal sense, that is, to be able to experience the pain of giving up childhood pleasures with appropriate sadness and to go on to the next stage of development in a healthy manner, free of childhood remnants. Mourning for the lost past is common to all ages, although it is usually associated with old age; it is not unhealthy because it provides continuity of development and allows one to keep alive the love objects in their mental images, yet altered with the new adolescent appreciation of reality by which the parents are seen more as they really are. If in adolescence the parental images are of reasonably good parents, then enough of the pain of childhood is forgiven, the good things are remembered, and the normal mourning process is successful; a healthy sadness for the lost childhood is experienced. Depression-prone adolescents cannot tolerate their affects well and tend to act out, for example, with drug abuse or with psychopathic antisocial acts, or to be inhibited and overcontrolled.

There are deficits in the self-image. Normal adolescents feel good about themselves; in fact, often they "know it all." Depressed and depression-prone adolescents do not feel good about themselves, although this attitude may be well defended in one way or another.

The borderline personality and delinquency come into the discussion here because often the borderline person, as understood today, has depressed feelings and not rarely makes suicidal attempts, as do delinquent adolescents in jail. It is possible occasionally for major depression to occur in conjunction with this type of personality, and, when it does, it is more likely that the personality is cyclothymic rather than borderline, an important distinction for purposes of therapy.

Adolescents with true affective disorders have a variety of personalities, but on the whole they tend to have reasonably good controls and to have a certain amount of integration and predictability. The borderline is more likely to be overwhelmed by fluctuating moods, including anger, and he comes to the therapist because of drug abuse, impulsive acting out, and delinquency, rather than by depression and suicidal acts. Persons in this group have more than the usual need for action because of a deficit in controls, so that one might expect impulsive and aggressive behavior, which is indeed the case. Homicide, suicide, and accidents occur, especially when confinement is forced. Suicides in jail, as well as in psychiatric hospitals, are not uncommon, where episodes of out-of-control behavior occur frequently.

Psychosocial Problems

In a broad sense, psychosocial refers to the environment with all the influences that impinge on the person from external sources.

These forces are of particular importance with children and adolescents because of their relative helplessness to change things to suit themselves and their dependency on their environment and family, who have power over them. Psychosocial influences from the family are of primary importance, but school, society, and the influence of peers also impinge on the adolescent and require evaluation.

The affects and moods described earlier derive from conflicts and are signals of internal struggles for which individuals may need external help. Many adolescents treat themselves, some with normal methods such as healthy sublimations, others with avoidance, school dropout, withdrawal, or the comfort or excitement of drugs, violence, and rebellion.

The particular issues of the adolescent revolve around practical and realistic problems and also intrapsychic issues causing conflicts which can generate shame and guilt or may lead to the sense of failure and helplessness. The practical issues of the early adolescent, from the age of about 11 to 15, have to do with growing awareness of changes in the body, the development of secondary sexual characteristics and sexual feelings, with the possibility of shame and guilt as well as loss of self-esteem over the changes themselves as they bear on or conflict with the established ideal self-image.

The therapist finds that the most intense conflicts arise around the questions of pleasing the parents, establishing peer relationships, and building or maintaining self-esteem in the face of burgeoning sexual and competitive feelings and the drive to find sexual and gender expression. Failure in any of these areas can lead to feelings of shame, guilt, frustration, and a sense of loss, causing suffering, mourning, and depression. Efforts to drive for success can be limiting and exhausting, can lead to loneliness and withdrawal, all of which promote depressive affect. Marital conflicts or divorce of parents can contribute, as well, to problems faced by the adolescent.

Family

Most children, and particularly adolescents with depressions, are found to have some problem within the immediate family. These problems include losses, or threatened losses, absence, either actual or emotional, particularly of the father, misunderstandings and failure of communication, or actual serious problems in the parents, either abuse, violence, alcoholism, or neglect, with or without separation of the parents.

These may be longstanding problems so that the responses have become part of the character structure by the time the child reaches adolescence, resulting in depressogenic ways of handling affects and in depressive ways of thinking (depressive cognitions), such as defeatism and alienation. The parental influence may impel the adolescent to attempt to live out the parent's role or the parent's fantasies, without finding an independent self, as for example, in those who see themselves as the one elected or fated to rescue the family from troubles

Society

It is possible that some of the changes in Western society have effected an increase in depressions and suicide in the young. For example, with increasing absence of parents from the home and the changes in the home environment, the children are thrown under the influence of peers, of ideas gleaned from the communciations media, and of impersonal relationships, so that there is less personal guidance and example in the immediate family. Parents are increasingly concerned with personal enrichment, so that they may be more detached from the children's concerns because of their own narcissistic orientation.

Puberty comes a year or two earlier than a generation ago, but society has not allowed adult opportunity for work, marriage, and responsibilities to come earlier, nor are the adolescents prepared for it.

School

Although some children who break down have been able to achieve in school, in general, a large number of depressed adolescents have poor school records, with truancy and failure not unusual. It is important to differentiate cause and effect, because depressed persons, occupied with their trouble and pain, cannot do well in matters requiring mental concentration and attention. Specific problems, such as undiagnosed dyslexia or other reading deficits, should receive attention, but often do not. By the time adolescence is reached, if a specific reading deficit has been unrecognized, children are likely to consider themselves "stupid" and can be quite seriously depressed and pessimistic.

Among upwardly mobile families, and other families of high achievers, school success is of such paramount importance that enormous amount of guilt and despair can result from failure to achieve at a high level. Also, the effort to succeed may be exhausting in itself and at least have the result of producing a personality based on limited self-regard.

It is to be hoped that schools will increase the efforts to recognize and direct students who have emotional problems, especially in a society where parents are increasingly absorbed in pursuits outside the home.

Chronic Illness

The psychotherapist sometimes has to deal with a chronically ill child, or with the child's parents, and must be prepared to deal with the sometimes severe depressions that complicate the damaging and debilitating illnesses adolescents occasionally have. Also, in contrast, there is the problem of the hypochondriacal youngster who is taken from one physician to another because of some vague physical complaint, because parents refuse to accept the reality of an emotional problem.

Several chronic illnesses make their appearance in adolescence, and can cause mood changes of a depressive nature. None is common, but together thy make up a fairly substantial group. These include ulcerative colitis and Crohn's disease, diabetes, cystic fibrosis, anorexia nervosa, schizophrenia, and a number of others which are less frequent, such as hypothyroidism and congenital anomalies persisting from birth. These latter have profound influences in adolescence, as the sufferers find themselves unable to follow a normal course of life along with their peers. Each of these separate illnesses requires special management to prevent serious depressive reactions and for improvement of the quality of life. The treatment, when depression does occur, has to be tailored to the individual, and all the modalities should be available, including individual and group therapy, family, special schools and classes, chemotherapy in severe cases, and, of course, whatever physical treatments are needed.

With regard to medicines, it has to be remembered that certain drugs which adolescents may receive, such as steroids, may cause depressive reactions themselves. Depressions that sometimes accompany schizophrenia can be severe and require very special treatment, possibly hospitalization and intensive treatment as with psychotic depressions of any kind.

In summary, psychosocial problems in adolescence are of primary importance in the treatment of affective and mood disturbances of all kinds. They require identification and assessment from the outset, along with formal diagnosis of the clinical disorder, the assessment of personality problems, and the physical examination.

TREATMENT AND PREVENTION

From the viewpoint of the therapist who works mainly with adults, the treatment of the adolescent for preventive purposes is an issue of utmost importance. This goes for the affective disorders of all kinds, whether bipolar, unipolar, or neurotic (dysthymic). It also goes for those without well-defined disorders who nevertheless suffer from personality problems related to depression, such as the masochistic, the dependent, the hypochondriacal, those with low self-esteem, or who are suicidal or guilt-ridden.

The impression held by therapists who work only with adults is that treatment of underlying character problems, and not simply limited treatment of presenting symptoms, might have gone a long way toward preventing some of the serious affective disabilities of adult life. Of course there is no statistical proof of this thesis, but there is empirical evidence from follow-up of those adolescents who have been fortunate enough to receive long-term, intensive treatment. They seem to do better than their peers who had the same problems or illness, for which they did not get thorough treatment but instead received only what might be called first aid, without proper follow-up and treatment for preventive purposes.

This section briefly outlines the appropriate treatments now available. It is in no way a substitute for a thorough study of the specialized field of adolescence, with the several highly developed techniques needed to treat the affectively disturbed adolescent. The list of references at the end of the book and the additional readings supply the reader with an entree to the subject. Treatment of the adolescent differs from both that of the child and that of the adult. Although the same modalities need to be available as for the child—parent guidance, play therapy, educational and remedial techniques, and socialization, as well as individual psychotherapy—the emphasis is more like that of adult therapy, because adult types of symptoms, symptom complexes, and adult conflicts, sometimes in florid form, are now developing. Yet adolescents require treatments that differ from those used for adults because they are still not entirely responsible for their own destiny, and the family's role is still very important. The methods most useful generally cut across diagnostic lines; whatever the diagnosis, whether a major affective disorder, a personality disorder, or a situational reaction, individual therapy is usually not enough, because the patient cannot be treated in isolation. The family and the environment have to be taken into account and brought into the therapy if necessary to relieve the situation or prevent recurrences.

Treatment of Major Affective Disorders

Although a relatively small number of adolescents suffer from major affective disorders, these illnesses occur frequently enough that one must be prepared with the appropriate techniques, which are not greatly different from those used with the adult. For bipolar disorder, which sometimes begins in adolescence, hospitalization and the use of neuroleptics and lithium for the manic attack follows the same schedule as for the adult. Unipolar major depressions respond to antidepressants in doses similar to those for adults. Because there are usually personality problems in those who have these illnesses, and because the family milieu is important as a precipitating influence and a meliorating influence, the family is brought into the therapy in some way, either with family therapy or with educational, supporting, or counseling treatment.

Individual and group psychotherapy are also very important. Intensive individual psychotherapy of a psychoanalytic technique is especially important for those with personality disorders, which includes a large proportion of the group. Psychotherapy of an educational type, and in some, an emphasis on interpersonal relations, should be available, especially when more intensive analytic treatment is not available.

For a few, where the family milieu is extremely unfavorable, placement in a long-term setting may be advisable, either in a hospital or in a facility specializing in the treatment of disturbed adolescents.

Treatment of Nonpsychotic Affective Disturbances

This group of depressed, discouraged, alienated, and possibly suicidal adolescents are described in the section on adolescent suicide. Here it should be emphasized that, although these patients do not present the picture of major depressive disorder, they can nevertheless be very disturbed and require some of the same treatment methods used for major affective disorders: medication, hospitalization, individual psychotherapy, family therapy, group therapy, and in some cases, placement. The borderline and delinquent adolescent is to be included in this group, as depressions and suicide are not rare. The specialized techniques needed for the borderline and delinquent (i.e., institutional treatment for control of behavior) are to be used also, in order to have the patient available for treatment and to prevent school dropout and neglect of education.

ADOLESCENT SUICIDE

Adolescent suicide is an object both of fascination and astonishment (Haim 1974). This is certainly true, but its frequency in our culture, that is, the Western world, makes it also an object of the gravest concern, especially to those in the healing professions. Even psychotherapists who treat only adults can find themselves involved with adolescent suicide in some way. For one thing, young adults in the age group of 18 to 25 years have certain characteristics of the adolescent and are considered by some professionals to be late adolescent; this is a group at great risk, and increasingly so in the last decade. Another reason for psychotherapists to be involved with adolescents is that the adult patients under treatment have adolescent children, and the psychotherapists are in a position to know what is going on with these children. They therefore may be able to advise or intervene, helping the parent to get help, or at least advice, for the purpose of identifying suicide risk in the child. It is essential for psychotherapists to know something of the special characteristics of the group if they are to perform their function adequately. This section summarizes the chief characteristics of adolescent suicide. A reading list for those who wish to study the subject more fully may be found at the end of the book.

Importance

Historically, adolescent suicide has received relatively little special attention until recently, in the last two decades, when the drastic increase in numbers of adolescent deaths by suicide has forced society to look at the causes. One notable exception to this neglect occurred in 1910 when the Vienna Psychoanalytic Society gave over a meeting to a discussion of the causes of suicide in the young (Friedman 1967). In this meeting, a number of causes were discussed. They included the role of aggression turned upon the self; the role of society, of the school and the examination system; examination anxiety; unresolved sexual tension; masturbation;

imitation; and the teacher–student relationship, as well as the role of mental illness. The revenge motive was discussed also, and the statement made that no one kills himself without first wishing to kill someone else. In this meeting Freud said that, although the school may not be responsible for the deaths, a school should do more than prevent the student from committing suicide, but should also promote the desire to live, and that adolescents should have an opportunity to be their age—that is, to linger long enough in adolescence to prepare themselves for adult life, and not be plunged into life before they are ready.

There has been a tripling of actual deaths by suicide in adolescents from the 1950s to the 1980s, with the result that a number of studies have been done, and the matter has been receiving a great deal of both public and professional scrutiny. In the United States, the Department of Health and Human Services, through the Public Health Service, for example, has issued a publication on adolescence and depression (National Institute of Mental Health 1984) containing a summary of some of the recent studies. One study describes the statistical importance of the recent increase in youthful suicide. Seventy-five percent of deaths of adolescents result from accidents, homicide, and suicide, all of which occur in considerable numbers. Suicide is the third most important cause, and is on the increase. It is quite possible that a good number of the accidents are based on self-destructive tendencies and excessive disregard for one's personal safety, if not on actual suicidal intent, so that the number of self-caused deaths is probably a good deal higher than the number of recorded suicides. Also, the increase in rates for males is considerably greater than that for females, although many more so-called suicide attempts are made by girls than boys, whose attempts are more likely to be fatal in outcome. Four times as many males in the age group from 15 through 24 kill themselves as do girls. In one study of high school students in New York City (Friedman et al. 1987), it was found that 62 percent have thought of suicide and 9 percent have actually attempted it.

Moreover, to bring it closer to home, everyone has had the experience of having someone he or she knew, or was close to, or heard about in the neighborhood or school, suddenly commit suicide, sometimes without apparent warning. The tragedy of high school or college students taking their own lives is reported fairly frequently in the press, and everyone is more and more aware of it. What comes to mind is the question of prevention. So often the story is of someone who allegedly gave no warning, but if you scan the story carefully you find something—a loss, an absent father, a disappointment, or a history of being depressed over something—and one could easily imagine seeing a warning of suicidal risk in the story.

The psychotherapist who deals with a fairly high-risk group sometimes has to make a decision about what to do, whether to get a consultation, to send the patient to an emergency service of a hospital, etc. In these cases, statistics and numbers no longer are of much help, and it is necessary to identify the dangers in the individual.

Phenomenology and Definitions

It has been estimated that only 10–30 percent of suicidal attempts among adolescents occur in the presence of a definite major psychiatric syndrome, such as a depressive or schizophrenic disorder, and that the majority of the acts occur in persons who cannot be identified as having such an obvious or gross disturbance as to be diagnosed as a major disorder, but instead have personality trends, immaturities of development, and vulnerabilities that have been unsuspected. As with adults, the presence of a depression, a schizophrenic disorder, or a schizoaffective psychosis makes the subject a person at high risk, but what about the others? Why do they commit suicide? Regardless of the clinical diagnosis, there are risk factors which cut across diagnostic lines.

There are degrees of severity of suicide proneness. Suicidal fantasies are at the start, but they occur in healthy people as well; next comes the group who makes suicidal gestures, then those who make suicidal attempts which fail or are inadequate, and then those who make fatal, completed attempts. Although there is a tendency among professional observers to differentiate the groups of suicide attempters who survive from those who make fatal attempts, one should not rest easy with this differentiation, because many persons who eventually do kill themselves have a history of previous failed attempts. Thus, although there are probably more than ten times as many attempts as fatal acts, these are all persons at risk, and the attempt, whether it seems like a mere gesture or not, must be taken seriously and investigated. Many more girls attempt suicide than boys, but they tend to use drugs and are saved, whereas the boys use guns, which are very often fatal.

Risk Factors

The misery and suffering that could induce anyone to take his or her own life is very great, and unbearable enough that the youngster must feel at the end of his or her rope and must, indeed, be convinced that there is no other way out. Clinically, the circumstances found to bring this conviction into action are several, and somewhat scattered, yet with certain common findings.

Affective or Feeling States

Depression, feelings of hoplessness, sleep disturbances, changes in eating habits, trouble concentrating, fatiguability, apathy, or agitation and anxiety can be observed in some.

Personality Problems

Some have a tendency to withdrawal and isolation, have poor personal relations, and poor school achievement. Worry over grades is seen, even among very good students. Low frustration tolerance and low impulse control is reported among a number of those who make attempts.

History

A history of previous depressive spells or previous suicidal attempt increases the risk considerably.

Social Aspects

Parental discord or neglect are not uncommon, but the problem may simply be a failure of ability to relate or to show interest rather than gross neglect. Moves and dislocations that cause a loss of usual social supports can be a factor. There are often issues and conflicts over pleasing the parents, establishing peer relationships, and building or maintaining self-esteem. Choosing a career and a mate present problems and conflicts, and dealing with burgeoning sexual feelings as well can bring out shame, guilt, and a sense of failure. These conflicts can then lead to the feeling of complete helplessness characteristic of the suicidal person.

Precipitating Factors

Immediate circumstantial factors that can be considered to precipitate the suicidal act can usually be found, although in some studies no precipitating factor can be found in a small proportion of the cases. The immediate precipitating event, in combination with some long-standing, ongoing problem, which is probably more important than the precipitating event, brings the youngster to the suicidal act.

In one study, 52 percent of the events involved problems with parents, 30 percent problems with the opposite sex, 30 percent problems with the school, 16 percent with the brothers or sisters, and 15 percent with peers. Only 5 percent had psychotic symptoms. The proportion in various categories varies with the population studied. It cannot be emphasized too much that the event itself has to be looked at and evaluated in terms of its meaning to the person to understand its importance as a precipitant. In addition, for complete understanding, one has to see the precipitant as the latest happening in a chain of events and developmental processes which made this particular person vulnerable to self-destructive acts.

The meaning of the events is usually of loss, failure, disappointment, or frustration causing shame, guilt, or a sense of despair. Sometimes the precipitating factor is the publicity given a suicide of a contemporary, so that a rash or epidemic of suicides may occur among the young following a publicized suicide.

Motivation

There is a striking difference between the motivation to make a suicidal attempt as it is reported by the adolescent and as it is viewed by the adults concerned (i.e., the clinicians and parents). The adult assessors usually attribute the attempt to punitive or manipulative reasons, and rarely to the wish to die. Adolescents state that they felt lonely or unwanted, or were angry with someone, and the attempt was to relieve the pain and distress. Also, many say that they want to die; for example, in one study, about one-third of the group reported that they wanted to die. Seldom do the victims report that the act represented an effort to get help, so that one is forced to assume that they considered the situation beyond help or that their caretakers would be unable to help.

In children under the age of 10, the concept of death is not realistic, and death usually does not mean an end, but instead often signifies going somewhere up in the sky or joining a lost person somewhere. In adolescence, some of these ideas may remain; they may be in the unconscious or in attenuated form, so that suicide may represent going somewhere else simply to get relief from intolerable pain and from the situation in which the suffering has occurred.

The children and adolescents who really want to die are at greatest risk and often use more lethal methods, such as firearms or hanging—methods employed much more frequently by males than by females.

The place of aggression also is important. Aggressive behaviors in adolescence probably account for the deaths of many more than are reported as suicides, if you add risk-taking, such as recklessness with cars and guns. Also, the suicidal act itself in some forms is an aggressive act of destruction, and, as might be expected, anger plays a part in the motivation. Anger toward someone else can easily be turned toward oneself in an act of self-destruction. It is well known among those who work with adolescents that impulsive people who have trouble containing their aggression, especially those who tend to act out, are at risk of suicide.

In recent studies, aggression and suicidal behavior, and the history of aggressive behaviors and suicide attempts, have been demonstrated to be associated with each other, and, also, these two behaviors are associated with abnormalities of serotonin metabolism, which can be detected by the finding of lower levels than normal of the metabolite of serotonin in the urine. The significance of this for the therapist is to be alert to the possibility that certain individuals with suicidal potential may require extra care and protection because they are struggling with a biological force which has greater than normal strength.

Comparison with Adult Suicide

Adult and the adolescent suicide victims have much in common. In both groups there is an increase in traumatic events, something that undermines the self, plus family stress or illness, and a decrease in family supportiveness and the ability to cope. However, there are important differences also. The adolescent, especially the male, feels a need for action, so that a suicidal idea may need to be carried out rather than contained. There is also likely to be less ability to defend oneself against impulses (i.e., somewhat less well-developed resources), so that the tendency, often found in adolescents, to silence and withdrawal may be reinforced. The divided responsibility, that is, the fact that the parents share some of the responsibility for the adolescent's actions, produces a dilution of responsibility, and the strength needed to take hold of the situation may not be exerted by either. Finally, the attitude of the adolescent toward adults, for example, "They wouldn't understand," may interfere with communication, and the attitude of the adult toward the youngster, perhaps taking the adolescent for granted, or underestimating his or her suffering, results in disbelief, denial, avoidance, and a low level of suspicion. Thus the problem is not identified until too late.

Predisposing Factors

Haim (1974, p. ix) has said, in his book on adolescent suicide, that adolescence is supposed to be associated with joy and hope, but that it is really the time of a renunciation of childhood pleasures, "for which some people retain a nostalgia throughout their lives, a renunciation of childhood dreams at a time when one has to confront the reality of the adult. It is a time of multiple loss, and sometimes of despair, as well as a revival of the most deeply buried emotions, the transitory disintegration of impulses, and the emergence of hetero-aggressivity and auto-aggressivity." Which is to say that the problems one sees in the adolescent have a developmental history and do not arise sui generis.

The earlier childhood history of the potential suicide tells of parental losses such as early absence of the father. These losses are especially likely to lead to suicidal ideas if they resulted in long-term disruptions in the family life. Where family life became stabilized, they had minimal influence. The quality and intensity of the parent–child relationship in the expression and management of aggression also has been found to be important; when anger is excessive and is not handled appropriately, then a contribution is made to suicide-proneness. There is some reason to implicate a lack of affection in the process also. Haim considers suicide a process with its beginning in remote childhood with a failure to protect against death tendencies, which then surface in adolescence when, with the resurgence of the Oedipus (sexual) complex, its resolution, and the loss of the love object, a disintegration or disorganization sets in. Any loss—grades, friends, lovers, or family—is felt as a narcissistic wound, and the pain may be unbearable.

Another dimension of the process of adolescence is the mourning for the lost past in order to be able to go on to new love objects and new defenses and abilities. This mourning process is likely to stir up old wounds in those who have deficits in self-regard or who have suffered too much in earlier life, so that they cannot mourn successfully, as the normal adolescent does, and are thus not prepared for the new challenges.

Treatment and Prevention

Identification

Treatment starts with identification of those at risk, which, for psychotherapists, means any of their depressed patients, no matter in what diagnostic category. Psychotic patients, whether schizophrenic or affective in classification, are prime risks, and one should be sure that proper precautions are taken, such as hospitalization. If you have a new psychotic patient in your office, you do not let him or her out of your sight until you are sure either that he or she is not suicidal or, if suicidal, that he or she is protected against acting out his or her impulses. If he or she cannot be admitted at once, then he or she must be under protective observation at home; this precaution holds true for the adolescent as well as for the adult.

The therapist, the pediatrician, the school nurse, the parent, in short, anyone with responsibility for the potential suicide, should not hesitate to find out just what the patient is thinking in respect to self-destruction. It can be done tactfully and inoffensively; it can be done without suggesting. Very seldom, for example, do pediatricians question their patients about suicidal fantasies or impulses. Not only should one question the emotionally disturbed patient as to the existence and presence of self-destructive ideas, but also their strength, the reason for such ideas, and the strength of the intention of carrying them out. Even the proposed or fantasied means should be queried. The risk factors described earlier should be kept in mind and reviewed in one's thinking as the patient is examined and his or her history reviewed.

Suicidal threats should never be ignored. The presence of a death wish in itself is a risk, even when patients say that their religion would not permit, or their parents would be too upset, or they "wouldn't do that" to their parents.

Suicidal wishes often occur in adolescents who cannot confide in their parents, and it is not to be expected that the parents in such cases will be the first to observe the danger. It is often a classmate or other peer, who generally is not in a position to act decisively to protect his or her friend, although many suicidal youths are brought to emergency rooms by peers. What is obviously needed is greater vigilance on the part of the "gatekeepers"— physicians, therapists, teachers, parents, peers, police, and clergy.

It is not clear that the suicide prevention centers have resulted in a drop in the death rate from suicide in any age group. Certainly the death rate among adolescents is rising and has been rising since the prevention centers were created. However, a greater involvement on the part of all those who have responsibility for the youth might greatly augment the effectiveness of the center, which largely relies on voluntary identification, which is not enough.

Treatment

The actual treatment of the suicidal person depends on the specific nature of the underlying disorder or causes, of which there are many, whether neurosis, psychosis, character disorder, or circumstances. Eclectic treatment, using whatever specifics are needed in the individual situation, is advisable—in fact, is demanded. There is no simple formula or cookbook approach to this problem, except to say that suicidal persons should be in the hands of a professional. It also should be added that when adolescents are treated, their family and their reality situation are also to be involved in whatever way and to whatever extent is needed to relieve the situation and to prevent recurrences.

There is one specific symptom characteristic of children and adolescents that should be taken into account, whatever the diagnosis, and whatever kind of global treatment is needed; that is, the adolescent's cognitive functions, ideas about death, and the realistic versus the fantasy nature of his or her thinking. It is not only the schizophrenic whose thought processes are not rational; others can have less than rational ideas, perhaps short of delusional, and more subtly pathological, but nevertheless capable of motivating the irrational act of suicide. It can seem merely immature, but can be childlike and regressive. The technique of bringing out this irrational process and working with it is discussed in the chapter on therapy, to which the reader is referred.

Primary Prevention

By definition, primary prevention means eliminating the social, environmental, and intrapsychic forces that originally made the person vulnerable to suicide. It is a large subject, encompassing the elimination of the neuroses, psychoses, and personality settings in which suicide occurs, as well as the specific suicidogenic factors in thinking, nurturance, object relations, etc. The challenge is awesome, yet there are some potentially helpful ideas to be had by examining the risk factors. It has been demonstrated, for example, that there is a high incidence of perinatal difficulties in the history of the suicidal child, so that there is justification in thinking that primary prevention should start at birth. Going from there, child-rearing should focus on healthy self-esteem, the construction of a positive self-image, the avoidance of experiences that cause excesses of aggression and hostility. However, the development of healthy expressions of aggression should nevertheless be permitted to occur. Premature and excessive guilt should be avoided. The child should be given time to be a child. Obviously, more research is needed, although at this time it can be reliably stated that, if there is a high genetic risk for the development of affective disorder by virtue of a strong family history of definitive illness of either the bipolar or unipolar type, the family should make every effort to rear the child in a normal way in order to avoid the development of serious illness.

Those who work with groups who are at high risk should be on the alert for potential suicide, for example, in psychiatric patients, especially depressed patients, and schizophrenics and other psychotic individuals. Delinquents, especially those in jail or other corrective institutions, are at risk. Students in trouble who come to teachers or counselors, or to clergy, should be carefully heard out, as should any youngster who has been heard to talk of suicide, whether threateningly or not. A high level of awareness is needed in all those persons responsible for this age group in order to enable society to reduce the numbers of victims.

Secondary Prevention

The work of the psychotherapist is a key factor here. By treatment of the patient, by helping identify and eliminate precipitating factors, the therapist becomes a strong force in prevention, especially with patients who have made a previous attempt. This is a group from whom many eventual suicides are known to come; they should be treated for both the underlying death wish and for the conditions that have brought it about, whether environmental or intrapsychic.

Special Methods

Crisis intervention, through the establishment of suicide prevention centers and crisis telephone numbers, is now well established and is available in most large cities. The method adds an important factor to the identification of potential suicides, whether or not it can be proven to have lowered the actual overall rate of deaths. The telephone numbers are listed, and the services are readily accessible. The service usually consists of a telephone conversation with a professional or a volunteer to tide the person over the crisis and a referral to an agency or private practitioner for further therapy. Follow-up is usually made also, so that case-finding is assured.

Family therapy has been used for the juvenile and adolescent potential suicide with good results. This method has the value of bringing the persons who are influential in the life of the patient into the therapeutic situation immediately, so that interpersonal relations can be modified, if necessary, with all concerned parties.

Intensive Psychotherapy

Psychoanalytic psychotherapy and psychoanalysis are the most clearly documented methods for the treatment of the personality tendencies that predispose to breakdown, and there is a good deal of convincing literature as to its effectiveness. It is the treatment of choice for anyone in whom the influences of the environment have already been internalized to the extent that death wishes and masochistic tendencies have become part of the character structure. Derivative methods, especially what is now called cognitive therapy, can be used for treatment of the thinking disorder that is at the source of the death wishes. Another derivative method, interpersonal therapy, is useful as part of the treatment program, when a relatively simple problem in the relationship with an individual seems to have precipitated the suicidal attempt.

Tertiary Prevention and Rehabilitation

The special methods just outlined are part of a rehabilitation program of long-range therapy, which often needs to be initiated when the crisis is over and an evaluation has been done that has turned up some long-range problems with intrapsychic roots. With adolescents, as with children, it is essential not to neglect one part of the program for another. Eclectic therapy, combined methods, and the use of whatever modality is appropriate together make up a comprehensive program of long-range prevention. Those patients who have a definite clinical disorder, such as bipolar illness, or a major depression, or who are cyclothymic, should receive the appropriate medication, whether lithium, antidepressants, or antipsychotics, or combinations.

An important preventive measure is the treatment of drug and alcohol abuse, which are often involved in suicidal acts. An increasing number of adolescents are using alcohol, and an appreciable number are abusing that drug, as well as cocaine, marijuana, and other street drugs. This group is very prone to taking overdoses, whether intentionally or accidentally, and are at risk for suicide. There are programs available for the adolescent drug abuser and the alcoholic, both inpatient and outpatient. Alcoholics Anonymous has excellent programs that are helpful to the older adolescent, and most large cities have groups organized for the adolescent drug abuser who is able to conform to the ambulatory therapy. Those who cannot be treated on an ambulatory basis should be treated in hospitals, where adolescent units are usually available in the larger cities. It may be necessary to force this treatment on the unwilling adolescent in the occasional cases where persuasion is unsuccessful.

Once the drug abuse is under some degree of control, then the suicidal tendency can be treated on an individual basis, and the underlying problems as well. Organized groups are very helpful in the treatment of these patients, but the individual psychotherapy and family involvement should not be neglected.

In summary, adolescent suicide has increased to the extent that it is the third most common cause of death in the age group. Identification of those at risk, vigorous treatment, and rehabilitation programs are needed for its control and eventual elimination.

19

EARLY ADULT LIFE

Affective disorders of early adults are likely to arise around problems associated with mating, marriage, divorce, pregnancy, childbirth, parenthood, and career. The types of illnesses that occur are the classical depressions and manias. Affective experiences such as disillusionment, boredom, grief over a lost childhood also are common, often projected on one's family or society. Separation from the family is common in the mobile society, and geographical moves to new jobs and strange surroundings all can be traumatic, or at least demanding.

When symptoms arise, usually some kind of an unfavorable climate exists in the love relationship, conflicts with the most important love object particularly, often the spouse. Either lack of nurturing, or excessive dependency and a need for nurturing sometimes beyond what the other can supply, can be present. In the case of a woman, is the young person ready for motherhood and separation from her own parents? The psychotherapist can be called upon even in what looks like a mild depression to confront very complex marital situations involving potential failures and their prevention, the management of parenting, and the rearing of children. The diagnosis and treatment of the depressive spell can be very simple compared with the treatment and management of the fostering pathological situation and the predicament that brought on the depression.

SEXUAL PROBLEMS

The sexual freedoms of the present day have gone far to foster an openness in society to discussions of sexuality. For individuals, this openness allows for acceptance of themselves as sexual persons. However, an open attitude does not, a priori, eliminate sexual problems; indeed, it may reveal how complex sexuality is and what problems exist. It is astonishing to find the numbers and seriousness of the sexual problems accompanying affective disorders in both young and middle aged adults. I refer not to the lack of sexual drive, which is a symptom of the depression itself, but to sexual problems preceding the illness. In simple situations it may be the predicament of a conscientious man with a frigid wife, or a timid woman with an overbearing husband, or a failure of communication.

The problems in those who are single generally are failures of identification in the early childhood developmental stages: latent homosexuality in men and women, inability to go beyond an oedipal stage of dependency on a parental figure, or such problems as ambivalence toward the loved one. Sometimes a lasting intimate relationship is not possible, and fixation remains at early stages – oral, narcissistic and anal retentive and aggressive – unless treatment is carried out against the depressogenic character traits and tendencies.

There are loveless, asexual marriages, there are problems in coordinating sexual drives, and some marriages are sexually frustrating to both parties, both to the one who has the illness and to the mate or spouse. There are struggles for dominance and pleas for support and nurturance.

Manic and hypomanic states increase sexual drive; the manic person tends to make excessive sexual demands on the partner, or, more likely, to get involved in sexual affairs outside the marriage, which generally are not appropriate. The elevated erotic state is relieved when the illness is treated, but it can leave in its path considerable anguish and regrets, unwanted pregnancies, and damaged marriages. It is vital to help the manic person avoid impulsive acts that will turn out to be damaging to him. The responsible physician has to make every effort to alert the patient and family to these dangers while they are still minor and do what is necessary to avoid them. Hospitalization for protection against this and other dangers may be necessary.

The relationships made in a manic state are not mature, but are demanding, controlling, and characterized by regressive aspects, so that they do not last and generally tend to be more promiscuous than monogamous, although the latter occur also. The presence of this hypersexuality suggests that there are compensatory drives acting here, such as an effort to make up for an unsatisfactory marital situation. This speculation turns out to be true when one examines the marriages of persons with both unipolar and bipolar disorders.

The initial breakdowns often occur in a marriage in which sexual satisfaction did not exist for years prior to the breakdown. Sometimes this deficit is based on difficulties in the patient in communicating desires because of his or her guilt over making any demands on the partner. Marital counseling may work for some of these patients, but some partners are uncooperative because of their own defensiveness. Referring the partner for individual treatment to another therapist is possible in some instances, and, if this is successful, the marriage may be saved, or at least the symptoms are relieved.

Sexual inhibitions can run deep, based not only on guilt but on gender and identity problems; latent homosexual trends, where satisfactions are oral and anal rather than genital, can be seen in both men and women. Treatment may run into masochistic and sadistic drives which have neither surfaced nor been acted out. Shame over desires act to prevent communication.

This is an area in which long-term psychodynamic therapy is indicated, and psychoanalysis has an important application. When such problems are treated intensively by analysis or analytic psychotherapy in young adults, it goes a long way toward preventing further breakdowns. Certainly the quality of the love relations is improved.

CAREER

Developing children who are destined to become depressed are usually conscientious and know how to work; they are usually able later on to choose careers and function in them effectively, because they are hard workers. Nevertheless, there are career problems. The need for approbation may be unusually strong, so that dissatisfaction with employers is not uncommon. Depressive people may set such high goals for themselves that achievement is impossible; in such cases, dissatisfaction with one's self can be excessive and unrealistic, as expected with the obsessive-compulsive person.

At the same time, the ambivalent tendencies and the passive-aggressive personality that goes along with many depressed personalities may cause interference with important relationships at work and interfere with effectiveness. Young adults may occasionally find that they unconsciously make other people angry with them by their perfectionism and excessive demands on them, but usually the problem is the opposite, namely, that they cannot defend themselves successfully, submit too readily to domination, are angry and hate themselves for it. A deficiency in self-esteem or at least in assertiveness, may become apparent for the first time when the young adult faces the challenges of that very harsh world in which he or she has to make his way. A tendency to react with retreat, sullenness, excessive self-blame, sadness, and other nonconstructive responses may occur in early adult life, before the onset of any major breakdown.

It is important to get treatment at this stage, directed toward improving the functioning and the quality of life and possibly preventing more serious developments. Insight therapy, that is, intensive analytic psychotherapy and psychoanalysis, is the best treatment of this kind of characterological symptom.

MOODS AND THE MENSTRUAL CYCLE

The menstrual cycle is often accompanied by changes in mood. These mood changes are discussed here because, while some of them are normal, some occur in relation to the mood disorders, and some in relation to a widespread heterogeneous and sometimes vague group of symptoms called premenstrual syndrome which often has to be distinguished from a mood disorder. These mood changes are best discussed as either normal, in relation to mood disorders, and as premenstrual syndromes.

Normal Moods

The hormonal changes in the menstrual cycle are complex, involving variations in the production of ten or more hormones (Halbreich and Endicott 1985a), the most obvious of which are the luteinizing hormones of the pituitary (luteinizing hormone and follicle-stimulating hormone), as well as estrogen and progesterone of the ovary. Water metabolism is affected and a water-retention syndrome (bloated feelings, shoes and rings tight) is common. Why some women complain and others do not is apparently related to both the individual severity and the psychology of the individual.

Also common are a labile mood, hypersomnia, irritability, anxiety, and other dysphoric feelings, in some resembling a mild depression but recognized as normal by most women, and relieved by the onset of menses. Some women, on the other hand, especially those of more active and vigorous temperament, become quite energetic, get a great deal done, sleep less, and are more sexually interested in the week preceding their menses.

Affective Disorders and the Menstrual Cycle

Women in the early stages of a depression or in the recovery stages often report that their symptoms are worse in the premenstrual period. Upon complete recovery, the premenstrual depressed period ends. There is yet another connection of mood disorders with the menstrual cycle. It has been reported (Halbreich and Endicott 1985b) that women with major depressions reported a much higher rate of premenstrual depressions than did women who had no mental illness, although the incidence of water-retention syndrome was the same in both groups.

Premenstrual Syndromes

The plural of "syndrome" is preferred because of the variety and varying significance of symptom groups. The concept of premenstrual syndrome has been popularized as PMS and has seized the public imagination as a single concrete entity, which it is not (Osofsky and Blumenthal 1985). One of the symptom clusters is the water-retention syndrome mentioned above; others are the hyperactivity syndrome and the depressive syndrome, as well as a number of less well-defined symptoms: irritability, sensitivity, excessive emotional responsiveness and dysphoria. Psychotherapists treating affective disorders may see some women whose symptoms overlap with genuine depression and are likely to find that standard treatment with psychotherapy and antidepressant medicines is effective. Hormone therapy has no consistent effect on the syndromes. In the appendix of *DSM-III-R* (Appendix A, p. 367) there is a discussion of a diagnostic term, late luteal phase dysphoric syndrome, which was considered for inclusion in *DSM-III-R*. Though not included because of insufficient data, it can be coded 300.90, unspecified mental disorder (late luteal phase dysphoric disorders).

PREGNANCY AND PARENTHOOD

Practical Issues Concerning Medications

Pregnancy itself can produce some very practical problems in those persons suffering from affective disorders. Three very important issues should be noted concerning the use of drugs.

1. The use of antidepressants and antipsychotic drugs should be avoided, especially in the first trimester. They do pass the blood–brain barrier and, though malformations are not reported, they may affect the physiology of the child. If really necessary in the final trimester, they are probably safer.
2. Lithium should not be given in pregnancy because of the incidence of congenital anomalies. Only if it is most urgent should it be employed, and then only in the last trimester.
3. Minor tranquilizers such as benzodiazepines should not be given regularly because of the effect on physiology, although

they do not cause anomalies. Use for transient panic or anxiety attacks or sleeplessness, or to avoid hypertension and promote rest, is acceptable.

Psychological Problems

When a deficiency has occurred in the parental nurturance, leaving the growing child with a deficit in self-esteem or a lack of satisfaction with its own identiy as a male or female or with problems in interpersonal relationships, it is to be expected that he or she will have difficulty psychologically in filling the role of the parent when the time comes. The typical difficulties are those in the parent–child relationship: ambivalence, difficulty experiencing healthy affects and emotions, excessively high expectations without the nurturing and tolerant quality a child requires. In addition, now that so many women have two jobs, one at home and one outside in the form of a career, and they are under enormous pressure to do well at both, one can expect something to suffer.

There is one singularly important issue in some cases, related to the reasons more women have depressions than men; this is the issue of passivity and submissiveness, which is part of the kind of predicament that fosters depressive reactions. One of the common predicaments seen is that of a rather submissive person, usually a woman in a marriage with a dominating spouse, silently living under a kind of repressive regime which is frustrating and defeating. Pregnancy can worsen this predicament and tighten the hold the situation has on the woman, even when she seems to want it. In some cases, to become pregnant is actually and realistically equivalent to submitting to an intolerable situation forever, with no chance of escape. As long as there are no children she sees a way out, but the escape is cut off when, with a new baby, she needs her husband. Especially to women whose tendency is to react to trying situations pessimistically, it looks hopeless, the final blow. This becomes a situation in which depressions are common. Also, unconscious rejection of the pregnancy may carry over to the baby, whose development suffers as a result.

Postpartum Depressions

Normally, pregnancy and bearing a child are looked upon by a woman as a high achievement, of which she is proud. Especially if the path of her development has been toward complete development of her femininity, she feels that she has a fuller self-realization as a result of this achievement, a feeling of omnipotence and conquest. Unfortunately, some women are not prepared so well or have such (unconscious) neurotic motives that they become pregnant to help their marriages, or because they think they ought to, or to diminish their self-doubts as women, or to compete with their mothers. A woman may even bring to her own mother the male child she thinks her mother always wanted instead of the woman herself.

Women with strong dependency needs themselves or a need to assert their independence are particularly susceptible to a letdown after the child is born. Identification with the baby may then increase the woman's own need for nurturance and cause jealousy of the baby or irritability toward the baby's needs. Certainly it must be a great shock to a woman who has had a career or a job that is well-controlled, 40 hours a week, and with pay, to give it up to take on a 24-hour-a-day, 7-day-a-week job with a constantly demanding subject. From a male standpoint, one shudders with sympathy.

Practical matters also enter the equation. Some women who are psychologically quite adequate to the task of pregnancy and childbirth may be so burdened with family responsibilities, financial burdens, numbers of children, poverty, or lack of supports, moral and practical, that they are taxed beyond their limits. Such situations are fertile ground for adverse emotional reactions.

Additionally, the father's attitude can have a great deal of influence. A supportive, sustaining attitude can go a long way toward giving the reassurance needed under difficult circumstances.

The physiological changes at childbirth are dramatic, to say the least. A drastic change occurs in the hormone balance. The corpus luteum of pregnancy resolves, the luteinizing hormone drops, and the lactogenic hormone begins to work. The altered fluid and circulatory system needed to sustain a pregnancy begin to resolve.

It seems likely that if a woman has a tendency to affective

disorders these profound changes could very well precipitate an episode. It is not rare to see a woman experience a major episode or a series of episodes upon leaving home as a young adult, then later after childbirth, and much later after menopause. Yet some women have an episode after the birth of a daughter, but not a son, or vice versa, depending on what the expectations are.

According to recent studies, most pregnancy-related affective episodes occur in the early puerperium. Frank and colleagues (1987) studied a group of fifty-two women with recurrent depressions, finding that those who had pregnancy-related attacks, mostly postpartum, scored less than normal controls in emotional stability and objectivity and had a lack of self-confidence. The vulnerability of women with a history of recurrent unipolar disorder is brought out in this study, which found that 33 percent of women with a history of depression had at least one episode of postpartum depression.

Vulnerable women should have a good deal of support during pregnancy and after delivery. Frequent visits, getting the husband's and family's support, are vital.

Symptoms of Normal Postpartum Reactions

Normally, many women experience a reaction to childbirth. Once the excitement has died down, there can be a let-down of spirits, usually not persistent. Others have a persistent kind of depression, not a major one, but enough to acknowledge "the blues." Having a child is a serious business, and to integrate the experience into one's life pattern is part of the process of growth and maturation, adding to the strength of character and confidence, but it also is a sobering experience.

Symptoms of Postpartum Depression

Preliminary symptoms may be present during the latter weeks of pregnancy—doubts, difficulty doing one's work. There is a tendency for the depressions to come on insidiously, unlike schizophrenic postpartum psychoses, which may be very sudden. However, in some women the episode may seem to begin suddenly because the patient has hidden her feelings through shame and guilt.

Psychotic and Nonpsychotic Depression

When the depression blossoms, the symptoms of classical major depression are all there, plus some atypical symptoms of persecution, ideas of influence, perverse sexual ideas, and mixed pictures of hysterical, schizoid, and compulsive or phobic nature that may not be verbalized. For the protection of both mother and child, anyone with a psychotic depression should be hospitalized at once because of the double danger of suicide and infanticide. The psychodynamics of infanticide may either rest on guilt or in the identification with the infant, who represents the bad part of the self.

Actual psychosis is unusual. In one study (Munoz 1985) only twelve cases with affective disorder of psychotic type requiring hospitalization were found in 30,000 records. The ages of the women were 18 to 31. Of the twelve, only four had had previous episodes, of whom one had had a previous postpartum depression. The onset was from a few to fifty-six days after delivery. The most common symptoms were insomnia, confusion, crying, agitation, paranoid thinking, and depression. Five of the twelve were bipolar; five others were atypical psychosis. The duration was usually less than two weeks.

Nonpsychotic depression, on the other hand, is frequent. In a very careful study (Kumar and Robeson 1978), two groups of women were described in whom the incidence was twenty-two of one group of seventy-nine, and seventeen of another group of 114. The latter group consisted of a very stable group of married women of higher socio-economic class who wanted their pregnancies. Psychological factors related to the occurrence were: marital tension, a history of original doubts about going through with the pregnancy, a history of difficulties in relations with their own parents, age of 30 years or more, and a history of trying to conceive for two or more years.

Probably more common than either an overtly psychotic or nonpsychotic type of postpartum depression is the more subtle, often unacknowledged depression, with its sadness, slowing down, and lowering of efficiency. Sometimes it progresses to apathy, but usually there is simply a lack of pleasure in taking care of the baby, with a consequent failure to develop a good relation ship. Sometimes this lack of pleasure becomes a generalized anhedonia and painful endogenous depression.

Although women who have this syndrome do not appear psychotic, they often feel so guilty about their feelings that one suspects unconscious murderous fantasies; consequently, questions about suicide should be asked and the mother and child given what help they need to prevent a real tragedy.

The psychological tragedy of a failure to develop a good relationship with the baby may repeat the mother's experience with her own mother. As so often happens in a depression, the long-repressed traumas of childhood tend to surface and demand resolution by psychotherapy.

An example is the experience of a 27-year-old mother who had appeared excited and happy to be pregnant, but when a daughter was born to her she became too depressed to care for the baby and had to be hospitalized and later treated (successfully) with electroconvulsant therapy. In subsequent psychotherapeutic work she worked through her main childhood trauma— the birth of a favored brother when she was 4½ years-old and the years of living with this new "little monster" who took over her mother and the house. For her, to bear a daughter was to repeat the trauma with dramatic finality.

Mild Cases. Women whose stories are not so dramatic, who verge on the normal but who suffer and have a deficit in the mother–child relationship, should still get some kind of psychotherapy in which they can work through their feelings. Especially important here is mother-guidance, with its impact on the development of a normal bonding and normal relationship with the infant. Pediatricians sometimes work closely with child therapists in dealing with such problems.

Treatment and Prognosis

The acute episode is usually responsive to combined biological and psychological treatment, as described in Chapter 15. Later, preventive psychotherapy, both for the mother and for reestablishing the mother–child relationship, is vital. Mother-guidance should be used, plus whatever psychotherapy is needed for her particular vulnerabilities. If this kind of therapy is carried out appropriately it also diminishes the risk of another episode, in case she wants another child.

Suicide and Unwanted Pregnancy

The psychiatrist and the psychotherapist are often consulted by women in the early stages of pregnancy as to the question of abortion. Sometimes the woman is happily married but has a history of previous mental illness, but more often she is a young woman, either married or unmarried, who is very upset by the pregnancy and is desirous of an abortion.

When the question of abortion arises it usually is found that the subject has had psychiatric problems, often of long-standing, and that she should have therapy, whether or not the pregnancy is to be interrupted, the kind and intensity of therapy, depending on the nature of her psychological problems.

Threats of suicide in the case of unwanted pregnancy are fairly common, and attempts are not rare, but actual suicide carried to completion is not frequent. In the adolescent who is unmarried, the incidence of suicidal attempts and completions is higher than expected for the age group. The significance of these matters for the consultant has been reported and summarized in a volume edited by Kleiner and Greston (1984), which includes an excellent bibliography. These authors believe that suicide associated with pregnancy and the puerperium is underreported and that, moreover, related issues should be discussed in this context, that is, the issues of the significantly higher risk of future suicide for teenage pregnant girls and the long-term sequelae of attempted suicide, such as congenital anomalies, psychological deprivation, and child abuse, "which may even lead to infanticide" (p. xv).

The danger of suicide is, therefore, to be taken seriously even in those who are thought to be using the threat of suicide as a manipulation to force an abortion, and a thorough evaluation of the mental state should be made.

Another group requiring thorough and prompt examination

and evaluation are those with a history of previous depressions, either related to pregnancy or unrelated, because some of the sicker patients who eventually commit suicide do not make any threat at all as a warning, but may suddenly and seemingly impulsively kill themselves.

Effect of Maternal Mental Illness on the Baby

A number of significant effects on the baby have been reported (Harvey 1978) as being associated with maternal neurotic illness, particularly depression. These include shorter gestation, more small babies, more illness in the babies, and more frequent intervention in the labor. There is also a greater risk of injury to the baby, although the battered child is more likely to be found with the psychotic mother, either schizophrenic or depressed. It has also been demonstrated that women who were separated before age 11 from their own mothers were more likely to have depressions in the first year after they themselves gave birth to a baby. Also, the babies of these women were much more likely to have both major and minor feeding and sleeping problems than babies whose mothers did not have childhood separations from their mothers.

Postabortion Depression

Psychiatric disorders of all kinds are said to be rarer after abortions than are postpartum disorders, although this view may be wrong. A number of careful studies (Brewer 1978) in England and the United States are in agreement and put the figures at 0.2–0.4 cases of postpartum disorder per 1,000 abortions. Nevertheless, one must be prepared to give psychological support and treatment to anyone who has had an abortion for psychiatric reasons, to work through the feelings about the experience, and to treat any depression that might result. Often women are so relieved that they do not immediately desire any psychotherapy, but there are those with guilt, remorse, anger, and a sense of loss; these may need therapy ranging from brief counseling to thorough working through of a grief reaction.

It is apparent that this is a complex subject with social, personal, and religious factors complicating the medical decision as to whether or not to interrupt the pregnancy. Punitive attitudes reflecting a drive to punish the "sinner" often affect the advice given the pregnant woman, creating guilt and suffering, which could have been avoided, but which, when present, can contribute to depression and despair. As to adolescent pregnancies, it is also important to take into account the impact on the future development of the adolescent who has a pregnancy before she is ready for it.

Fortunately for those immature and emotionally disturbed adolescents, it is possible nowadays legally to interrupt a pregnancy if there is excessive risk to the girl's mental health and to her future development.

Fatherhood

Although a man does not go through the physical upheaval that a woman has in childbirth, he does experience a major developmental transition when he becomes a father; the new responsibilities require him to call on resources he may not have. Occasionally you see a man who develops symptoms at this stage that directly result from jealousy of the child, anxiety over the responsibility, doubts over being the father, or other negative reactions. Most of the time these take the form of some disguise—alcoholism, having affairs, or neurotic hypochondrial symptoms. Openly expressed affects can make the matter easier to deal with. Major episodes are not seen commonly. However, when the mother has become mentally ill, the father's situation must then be addressed very thoroughly. What part, if any, does he play in the environment for the mother? Is he part of her predicament? What is his attitude, his contribution? He must be helped to overcome any trouble he has in assuming his new function, both to help the mother through her crisis and for the future of the child. The child of a mother who has a postpartum depression is at risk, and the father's understanding of this and his cooperation are needed for whatever help he can give. Fathers have been neglected, mainly because the mother's illness is so dramatic that it covers up all other considerations.

20

LATE LIFE

IMPORTANCE OF AFFECTIVE DISORDERS
IN THE ELDERLY

The majority of first attacks of severe depression occur in the second half of life. For men, the highest incidence is from age 55 to 65; for women it is 50 to 60. Moreover, the incidence of suicide rises, especially with men, so that the highest rate is in elderly men, giving an opportunity for preventive measures. The death rates of the elderly with depressions is higher than that of others in the same age group who die from natural causes. Persons with affective disorders that started earlier in life are sometimes more difficult to treat or maintain in functioning condition as they age because of losses, ill health, and changing conditions which go with the later years of life.

In addition to the major affective disorders, there is the variety of depressive reactions that do not appear as major disorders, but which can be extremely disrupting, cause disability, and interfere seriously with the quality of life. Aging, with its inevitable losses—loss of strength, resources, mastery and control, sexual function, mental faculties, and supports—is especially conducive to this kind of secondary depression, and normally people find these losses traumatic. When aging comes slowly and insidiously, people can continue to deny their losses and can accommodate to the changes.

When something catastrophic happens suddenly—a stroke,

cancer, loss of resources, retirement for which one was unprepared, a heart attack, debilitating illness—then defenses may not be adequate, and some kind of a depression can occur that may bring the suffering person to the psychotherapist or psychiatrist. In the past, psychotherapy has been underused in the elderly; this tendency is slowly being reversed.

Major Disorders

One has to be able to distinguish the unhappiness of aging from the actual depressive disorders themselves. Diagnosis requires particular alertness to distinguish the sadness, grief, and despair of an especially painful loss from the symptoms of depressive illness. The following features of depressive illness are particularly important to look for, especially when they constitute a change from the usual state of the patient:

- Psychomotor retardation. Persistent difficulty in concentrating, slowing-down of thinking. The pathognomonic sign.

- Regular early morning waking, 1–5 hours before the usual time.

- Persistent loss of weight and appetite.

- Agitation and restlessness.

- Suicidal preoccupation, possibly disguised, for example, overconcern with health.

- Guilt and self-blame, sometimes with delusional intensity.

- Loss of pleasure in normal activities. Inability to enjoy anything—anhedonia.

- Persistence of the symptoms with an unremitting, unrelenting quality.

Secondary Depressions

In the elderly, physical disease often has to be considered. Separating depression from the effect of an organic disease can be difficult because they often coexist. The *DSM-III-R* diagnosis of organic mood disorder (293.83) describes an episode, either manic or depressed, without much in the way of clouding of consciousness or loss of intellectual abilities. It is usually caused by a toxic or metabolic factor. Reserpine, or its derivatives, given for hypertension, is a common offender; methyldopa and hallucinogens can produce something that is hard to distinguish from a spontaneous depression. In fact it *is* a depression, but goes away when the medication is stopped. Phenobarbital, which used to be very widely used for anxiety, can produce depression. Tranquilizers of the benzodiazepine family are less likely to cause depressions than barbiturates, but an occasional patient who feels enough loss of drive from phenothiazines or benzodiazepines given for anxiety can feel depressed also.

Steroids, now widely used, can precipitate affective disorders. The steroids given to an elderly person for arthritis or a skin disease can precipitate a manic attack or a depression in a susceptible person with a previous history of affective disorders.

One occasionally sees a depressed person with a hidden, advanced carcinoma that has been missed (liver metastases, pancreatic tumors, etc.). The depletion and loss of energy resulting from the illness has precipitated a depression. First comes lowering of drive, then a feeling of inadequacy, guilt, lowered self-esteem, and possibly death wishes. More than a few suicides occur every year in medical and surgical wards from this kind of depression secondary to physical disease.

One should always insist on a thorough physical examination in the case of a new elderly patient when weakness, fatigue, and weight loss are present. The physical examination is necessary; for all depressed persons, but especially for the elderly; the symptoms of physical disease overlap with these symptoms.

Depression and Organic Brain Disease

The organic brain disease of old age can have secondary depressive symptoms or can, in susceptible persons, cause a primary major depression. Primary degenerative dementia, with depression (coded 290.13)* includes Alzheimer's and Pick's disease. Other cerebral diseases that can give a similar clinical feature must be ruled out, including subdural hematoma, brain tumor, vitamin B_{12} deficiency, hypothyroidism, and substance intoxication. The other common illness is multiinfarct dementia, with depression (coded 290.43) in which repeated episodes of strokes, large or small, have resulted in sufficient brain damage to cause dementia. Other disorders in the organic class are substance-induced mood disorder (coded 292.83) caused by alcohol, barbiturates, hypnotics, tranquilizers, or other drugs. Many suicides, including those in the elderly, intentional or not, occur in people under the influence of alcohol. The tolerance of the elderly for drugs is notoriously reduced; irrational behavior, including suicide, occurs often in lonely or depressed elderly people after a moderate amount of alcohol is consumed.

Also, an irritable or depressed mood is common during withdrawal from chronic alcohol or drug abuse. Be on the alert for this in patients recently admitted to hospitals, and those practicing self-withdrawal.

Pseudodementia

Elderly, depressed persons can give the appearance of a dementia (defects of memory, orientation, judgment, abstract thinking, neglect of personal hygiene, etc.) Upon careful testing it is discovered that lack of attention and concentration and a preoccupation with depressive thoughts is the apparent cause, and a true dementia is not present.

Often depressed people, because of the tendency to self-

---

*The ICD-9-CM terms are slightly different, but the code numbers are identical.

criticize, complain of poor memory, but when one tests the intellectual faculties, they turn out to be intact. On the other hand, usually persons with true dementia lack insight and often do not complain of loss of faculties even when the dementia is obvious. (See Chapter 9 on differential diagnosis.) When the depression clears up, the memory loss complained of clears up also.

Depressive Affects and Existential Suffering

Many unhappy, apathetic, defeated, hopeless-feeling elderly people do not have a true depressive disorder, but are reacting to their situation, the adjustment disorder with depressed mood (*DSM-III-R*). Often one has to institute a vigorous treatment program to determine whether a person is in an early stage of major depressive disorder or is demoralized and defeated by his or her circumstances. Sometimes it is both.

As with children, these affects have an evolution, a cause-and-effect psychological basis. This is fertile ground for psychotherapy, which can bring to light the patient's feelings. Being able to ventilate feelings either in group or individual therapy can give relief and, equally important, can possibly be a starting point for an improvement in the troublesome situation.

Sufferers may be unaware of what is bothering them; painful conflicts often are at a preconscious or unconscious level. Withdrawal, retreat, or even fighting are their way of warding off the pain. Making conscious the feelings that are warded off may temporarily cause more pain and suffering, for which one has to be prepared. The psychotherapy of the elderly requires a great deal of skill, insight, and empathy, because often they are up against situations which cannot be changed. The ability to come to terms with losses, decline, and even approaching death requires enormous internal philosophical resources, as well as a sustaining support system. Recovery from major illness can get more difficult as age advances, if losses have been overwhelming and support systems are deficient. Some people who had occasional, circumscribed attacks of major affective disorders lasting weeks or months, tend, as they get older, to have longer spells, more resistant to treatment. Those who had a great deal of insight therapy in the early years tend to do better as they get older.

In persons with bipolar illness, the tendency is for late-life attacks to be more and more on the depressive rather than the manic side and for the attacks to become longer, especially if there is cerebral deterioration and loss of sensorium caused by organic disease.

It is not yet known what effect the widespread use of antidepressant drugs and lithium may have on the occurrence and seriousness of the formerly very long-term depressive illnesses of late life. It has not been necessary to use electroconvulsive treatment as much as formerly, before the advent of the modern drugs. In some cases nowadays, this treatment is not used as often as it should be, in the zeal to try medications. The pendulum may have to swing back a little.

INTEGRATED THERAPY

Psychological improvements may help in prevention, for example, the development of education for retirement, the use of preventive work with families and individuals, the increasing awareness of the need for support systems, improved medical care, and financial security.

Social agencies and hospitals now have geriatric assessment, treatment, and support programs that employ a multidiscipline team approach, using individual and group therapy. These programs are very helpful to the individual practitioner because they have resources for support and rehabilitation that individual therapists can use to supplement their efforts and those of the family.

Individual psychotherapy tends to be neglected in the elderly, especially when medication gives temporary relief. Many elderly people are given antidepressant drugs by internists, who may not go into the psychological background of the depression, and some psychiatrists might find it simpler just to medicate.

BIOLOGICAL TREATMENT IN THE ELDERLY

Psychopharmacological agents can be very useful in the actual depressive disorders of the elderly, and sometimes in the adjustment disorder as well. There are some special considerations about medicines, some of them very serious, because neglect of them can lead to overdosing, to side effects, and to dangerous overreactions. There are a number of age-related effects worth noting. For example, the elderly do not tolerate the same doses of drugs, especially the potent antidepressants, as used in younger people. Antidepressants diminish some secretions; for example, they may cause diminution in the production of tears, and if a patient has a cataract removed, this effect can prevent proper healing. The effect of tricyclic antidepressants on the urinary sphincter does not trouble the younger people, but in an older man with some enlargement of the prostate gland, it can produce urinary retention. If a hypertensive patient who is receiving lithium happens also to be given a diuretic drug such as hydrochlorothiazide, which lowers sodium levels in the body, the levels of lithium may become toxic. Constipation with tricyclic antidepressants tends to be worse in older people, as is the risk of cardiac arrhythmias.

The most important rule of thumb with the elderly is if drugs are to be given, they should be started in doses of half-strength or less to test for tolerance, which diminishes with age.

Polypharmacy

It is very easy with elderly patients to get into the pitfall of polypharmacy and overmedication. For one thing, the nonpsychiatric physician today often gives antidepressants and tranquilizers along with other medicines, and the patients continue to take them, often because they have a medically treatable disease such as hypertension. Drug interactions are common and the psychotherapist, seeing the patient regularly, may have a better opportunity to see the effects than the medical doctor. The psychotherapist should look for the mental confusion caused by overdosage with tranquilizers, the depressions that result from the reserpine, phenothiazines, propanolol, barbiturates, and some other drugs. The elderly sometimes passively accept directions, and may continue to take medicines against which a younger person might rebel. With this age group, communication between those responsible for care is vital. A psychiatrist treating a medical patient ought to be in touch with any physician who is giving that patient medicines, and the two ought to understand and approve of each other's prescriptions.

Some multiple drug combinations are legitimate; for example, the nonsedating tricyclic antidepressants may have to be supplemented with a tranquilizer. Lithium may not, and often does not, completely eliminate the occurrence of depressive attacks, however diminished they may be, and has to be supplemented with antidepressants and sometimes tranquilizers.

Electroconvulsant Treatment

Electroconvulsant treatment can be life-saving for a deeply depressed patient who cannot function, or cannot eat, or is so agitated and restless that exhaustion to the point of collapse is inevitable, especially when drugs are not tolerated well. The number of treatments may be very small. There are cases where one or two treatments were enough to stop what was otherwise a disaster, but generally six to eight treatments will suffice. Some very aged and infirm patients who cannot tolerate medicines can take electroconvulsant treatment.

PSYCHOTHERAPY

Talking to the Elderly Depressed Patient

There are some physical problems that may interfere with communication, for example, hearing or visual losses. Sometimes mental confusion on the patient's part may go unnoticed, but is serious enough that the patient does not really know what you are trying to say. Hearing loss can give the impression of confusion, and sometimes a simple question, "Do you hear me?" or "Can you hear what I am saying?" will clear the air.

The psychological aspects of the interview is important. Young therapists sometimes think that older persons do not pay any attention to them or do not respect their function, but this is not the case. When one is a patient, age does not matter as much as is generally thought, and the older patient will listen, talk, confide, and depend on a much younger therapist. Of course, if the younger person cannot appreciate what the older one is experiencing, it is usually not a matter of age, but of personality. A good deal of the atmosphere of the interview and examination depends on the situation. With a disabled, sick, suffering older person, it helps to show a great deal of consideration and warmth, without talking down to the patient. If a well-preserved, functioning, depressed woman of 60 brings her husband in for you to explain to him why she has lost her sexual desire, an explanation of this as a common symptom of depression may clear the air.

The older person who tends to be private about sexual matters and intimate relationships can nevertheless discuss these matters if they are coached in appropriate language. The language of the street is generally to be avoided, especially with the elderly, but reasonable questions, properly asked, get answers, even if patients have not volunteered the information themselves. The same may be true of feelings, because more reserved older persons may not volunteer their feelings and will have to be asked if they are sad, lonely, grieving, miserable, or hopeless, before they can open up and cry or otherwise reveal themselves.

Privacy is also important. In the hospital, one should be sure that patients do not have to express their feelings or tell their history in the presence of roommates, family, or nurses, unless, of course, part of your program is to bring other key persons into the discussion. In the office, always give the patient a chance to talk alone, even if the spouse has accompanied him or her. There is plenty of time to get the spouse in also, either alone or together; and this should be done also in most cases, especially where a major disorder is suspected, because the whole story may not be forthcoming from the patient alone.

Individual Psychotherapy

Insight therapy, even analysis, can be used with intact elderly persons. There has been a tradition that persons over the age of 50 should not be psychoanalyzed, but actually some excellent results can be achieved, even where working through of childhood residue is needed. One man of 70 years, after a psychotic depression, went into a short analysis, worked through his childhood feelings about his parents, recovered, and was freed up from a long-standing, chronic depression which had haunted him all his life. He lived actively for 10 years, without a recurrence.

Grieving

Grieving is often a part of the psychotherapy of the older group. For example, a woman of 75 years, with a history of two depressive attacks with recovery, was in a chronic depression for several years, ambulatory and functioning, but requiring medication and frequent monitoring to keep going. Ambivalence about her husband, deceased 25 years earlier, led the therapist to help her discuss this feeling, which also brought out the griefs of her childhood, with a depressed mother and premature responsibilities on the patient's part. For the first time, after several sessions of this mourning process, her depression lifted, without any change in medication.

Sadness

Sadness can be a normal part of old age. Older persons may use and experience sadness as a way of keeping contact with their relationships with those who have died. Depressed people often cannot experience sadness in a normal healthy fashion and may have to learn to feel their sadness and grief when they recover from the depression in order to come to terms with the loss which caused the depression in the first place. Depressed people often say that they cannot cry and wish that they could. When they recover, they may have to learn to cry about the things that are worth crying about, and in older people there is usually something lost that is worth crying about.

Therapy of Depressive Thinking and Personality Disorders

Older persons who have tended to be pessimistic all their lives and have expected the worst possible outcome of events, who put negative interpretations on events and expectations, are depression-prone and, in a depression, usually keep or expand on their original depressive thinking because it is their character trait, their way of looking at life. As in younger persons, this symptom can provide an entree to treatment, because if it can be identified for patients and demonstrated to them, they may learn to combat it. This kind of educational approach can be helpful with certain people in giving them some insight into how to control their depression. Or it may open the door to more insight by providing a clue as to the development of their patterns of thought, their early object relations, and the childhood depressive neurosis that has provided the template from which even old-age depressions take shape. Older persons may prefer something intellectual rather than something that might touch on hidden anger or sexual frustration, and indeed there are many cases in which fortifying the defenses is preferable to eroding them.

The dependent and the masochistic personality seen in midlife depressives can still be found in the older age group and may provide a focus for individual psychotherapy.

Psychosocial Therapy

Nowhere is the subject of psychosocial problems more important than with older persons, especially with those who are dependent or have had irreplacable losses, such as death of a spouse, disabling sickness, loss of children upon whom they depended, and so forth. In somewhat the same manner as children, older persons may have become dependent on some one person or thing, or on an environment that provided status, support, or satisfaction. When it is gone, the loss is very depressing, whether with the picture of a major depression or simply a depressive reaction to the situation.

The diagnostic importance of finding out the nature of the precipitating or ongoing situation cannot be overestimated, because it allows for some kind of environmental manipulation, or therapy, to try to make up the loss or to help the suffering individual recover. The losses may be real, such as death, retirement, or illness, or they may be symbolic, such as the loss of ideals or hope for some goal. One loss that seems to be common in older depressed persons is the loss of sexual function, which is generally preserved in most nondepressed persons. This should be discussed with patients, and their feelings worked through, if they are able.

Group therapy

Group therapy, which can be very useful with persons who are mourning a death, can also be helpful with depressed older people, with whom a replacement can be found in the group. Either the peers or the leader may perform the function of a parent to whom they can bring their grief.

Couple and Family Therapy

Often the older depressed person prefers to have the spouse or a supportive other person, sister, friend, aunt, or grown child, sit in with them when visiting the therapist. This can be very helpful in some cases where something has to come out that the patient could not formulate alone or did not dare to say alone, to the spouse. Contrariwise, it can be used as a defense against having to deal with feelings that might come out if the patient were seen alone, and sometimes the patient needs that protection, especially in major depressions in which loss of control is imminent, or threatened, or if for some other reason the patient is too uncomfortable to be alone with the therapist. It is perhaps a signal, when a couple prefers to sit together in the therapist's office, that after 30, 40, or even 50 years of marriage, they do everything together or feel involved inseparably in each other's troubles. Nevertheless, it can be helpful and revealing to give each a chance to be alone to give the individual side of the picture, if it can be arranged.

More than this, it can be very helpful to have a retired spouse to nurse a depressed elderly woman, and it can make it possible to treat her at home, when otherwise she would have to be in the hospital.

Actual couples therapy, with the process of working through the interpersonal relations together, can also be used with the older group, just as in the younger age groups, although the motivation to change may not be as great, and there may be so much acceptance and resignation that intervention is not feasible.

The use of grown children can be constructive in some cases, where actual improvement in the quality of life can be made through the assistance of the available adult children. Or information can be provided which helps one understand the situation better. Sometimes, however, the patient and spouse are so protective of their independence and privacy that the children have to be left out of it, unless it is obviously necessary for outside intervention because the patient, though refusing assistance, is actually helpless and in an intolerable situation.

Affective disorders in the elderly may be complicated by certain problems that need special handling: exceptional loading of actual losses and of grief and mourning, sensitivity to medication, the complication of other illnesses, brain disease, and physical disability. Yet they are often treatable, and good results can be obtained with therapy. Specific diagnosis of disorder, of physical condition, and social situation is vital. Psychotherapy of the elderly has often been neglected, but can be used in whatever way is appropriate, whether insight, supportive, group, individual, couple, or family. Integration of therapies is especially important with the elderly, as is attention to the bolstering of support systems.

REFERENCES

Abraham, K. (1949). Notes on the psycho-analytical investigation and treatment of manic-depressive insanity and allied conditions. In *Selected Papers of Karl Abraham*, trans. D. Bryan and A. Strachey, pp. 137–156. London: Hogarth Press. (Original work published 1911)

Abrams, R., Taylor, M. A., and Faber, R., et al. (1983). Bilateral versus unilateral electroconvulsive therapy: efficacy in melancholia. *American Journal of Psychiatry* 140:463–465.

Alexander, L. (1954). The commitment and suicide of King Ludwig II of Bavaria. *American Journal of Psychiatry* 111:100–107.

AMA Drug Evaluation (1983). 5th ed. Prepared by the AMA Division of Drugs. Washington, DC: American Medical Association.

American Heritage Dictionary (1983). Based on the new second edition. New York: Dell.

American Psychiatric Association (1987). *Diagnostic and Statistical Manual of Mental Disorders*. 3d ed. (Revised). (*DSM-III-R*). Washington, DC: American Psychiatric Association.

American Psychiatric Association Committee on Nomenclature and Statistics (1968). *Diagnostic and Statistical Manual of Mental Disorders (DSM-II)*. Washington, DC: American Psychiatric Association.

American Psychiatric Association. Task Force on Electroconvulsive Therapy (1978). Washington, DC: American Psychiatric Association.

American Psychiatric Association Task Force on Nomenclature and Statistics (1980). *Diagnostic and Statistical Manual of*

Mental Disorders. 3d ed. (*DSM-III*). Washington, DC: American Psychiatric Association.

American Psychiatric Association Task Force on the Use of Laboratory Tests in Psychiatry (1985). Tricyclic antidepressants—blood level measurements and clinical outcome: an APA task force report. *American Journal of Psychiatry* 142:155-162.

American Psychiatric Association (1987). *Diagnostic and Statistical Manual of Mental Disorders.* 3d ed. (Revised). (*DSM-III-R*). Washington, DC: American Psychiatric Association.

Angel, A. (1934). Einige bemerkugen über den optimismus. *Internationale Zeitschrift fur Psychoanalyse und "Imago"* 20:191-199.

Anthony, E. J. (1970). Two contrasting types of adolescent depression and their treatment. *Journal of the American Psychoanalytic Association* 18:841-859.

Arieti, S. (1977). Psychotherapy of severe depression. *American Journal of Psychiatry* 134:864-868.

Badal, D. W. (1981). Treatment combinations in long term depressions (Summary). In *Continuing Medical Education Syllabus and Scientific Proceedings in Summary Form: The One Hundred and Thirty-Fourth Annual Meeting of the American Psychiatric Association*, pp. 229-230. Washington, DC: American Psychiatric Association.

Bailey, J., and Coppen, A. (1976). A comparison between the Hamilton Rating Scale and the Beck Inventory in the measurement of depression. *British Journal of Psychiatry* 128:486-489.

Baldessarini, R. J. (1977). *Chemotherapy in Psychiatry.* Cambridge: Harvard University Press.

———— (1983). *Biomedical Aspects of Depression and Its Treatment.* Washington, DC: American Psychiatric Press.

Beck, A. T. (1973). *The Diagnosis and Management of Depression.* Philadelphia: University of Pennsylvania Press. (Abridged edition of *Depression: Causes and Treatment*, by A. T. Beck published 1967).

Beck, A. T., Rial, W. Y., and Rickels, K. (1974). Short form of depression inventory: cross-validation. *Psychological Reports* 34:1184-1186.

Beck, A. T., Ward, C. H., Mendelson, M., Mock, J., and Erbaugh,

J. (1961). An inventory for measuring depression. *Archives of General Psychiatry* 4:561–571.

Bemporad, J. R. (1982). Childhood depression from a developmental perspective. In *Psychiatry 1982: The American Psychiatric Association Annual Review*, ed. L. Grinspoon, pp. 272–281. Washington, DC: American Psychiatric Press.

Benson, R. (1976). Psychological stress as a cause of lithium prophylaxis failure: a report of three cases. *Diseases of the Nervous System* 37:699–700.

Berger, D. M. (1987). *Clinical Empathy.* Northvale, NJ: Jason Aronson.

Bibring, E. (1953). The mechanism of depression. In *Affective Disorders: Psychoanalytic Contribution to Their Study*, ed. P. Greenacre, pp. 13–48. New York: International Universities Press.

Bick, P. (1986). Seasonal major affective disorder. *American Journal of Psychiatry* 143:90–91.

Blehar, M. C., Weissman, M. M., Gershon, E. S., and Hirschfeld, R. M. A. (1988). Family and genetic studies of affective disorders. *Archives of General Psychiatry* 45:289–292.

Bowlby, J. (1961a). Childhood mourning and its implications for psychiatry. *American Journal of Psychiatry* 118:481–498.

———— (1961b). Processes of mourning. *International Journal of Psycho-Analysis* 42:317–340.

Boyce, P., and Parker, G. (1988). Seasonal affective disorder in the Southern Hemisphere. *American Journal of Psychiatry* 145:1, 96–99.

Brenner, C. (1982). *The Mind in Conflict.* New York: International Universities Press.

Brewer, C. (1978). Post-abortion psychosis. In *Mental Illness in Pregnancy and the Puerperium*, ed. M. Sandler, pp. 52–58. New York: Oxford University Press.

Carroll, B. J., Fielding, J. M., and Blashki, T. G. (1973). Depression rating scales: a critical review. *Archives of General Psychiatry* 28:361–366.

Cohen, M. B., Baker, G., Cohen, R. A., Fromm-Reichmann, F., and Weigert, E. V. (1954). An intensive study of twelve cases of manic-depressive psychosis. *Psychiatry* 17:103–137.

Compendium of Drug Therapy, 1985–86 (1985). New York: Biomedical Information.

Cytryn, L., McKnew, D. H., Zahn-Waxler, C., Radke-Yarrow, M., Gaensbauer, T. J., Harmon, R. J., and Lamour, M. (1984). A developmental view of affective disturbances in the children of affectively ill parents. *American Journal of Psychiatry* 141:219–222.

Davenport, Y. B., Zahn-Waxler, C., Adland, M. L., and Mayfield, A. (1984). Early child-rearing practices in families with a manic-depressive parent. *American Journal of Psychiatry* 141:230–235.

Decina, P., Kestenbaum, C. J., Farber, S., Kron, L., Gargan, M., Sackeim, H. A., and Fieve, R. R. (1983). Clinical and psychological assessment of children of bipolar probands. *American Journal of Psychiatry* 140:548–553.

Dempsey, P. (1964). A unidimensional depression scale for the MMPI. *Journal of Consulting Psychology* 28:364–370.

Deutsch, H. (1933). Zur psychologie der manisch-depressiven zustände, insbesondere der chronischen hypomanie. *Internationale Zeitschrift für Psychoanalyse* 19:358–371.

Dorpat, T. L. (1977). Depressive affect. *Psychoanalytic Study of the Child* 32:3–27.

Dweck, C. S., Gittleman-Klein, R., McKinney, W. T., and Watson, J. S. (1977). Summary of the Subcommittee on Clinical Criteria for Diagnosis of Depression in Children. In *Depression in Childhood: Diagnosis, Treatment, and Conceptual Models*, ed. J. G. Schulterbrandt and A. Raskin, pp. 153–154. New York: Raven Press.

Ehrenwald, E., ed. (1976). *The History of Psychotherapy: From Healing Magic to Encounter.* New York: Jason Aronson.

Erikson, E. H. (1963). *Childhood and Society.* 2nd ed. (Revised). New York: Norton.

Farberow, N. L., and Shneidman, E. S. (1983). Suicide and age. In *The Psychology of Suicide*, ed E. S. Shneidman, N. L. Farberow, and R. E. Litman, pp. 165–174. New York: Jason Aronson.

Fawcett, M. D., Scheftner, M. D., Clark, D., Hedeker, D., Gibbons, R., and Coryell, W. (1987). Clinical predictors of suicide in patients with major affective disorders: a controlled prospective study. *American Journal of Psychiatry* 144:35–40.

Feighner, J. P., Robins, E., Guze, S. B., Woodruff, R. A., Winokur, G., and Munoz, R. (1972). Diagnostic criteria for use in psychiatric research. *Archives of General Psychiatry* 26:57–63.

Fenichel, O. (1945). *The Psychoanalytic Theory of Neurosis*. New York: Norton.

Frank, E., Kupfer, D. J., Jacob, M., Blumenthal, S. J., and Jarrett, D. B. (1987). Pregnancy-related affective episodes among women with recurrent depression. *American Journal of Psychiatry* 144:288–293.

Frank, J. D. (1961). *Persuasion and Healing: A Comparative Study of Psychotherapy*. Baltimore: Johns Hopkins Press.

Freeman, T. (1976). *Childhood Psychopathology and Adult Psychoses*. New York: International Universities Press.

Freud, A. (1937). *The Ego and the Mechanism of Defense*, trans. C. Baines. International Psycho-Analytical Library, no. 30. London: Hogarth Press. (Original work published 1936)

––––––– (1971a). A letter from Anna Freud. *American Journal of Psychiatry* 140:1583.

––––––– (1971b). *The Writings of Anna Freud*. Vol. 7: *Problems of Psychoanalytic Training, Diagnosis, and the Technique of Therapy, 1966–1970*. New York: International Universities Press.

Freud, S. (1917). Mourning and melancholia. *Standard Edition* 14:237–258.

––––––– (1930). *Civilization and Its Discontents*, trans. J. Riviere. International Psycho-Analytical Library, no. 17. London: Hogarth Press.

––––––– (1960). Letter to Ludwig Binswanger, April 12, 1929. In *Letters of Sigmund Freud,* trans. T. Stern and J. Stern, ed. E. L. Freud, p. 386. New York: Basic Books.

Friedman, J. M. H., Asnis, G. M., Boeck, M., and DiFiore, J. (1987). Prevalence of specific suicidal behaviors in a high school sample. *American Journal of Psychiatry* 144:1203–1206.

Friedman, P. (1967). *On Suicide, with Particular Reference to Suicide Among Young Students: Discussions of the Vienna Psychoanalytic Society–1910.* New York: International Universities Press.

Frosch, J. (1983). Psychotic affective disorders. In *The Psychotic Process*, pp. 177–195. New York: International Universities Press.

Furman, E. (1984). Some difficulties in assessing depressions and suicide in childhood. In *Suicide in the Young*, ed. H. S. Sudak, A. B. Ford, and N. B. Rushforth, pp. 245–258. Boston: John Wright-PSG, Inc.

———— (1985). Some difficulties in defining and assessing depression in childhood. Paper presented at the Monday Conference Series, Division of Child Psychiatry, University Hospitals of Cleveland, Ohio, December 2.

Gammon, G. D., John, K., Rothblume, E. D., Mullen, K., Tischler, G. L., and Weissman, M. M. (1983). Use of a structured diagnostic interview to identify bipolar disorder in adolescent inpatients: frequency and manifestations of the disorder. *American Journal of Psychiatry* 140:543–547.

Gershon, E. S. (1983). The genetics of affective disorders. In *Psychiatry Update: The American Psychiatric Association Annual Review*, vol. 2, ed. L. Grinspoon, pp. 434–457. Washington, DC: American Psychiatric Press.

Glassman, A. H., Perel, J. M., Shostak, M., Kantor, S. J., and Fleiss, J. L. (1977). Clinical implications of imipramine plasma levels for depressive illness. *Archives of General Psychiatry* 34:197–204.

Goodman and Gilman's The Pharmacological Basis of Therapeutics (1985). 7th ed. New York: Macmillan.

Greenson, R. R. (1953). On boredom. *Journal of the American Psychoanalytic Association.* 1:7–21.

Gunderson, J. G. (1983). DSM-III diagnoses of personality disorders. In *Current Perspectives on Personality Disorders*, ed. J. P. Frosels, pp. 19–39. Washington, DC: American Psychiatric Press.

Haim, A. (1974). *Adolescent Suicide*, trans. A. M. Sheridan Smith. New York: International Universities Press. (Original work published 1970)

Halbreich, U., and Endicott, J. (1985a). The biology of premenstrual changes: what do we really know? In *Premenstrual Syndrome: Current Findings and Future Directions*, ed. H. J.

Osofsky and S. J. Blumenthal, pp. 13–24. Washington, DC: American Psychiatric Press.

_____ (1985b). Relationship of dysphoric premenstrual changes to depressive disorders. *Acta Psychiatrica Scandinavica* 71:331–338.

Hamilton, M. (1960). A rating scale for depression. *Journal of Neurology, Neurosurgery, and Psychiatry* 23:56–62.

Harvey, D. (1978). Maternal mental illness—the effect on the baby. In *Mental Illness in Pregnancy and the Puerperium,* ed. M. Sandler, pp. 112–119. New York: Oxford University Press.

Hendin, H. (1969). Black suicide. *Archives of General Psychiatry* 21:407–422.

International Drug Therapy Newsletter (1986). Carbamazepine therapy for manic depressive illness: an update. March, pp. 9–12.

Jackson, S. W. (1986). *Melancholia and Depression: From Hippocratic Times to Modern Times.* New Haven: Yale University Press.

Jacobson, E. (1953). Contribution to the metapsychology of cyclothymic depression. In *Affective Disorders: Psychoanalytic Contribution to Their Study,* ed. P. Greenacre, pp. 49–83. New York: International Universities Press.

_____ (1971). *Depression: Comparative Studies of Normal, Neurotic, and Psychotic Conditions.* New York: International Universities Press.

Janicak, P. G., Pandy, G. N., Davis, J. M., Boshes, R., Bresnahan, D., and Sharma, R. (1988). Response of psychotic and nonpsychotic depression to phenelzine. *American Journal of Psychiatry* 145:93–95.

Joffe, W. G., and Sandler, J. (1968). Comments on the psychoanalytic psychology of adaptation, with special reference to the role of affects and the representational world. *International Journal of Psycho-Analysis* 49:445–454.

Kashani, J. H., Carlson, G. A., et al. (1987). Depression, depressive symptoms, and depressed mood among a community sample of adolescents. *American Journal of Psychiatry* 144:931–934.

Katan, A. (1961). Some thoughts about the role of verbalization in early childhood. *Psychoanalytic Study of the Child* 16:184–188.

Kernberg, O. F. (1975). *Borderline Conditions and Pathological Narcissism*. New York: Jason Aronson.

——— (1976). *Object-Relations Theory and Clinical Psychoanalysis*. New York: Jason Aronson.

Kerr, W. (1962). *The Decline of Pleasure*. New York: Simon & Schuster.

Kleiner, G. J. (1970). On nostalgia. *Bulletin of the Philadelphia Association for Psychoanalysis* 20:11–30.

Kleiner, G. J., and Greston, W. M., eds. (1984). *Suicide in Pregnancy*. Boston: John Wright-PSG, Inc.

Kohut, H. (1971). *The Analysis of the Self*. New York: International Universities Press.

——— (1977). *The Restoration of the Self*. New York: International Universities Press.

Kraepelin, E. (1921). *Manic-Depressive Insanity and Paranoia*. Trans. R. M. Barclay, ed. G. M. Robertson, Edinburgh: E. & S. Livingstone. (Original work published 1909–1913)

Kumar, R., and Robson, K. (1978). Neurotic disturbance during pregnancy and the puerperium: preliminary report of a prospective survey of 119 primiparae. In *Mental Illness in Pregnancy and the Puerperium*, ed. M. Sandler, pp. 40–51. New York: Oxford University Press.

Leff, M. J., Roatch, J. F., and Bunney, W. E., Jr. (1970). Environmental factors preceding the onset of severe depressions. *Psychiatry* 33:293–311.

Lesse, S., ed. (1974). *Masked Depression*. New York: Jason Aronson.

Lewin, B. D. (1932). Analysis and structure of a transient hypomania. *Psychoanalytic Quarterly* 1:43–58.

——— (1950). *The Psychoanalysis of Elation*. New York: Norton.

Lewy, A. J. (1987). Treating chronobiologic sleep and mood disorders with bright light. *Psychiatric Annals* 17(10): 664–669.

Lewy, A., Wehr, T., Goodwin, F., et al. (1980). Light suppresses melatonin secretion in humans. *Science 1980* 210: 1267–1269.

Lewy, A., et al. (1982). Bright artificial light treatment of a manic-depressive patient with a seasonal mood cycle. *American Journal of Psychiatry* 139:1496–1498.

Lindemann, E. (1944). Symptomatology and management of acute grief. *American Journal of Psychiatry* 101:141–148.

_____ (1979). Mental health aspects of rapid social change. In *Beyond Grief: Studies in Crisis Intervention*, pp. 190–201. New York: Jason Aronson. (Abridged from original work published 1969)

Litman, R. E. (1983a). Medical-legal aspects of suicide. In *The Psychology of Suicide*, ed. E. S. Shneidman, N. L. Farberow, and R. E. Litman, pp. 511–518. New York: Jason Aronson.

_____ (1983b). Police aspects of suicide. In *The Psychology of Suicide*, ed. E. S. Shneidman, N. L. Farberow, and R. E. Litman, pp. 519–530. New York: Jason Aronson.

Lukas, C., and Seiden, H. M. (1987). *Silent Grief: Living in the Wake of Suicide*. New York: Scribner's.

Mahler, M. S. (1979a). Notes on the development of basic moods: the depressive affect. In *Selected Papers of Margaret S. Mahler*, vol. 2: *Separation-Individuation*, pp. 59–75. New York: Jason Aronson. (Original work published 1966)

_____ (1979b). On sadness and grief in infancy and childhood: loss and restoration of the symbiotic love object. In *Selected Papers of Margaret S. Mahler*, vol. 1. *Infantile Psychosis and Early Contributions*, pp. 261–279. New York: Jason Aronson. (Original work published 1961)

Mahler, M. S., Pine, F., and Bergman, A. (1975). *The Psychological Birth of the Human Infant: Symbiosis and Individuation*. New York: Basic Books.

Malan, D. H. (1973). The outcome problem in psychotherapy research: a historical review. *Archives of General Psychiatry* 29:719–729.

Manual of the International Statistical Classification of Diseases, Injuries, and Causes of Death, Based on the Recommendations of the Ninth Revision Conference, 1975, and Adopted by the Twenty-ninth World Assembly (ICDM-9). (1977–1978). 2 vols. Geneva: World Health Organization.

Martin, F. M., Brotherston, J. H. F., and Chave, S. P. W. (1957). The incidence of neurosis in a new housing estate. *British Journal of Preventive and Social Medicine* 11:196–202.

Meltzer, H., ed. (1987). *Psychopharmacology. The Third Generation of Progress.* New York: Raven Press.

Meyer, A. (1948a). *The Commonsense Psychiatry of Dr. Adolf Meyer,* ed., with Biographical Narrative, A. Lief. New York: McGraw-Hill.

—— (1948b). Interrelations of the domain of neuropsychiatry. In *The Commonsense Psychiatry of Dr. Adolf Meyer,* ed. A. Lief, pp. 565–575. New York: McGraw-Hill. (Original work published 1922)

—— (1948c). Mental and moral health in a constructive school program. In *The Commonsense Psychiatry of Dr. Adolf Meyer,* ed. A. Lief, pp. 491–500. New York: McGraw-Hill. (Original work published 1917)

Moore, B. E., and Fine, B. D., eds. (1967). *A Glossary of Psychoanalytic Terms and Concepts.* New York: American Psychoanalytic Association.

Morrison, H. L., ed. (1983). *Children of Depressed Parents: Risk, Identification, and Intervention.* New York: Grune & Stratton.

Munoz, R. A. (1985). Postpartum psychosis as a discrete entity. *Journal of Clinical Psychiatry* 46:182–184.

National Institute of Mental Health (1984). *Adolescence and Depression.* DHHS Publication no. ADM 84-1337. Washington, DC: U.S. Dept. of Health and Human Services, Public Health Service.

Nemiah, J. C. (1978). Alexithymia and psychosomatic illness. *Journal of Continuing Education in Psychiatry,* October, pp. 25–37.

The New York Times (1985). Increase in young men's suicides arouses concern of healthy aides. June 24, Section B, page 7.

Ogden, T. H. (1983). The concept of internal object relations. *International Journal of Psychoanalysis* 64:227–241.

Osofsky, H. J. and Blumenthal, S. J., eds. (1985). *Premenstrual*

Syndrome: Current Findings and Future Directions. Washington, DC: American Psychiatric Press.

Paykel, E. S., Myers, J. K., Dienelt, M. N., Klerman, G. L., Lindenthal, J. J., and Pepper, M. P. (1969). Life events and depressions: a controlled study. *Archives of General Psychiatry* 21:753–760.

Perry, S., Cooper, A. M., and Michels, R. (1987). The psychodynamic formulation: its purpose, structure, and clinical application. *American Journal of Psychiatry* 144:3, May.

Physician's Desk Reference (1988). 42nd ed. Oradell, NJ: Medical Economics Books.

Post, R. M., Uhde, T. W., Ballenger, J. C., and Squillace, K. M. (1983). Prophylactic efficacy of carbamazepine in manic-depressive illness. *American Journal of Psychiatry* 140:1602–1604.

Poznanski, E. O., Cook, S. C., Carroll, B. J., and Corzo, H. (1983). Use of the children's depression rating scale in an inpatient psychiatric population. *Journal of Clinical Psychiatry* 44:200–203.

Psychiatric News (1986a). Phototherapy, sleep deprivation. Effective nondrug treatments. p. 15, November 21.

———— (1986b). Two psychotherapies as effective as drug. July 4, pp. 1, 24–25.

Quitkin, F. M., Stewart, J. W., McGrath, P. J., et al. (1988). Phenelzine versus imipramine in the treatment of probable atypical depression: defining syndrome boundaries of selective MAOI responders. *American Journal of Psychiatry* 145:306–311.

Reid, W. H., and Morrison, H. L. (1983). Risk factors in children of depressed parents. In *Children of Depressed Parents: Risk, Identification, and Intervention*, ed. H. L. Morrison, pp. 33–46. New York: Grune & Stratton.

Rifkin, A. (1988). ECT versus tricyclic antidepressants in depression: a review of the evidence. *Journal of Clinical Psychiatry* 49:3–7.

Risch, S. C., Huey, L. Y., and Janowsky, D. S. (1979). Plasma levels of tricyclic antidepressants and clinical efficacy: review of the literature. *Journal of Clinical Psychiatry* 40:4–16, 58–69.

Robins, L. N., Helzer, J. E., Weissman, M. M., Orvaschel, H., Gruenberg, E., Burke, J. D., Jr., and Regier, D. A. (1984). Lifetime prevalence of specific psychiatric disorders in three sites. *Archives of General Psychiatry* 41:949–958.

Rome, H. P. (1974). Depressive illness: its sociopsychiatric implications. *Psychiatric Annals* 4:54–68.

Rosenthal, N, et al. (1984). Seasonal affective disorder: a description of the syndrome and preliminary findings with light therapy. *Archives of General Psychiatry* 41:72–80.

Rosenthal, N., and Wehr, T. (1987). Seasonal affective disorders. *Psychiatric Annals* 17:670–674.

Sackeim, H. A., Decina, P., Kanzler, M., Kerr, B., and Malitz, S. (1987). Effects of electrode placement of efficacy of titrated low-dose ECT. *American Journal of Psychiatry* 144(11): 1444–1459.

Saletu, B., Dietzel, M., Lesch, O. M., et al. (1986). Effect of biologically active light and partial sleep deprivation on sleep, awakening, and circadian rhythm in normals. *European Neurology* (suppl.) 25, 22:82–92.

Sandler, J., and Joffe, W. G. (1965). Notes on childhood depression. *International Journal of Psycho-Analysis* 46:88–96.

Schmale, A. H., and Engel, G. L. (1975). The role of conservation–withdrawal in depressive reactions. In *Depression and Human Existence*, ed. E. J. Anthony and T. Benedek, pp.183–198. Boston: Little, Brown.

Seligman, E. P. (1975). *Helplessness: On Depression, Development and Death*. San Francisco: Freeman, Cooper.

Sherrill, R. (1982). Review of *America in Search of Itself: The Making of the President, 1956–1980,* by Theodore H. White. In *The New York Times Book Review*, pp. 1, 26–28, May 9.

Shneidman, E. S., and Farberow, N. L. (1983). Feasibilities of the Los Angeles Suicide Prevention Center. In *The Psychology of Suicide*, ed. E. S. Shneidman, N. L. Farberow, and R. E. Litman, pp. 98–107. New York: Jason Aronson.

Sifneos, P. E. (1972). *Short-Term Psychotherapy and Emotional Crisis.* Cambridge: Harvard University Press.

Silverman, C. (1968). *The Epidemiology of Depression.* Baltimore: Johns Hopkins University Press.

Solnit, A. J., and Leckman, J. F. (1984). On the study of children of parents with affective disorders. *American Journal of Psychiatry* 141:241–242.

Spitz, R. A. (1946). Anaclitic depression. *Psychoanalytic Study of the Child* 2:313–342.

Srole, L., Langner, T. S., Michael, S. T., Kirkpatrick, P., Opler, M. K., and Reenie, T. A. (1978). *Mental Health in the Metropolis: The Midtown Manhattan Study*, Rev. ed., ed. L. Srole and A. K. Fischer. New York: New York University Press.

Stoller, R. J. (1984). Psychiatry's mind-brain dialectic, or the *Mona Lisa* has no eyebrows. *American Journal of Psychiatry* 141:554–558.

Stone, L. (1954). The widening scope of indications for psychoanalysis. In *Transference and Its Context: Selected Papers on Psychoanalysis*, ed. L. Stone, pp. 21–42. New York: Jason Aronson, (1984).

Strober, M. (1985). Depressive illness in adolescence. *Psychiatric Annals* 15:375–378.

Summers, A. (1985). *Goddess: The Secret Lives of Marilyn Monroe.* New York: Macmillan.

Volkan, V. D., ed. (1985). *Depressive States and Their Treatment.* Northvale, NJ: Jason Aronson.

Werman, D. S. (1977). Normal and pathological nostalgia. *Journal of the American Psychoanalytic Association* 25:387–398.

Wolpert, E. A., ed. (1977). *Manic-Depressive Illness: History of a Syndrome.* New York: International Universities Press.

Zahn-Waxler, C., McKnew, D. H., Cummings, E. M., Davenport, Y. B., and Radke-Yarrow, M. (1984). Problem behaviors and peer interactions of young children with a manic-depressive parent. *American Journal of Psychiatry* 141:236–240.

Zilboorg, G., and Henry, G. W. (1941). *A History of Medical Psychology.* New York: Norton.

Zung, W. W. K. (1965). A self-rating depression scale. *Archives of General Psychiatry* 12:63–70.

ADDITIONAL READING

CHAPTER 2

Dunner, D. L. (1983). Recent genetic studies of bipolar and unipolar depression. In *The Affective Disorders*, ed. J.. M. Davis and J. W. Maas, pp. 183–191. Washington, DC: American Psychiatric Press.

CHAPTER 3

Craig, T. J., and Van Natta, P. A. (1983). Disability and depressive symptoms in two communities. *American Journal of Psychiatry* 140:598–601.

Myers, J. K. et al. (1984). Six-month prevalence of psychiatric disorders in three communities. *Archives of General Psychiatry* 4:959–967.

Regier, D. A. et al. (1984). The NIMH Epidemiologic Catchment Area program. *Archives of General Psychiatry* 41:934–941.

Stainbrook, E. J. (1954). A cross-cultural evaluation of depressive reactions. In *Depression*, ed. P. H. Hoch and J. Zubin, pp. 39–50. New York: Grune & Stratton.

CHAPTER 4

Abraham, K. (1924). Short study of the development of the libido, viewed in the light of mental disorders. In *Selected Papers of*

Karl Abraham, trans. D. Bryan and A. Strachey, pp. 418–501. London: Hogarth Press, 1949.

Gaylin, W., ed. (1983). *Psychodynamic Understanding of Depression: The Meaning of Despair.* New York: Jason Aronson.

Hofling, C. K. (1977). The treatment of depression: a selective historical review. In *Depression: Clinical, Biological and Psychological Perspectives,* ed. G. Usdin, pp. 52–72. New York: Brunner/Mazel.

Klaus, M. H., and Kennell, J. H. (1976). *Maternal-Infant Bonding: The Impact of Early Separation or Loss on Family Development.* St. Louis: C. V. Mosby.

Mendelson, M. (1974). *Psychoanalytic Concepts of Depression.* 2d ed. Flushing, NY: Spectrum, dist. by Halsted Press.

Meyer, A. (1906). Principles in grouping facts in psychiatry. In *The Commonsense Psychiatry of Dr. Adolf Meyer,* ed. A. Lief, pp. 153–168. New York: McGraw-Hill, 1948.

Pollock, G. H. (1977). Foreword to *Manic-Depressive Illness: History of a Syndrome,* ed. E. A. Wolpert, pp. 1–2. New York: International Universities Press.

Wolpert, E. A. (1977). Manic-depressive illness as an actual neurosis. In *Depression and Human Existence,* ed. E. J. Anthony and T. Benedek, pp. 199–221. Boston: Little, Brown.

CHAPTER 6

Bird, B. R. (1973). *Talking with Patients.* 2d ed. Philadelphia: J. B. Lippincott.

Frazier, S. H., and Carr, A. C. (1983). *Introduction to Psychopathology.* New York: Jason Aronson.

MacKinnon, R. A., and Michels, R. (1971). *The Psychiatric Interview in Clinical Practice.* Philadelphia: W. B. Saunders.

Merikangas, K. R., Leckman, J. F., Prusoff, B. A., Pauls, D. L., and Weissman, M. M. (1985). Familial transmission of depression and alcoholism. *Archives of General Psychiatry* 42:367–372.

Nemiah, J. C. (1973). *Foundations of Psychopathology.* New York: Jason Aronson.

Nicholi, A. M., Jr., ed. (1978). *The Harvard Guide to Modern Psychiatry.* Cambridge: Belknap Press of Harvard University.

Volkan, V. D., ed. (1985). *Depressive States and Their Treatment*. Northvale, NJ: Jason Aronson.

CHAPTER 7

Carlson, G. A., and Goodwin, F. K. (1973). The stages of mania: a longitudinal analysis of the manic episode. *Archives of General Psychiatry* 28:221–228.

Lalinec-Michaud, M., and Engelsmann, F. (1985). Anxiety, fears, and depression related to hysterectomy. *Canadian Journal of Psychiatry* 30:44–47.

Leckman, J. F., Weissman, M. M., Merikangas, K. R., Pauls, D. L., and Prusoff, B. A. (1983). Panic disorder and major depression: increased risk of depression, alcoholism, panic, and phobic disorders in families of depressed probands with panic disorder. *Archives of General Psychiatry* 40: 1055–1060.

Lewin, B. D. (1941). Comments on hypomanic and related states. *Psychoanalytic Review* 28:86–91.

Logan, J. (1976). *Josh: My Up and Down, In and Out Life*. New York: Delacorte.

Murphy, G. E., Woodruff, R. A., and Herjanic, M. (1974). Primary affective disorder: selection efficiency of two sets of diagnostic criteria. *Archives of General Psychiatry* 31:181–184.

Rivinus, T. M., Biederman, J., Herzog, D. B., Kemper, K., Harper, G. P., Harmatz, J. S., and Houseworth, S. (1984). Anorexia nervosa and affective disorders: a controlled family history study. *American Journal of Psychiatry* 141:1414–1418.

Spitzer, R. L., Endicott, J., and Robins, E. (1978). Research diagnostic criteria: rationale and reliability. *Archives of General Psychiatry* 35:773–782.

Stasiek, C., and Zetin, M. (1985). Organic manic disorders. *Psychosomatics* 26:394–402.

CHAPTER 9

Bibring, E. (1953). The mechanism of depression. In *Affective Disorders: Psychoanalytic Contribution to Their Study*, ed. P.

Greenacre, pp. 13–48. New York: International Universities Press.

Chodoff, P. (1972). The depressive personality: a critical review. *Archives of General Psychiatry* 27:666–673.

Gaylin, W., ed. (1983). *Psychodynamic Understanding of Depression: The Meaning of Despair*. New York: Jason Aronson.

Gunderson, J. G., and Elliott, G. R. (1985). The interface between borderline personality disorder and affective disorder. *American Journal of Psychiatry* 142:277–288.

Hirschfeld, R. M. A., and Klerman, G. L. (1979). Personality attributes and affective disorders. *American Journal of Psychiatry* 136:67–70.

Hirschfeld, R. M. A., Klerman, G. L., Clayton, P. J., Keller, M. B., McDonald-Scott, P., and Larkin, B. H. (1983). Assessing personality: effects of the depressive state on trait measurement. *American Journal of Psychiatry* 140:695–699.

Jacobson, E. (1953). Contribution to the metapsychology of cyclothymic depression. In *Affective Disorders: Psychoanalytic Contribution to Their Study*, ed. P. Greenacre, pp. 49–83. New York: International Universities Press.

———— (1971). *Depression: Comparative Studies of Normal, Neurotic and Psychotic Conditions*. New York: International Universities Press.

Kernberg, O. F. (1975). *Borderline Conditions and Pathological Narcissism*. New York: Jason Aronson.

———— (1976). *Object-Relations Theory and Clinical Psychoanalysis*. New York: Jason Aronson.

Loewenstein, R. M., ed. (1953). *Drives, Affects, Behavior*. New York: International Universities Press.

Mazer, M. (1976). *People and Predicaments*. Cambridge: Harvard University Press.

Paykel, E. S. (1974). Recent life events and clinical depression. In *Life Stress and Illness*, ed. E. K. E. Gunderson and R. H. Rahe, pp. 134–163. Springfield, IL: Charles C Thomas.

Prego-Silva, L. E. (1978). Dialogue on "Depression and Other Painful Affects." *International Journal of Psycho-Analysis* 59:517–532.

Rado, S. (1928). The problem of melancholia. *International Journal of Psycho-Analysis* 9:420–438.

Scott, J. P., and Senay, E. C. (1973). *Separation and Depression: Clinical and Research Aspects*. American Association for the Advancement of Science, Publication no. 94. Washington, DC.

Stangl, D., Pfohl, B., Zimmerman, M., Bowers, W., and Corenthal, C. (1985). A structured interview for the *DSM-III* personality disorders: a preliminary report. *Archives of General Psychiatry* 42:591–596.

Vaillant, G. E., Bond, M., and Vaillant, C. O. (1986). An empirically validated hierarchy of defense mechanisms. *Archives of General Psychiatry* 43:786–794.

Vaillant, G. E., and Drake, R. E. (1985). Maturity of ego defenses in relation to *DSM-III* Axis II personality disorder. *Archives of General Psychiatry* 42:597–601.

Widiger, T. A., and Frances, A. (1985). The *DSM-III* personality disorders: perspective from psychology. *Archives of General Psychiatry* 42:615–623.

CHAPTER 11

Carr, A. C., Schoenberg, B., Peretz, D., Kutscher, A. H., and Goldberg, I. K., eds. (1975). *Grief: Selected Readings*. Health Sciences Publishing Corp.

Colgrove, M., Bloomfield, H. H., and McWilliams, P. (1976). *How to Survive the Loss of a Love: 58 Things to Do When There Is Nothing to Be Done*. Leo Press.

Dunlop, R. S. (1978). *Helping the Bereaved*. Bowie, MD: Charles C Thomas.

Guest, J. (1976). *Ordinary People*. New York: Ballantine.

Kreis, B., and Pattie, A. (1969). *Up from Grief: Patterns of Recovery*. New York: Seabury Press.

Kubler-Ross, E. (1969). *On Death and Dying*. New York: MacMillan.

Kushner, H. S. (1981). *When Bad Things Happen to Good People*. New York: Schocken Books.

Lindemann, E. (1979). *Beyond Grief: Studies in Crisis Intervention*. New York: Jason Aronson.

Parkes, C. M. (1972). *Bereavement: Studies of Grief in Adult Life.* New York: International Universities Press.

Seligman, M. E. P. (1975). Helplessness: On Depression, Development, and Death. San Francisco: W. H. Freeman.

Socarides, C. W., ed. (1977). *The World of Emotions: Clinical Studies of Affects and Their Expression.* New York: International Universities Press.

Thorton, A. (1983). Triumph Born of Tragedy. Eugene, OR: Harvest House.

Zisook, S., and DeVaul, R. A. (1983). Grief, unresolved grief, and depression. *Psychosomatics* 24:247–256.

CHAPTER 12

Clayton, P. J. (1983). Epidemiologic and risk factors in suicide. In *Psychiatry Update: The American Psychiatric Association Annual Review,* vol. 2, ed. L. Grinspoon, pp. 428–434. Washington, DC: American Psychiatric Press.

Friedman, P. (1967). *On Suicide, with Particular Reference to Suicide Among Young Students: Discussions of the Vienna Psychoanalytic Society—1910.* New York: International Universities Press.

Shneidman, E. S., ed. (1976). *Suicidology: Contemporary Developments.* New York: Grune & Stratton.

Shneidman, E. S., Farberow, N. L., and Litman, R. E., eds. (1983). *The Psychology of Suicide.* New York: Jason Aronson.

Sudak, H. S., Ford, A. B., and Rushforth, N. B., eds. (1984). *Suicide in the Young.* Boston: John Wright-PSG Inc.

CHAPTER 13

Apfel, R. J., and Simon, B. (1985). Patient–therapist sexual contact. *Psychotherapy and Psychosomatics* 43:57–62.

CHAPTER 14

Biological Therapies in Psychiatry. The Massachusetts General Hospital, Department of Psychiatry. Littleton, MA: PSG Publishing Company, Inc.

Coyle, J. T. (1985). Introduction to the pharmacology of the synapse. In *American Psychiatric Association Annual Review* vol. 4, ed. R. E. Hales and A. J. Frances, pp. 6–16. Washington, DC: American Psychiatric Press.

Currents in Affective Illness: Literature Review and Commentary. Currents Publications, Ltd., Bethesda, MD.

Gershon, S., and Shopsin, B. (1973). *Lithium: Its Role in Psychiatric Research and Treatment.* New York: Plenum.

Guggenheim, F. G., and Weiner, M. F., eds. (1984). *Manual of Psychiatric Consultation and Emergency Care.* New York: Jason Aronson.

The Harvard Medical School Mental Health Letter. Harvard Medical School, Department of Continuing Education, Farmingdale, NY.

Johnson, F. N., ed. (1980). *Handbook of Lithium Therapy.* Baltimore: University Park Press.

Praag, H. M., van (1977). *Depression and Schizophrenia: A Contribution on Their Chemical Pathologies.* New York: Spectrum.

Shader, R. I., ed. (1975). *Manual of Psychiatric Therapeutics: Practical Psychopharmacology and Psychiatry.* Boston: Little, Brown.

Shader, R. I., Greenblatt, D. J., and Ciraulo, D. A. (1981). Benzodiazepine treatment of specific anxiety states. *Psychiatric Annals* 11,1:30–40.

CHAPTER 15

Weissman, M. M., Prusoff, B. A., DiMascio, A., Neu, C., Goklaney, M., and Klerman, G. L. (1979). The efficacy of drugs and psychotherapy in the treatment of acute depressive episodes. *American Journal of Psychiatry* 136:555–558.

CHAPTER 16

Coryell, W., Lavori, P., Endicott, J., Keller, M., and Van Eerdewegh, M. (1984). Outcome in schizoaffective, psychotic, and nonpsychotic depression: course during a six- to 24-month follow-up. *Archives of General Psychiatry* 41:787-791.

Gammon, G. D., John, K., Rothblum, E. D., Mullen, K., Tischler, G. L., and Weissman, M. M. (1983). Use of a structured diagnostic interview to identify bipolar disorder in adolescent inpatients: frequency and manifestations of the disorder. *American Journal of Psychiatry* 140:543-547.

Keller, M. B., Lavori, P. W., Endicott, J., Coryell, W., and Klerman, G. L. (1983). "Double depression": two-year follow-up. *American Journal of Psychiatry* 140:689-694.

Poznanski, E. O., Cook, S. C., Carroll, B. J., and Corzo, H. (1983). Use of the children's depression rating scale in an inpatient psychiatric population. *Journal of Clinical Psychiatry* 44:200-203.

CHAPTER 20

Annell, A.-L. (Ed). (1972). *Depressive States in Childhood and Adolescence*. 4th European Congress of Pedopsychiatry, Stockholm, 1971. Stockholm: Almqvist & Wiksell.

Anthony, E. J. (1975). Childhood depression. In *Depression and Human Existence*, ed. E. J. Anthony and T. Benedek, pp. 231-277. Boston: Little, Brown.

———— (1978). Affective disorders in children and adolescents with special emphasis on depression. In *Depression: Biology, Psychodynamics and Treatment*, ed. J. O. Cole, A. F. Schatzberg, and S. H. Frazier,pp. 173-184. New York: Plenum.

Anthony, J., and Scott, P. (1960). Manic-depressive psychosis in childhood. *Journal of Child Psychology and Psychiatry* 1:53-72.

Bene, A. (1975). Depressive phenomena in childhood: their open and disguised manifestations in analytic treatment. In *Studies in Child Psychoanalysis: Pure and Applied*. The Scientific Proceedings of the 20th Anniversary Celebrations of the Hampstead Child-Therapy Course and Clinic. Monograph Series of the Psychoanalytic Study of the Child, no. 5, pp. 33-36. New Haven: Yale University Press.

Berezin, M. A. (1972). Psychodynamic considerations of aging and the aged: an overview. *American Journal of Psychiatry* 128:1483–1491.

Bowlby, J. (1960). Grief and mourning in infancy and early childhood. *Psychoanalytic Study of the Child* 15:9–52.

_____ (1960). Separation anxiety. *International Journal of Psycho-Analysis* 41:89–113.

_____ (1961). Childhood mourning and its implications for psychiatry. *American Journal of Psychiatry* 118:481–498.

Brockman, D. D., ed. (1984). *Late Adolescence: Psychoanalytic Studies*. New York: International Universities Press.

Carlson, G. A. (1984). A comparison of early and late onset adolescent affective disorder. *Journal of Operational Psychiatry* 15:46–50.

Cath, S. H. (1965). Some dynamics of middle and later years: a study in depletion and restitution. In *Geriatric Psychiatry: Grief, Loss, and Emotional Disorder in the Aging Process*, ed. M. A. Berezin and S. H. Cath. New York: International Universities Press.

_____ (1966). Beyond depression—the depleted state: a study in ego psychology in the aged. *Canadian Psychiatric Association Journal (Special Suppl.)* 11:S329–S339.

_____ (1969). Discussion of A survey of the literature on the adjustment of the aged to retirement, by T. Nadelson. *Journal of Geriatric Psychiatry* 3:21–32.

Cohen, D. J. (1980). Constructive and reconstructive activities in the analysis of a depressed child. *Psychoanalytic Study of the Child* 35:237–266.

Crook, T., Ferris, S., and Bartus, R., eds. (1983). *Assessment in Geriatric Psychopharmacology*. New Canaan, CT: Mark Powley.

Dorpat, T. L. (1977). Depressive affect. *Psychoanalytic Study of the Child* 32:3–27.

Evans, J. (1982). *Adolescent and Pre-Adolescent Psychiatry*. New York: Grune & Stratton.

Feinstein, S. C. (1975). Adolescent depression. In *Depression and Human Existence*, ed. E. J. Anthony and T. Benedek, pp. 317–336. Boston: Little, Brown.

Feinstein, S. C., and Wolpert, E. A. (1973). Juvenile manic-depressive illness: clinical and therapeutic considerations. *Journal of the American Academy of Child Psychiatry* 12: 123–136.

Furman, R. A. (1964). Death and the young child: some preliminary considerations. *Psychoanalytic Study of the Child* 19:321–333.

Geller, B., Rogol, A. D., and Knitter, E. F. (1983). Preliminary data on the dexamethasone suppression test in children with major affective disorder. *American Journal of Psychiatry* 140:620–622.

Golombek, H., and Garfinkel, B. D., eds. (1983). *The Adolescent and Mood Disturbance*. New York: International Universities Press.

Hamilton, J. A. (1962). *Postpartum Psychiatric Problems*. St. Louis: C.V. Mosby.

Harvard Medical School Mental Health Letter (1985). Senile dementia, part I. vol. 1, no. 11 (May), pp. 1–4; Senile dementia, part II. vol. 1, no. 12 (June), pp. 1–4.

Kahana, R. J. (1979). Strategies of dynamic psychotherapy with the wide range of older individuals. *Journal of Geriatric Psychiatry* 12:71–100.

Keckich, W. A., and Young, M. (1983). Anaclitic depression in the elderly. *Psychiatric Annals* 13:691–696.

Klaus, M. H., and Kennell, J. H. (1982). *Parent–Infant Bonding*. 2d ed. St. Louis: CV. Mosby.

Lipton, M. A. (1980). Pharmacotherapy of depression in the elderly. *Psychosomatics* 21:816–824.

Malmquist, C. P. (1975). Depression in childhood. In *The Nature and Treatment of Depression*, ed. F. F. Flach and S. C. Draghi, pp. 73–98. New York: Wiley.

———— (1978). *Handbook of Adolescence: Psychopathology, Antisocial Development, Psychotherapy*. New York: Jason Aronson.

Rie, H. E. (1966). Depression in childhood: a survey of some pertinent contributions. *Journal of the Academy of Child Psychiatry* 5:653–685.

Rosenthal, P. A., and Rosenthal, S. (1984). Suicidal behavior by preschool children. *American Journal of Psychiatry* 141: 520–525.

Rubin, I. (1965). *Sexual Life after Sixty*. New York: Basic Books.

Sandler, M., ed. (1978). *Mental Illness in Pregnancy and the Puerperium*. New York: Oxford University Press.

Sandler, A. M. (1982). Psychoanalysis and psychoanalytic psychotherapy of the older patient: a developmental crisis in an aging patient: comments on development and adaptation. *Journal of Geriatric Psychiatry* 15:11–32.

Schatzberg, A. F., Liptzin, B., Satlin, A., and Cole, J. O. (1984). Diagnosis of affective disorders in the elderly. *Psychosomatics* 25:126–131.

Schulterbrandt, J. G., and Raskin, A., eds. (1977). *Depression in Childhood: Diagnosis, Treatment and Conceptual Models*. New York: Raven Press.

Shaffer, D. (1974). Suicide in childhood and early adolescence. *Journal of Child Psychology and Psychiatry* 15:275–291.

Spar, J. E., and La Rue, A. (1983). Major depression in the elderly: DSM-III criteria and the dexamethasone suppression test as predictors of treatment response. *American Journal of Psychiatry* 140:844–847.

Sudak, H. S., Ford, A. B., and Rushforth, N. B., eds. (1984). *Suicide in the Young*. Boston: John Wright—PSG, Inc.

Weiner, I. B. (1975). Depression in adolescence. In *The Nature and Treatment of Depression*, ed. F. F. Flach and S. C. Draghi, pp. 99–117. New York: Wiley.

Weller, E. B., and Weller, R. A., eds. (1984). *Current Perspectives on Major Depressive Disorders in Children*. Washington, DC: American Psychiatric Press.

Weller, R. A., Weller, E. B., and Herjanic, B. (1983). Adult psychiatric disorders in psychiatrically ill young adolescents. *American Journal of Psychiatry* 140:1585–1588.

White, J. H,., and O'Shanick, G. (1977). Juvenile manic-depressive illness. *American Journal of Psychiatry* 134:1035–1036.

Wolpert, E. A., ed. (1977). *Manic-Depressive Illness: History of a Syndrome*. New York: International Universities Press.

INDEX

Abortion, and depression,
    393–394
Abraham, K., 114, 325
Abrams, R., 265
Accountability, 63
Addison's disease, 86
Adjustment disorder with
    depressed mood, 84, 120
    in adolescence, 355–356
    in childhood, 335–337
    in the elderly, 401–402
Adolescence, 345–380
    bipolar disorder in, 352–354
    borderline personality in, 360
    characteristics of depression in,
        354–355
    chronic illness in, 363–364
    depression-related moods and
        effects in, 356–357
    disguises of depression in,
        349–351
    dysthymia, adjustment disorder
        with depressed mood, and
        cyclothymia in, 355–356
    family problems in, 361–362
    and history of individual,
        358–359
    major affective disorders in,
        365–366

moodiness and, 348–349
mourning in, 359–360, 374–375
nonpsychotic affective distur-
    bances in, 366
normal depression in, 348
personality disorders and trends
    in, 357–358
poor performance in, 350
psychopathology and diagnosis
    in, 346–364
psychosocial problems in,
    360–363
regression in, 350–351
suicide in, see Adolescent sui-
    cide
treatment and prevention in,
    364–366
unipolar disorder in, 354
Adolescent suicide, 324, 347,
    367–380
    compared with adult suicide,
        373–374
    dramatic rise in, 368
    motivation, 372–373
    phenomenology of, 369–370
    precipitating factors in,
        371–373
    predisposing factors in,
        374–375

Adolescent suicide (*continued*)
  prevention of, 377–380
  risk factors in, 370–371
  treatment of, 375–377
Adolescent turmoil, 350
Affect
  biological function and, 4–5,
    163–164
  clinical manifestations of, 5–6
  difficulty experiencing, 126,
    129
  inability to perceive, 165–166
  mood and, 3–6
  resulting from loss of defenses,
    162–163
  as signal, 148–149
Affective disorders, 6; *see also*
    Mood disorders
  in adolescence, 345–380
  biological psychiatry and, 9–12
  "borderlands" of, 147–168
  in children, 325–344
  drugs used in, 225–240
  of early adults, 381–395
  effectiveness of psychotherapy
    in, 271–273
  in the elderly, 397–410
  genetic components and, 18
  moodiness versus, 348–349
  seasonal, 102–104
  treatment in adolescence,
    365–366
  types of, 83–102
Affective psychoses, 93
Aftercare, 186–187
Age
  and suicide, 170–171
  variations in signs and symp-
    toms with, 323–324
Aggression
  fusion with sexuality, 292
  identification with, 289–290
  suppressed, 114
  vicissitudes of, 291–292
Agitated depression, 138
Akiskal, H. S., 352
Alcoholism
  and adolescent suicide, 379
  and cylothymia, 101
  and depression, 65, 75, 85, 167
Alexander, L., 30
Alexithymia, 166
Alzheimer's disease, 106, 121,
    137
Ambivalence, 126
Ambulatory patients, 190–191
America in Search of Itself
    (White), 162–163
American Heritage Dictionary,
    298
American Psychiatric Association
    Task Force on Electroconvul-
    sant Therapy, 265
American Psychiatric Association
    Task Force on Nomenclature
    and Statistics (1980), 3
American Psychiatric Association
    Task Force on the Use of
    Laboratory Tests in Psychia-
    try, 241
Anemia, 247–248
Anger, and suicide, 175
Anhedonia, 7
Anniversaries, of suicides, 176
Anorexia, 143, 167
Anthony, E. J., 358
Antidepressants; *see also* MAOs
  administration of, 241
  carbamazepine as, 247–249
  and children, 343
  miscellaneous, 237
  results of treatment with,
    241–243
  side effects of, 243–244

tricyclic, see tricyclic antide-
pressants
Antisocial symptoms, 350
Anxiety
and depression, 139, 143
drugs used for, 225, 229
fear of losing control, 282
Appearance of patient, 67–68
Appetite, lack of, 85
Arieti, S., 148
Arteriosclerotic dementia, 106
Attraction, 53
Atypical bipolar disorder, 93
Atypical depression, 104–105

Baldessarini, R. J., 220–221
Beck, A. T., 40
Bemporad, R. J., 323
Benson, R., 247
Bereavement, 120, 153–154
Berger, D. M., 52
Bibring, E., 39–40
Bick, P., 104
Biological function, 4–5
Biological psychiatry, 9–12
Biological therapy, 217–270
clinical basis for, 217–219
definition of, 217
in late life, 403–404
Bipolar disorders, 9, 93–102,
117–118
in adolescence, 352–354
aspects and varieties of, 94–95
carbamazepine for, 247–249
in childhood, 333–335
course and outcome of, 97–99
and cyclothymia, 100–102
genetic factors in, 15–22
manic attacks in, 96–97
mixed, 303
onset of, 96
psychology of, 99–100

Blehar, M. C., 17
Bleuler, E., 33
Blumenthal, S. J., 386
Boleyn, A., 30
Borderline individuals
adolescent, 360
with depressive neurosis, 88
Boredom, and apathy, 160–163
Bowlby, J., 153
Boyce, P., 104
Brain tumors, 136
Breakdown
general, 36–37
and restitution, 129–130
Brewer, C., 393
Brief depressive reaction, 84
Bulimia, 144
Business preoccupations, 76

Carbamazepine (Tegretol),
247–249
Career, and depression, 383–384
Castration complex, 292–293
Catharsis, 275–276
Childhood depression
and adult memories, 328–329
bipopular and major depressive
disorder, 333–335
clinical features of, 332–333
and damage to self-esteem, 339
definition of, 328
dysthymia and adjustment disorder with depressed mood,
335–337
in early childhood, 341–342
and helplessness, 339–340
identifications in, 340
and mourning, 337–339
and object relations, 340–341
and suicide, 332
Child Psychopathology and Adult
Psychoses (Freeman), 341

Children
  affective disorders in, 325–344
  of depressed mothers, 343–344
  depressive potentials in, 323,
    337
  diagnosis of, 66, 123–124,
    329–333
  of hospitalized parents, 208
  and loss, 156, 206, 336–338
  of parents with bipolar and uni-
    polar disorder, 18–19
  special problems of diagnosis
    in, 331–333
  treatment of, 342–344
A Child's Parent Dies (Furman),
  206
Chronic depressive personality
  disorder, 84–88
Chronic disability, 249–250,
  306–308
Chronobiology, 104
Churchill, W., 29
Circadian rhythms, 103–104
Clinical disorders, 80–83
Code numbers
  and confidentiality, 78
  fifth-digit subclassifications, 123
Cognition
  and depressive personality,
    70–71, 127–128
  general, 40–41
Cohen, M. B., 44, 128
Compassion, 52–53
Confidentiality, 58–59
  code numbers and, 78
  and suicidal patients, 189
Conservation-withdrawal state,
  164
Countertransference, 55–56
Criminal, convicted, 177–178
Crisis intervention, 378

Cyclothymia, 5–6, 18, 21,
  100–102, 119
  adolescent, 355–356
  psychodynamics of, 101–102
Cytryn, L., 19, 98

Davenport, Y. B., 341–342
Death, preoccupation with, 126
Decina, P., 20, 98
Defenses
  affects resulting from loss of,
    162–163
  and depressive affect, 4–5, 130
  pathological, 126
  rationalization, 75
Delirium
  and manic states, 145
  and suicide, 176–177
Delusions
  in severe depression, 92, 165
  of sins, 175–176, 204
  of somatic disease, 71, 74–75,
    204
Dementia
  Alzheimer type, 106
  and depression, 110–111, 137
  multiinfarct, 106, 121
  and pseudodementia, 111–112,
    400–401
Dependency, 126, 128–129
  on medication, 298–299
  and risk of suicide, 182–183
Depressed person, living with,
  214–215
Depression, 6–9
  acute, 206–207, 317–319
  adult versus adolescent,
    354–355
  agitated, 138
  and anorexia, 144
  and anxiety, 139, 143

atypical, 104–105
boredom and apathy, 160–163
and bulimia, 144
and business preoccupations, 76
career and, 383–384
chemotherapy and types of, 222–223
childhood, see Childhood depression
current concepts of, 33–45
and delusion, 165
dementia and, 110–111, 137
and disability, 31–32, 249–250
disguises of, 73–76
electroconvulsant treatment for, 267
epidemiology of, 23–32
and fatigue, 149–150
illness-induced, 108–109, 135–136, 399
in loss, grief, and mourning, 151–158
major, see Major depression
MAOs used in, 237
and marital preoccupations, 76
midlife, 93
misdiagnosed as medical illness, 137
normal, see Normal depression
normal adolescent, 348
and organic brain disease, 400–401
and other psychiatric illnesses, panic and, 143-144
and the personality, 28–32
postabortion, 393–394
postpartum, 388–392
with prescribed medications, 107–109, 136–137
psychodynamics of, 125–133

psychotic, 28–29
recurrent, 176
rejection and, 150–151
the return of the repressed and, 159–160
secondary, 399
separation and nostalgia, 158–159
seriousness of, 30–31
sex and race differences in, 25–26
"smiling," 67
and stimulants, 237, 239
and suicide, see Suicide
and tricyclics, 233, 237
and withdrawal, alienation, or retreat, 164
Depression-proneness, 337
Depressive disorders, 6, 119–120
Depressive equivalents, 166–167
Depressive neurosis, 84–88
diagnosis of, 301
and major depression, 86–87
and other symptoms, 87–88
Depressive personality, cognition and, 70–71
Depressive States and Their Treatment (Volkan), 157
Dermatitis, 247–248
Deutsch, H., 39, 338
Dexamethazone suppression test, 141, 240
Diagnosis
and aggression, 114
differential, 135–145, 351–354
and evaluation, 63–76
frequency of types, 105–106
limitations of, 64–65
longitudinal, 92–93
of organic mood disorders, 106–112

Diagnosis (*continued*)
and outcome, 316
of personality disorders,
112–115
in practice, 80–83
preparation for, 49–62
psychodynamic appraisal,
125–133
Diagnostic classifications, 77–115
Disability
chronic, 249–250, 306–308
depression and, 31–32
Disillusionment, 162–163
Diuretics, and low potassium levels, 86, 136
Drug abuse, 75, 85, 121
and cyclothymia, 101
and manic attacks, 109
and suicide, 379–380
DSM III-R (Diagnostic and
Statistical Manual of Mental
Disorders, 3rd edition), 3, 23,
34–35, 38, 138, 353
DSM-III-R, 77–79, 112–113, 115,
334–335, 349, 386, 399
axes of, 80–83
and *ICD-9-CM*, 83–84, 88,
92–95, 100, 106–107,
117–124
DSM-II, 34, 77
Dweck, C. S., 332
Dysthymia, 29, 84–88, 119, 305;
see also Depressive neurosis
adolescent, 355–356
childhood, 335–337

Eagleton, T., 28
Early development, 127–128
Eclectic therapy, 297–298
Ehrenwald, E., 45
Electroconvulsant treatment
(ECT), 97, 142–143, 255,
265–267
for depression, 267
effectiveness of, 268
for elderly patients, 404
and lithium therapy, 245
for mania, 267–268
side effects of, 268–270
Elizabeth I, Queen of England,
29–30
Emergency room, 186–187
Emergency situations
acute depression, 206–207
helping families in, 207–208
in hospitalized medical and surgical patients, 208
suicidal risk, 203–205
Empathy, 51–52
Endicott, J., 385
Engel, G. L., 164
Epidemiology of suicide, 169–170
Erikson, E. H., 325
Ethics, 57–58
Evaluation
diagnosis and, 63–76
of risk of suicide, 173–174

Family
of adolescents, 361–362
advice to, 212–213
first aid for, 205–208
history of suicide in, 176
patient in savior role in, 128
role of, 211–212
Farberow, N. L., 170, 186
Fatherhood, 394–395
Fatigue, 149–150, 174–175
Fawcett, M. D., 174
Feelings of therapist, 51–75
Fine, B. D., 4
Fixations, early, 126
Forrestal, J., 28, 30

Frank, E., 389
Frank, J., *Persuasion and Healing,* 23
Freeman, T., *Child Psychopathology and Adult Psychoses,* 341
Freud, A., 39, 297, 330–331, 335–336
Freud, S., 10, 114, 149, 153, 159
  on adolescence, 368
  "Mourning and Melancholia," 33, 38, 154
Friedman, J. M. H., 27, 368
Friedman, P., 367
Functioning
  cessation of, 91, 204
  global assessment of, 80
Furman, E., 206, 333, 336–339

Gammon, G. D., 353–354
Genetics, importance of, 14–22, 94
Gershon, E. S., 16–18, 94
Glassman, A. H., 241
A Glossary of Psychoanalytic Terms and Concepts (Moore and Fine), 4
Greenson, R. R., 160
Greston, W. M., 392
Grief, 155–157
  acute, 151–153
  normal states of, 83
  unresolved, 157–158, 406
Grief work, 154–155
Guilt
  and childhood depression, 340
  unrealistic, 175–176

Haim, A., 367, 374
Halbreich, U., 385
Hamilton, M., 271
Happiness, 149

Harvey, D., 393
Heart disease, 243–244
Helplessness, 162, 339–340
  learned, 40, 45, 163
  and suicide, 181–182
Hendin, H., 26–27
Henry VIII, King of England, 30
Hepatitis, 247
Heredity, 14–22
Hippocratic oath, 57–58
History, 65–66
  of adolescents, 358–359
  and longitudinal diagnosis, 92–93
  and suicide risk, 173–174
Hoarders, 262–263
Homesickness, 158
Honesty, 54–55
Hopelessness, 162, 181–182
Hospitals, 197–200
  daycare, 197
  management of patient in, 199–200
House calls, 196–197
Hypersomnia, 85
Hypertension, and effects of diuretics, 86, 136
Hypochondriasis, 167, 344–350
Hypomania, 94–95
Hypothyroidism, 86, 135–137
Hysteria, 6

ICD-9-CM (International Classification of Diseases), 77–78, 138, 141, 335, 349
  DSM-III-R and, 83–84, 88, 92–94, 100, 106, 117–124
Ideation, 69–70
Identifications
  with the aggressor, 289–290
  pathological, 126–127, 340

Illness
  depressions induced by,
    108–109
  other affective reactions to,
    109–110
  physical, 74–75
  as "reactions," 36
  unrecognized, 107
Impatience, 54
Impulsive behavior, 88
Infantile sexuality, 292–293
Infants, of parents with bipolar
    disorder, 19–20, 98–99
Insight, 56–57, 72–73, 276
Insomnia
  drugs used for, 229, 233
  general, 68, 85
Instinctual drives
  importance of, 325
  as risk factors, 183
Insurance, 63
Intellectual functions, 71–72
Interpersonal psychiatry, 37–38,
    45
Interventions
  early, 282–283
  interpersonal, 284–285
  and medication, 312–313
Interview, initial, 58–62
Introspection, 129–130
Involutional melancholia, 88, 138

Jackson, S. W., 33
Jacobson, E., 39, 44
James, W., 29
Janicak, P. G., 221
Judgment, 72–73

Kashani, J. H., 345
Katan, A., 323
Kernberg, O., 41
Kerr, W., 147–148
Kindness, 52

Kleiner, G. J., 159, 392
Kohut, H., 41, 130–131
Kraepelin, E., 33–35, 81, 95, 334
Kumar, R., 390

Labile affect, 6
Late life
  affective disorders in, 397–402
  biological treatment in,
    403–404
  psychotherapy in, 404–409
Learned helplessness, 40, 45, 163
Leckman, J. F., 342
Leff, M. J., 284
Lesse, S., Masked depression,
    166, 349
Lewin, B. D., The Psychoanalysis
    of Elation, 35
Lewy, A., 102, 104
Life cycle, 324–325
Lighty therapy (phototherapy),
    103–104, 264–265
Lincoln, A., 29–30
Lindemann, E., 39, 151–152
Listening, 73
Lithium, 96–98
  administration of, 244–246
  for children, 343
  medical clearance for, 245
  and noncompliance, 261
  and pregnancy, 386
  prolonged administration of,
    246–247
  and psychosocial stress, 247
  side effects of, 246
Litman, R. E., 177, 189
Loneliness, 156, 163, 181
Longitudinal diagnosis, 92–93
Loss, importance of, 151
Love, "supplies" of, 129
Lukas, C., 187
Ludwig II, King of Bavaria,
    29–30

Mahler, M., 39, 341
Major depression, 88–93, 119
  in childhood, 333–335,
    342–343
  depressive neurosis and, 86–87
  early stages of, 89–90,
    251–252
  in the elderly, 398–399
  longitudinal diagnosis of, 92–93
  moderately severe stage of,
    90–91, 252–254
  recovery from, 255
  severe stage of, 91–92, 254–255
  timing of medication in,
    250–258
  well stage after recovery
    from, 255, 258
Malan, D. H., 39
Malpractice, 52–53, 58, 188–190,
  206
Mania, 8–9
  drugs used in, 233
  electroconvulsant therapy for,
    267–268
  and sexual drive, 382–383
Manic attack
  and delirium, 145
  development of, 93–94
  drug-induced, 109
  established, 96–97
  precipitation of, 99–100
Manic-Depressive Insanity
    and Paranoia (Kraepelin), 34,
    334
Manic-depressive psychosis,
  93–94
Manic patient
  hospitalization of, 209–211
  living with, 213–214
  noncompliance of, 260
MAOs (Monoamine oxidase in-
    hibitors), 88
  and atypical depression, 105

and biogenic amine theory, 224
and carbamazepine, 248
and nonpsychotic depression,
  221
use of, 237, 254
Marijuana, 352
Marital preoccupations, 76
Martin, F. M., 24–25
Masked Depression (Lesse), 166,
  349
McGovern, G., 28
Medication, 225–240; see also
    individual types
  administration of, 308–310
  and children, 331, 343
  clusters of symptoms and,
    258–259
  combined with psychotherapy,
    297–313
  discontinuation of, 313
  effects of, 135–137
  noncompliance with; see Non-
    compliance
  polypharmacy, 403–404
  precipitating attacks, 107–109,
    399
  and pregnancy, 386–387
  and prevention, 259
  purposes and functions of,
    223–224
  resistance to, 50, 214
  responses to, 241–243
  and responsibility, 219–220
  selection criteria for, 239–240
  side effects of; see Side effects
  timing of, 250–258
  and types of depression,
    222–223
Melancholia, 33, 91–92, 159–160
Meltzer, H., 9
Memory, sudden bursts of,
  139–140
Menstrual cycle, 384–386

Menstrual cycle (*continued*)
affective disorders and, 385
normal moods and, 385
premenstrual syndromes,
385–386
Mental status, 66–73
Meyer, A., 35–37
Midlife depression, 93
Midtown Manhattan Study (Srole
et al.), 23–24
Monamine oxidase inhibitors, *see*
MAOs
Monopolar depression, 88
Monroe, M., 29–30
Mood disorders, 6, 34–35, 83,
117–120, 333; *see also* Affective disorders
causes of, 13–22
fluid nature of, 78
function of psychotheraphy in,
275
organic, 106–112
subtypes of, 102–1055
suicide and, 169–191
Moods
and adolescence, 348–349
and affect, 3–6
clinical manifestations of, 5–6
and the menstrual cycle,
384–386
as signals, 148–149
Moore, B. E., 4
Morrison, H. L., 19, 344
Mother
depressed, 19–20, 98–99, 341,
343–344
effect of mental illness on baby,
393
interaction with child, 127
manic-depressive, 341–342
Mourning, 130, 153–154
in adolescence, 359–360,
374–375

in childhood, 338–339
uncompleted, 126, 157–158
"Mourning and Melancholia"
(Freud), 33, 38, 154
Moving, as stress, 280–281, 300
Multiinfarct dementia, 106, 121
Munoz, R. A., 390
Murder, suicide and, 26–27
Myth, unconscious, 128
Myxedema, 86, 136

Narcissistic personality disorder,
131
National Institute of Mental
Health, 23, 271, 368
Nemiah, J. C., 166
Neurasthenia, 150
Neuroleptics, 233
Neurotic depression, 84–88
Noncompliance, 259–264
and manic patients, 260
overmedicators and hoarders,
262–263
reduction of, 263–264
and severe depression, 260
and side affects, 260–261
Normal depression, 147–149
bordeom and apathy, 160–163
and fatigue, 149
loneliness, 163
in loss, grief, and mourning,
151–158
and rejection, 150–151
and self-esteem, 165–166
separation and nostalgia,
158–159

Object relations, 41
and childhood depression,
340–341
with self-object, 131
Obsessive-compulsive symptoms,
98

Oedipus complex, and adolescent suicide, 374
Ogden, T. H., 41
Oncology, psychiatric, 110
Organic disease, 83, 400–401
Organic mood disorders, 106–112, 120–121
Osofsky, H. J., 386
Outcome, factors influencing, 315–317
Overdose potential
    and adolescent suicide, 379
    for anxiolytics, 225, 229
Overeating, 85

Pain
    atypical, 167
    struggle against, 73–76
    and suicide, 179–180
Panic, and depression, 143
Parenthood, 386–395
Parents
    with bipolar disorder, 98–99
    with depressive neurosis, 87
    and risk of inheritance, 14–15
Parker, G., 104
Passive–aggressive personality, 85, 127
Patient
    advice to, 215–216
    ambulatory, 190–191, 317–319
    angry, 175
    appearance, behavior, and speech of, 67–68
    attraction to, 53
    with chronic disability, 249–250, 306–308
    clinical history of, 65–66
    compassion for, 52–53
    confidentiality of, see Confidentiality
    and countertransference, 55–56
    in crisis, 128–130, 184–186

delirious, 176–177
despairing and overwhelmed, 174
dislike of, 53–54
elderly, 397–400
empathy with, 51–52
exhausted, 174–175
guilty, 175
honesty with, 54–55
hospitalized, 197–200, 319–320
house calls to, 196–197
ideation and thought of, 70
immediate problems of, 283–284
impatience with, 54
initial interview with, 58–62
insight into, 56–57
intellectual functions of, 71–72
judgment of, 72–73
manic, see Manic patient
medical and surgical, 208
mental status of, 66–73
mood and affect of, 68–69
need for relief of, 180–181
noncompliance of, 259–264
private misery of, 125
and psychopharmacology, 221–223, 312
response to medication, 242–243
responsibility of, 211–212
in savior role, 128
and sexual relations, 58
in therapy, 178–179
workplace of, 197
Paykel, E. S., 105, 113, 273, 284, 318
Perry, S., 125
Personality
    depressive, 70–71
    and outcome, 316–317
    passive–aggressive, 85, 127
    and suicide, 182–184

Personality disorders, 80–83,
121–123
in adolescence, 357–358
diagnosis of, 112–115
narcissistic, 131
Persuasion and Healing (Frank),
23
Phototherapy, 103–104, 264–265
Physical illness, 74–75, 80, 86,
108–110; *see also* Organic
disease
in adolescence, 363–364
and effects of medication,
135–137
and self-esteem, 183–184
and suicide, 176–177, 399
unrecognized, 107
Physicians, and administration of
medication, 308–309, 311
Pilkonis, P. A., 113–114
Pituitary tumors, 136
Postabortion depression, 393–394
Postpartum depression, 388–392
psychotic and nonpsychotic,
390–391
symptoms of, 389
treatment and prognosis,
391–392
Post, R. M., 247
Potassium, lowered levels of, 86,
136
Poznanski, E. O., 331–332
Pregnancy, 386–394
Premenstrual syndromes, 385–386
Prisons, 177–178
Privacy, 58–59
Prognosis, 315
Projective identification, 41
Prolonged depressive reaction, 84
Pseudodementia, 72, 111–112,
400–401
Psychiatric News, 265, 271

Psychiatric oncology, 110
Psychiatrists, and administration
of medication, 308–311
Psychiatry
biological, 9–12
interpersonal, 37–38, 45
social, 39
Psychoanalysis, 39–40
long-term, 125–126, 139,
278–279
and medication, 310
and suppressed aggression, 114
as training, 56–57
widening scope of, 44–45
The Psychoanalysis of Elation (Lewin), 35
Psychobiology, 35–37
Psychodynamics, 38–41, 125–133
Psychomotor retardation, 67, 91,
332
Psychopharmacology, 224–225
attitudes toward, 49–50, 220
the patient and, 221–223
Psychosis, 91–92
Psychosocial stresses, 80
in adolescence, 360–363
and chronic disability, 249–250
and the elderly, 407–408
and lithium therapy, 247
moving house as, 280–281, 300
and outcome, 317
and psychotherapy, 278
Psychosomatic processes, 219
Psychosomatic symptoms,
166–167, 251
Psychotherapy, 271–296
and adolescent suicide,
378–379
aggression in, 291–292
cathartic, 275–276
combined with drugs, 297–313
for depressive neurosis, 87

early stages of, 279–285
educational, 276
effectiveness of, 271–273
function in mood disorders, 275
goals of, 273
in late life, 404–409
long-term, 125–126, 139,
    289–296
and medication, 223
prevailing attitudes toward,
    274–275
psychodynamic and abreactive,
    276–277
psychodynamic and insight-
    providing, 276
regression in, 292–293
renewed interest in, 39–40
short-term without medication,
    285–289
supportive, 275
target of, 277–279
termination of, 295–296
and third-party payers, 272
transference methods of, 277,
    293–295
unresponsiveness to, 218–219
Psychotic depression, 29, 88

Quitkin, F. M., 105

Race, and depression, 26–27
Rado, S., 39
Rationalization, 75
Referrals, 178
Regression
    in adolescence, 350–351
    general, 292–293
Reid, W. H., 19
Rejection, 150–151
Repression, 41
Reserpine, 136–137
Restitution, 129–130

Return of the repressed, 139–140,
    159–160
Rifkin, A., 220, 265, 268
Risch, S. C., 241
Risk factors for suicide, 171–179
Robins, L. N., 23
Robson, K., 390
Rome, H. P., 27–28
Rossini, G., 29

Sackeim, 265
Sadness, 406–407
Saletua, B., 265
Schizoaffective disorder, 18, 121,
    141–142, 222
Schizophrenia, diagnosis of,
    140–143
Schmale, A. H., 164
School, adolescents in, 362–363
Schumann, R., 29
Seasonal affective disorders,
    102–104, 264–265
Seiden, H. M., 187
Self-esteem
    deficits in, 126, 128, 165, 182,
        339
    physical illness and, 183–184
Self-images, 131, 165
Self-objects, 131
Self psychology, 41–44, 130–132
Seligman, E. P., 45
Separation-individuation, 127
Separation, and nostalgia,
    158–159
Sex, and depression, 25–26
Sexuality
    in adolescence, 346
    aggression fused with, 292
    infantile, 292–293
    and relations with patients, 58
Sexual problems, 302–303
    in bipolar disorder, 98

in depressed patients, 81,
130–131, 284–285
in young adults, 381–383
Sherrill, R., 162–163
Shneidman, E. S., 170, 184, 186
Side effects
of antidepressants, 243–244,
247–248
of electroconvulsant therapy,
268–270
of lithium therapy, 246
and noncompliance, 260–261
Sifneos, P. E., 166
Silverman, C., 25–26
Sleep deprivation, 265
"Smiling depression," 67
Social psychiatry, 39
Solnit, A. J., 342
Somatic symptoms, 92
Speech, of patient, 67
Splitting, 40–41
Srole, L., 23–24, 32
Stages of treatment
early, middle, and late, 202
first contact, 201–202
follow-up, 203
Steroids, precipitating attacks,
107–108, 136
Stimulants, use of, 237, 239, 244
Stoller, R., "Psychiatry's Mind–
Brain Dialectic," 49, 51
Stone, L., 44
Strober, M., 354
Suffering, and suicide, 179–180
Suicidal crisis, 184–186, 295
Suicide, 25–28, 91, 169–191
adolescent, see Adolescent sui-
cide
and age, 170–171
and anorexia, 144
and childhood depression, 332

and convicted criminal,
177–178
epidemiology of, 169–170
and failure in school, 76
family history of, 176
and first aid for family, 205–206
loneliness and, 181
medical–legal considerations,
188–191
and personality, 182–184
physical illness and, 176–177
precautions against, 172–173
preoccupation with, 71, 85, 204
psychology and motivation,
179–182
responsibility for, 188
risk factors, 171–179, 203–205
rumination and, 139
separation and, 158
and splitting, 40
and treatment, 184–187
and unwanted pregnancy,
392–393
and the young, 27–28
Suicide prevention centers, 186,
376, 378
Summers, A., 30
Superego, punishing, 126
Symptoms
psychosomatic, 166–167, 251
variations with age, 323–324

Termination, 295–296
Therapist, 49–51, 308–310
and administration of medicine,
308–310
countertransference of, 55–56
in early stage of therapy,
281–282
ethics of, 57–58
feelings of, 51–57

importance of bipolar disorder
to, 98
and loss of patient, 206
mourning assisted by, 338–339
office of, 195–196
psychoanalytically trained,
56–57
psychopharmacological knowledge of, 219–220
and suicidal crisis, 184–186,
295
Therapy
for children, 342–344
couple and family, 408–409
eclectic, 297–298
geographical setting for,
195–200
group, 408
planning of 63–64
process of, 200–201
psychosocial, 407–408
stages of, see Stages of treatment and suicide, 184–187
Third-party payers, and psychotherapy, 272
Thought, content of, 69–70
Timing, of medication, 250–258
Tranquilizers, 244, 313
Transference, 44, 277, 293–295
and aggression, 291
negative, 178–179
and parentol role, 132

Tricyclic antidepressants,
224–225, 233, 237
administration of, 241
results of treatment with,
241–243
side effects of, 243–244
and stages of major depression,
250–258
Tumors, 107, 136
Twin studies, 15–16

Unipolar disorder
in adolescence, 354
genetic factors in, 15–22
Unresolved grief, 157–158
Usdin, G., 10

Volkan, V. D., *Depressive States
and Their Treatment,* 157

Warm, T. R., 330
Webster's New World Dictionary
(1966), 158
Wehr, T., 103
Weissman, M. M., 105, 113, 273,
318
Werman, D. S., 158–159
White, T. H., *America in Search
of Itself,* 162–163
Withdrawal, 67–68, 204, 350
Wolpert, E. A., 95
Working through, 283, 289–296
World Health Organization, 77

Zahn-Waxler, C., 342